KU-029-297

Virtue, Learning
and the Scottish Enlightenment

Virtue, Learning and the Scottish Enlightenment

Ideas of Scholarship in Early Modern History

DAVID ALLAN

EDINBURGH UNIVERSITY PRESS

© David Allan 1993

Edinburgh University Press Ltd
22 George Square, Edinburgh

Typeset in Lasercomp Ehrhardt
and printed and bound in Great Britain by
the University Press, Cambridge

A CIP record for this book is
available from the British Library.

ISBN 0 7486 0434 0 (cased)
ISBN 0 7486 0438 3 (paper)

The Publisher acknowledges
subsidy from the Scottish Arts
Council towards the publication
of this volume.

Contents

Note on Reference Style

MANY BOOKS OF the sixteenth and seventeenth centuries possess incomplete, and occasionally no, pagination. Quotations from such works refer instead to the printers' signatures, marked on most of the original folios to aid the origamic process of binding and cutting. These commonly comprise three characters: a letter (A, B, C, ... or a, b, c, ...) indicating the first and subsequent four-folio partitions of a quarto volume or the eight-folio partitions of an octavo volume; a numeral, invariably in Arabic, describing the place of the individual folio in the four- or eight-page partition; and lastly a lower-case letter (r or v) indicating the side of the folio, recto (front/right page) or verso (back/left page), to which the particular reference relates. A typical pseudo-pagination thus runs: A1r, A1v, A2r, A2v, A3r, A3v, A4r, A4v, B1r, etc. However, marks do not occur on all folios, and identification of the intervening unmarked folios is a matter of counting forwards or backwards from the closest printer's mark and constructing a unique reference according to the same basic rules. For other works, in which a variety of unusual printers' marks have obtruded into an otherwise normal pagination system, I have likewise followed strictly the notations found in the original.

Acknowledgements

T HE HELP OF many people, both individuals and institutions, has been invaluable in the preparation of this study.

The Rare Books Department of Cambridge University Library bore the brunt of my demands for printed books. Its staff, as well as those of Emmanuel College Library and the Seeley Historical Library, deserve special thanks. Elsewhere, the British Library in London, the John Rylands University Library of Manchester, and on a number of occasions the Bodleian Library, Oxford were of signal service to an otherwise isolated student of Scotland's history. The collections of the National Library of Scotland pre-eminently, and also of the University Library and New College Library, Edinburgh were unsurpassed in their richness. Along with Glasgow University Library and the libraries of the universities of Aberdeen and St Andrews, I found my work in their portals as fruitful as it was unfailingly agreeable. To each, in addition, I should express my gratitude for being allowed to consult the unique manuscripts in their care.

More personal debts also accrued along the way. My former tutors at the University of Edinburgh, Nicholas Phillipson and Richard Mackenney, were enthusiastic in first motivating my studies, and offered periodic advice and encouragement as my work progressed – frequently in the inspirational surroundings of an Edinburgh hostelry not twenty yards from the residences of James Boswell and David Hume. I would also like to think, however, that several other members of the Department of History there might recognise their benign influence in the succeeding pages. In Cambridge I was well served in having Mark Goldie as a perceptive supervisory critic of my developing ideas – though it would be remiss of me not to acknowledge the value of later having had Istvan Hont and J. H. Burns as doctoral examiners, both of them subjecting my fledgeling arguments to the most rigorous and penetrating scepticism. Among the other scholars who offered help or advice at different stages were Duncan Forbes, Jan Golinski, Peter Burke, Peter Jones, Clare O'Halloran, Roger Mason, Richard Sher, Jeremy Black, Ian Rae, Jonathan Clark and Antony Flew. Each allowed me to discuss matters Scottish and to develop further the arguments deployed herein – though of course, any culpability attaching to this study remains entirely my own.

The assistance of Penny Clarke and her colleagues at Edinburgh University Press in guiding this study to publication is something for which I am particularly grateful. I am also obliged to three anonymous publishers' readers, whose constructive criticism and helpful suggestions have made this work more, I think, than it would otherwise have been.

Finally I should confess that I was fortunate in securing the material support of several academic bodies. The British Academy initially made my doctoral research possible. An External Research Studentship awarded by the Master and Fellows of Emmanuel College, Cambridge made it much more comfortable. At the last the gainful employment and academic services provided by the University of Lancaster made the completion of this study less onerous than it might otherwise have been. This is, of course, fitting, for in the absence of such generous and unquestioning support it could not even have been begun.

INTRODUCTION

'Fable and Falshood'
The Historiographical Context

I

THE SCOTTISH ENLIGHTENMENT has in recent years re-emerged as a major historical issue. The location of Scottish political economy and moral philosophy in the mainstream of academic debate has allowed Scotland to be seen as a singularly important centre within the celebrated eighteenth-century European revival of learning. Many attempts have been made to explain the vigorous culture and climate of infectious intellectual endeavour which are now synonymous with the age of Adam Smith and David Hume. It has become acceptable, even fashionable, to consider the 'hotbed of genius' which excited the admiration of Carlo Denina and the exclamations of Matthew Bramble as a pre-eminently enlightened community.[1] A great deal has been written, moreover, about the leading Scottish men of letters, their works and their formidable legacies. If Hume awoke Kant from his slumbers, then we now know that the ideas associated with men like Adam Ferguson, Hugh Blair, and Thomas Reid, were to be of comparable influence among succeeding generations of intellectuals. Yet, despite the vivacity with which Scottish Enlightenment studies have been taken up, and the enthusiasm displayed in scholarly debates which have generated both heat and light, one view of its intellectual origins has to a considerable extent prevailed. This view, which has grown into a historiographical juggernaut with its own formidable momentum, characterises the Enlightenment in Scotland as a revolutionary phenomenon, to be contrasted sharply with an intolerant and benighted past. In other words, it can safely be regarded as an aberration in Scotland's otherwise unblemished record of internecine bickering and cultural sterility.

For Henry Buckle, perhaps the most famous and controversial Victorian commentator on this question, the Scottish Enlightenment consisted in an escape from the clutches of the Kirk's theological embrace. If Scottish philosophy remained tainted with a deductive method, it could nevertheless be regarded essentially as a reaction against 'one of the most detestable tyrannies ever seen on earth'.[2] Other Victorian and Edwardian scholars like H. G. Graham and Hector Macpherson, meanwhile, put flesh upon the gaunt skeleton of Buckle's schema. Having dismissed the seventeenth century in a brief opening chapter, Macpherson actually proceeded to portray the eighteenth beneath the bold and unambiguous title 'The Reaction: Moderatism'.[3] In an earlier work, moreover, he had foreshadowed something of the flavour of this interpretation in referring to 'the somewhat narrow ideals of Puritanism, which, by frowning upon philosophy and literature, and by drawing a sharp line between the sacred and the secular, helped to create a gulf between religion and culture'.[4] Similarly, to William Law Mathieson, writing in 1910, it was 'the noontide of Moderatism', a development with many novel 'ecclesiastical demerits', which was also 'the master spirit' of an enlightened age.[5] Yet, by employing the language of discontinuity and reaction in this way, these scholars were building an interpretation of the Scottish Enlightenment which itself relied heavily upon particular and somewhat questionable sources. Some appreciation of the provenance of their views, then, would clearly help us put into relief the more invidious suppositions, that modern blend of 'fable and falshood',[6] with which they have burdened us.

For example, the vibrancy of Scottish intellectual activity had certainly impressed the many visitors to eighteenth-century Edinburgh and Glasgow. But their surprise at finding such a ferment in the far north lent itself perhaps too easily to the Victorian view. After all, the opportunity of a leisurely progress through Scotland was a new experience for the eighteenth-century European traveller. With Scotsmen increasingly prominent in the world of letters, there were many things for him to look out for, and many new experiences to be recounted: so as the influential Dugald Stewart was afterwards to observe, the Scottish Enlightenment had seemed like 'a sudden burst of genius', and, as others would later agree, one 'which to the foreigner must seem to have sprung up in this country by a sort of enchantment soon after the rebellion of 1745'.[7] Similarly, several great enlightened men of letters were found to have pronounced on the novelty of their own achievements from the commanding heights of what had by 1760 become a self-confident Scottish 'Athens'.[8] But again, too much concentration on this chorus of self-congratulation emanating from the Acropolis, a phenomenon at which we shall later have to look in much greater detail, might also tend to encourage the view that the literati had indeed left behind all that had gone before. That this very clamour of adulation was itself misleading, perhaps even dishonest, was a thought which certainly crossed the sceptical minds of less Scotophile contemporaries, among them Byron at his most satirical.[9] In understanding the factors which shaped the characteristic Victorian view of the relatively recent Scottish past, moreover, it would be fatal for us to underestimate the importance of the continuing fissure in the Scottish church after 1843. This inevitably led the Free Kirk and its subscribers to condemn the Moderates as a pernicious deviation in the linear development of the Scottish Calvinist tradition. To latter-day cynics like the influential James McCosh, therefore, the Enlightenment was simply the cultural manifestation both of theological heterodoxy and of ecclesiastical schism.[10] Equally, the highly motivated and retrospective secular critique of Whig and Tory intellectual achievements formed by nineteenth-century observers also needs to be recognised. In the trenchant polemic of dogmatists as opposed as Robert Mudie and John Gibson Lockhart, one finds attitudes strongly conducive to the consolidation of a historiographical convention arguing that the enlightened literati were both marginal and exceptional.[11] Even in the 'inimitable Author of Waverley', so rightly seen by a Georgian admirer as uniquely responsible for the 'powerful interest' and 'intense value' of the Scottish past to a voracious nineteenth-century public, one might again legitimately detect a tendency to propagate a definitive view of Scotland's history which was as misleadingly contrasting as it was engagingly colourful:[12] darkness and light, heroism and mendacity, are the natural stuff of the novels by which the Scottish past has overwhelmingly been presented to posterity. All these influences acted simultaneously upon those who were favourable as well as those who were instinctively opposed to the literati. And they combined successfully to suggest the isolation of the Enlightenment within Scotland's intellectual and theological history. On this basis, then, historians like Buckle and Macpherson were able to articulate by the end of the nineteenth century that broadly consensual view of the Scottish Enlightenment which was to inform the modern revival of interest in the phenomenon.

Though the writings of historians like Agnes Mure Mackenzie remind us that it was never even wholly buried, the full disinterment of Buckle's view can be dated with some accuracy to Trevor-Roper's seminal article in 1967, an event which significantly coincided with Peter Gay's complementary work on the European Enlightenment.[13] Trevor-Roper focused our attention on a small group of the most brilliant Scottish literati, dismissing other writers as 'camp-followers' and the rest of Scotland as backward and moribund.[14] This chimed euphonically with Gay's emphasis upon élite coteries of Francophonic intellectuals, seen as practising a rationalist and militantly secular form of Enlightenment in the face of open clerical hostility. It soon became clear, moreover, that in the process a sound interpretative model had been fashioned with which it would be possible to integrate Scotland into the better-known European Enlightenment. The resulting impetus given to studies of the Scottish Enlightenment, and the open admission of a few Scotsmen, albeit briefly, to the ranks of the great European intellectuals, thereafter stimulated a considerable body of work devoted to opening up the cultural life of eighteenth-century Scotland as never before. Yet, in the final analysis, escape from the prescribed Victorian picture of the Scottish Enlightenment has been a very laboured affair. In substantial part Buckle's view remains alive and well. In the manner of Black and Horn,[15] it is apparently still possible for scholars to confine the Scottish Enlightenment to a handful of chosen individuals. These, in the *reductio ad absurdam* of this approach, have, for example, been minutely scrutinised by the sociologist Charles Camic to betray their allegedly impeccable anti-Calvinist credentials.[16] David Hoeveler, meanwhile, has lately described 'the world of the

Moderates and the philosophers' as cut off from and 'largely irrelevant to the Scottish population'.[17] And another recent scholar, John Lough, has even chastised Trevor-Roper for his leniency. He actually missed, we are told, 'the obvious point that such Enlightenment as existed in eighteenth-century Scotland was confined to a tiny minority who lived surrounded by a narrow-minded nationalism and bigoted puritanism which have survived in part down to our own day'.[18]

Such intemperate outbursts are fortunately rare. But they are merely the most unpleasant result of the prevailing model of the Scottish Enlightenment. Perhaps more damaging, however, is the tendency to approach the achievements of eighteenth-century Scotland in a teleological manner, as though they are to be understood principally in terms of their contribution to nineteenth-century Western thought. Even those scholars most sensitive to the contours of Scottish thinking, like John Robertson, are led to concede that Scotland had no intellectual tradition of interest to nascent Enlightenment minds; that 'what Scotland could not provide were the intellectual resources to pursue the interest'.[19] So it can be no surprise that other historians of the Enlightenment have tended simply to stress those identifiable elements in the Scottish enquiry which most obviously fed into subsequent strands of thought. This approach has undoubtedly produced a number of valuable studies, perhaps most notably those by Chitnis and Kuehn, each of them revealing debts to Scottish work which, though again anticipated in isolated earlier works, long remained relatively neglected.[20] Equally numerous, however, have been interpretations after the style of Ronald Meek. These focus our minds upon the materialist element in the Scottish Enlightenment, especially its political economy and social history, in an effort to trace the origins of Marxist thought or the various social sciences in the ideas of a small body of Scottish writers.[21] These are questions of understandable interest to the modern micro-economist, structuralist, or behavioural scientist. Eighteenth-century Scotland may offer much-needed illumination within the murkier recesses of *Das Kapital*. But it is arguable that such forward-looking concerns necessarily distort the substance and purpose of the Enlightenment itself as it was understood by those who actually fashioned it.

A somewhat different and more imaginative approach has, however, developed in recent years. This does not in fact abandon the postulates of the Buckle and Trevor-Roper interpretation as regards a discontinuous and quantitatively marginal Enlightenment in Scotland. But in its development historians like Nicholas Phillipson have been able to open up the wide and fertile pastures of the English and Continental intellectual landscape in search of the origins of the Scottish Enlightenment. If, as Carlo Denina claimed, 'Scotland for a long succession of ages had hardly given birth to one author of eminence',[22] it seemed logically to follow that the necessary impetus for enlightened discourse must have entered Scotland from abroad: its Enlightenment could thus be understood as an episode in the diasporic history of essentially foreign intellectual traditions. In this view, of course, understanding the Enlightenment, as Phillipson suggests, becomes a matter of explaining 'the intense interest [the] Scots showed in importing whole systems of foreign knowledge at the turn of the seventeenth and eighteenth centuries'.[23] The more narrow version of this interpretation, it should be noted, remains not incompatible with the emphasis of those principally concerned with the nineteenth-century fruits of the Scottish endeavour. This, in Meek's expert hands, has attempted to focus attention upon Scotland as the recipient of the materialist social categorisation identified in earlier French, English and Dutch writers.[24] But this rather limited debate has given way to a much broader and wide-ranging discussion. The two chief contenders for a more comprehensive, if rather speculative, Continental interpretation of Scottish developments, particularly in the field of political economy, have surely been the natural law and classical republican traditions, influentially assessed in the collection of papers edited in 1983 by Michael Ignatieff and Istvan Hont.[25] This argument centres essentially upon the rival claims of the lawyers' *jus*[26] and the political philosophers' *virtù*[27] to be the paradigmatic concept at the heart of classical political economy as developed by Hume and Smith. Yet, the ensuing and highly-technical debate has probably provoked more questions than it has provided answers. And whichever interpretation is held to have won the field, the central problem of accounting for the sudden emergence of a Scottish Enlightenment, foreign traditions and all, surely remains.

Attention has therefore remained on the headlong search for the contingent factors which might have rendered these Continental and English intellectual traditions suddenly accessible and so attractive to Scotsmen. In their quest, historians have once again been able to draw upon the reasons offered by assorted literati in their more reflective moments. Among late eighteenth-century Scotsmen like John Ramsay of Ochtertyre the pre-eminent explanation for their unexpected emergence as a polite and learned community focused on the role of the Glorious Revolution in 1688 and the Act of Union of 1707 in securing political stability and injecting the civilising influence of Augustan England into Scottish life.[28] This first-hand impression has long been supported by the weight of subsequent historiography. It has now been substantially buttressed by an array of parallel explanations brought over from economic and social history so as to portray early eighteenth-century Scotland as an increasingly provincial society undergoing the most profound social, economic and constitutional change.[29] Without significantly deviating from the received wisdom on the revolutionary nature and limited scope of the Enlightenment, it has been possible for historians such as Tom Devine to construct an arresting image of commercial and agricultural development in eighteenth-century Scotland. Since the leading role in this social revolution is naturally played by an emergent mercantile and urban class, innovative cultural forms and ambitious intellectual inquiries might indeed have found in them a new and welcoming audience.[30]

The controversy surrounding the enactment of the Union itself and the subsequent development of a political vocabulary appropriate to the changed institutional circumstances of Scotland have lent particular weight to the argument that republican thought was a crucial stimulus to an Enlightenment. Moreover, there has in addition been skilful refinement of the traditional emphasis on the importance of the first decade of the eighteenth century. This has led to the contention of authors like Phillipson and Neil McCallum that, for the lawyers and merchants who comprised the prospective 'leaders of a polite commonwealth ',[31] perhaps the most important benefit of the closer relationship with England at this juncture was the arrival in Scotland of the cult of Addisonian politeness, associated with the urbane clubs and coffee-house journals of Augustan England.[32] In this view, politeness was the fashionable pursuit of a new urban elite. Any importation of philosophy and literature into Scotland could be regarded as a response to their eager demand for entertainment, instruction and justification. Furthermore, if the Union was indeed a crucial intellectual landmark, then it has been possible for Rosalind Mitchison and T. C. Smout to consider the Enlightenment as also playing some part in the evolution of a new national identity for a deracinated Scotland, with politics and patriotism largely sublimated within a burning Scottish desire for the acquisition of English rights and manners, and English commerce.[33] Edinburgh in particular, and Scotland in general, it is therefore concluded by Phillipson, was by the 1720s involved in 'a remarkable experiment in rebuilding the country's political and religious culture'.[34]

Another eighteenth-century development has perhaps inevitably been seen as a prominent contributory factor in an unanticipated Enlightenment which was long ago recognised by Walter Bagehot and others as owing a very special debt to the Scottish universities.[35] This is the reform of the curriculum and of the professorial system at Glasgow, Edinburgh, St Andrews and the colleges of Aberdeen.[36] Again, the post-Union relationship with England can be seen as very significant in this respect, with the connection between the Dissenting academies and the reformed Scottish universities already convincingly established by Peter Jones.[37] Within Scotland itself the effect of university reform, as George Davie claims in a justly-celebrated assessment, was to produce an educational system capable of producing men imbued with a rigorous training in moral philosophy, rhetoric, science and letters.[38] This, it is clear, would have rendered them amenable not only to the attractions of polite culture but particularly to the intellectual and scientific inquiries of the learned societies which we know they spawned and supported.[39] The reform of the universities, Roger Emerson also tells us, was followed by the emergence of a thriving community of clubs and societies, all of them dedicated to the promotion of polite values, speculative discussion and particular projects.[40] These provided the educational infrastructure within which the characteristic preoccupations of the Scottish Enlightenment could develop and diversify. Once again, however, a quite profound and far-reaching transformation has been used to account for the assumed discontinuity in Scottish intellectual life. Yet this has not in itself overturned the conventional wisdom that no obligation has been incurred to question either the apparently limited scale of the Enlightenment thus explained, or the more fundamental premise that it represented a decisive break with the past.[41]

The current approach to our problem, then, betrays its origins in a deeply untrustworthy Victorian historiography. It argues, or else insinuates, that what became the 'Science of Man' could be constructed by Scotsmen only once the institutional and social foundations had been laid and the intellectual apparatus imported. Modern Scotland, it has therefore been concluded, like Edinburgh in Youngson's widely-influential survey, basks merely in the glory of a 'late and sudden flowering of Scottish culture, when, as Balfour put it, a country "which had done nothing up to the eighteenth century, after the eighteenth century began seemed almost to do everything"'.[42] Indeed, the awesome application of geometrical principles and the self-conscious grandeur of the New Town, so clearly identified by all subsequent commentators as the dominant legacy of Georgian Edinburgh, have been taken straightforwardly to confirm the belief that the visionaries who conceived and first inhabited it simply *must* have stood boldly, even brazenly, apart from a chaotic and unseemly Scottish past.[43] Not surprisingly, however, as this interpretation so consistently misrepresents the Enlightenment by its concentration on those facets of eighteenth-century Scotland most readily explicable in terms of its own assumptions, discordant voices have been heard. The findings of empirical work on the social and institutional changes of the early eighteenth century, of course, cannot seriously be cast aside. There is now little doubt that Scotland at this time was indeed witnessing changes which might allow an Enlightenment to develop and prosper; or that these changes were a prerequisite to a flowering of intellectual energy such as the Scottish Enlightenment represented. Nor are many of the otherwise illuminating studies which have contributed to the unhappy disjunction of Scotland's cultural traditions and her Enlightenment exactly in need of demolition. But the underlying implication of intellectual discontinuity certainly is. Recent criticism has therefore rightly focused on the lack of emphasis given to particular aspects of the Enlightenment, as well as on the continuing failure to pay due attention to developments in what has traditionally been regarded as the pre-Enlightenment period.

The importance of the late seventeenth century in explaining the later Enlightenment has been periodically canvassed but never wholly accepted.[44] The works of Mackenzie, Stair and Fletcher have long been assimilated into the story of the arrival of natural law and republican ideas in Scotland. But the wider significance of the period, especially in terms of domestic traditions of thought and learning, has been largely ignored until recently. As Gordon Donaldson drily observed only a decade ago, and as is still very often the case (despite some strenuous protestations of innocence), 'too many who babble about "The Enlightenment" of the eighteenth century have not taken the trouble to find out about Scottish culture in the seventeenth'.[45] Now, with the role of Newtonian science in early eighteenth-century Scotland more widely recognised, however, the importance of men like Sibbald and Moray in promoting Scottish natural philosophy before 1700 has been affirmed.[46] This argument has been carried furthest by Roger Emerson, and in ways which seem intriguingly to offer a plausible connection with Scotland's theological heritage. If natural philosophy sought to encompass order, reason, and regularity in Nature, then these priorities, it seems, might have had affinities with traditional Calvinist attempts to comprehend the systematic design and diversity of Creation. Equally, the antiquarian interests of men of science like Sir Robert Sibbald, and particularly of successive Clerks of Penicuik, at the beginning of the eighteenth century, are now regarded as having had a significant impact upon the subsequent character of the Enlightenment in Scotland.[47] And it is now seen as more than likely, as Alex Broadie has claimed, that eighteenth-century moral philosophers such as Hutcheson, Hume and Reid were in important respects merely reviving an intellectual tradition which had flourished in Scotland at least two centuries earlier.[48] It would be wise to avoid the accusation that one is seeking to shade the Scottish Enlightenment itself back into the period before 1700. But there are clearly avenues available down which explanations of domestic traditions conducive to an Enlightenment might legitimately proceed. The argument founded upon the significance of experimental science has, as yet, merely shown the way. If circumstances in Scotland by 1700 were indeed becoming increasingly propitious to the development of an Enlightenment, then our understanding of the relationship between Scottish Calvinism, humanism, and the enlightened 'Science of Man', would also have to be somewhat revised.

There have, at least, been encouraging collateral developments in our knowledge of the part played by the Kirk in Scotland's Enlightenment. And this is a trend in broad sympathy with the recent frontal assaults of scholars such as Derek Beales and Tim Blanning upon Gay's determinedly irreligious model of its Continental equivalent.[49] For their criticis there has long been a convention of equating Moderatism and Enlightenment for polemical purposes.[50] Meanwhile the long-recognised role of toleration in creating a climate in which speculation and polite learning could flourish has also, rather ironically, always provided a useful guide for the enthusiasts of Enlightenment to explain it at the personal and institutional level as a by-product of Kirk factionalism. We can now reassure ourselves, with Anand Chitnis, that Scotland was indeed a 'religiously-aware society.... So many different areas of Scottish life were impregnated by religion that to dissociate it from the origins of the Scottish intellectual inquiry would be curious, to say the least'.[51] It is abundantly clear from Ian Clark's work, moreover, that a Moderate minority controlled the late eighteenth-century Kirk in their own interest.[52] We can appreciate, because David Lachman's study has shown us, how in the earlier part of the century the Kirk's ugly theological controversies came increasingly to seem one of the best arguments in favour of greater tolerance and moderation.[53] More recently, we have also begun to re-evaluate the educational and cultural position of the Kirk in order to account for the manifest centrality of ministers like Robertson, Blair and Ferguson in the Edinburgh Enlightenment. What has been revealed, most impressively by Richard Sher, has been the extent to which the Moderates actually employed the lectern and the pulpit to propagate notions of polite morality. The Kirk and university, it appears, were nothing less than the principal organs for the dissemination of the enlightened values of tolerance, politeness and learning.[54] Even the sermons delivered by the Moderate leadership have been shown by John Dwyer, following Carl Becker's masterly reappraisal of the Continental intellectual scene, to have been vehicles essentially for the conveyance of a practical Christian morality reconciled to the enlightened principles of sociability.[55] The Scottish Kirk and the Scottish Enlightenment, it therefore transpires, were probably far from being the distant and cantankerous relations portrayed in the conventional account.

Significant steps are thus being taken to correct an inherited picture which, I have suggested, is insidiously warped both in terms of its content and its chronology. Just as Pater and Burckhardt managed to discover the kind of Renaissance which appealed to their own tastes and prejudices, it seems that their Victorian contemporaries, and chiefly the influential Henry Buckle, had fashioned for themselves an unholy Enlightenment which stood triumphant and unrepentant above a pious and utterly bleak Scottish past. As a result it is increasingly difficult to regard the Enlightenment simply as a narrow and temporary reaction against the role of the Kirk, or as a flat rejection of the native theological tradition. It is also less easy to accept the millenarian fervour of enlightened commentators like Thomas Somerville, who suggested – and not without a modicum of personal interest – that under their own stewardship Scotland had 'made advances perhaps unparalleled in any former age'.[56] Nor in particular, given the work appearing only in the last two or three years, can we now tolerate the outmoded assumption that vigorous presbyterianism was necessarily hostile towards the rational and reformist programmes which grew out of the Scottish intellectual inquiry.[57] There is beyond doubt an increasingly convincing argument to be heard for early eighteenth-century Scottish science. We also have the elaborate re-working of the polemical convention that the mid-century Kirk was itself instrumental in fostering the Enlightenment. But much more clearly needs to be done. In broadening this perspective, it would in fact be necessary to enter the historical and literary heartlands of the orthodox model of the Scottish Enlightenment. And we would need to ask, in unison with bolder students of imaginative literature like John MacQueen, whether some elements of enlightened discourse were not only more widely prevalent but also more deeply rooted in a Scottish tradition than has commonly been supposed.[58]

II

It would certainly be no departure from the orthodoxy to suggest that the historical writings associated with the Enlightenment provide the central testament of the eighteenth-century Scottish achievement. On this much at least all current historians could probably agree. In their historical works the great literati gathered the evidence and deduced the explanatory schemes upon which their definitive pronouncements on political economy and social development would ultimately rest. When Smith approached the transformations in economic organisation, when Ferguson considered different social structures or Kames the unique character of Scottish property law, each did so from a profoundly historical perspective. Nor was straightforward factual scholarship of this kind the only area of Scottish cultural activity to reap dividends from a quite extraordinary upsurge in historical interest. Arguably, those most enduring and influential products of Scotland's enlightened age, the *Waverley Novels* of Sir Walter Scott, were themselves saturated with the same historical obsessions and antiquarian curiosity which had so characterised the academics and gentlemen-lawyers of eighteenth-century Edinburgh.[59] Men like Ferguson, as well as James Dunbar and William Maitland, certainly understood that many aspects of human society were highly developmental, and that as a result they could only be explained historically. Others, among them Scott and the poets, painters and philosophers of the 'Athens of the North', found in the past the vivid illustrations and inspirational examples with which to engage the attention of a transfixed public. Not without considerable justification, therefore, did David Hume in 1770 proclaim that 'this is the historical Age, and this the historical Nation'.[60]

Yet I have already suggested that our own understanding of the Enlightenment historical canon in Scotland has itself fallen prey to a teleological approach; that it is frequently regarded as a handmaid of political economy and therefore as the preface to an account of modern historical materialism. Only slightly less damaging in this respect have been the ruminations of those from Albion Small to George Stocking who have been concerned principally, if not exclusively, with the origins of modern sociology and anthropology. Poring over the central texts in search of the birth of their own discipline, they have been utterly unable, it seems, to recognise its theological parentage.[61] With scholars such as Gladys Bryson and Louis Schneider approaching the Scottish Enlightenment from avowedly modern and secular disciplines, there are even problems when they have been prepared to embrace a wider constituency of enlightened authors. It has been all too easy simply to highlight the perceptible glimmerings of modernity, and to do so at the expense of the seemingly unfamiliar and uncongenial residuum from a preceding age.[62] The result has been a reading which too often assumes that the texts were written for the analytical purposes familiar to the modern social scientist. There has followed a devaluation of the moral and religious functions of enlightened historical writing which has drawn some comment (notably again from Phillipson) but little corrective action.[63] This state of affairs is as deeply frustrating as it is profoundly unfortunate. For it is evident that whilst inflicting their own misleading teleologies upon the authors of eighteenth-century Scottish texts, later scholars have actually ignored the testimony of those authors themselves. This is in fact freely available in their voluminous works. It is couched in some of the most eloquent and carefully worded enunciations of scholarly purpose and intention one could hope to find. Enlightened Scotsmen and their predecessors made explicit statements of their own aims and aspirations as scholars. These, as I hope to demonstrate in considerable detail, deserve from the modern student at least a closer inspection.

It is arguable, moreover, that other significant elements in the Enlightenment historical texts have suffered correspondingly from this distorted and highly partial perspective. There has, for example, been no serious consideration of the possible relationship between the classic historical writings attributable to the recognised literati and the prolific outpourings of the more anonymous Scotsmen of the same period, scholars who look much less like the ancestors an economist or sociologist might choose. As John Dwyer perceptively remarks, and despite the recent reawakening of interest in the moralistic component of enlightened Scottish thought led by Nicholas Phillipson and Donald Winch, too often there has survived 'a tendency to reduce cultural discourse to a handful of thinkers, texts, or issues'.[64] There is also still a marked preference for regarding the work of the literati themselves as *sui generis*. This is the case even though our scholarship has yet fully to assess the extent of eighteenth-century Scottish intellectual activity.[65] These would of course be grave deficiencies in themselves. Yet perhaps an even greater deficiency remains the continuing failure to explore the Scottish origins of enlightened historical writing, a problem in part traceable to Trevor-Roper but again possessing a quite remarkable scholarly pedigree.[66] This astonishing lapse is surely symptomatic of the broader malaise which, I have argued, has so debilitated our own efforts to engage with and to understand the significance of the Enlightenment experience in Scotland. It is one which it will be the principal purpose of this study to make good.

The large historical literature of sixteenth- and seventeenth-century Scotland, like the less well-known majority from the eighteenth, turns out to be as intriguing as it is diverse. That so little attention has been accorded to it is a situation due not least to the malign influence, in Scottish studies at least as much as elsewhere, of historians' excessive specialisation. [67] Many, as I have so far insisted, have proceeded by concentrating solely upon a charmed inner circle of major authors, comprising the more famous figures of Scotland's Enlightenment – Hume, Smith, Robertson, Blair and the like. Some seem to have taken seriously C. S. Lewis's mischievous and quite preposterous contentions regarding the absence of worthwhile early modern Scottish literature.[68] Others, like Arthur Williamson (again following an older historiographical tendency), have focused instead on the brilliant but brief reign of those historians and propagandists – principally Boece, Major and Buchanan – who illuminated sixteenth-century Scotland in a golden age. This, tradition argues, was brought to an abrupt conclusion by the final triumph in the early seventeenth century of a basically philistine Reformation.[69] Of the literally dozens of energetic and productive historians who were the contemporaries and colleagues of David Hume, virtually nothing has been heard.[70] The silence regarding the shrill, combative and violently polemical historians of Caroline and Restoration Scotland – including such colourful, hard-bitten cynics as the two loquacious Alexanders, Shields and Ross – has, if anything, been even more deafening. In permitting the impression to survive that pre-Enlightenment Scotland actually fits its received image of grinding intellectual poverty this oversight of course has the conspicuous merit of convenience. It fits equally the presupposition, deeply ingrained though decisively despatched by Donald Kelley, that one should not even *expect* to find significant historical discussion in a land given to endemic civil disorder and religious strife.[71] Yet it is also profoundly misleading. It denies vital critical limelight to a panoply of acute early-modern minds, each of them intriguing in their own right but even more valuable for what they can tell us about the moral and intellectual worlds out of which a Scottish Enlightenment was eventually to condense. To read and draw conclusions from the fevered ruminations of Robert Monro, from the elegant Jacobean prose of John Spotswood, or the very different minds of Sir Thomas Urquhart, Thomas Dempster and Gilbert Burnet, is not only belatedly to redress the basic imbalance in our own coverage and understanding of the Scottish past. It is to encounter the compelling moral vision of Scotsmen who were actively engaged in the affairs of their own world, men who satisfied to the full Montaigne's classic humanist dictum that the 'only good histories are those that are written by such as commanded or were employed in weighty affairs'.[72] It is also, I will suggest, to reveal the essential underpinning of habitual scholarly concerns and of common cultural assumptions which united them. These are facets of discourse which are easily dismissed as 'commonplace'. But upon them the prodigious edifice of Scotland's Enlightenment was fundamentally to rely.

Foremost among the questions at which we shall necessarily be looking in this exploration of Scottish scholarship must be the purposes to which these scholars invariably took themselves to be contributing; in shorthand, what they thought they were trying to *do* in writing history. Scholarship in this period offered much more than the mere individual acquisition of knowledge, the personal intellectual gratification of a 'fugitive and cloister'd virtue' so contemptuously dismissed by John Milton, England's greatest spokesman for the Calvinist verities.[73] It promised actual moral improvement, an incalculable benefit to which troubled Scottish minds of all persuasions were irresistably drawn. I shall argue that, because of the oratorical role which they believed their scholarship also gave them, the successors of Boece and Major set out directly to harangue and to edify the nation's sadly nebulous social leadership. But more than this – and in a sense unsurprisingly for they were clearly Scotland's pre-eminent scholars – we shall see that they were tied intellectually as well as emotionally to Calvinist and humanist arguments for the social utility of a deeply rational and learned moral virtue. To this ideal as an incessant and persuasive chorus the Scottish historians of the sixteenth and seventeenth centuries turn out to have committed themselves and, they earnestly hoped, a compliant native audience. This self-consciously moralistic function, moreover, also led early modern historians to discuss with heightened urgency the vexed question of causality. Like their enlightened successors, they knew that without a satisfactory account of the historical processes by which change and development occur any programme so strenuously bent upon the moral regeneration of Scotland and its social leadership would be seriously weakened.[74] As a result the problem of historical causality came to acquire, as Ronald Hamowy has recently highlighted, a disproportionate importance in Scottish thought.[75] These discussions certainly attained their maturity only in the speculations of Ferguson and Smith. But they also possessed a native ancestry at least as far back as the early sixteenth century, a lineage which seems to have held an inescapable grip on even the most enlightened of minds. As basic themes, however, the issues of moral leadership and historical causality were not only to remain alive and extremely fruitful in eighteenth-century Scottish discourse. I shall argue that profound contra-dictions within them, when embodied in strenuous exhortation and argument, were also to have the most damaging consequences for the eventual attempt by Scottish historians to mount an ideological defence of the Enlightenment as a social and intellectual achievement. Indeed, we will see that these inconsistencies were fundamentally to undermine the very social theory of leadership which it had been the dearest wish of Scottish scholars since the sixteenth century to entrench. Few things, then, will emerge more clearly from our own study than that Scotland's eloquent, complex and highly motivated Calvinist and humanist scholars entirely deserve their overdue second hearing.

III

This study takes the form of an extended exploration in the Scottish history of ideas. As a result, the methods employed must seek to tease out from the textual evidence the extent to which the writers actually saw themselves as influential pedagogues. It should reveal them as purposeful Calvinists and committed humanists trying to use history as a vehicle for offering solutions to the most deeply-felt moral problems. The question of authorial intent of course remains a vexed one. Indeed, it is one which for early modern Scotland has rarely been tackled.[76] But in this case we shall at least be able to make use of the dedications, prefaces, and methodological comments provided in the texts. Few Scottish authors seem in their scholarship simply to have plunged *in media res*. Almost all in fact turn out to have made a rhetorical attempt to vindicate their own stance and to theorise their scholarly intentions. This allows the later reader, when willing, to tap into a vein of brooding deliberation, to mine a rich seam of self-conscious purpose which runs throughout the Calvinist and humanist texts, sometimes brilliantly illuminating their authors' own sense of direction. We can therefore with some confidence begin to question the motives which gave rise to the texts. In Quentin Skinner's preferred idiom, we may ask what the authors actually 'were *doing* in writing them'.[77] We might even hope, as I shall later claim, that we are in a position substantially to reconstruct and subject to scrutiny the unfamiliar assumptions, interests and attitudes which characterised men's intellectual response to the peculiar circumstances of a sometimes baffling Scottish past. Adam Ferguson's humanist confidence that 'An author and a work, like cause and effect, are perpetually coupled together'[78] may now seem rather misplaced in the face of Derrida, Lacan, and post-structuralist critical theory. But our frank and sometimes even apologetic authors nevertheless provided us with the most unambiguous statements of their scholarly intent. This surely obliges us as historians to take them into account when we strive, as Pocock and Skinner exhort us, to understand the *historical* meaning of the texts.[79] Whether carefully and deliberately constructing their statements of intention, as most modern historians would accept, or acting merely as conduits for an obligatory rhetoric which they scarcely considered or understood, as some literary theorists would prefer, Scottish authors of this period still delivered surprisingly eloquent and deeply suggestive claims as to the nature and purpose of history. Such clear utterances of the authorial voice offer us from any theoretical perspective a welcome alternative to the mere imputation of intention and purpose to earlier authors and to older forms of scholarship. It is certainly an alternative which no serious modern assessment of its contemporary meaning and function can afford to ignore.

A study of what is essentially a historical discourse must also, of course, pay close attention to the use of contemporary vocabularies in the texts. The vocabulary of moral and political corruption, for example, with its resonant polarities of 'public' and 'private', 'virtue' and 'luxury', was an essential component in the discursive armoury of most Scottish writers, before as well as during the Enlightenment – though we shall sometimes see that the comfortable theoretical oppositions actually conceal less difference and much more awkward ambiguity than is usually presupposed. Similarly, a range of less well-known terms, including such suggestive dualities as 'cause and effect', 'eloquent and learned' and 'honour and greatness', enjoyed a remarkable currency in Scottish historical thinking throughout the period under consideration. These characteristic and usually coherent registers, moreover, were to seem indispensable to the discussions evolving within Scotland's early modern scholarly community. For the exposition of a historical causality, for the propagation of virtue and the creation of a sound and reliable social leadership in Scotland, they were to prove both an instinctive and an appropriate idiom in which to conduct moral discussion. So their historical meaning, which is to say the likely construction put upon them by a contemporary audience comprising other active scholars as well as mute listeners, will emerge as another main preoccupation of our own inquiries.

Fortunately this sensitivity to the full range of potential historical meaning is entirely compatible with the other requirements of this study. I have already argued that the nature and extent of scholarly discourse in Scotland needs urgent reconsideration. By implication this demands, as Pocock has persuasively insisted, a much broader survey of historical texts from the relevant periods: when studying rhetorics, vocabularies or other 'continuities of discourse', the 'more authors you can show to have made use of it the better' and accordingly the less likely that one is guilty of having simply 'read it into the text'.[80] The study of 'discourse' in any case etymologically implies an attempt to recover a complex and interactive discussion. Discourse, at least according to the more plausible modern theoreticians, might even be thought of as a conversation between various participants rather than as a limited and discrete series of monologues, and thus as a conclusive argument for the analysis of a sufficiently large number of texts.[81] Yet, even if it were only a means to breaking out of the 'hermeneutic circle' identified by Pocock in interpreting the texts merely of the famous few, our examination of this much wider selection of contributions to Scottish moral debate would still be amply justified.[82] As an interpretative strategy it tends effectively to limit the scope for a significant misrepresentation of meaning. But at the same time it promises to reveal something of the conventions and purposes leading to the creation of such a remarkable array of early modern literary offerings.

These are the methodological premises upon which this study will proceed. At least, they explain both the priority accorded to historical semantics and the wide selection of texts which it must unapologetically entail. But in the interests of clarity, I must also confess to having divided the material under discussion into two separate chronological sections. This perhaps may seem implicitly to contradict my own special pleading on behalf of cultural continuity and the longer historical perspective. The year 1740, however, at least makes a particularly good dividing point for this entirely pragmatic purpose. It was the year in which David Hume's great *Treatise* notably failed to attract the critical acclaim sought by its young and ambitious author. It was also the year in which considerably more literary attention was lavished on the republication, by popular subscription, of John Major's Latin classic *Historia Majoris Britanniae*. In addition, George Turnbull published his rich and penetrating study of the historical relationship between morality and art, entitled *A Treatise on Ancient Painting*, which generously repays the consideration which we shall give it. But it should by now have become apparent that 1740 also marks a pivotal point in the problematic historiography of Scotland's intellectual life. Hereafter, Scotland is unashamedly regarded as a country in the grip of an Enlightenment. It has duly been rewarded with the attention of students of political thought, social theory and of European discourses. The generations of Scottish scholars writing before 1740, however, were still in touch with an older society and its less familiar intellectual life. The further back one proceeds, their worlds have seemed the private domain of the academic historians inhabiting a few Scottish History departments, as well as of antiquarian researchers. The conventional and disjointed historiography of Scotland's intellectual past, at which I have already substantially gestured, bears an obvious relation to this unfortunate professional dichotomy. It has, not surprisingly, been difficult for intellectual historians unfamiliar with the specifically Scottish writings of the sixteenth and seventeenth centuries properly to question the apparently impressive case for seeing an intellectual revolution in eighteenth-century Scotland. An outmoded academic division-of-labour will therefore also have to be overturned as we now move on to seek an alternative to the traditional historiography by which, I will suggest, the Enlightenment in Scotland has been so sorely abused.

NOTES

1. Carlo Denina's enthusiasm emerges repeatedly in *An Essay on the Revolutions of Literature* (ed.), J. Murdoch (London, 1771). Bramble's famous eulogy is in Tobias Smollett, *The Expedition of Humphry Clinker*, (ed.), L. M. Knapp (London, 1966), p. 233.

2. *On Scotland and the Scotch Intellect*, (ed.), H. J. Hanham (Chicago, 1970), p. 234. This is extracted from the highly influential H. T. Buckle, *History of Civilization in England*, 2 vols (London, 1857–61). See also H. G. Graham's vision of 'the burden of religious tyranny ... the censures levelled at all who indulged in prophane literature, against which ministers inveighed and the pious frowned', *Scottish Men of Letters in the Eighteenth Century* (London, 1901), p. 3.

3. His analysis went on to conflate Moderatism with Deism, and by this disservice was able to represent the Enlightenment as nothing short of a 'new line of anti-Calvinist thought'. H. Macpherson, *The Intellectual Development of Scotland* (London, 1911), pp. 25–6.

4. H. Macpherson, *A Century of Intellectual Development* (Edinburgh, 1907), p. 6.

5. W. L. Mathieson, *The Awakening of Scotland: A History from 1747 to 1797* (Glasgow, 1910), pp. 186–241.

6. William Maitland, *The History and Antiquities of Scotland*, 2 vols (London, 1757), I, 52. Maitland believed that previous Scottish scholarship had been characterised by 'fable and falshood', a description which we shall see could with perhaps greater accuracy be applied to many recent assessments of the Scottish Enlightenment.

7. 'Dissertation Exhibiting a General View of the Progress of Metaphysical, Ethical, and Political Philosophy, Since the Revival of Letters in Europe', *Supplement to the 4th, 5th, and 6th Editions of the Encyclopaedia Britannica*, 6 vols., (Edinburgh, 1815–24), V, 211 n. Significantly, as we shall see, Stewart's conclusion was that the 'constant influx of information and of liberality from abroad' had been responsible. These sentiments found their Edwardian echo when Sir Henry Craik wrote that 'Seldom has a country started more suddenly upon a new career than Scotland did after the Rebellion', *A Century of Scottish History. From the Days Before the '45 to Those Within Living Memory* (Edinburgh, 1911), p. 228. More recently, Tom Nairn has shown how this interpretation can even be integrated into Nationalist cultural politics, with the observation that 'in comparison with the theocratic gloom of the seventeenth century, this [Enlightenment] appeared strange even to some of its protagonists', *The Break-Up of Britain. Crisis and Neo-Nationalism*, 2nd ed (London, 1981), p. 139.

8. Typical of the sententiousness underpinning Edinburgh's publicising of herself as the 'Athens of the North' are references like that to 'this enlightened age of philosophy and reflexion' in Gilbert Stuart, *The History of the Establishment of the Reformation of Religion in Scotland* (London, 1780), p. 206. On Enlightenment triumphalism see J. S. Gibson 'How did the Enlightenment seem to the Edinburgh Enlightened?', *British Journal of Eighteenth Century Studies*, 1 (1978), 46–50. More generally, the flavour of enlightened meditations on their own society and culture may be tasted in some of the excerpts gathered together in E. Dunlop and A. Kamm (eds), *A Book of Old Edinburgh* (Edinburgh, 1983), and in O. D. Edwards and G. Richardson (eds), *Edinburgh* (Edinburgh, 1983).

9. To the wounded English poet, Jeffrey, Scott and Brougham among the authors of the opinionated *Edinburgh Review* were nothing less than the 'Northern wolves', a 'coward brood which mangle as they prey,| By hellish instinct all that cross their way', *English Bards and Scotch Reviewers*, 3rd ed (London, 1810), p. 34. Anger at Scotland's presumptuous and self-appointed cultural arbiters who 'O'er politics and poesy preside', and sheer frustration that 'Scottish taste decides on English wit', only helped foster the impression that its Enlightenment was basically tenuous, unprecedented and, most of all, undeserved.

10. A typical criticism of schismatic Moderatism was McCosh's, that their doctrine 'did not gain, as it did not warm, the hearts of the common people, who either became callous to all religion, without any zealous efforts being made to stir them up, or longed and prayed for a better state of things'. *The Scottish Philosophy: Biographical, Expository, Critical, From Hutcheson to Hamilton* (London, 1875), p. 18. The continuity in this caricature is underlined when it is remembered that in 1868 McCosh had become the President of the College of New Jersey, now Princeton University, exactly one hundred years after the installation of John Witherspoon, to whose contemporary attacks on the Moderates we shall later refer. Princeton was a traditional seat of energetic Presbyterianism with strong Scottish connections, and a prominent home of those 'New England Calvinist clergy' who, according to one recent scholar, after 1798 began to put it about that 'the whole Enlightenment had been a conspiracy' and 'who recited the exciting legend of the near triumph of "French" atheism', H. F. May, 'The Decline of Providence?', *Studies on Voltaire and the Eighteenth Century*, 154 (1976), 1404–5. Modern America, like Scotland, thus inherits from its evangelical past a distinctly partial, almost Manichaean, commentary on the character and achievements of the Enlightenment.

11. Whig antipathy towards the fag-end of enlightened culture in Tory Edinburgh was responsible for a strikingly similar view of the Enlightenment to that propagated by its most malicious evangelical enemies. An irate and anonymous Tory scribbler in the margins of Edinburgh University Library's copy of Mudie's *The Modern Athens* (London, 1825), leaves us in little doubt that his author's Whig disdain for enlightened classicism and triumphalism, for 'Mrs Macspire, who studies the Differential Calculus' and for a society which affected to be 'religiously irreligious', had struck its intended target. That the Enlightenment was thus pretentious, ephemeral, marginal, or even vaguely ridiculous, was also the equivalent Tory charge levelled at the Whig 'high' Enlightenment of the previous century, and its surviving vestiges like the second *Edinburgh Review*. Lockhart in particular, as may be seen in his satirical *Peter's Letters to His Kinsfolk* (ed.), W. Ruddick (Edinburgh, 1977), could purvey a scathing conservative critique of the Enlightenment as deviant, decadent and dangerous. Like his mentor Scott, moreover, Lockhart's opinions of the Scottish past were to be as widely influential as they were blatantly partial.

12. [John Britton], *Modern Athens! Displayed in a Series of Views* (London, 1829), p. 1.

13. H. R. Trevor-Roper, 'The Scottish Enlightenment', *Studies on Voltaire and the Eighteenth Century*, 58 (1967), 1635–58; P. Gay, *The Enlightenment*, 2 vols (New York, 1966–9). Mackenzie claimed that before 1700 in Scotland 'Trade, farming, scholarship, the arts, were a desert', *Scotland in Modern Times*, 1720–1939 (London, 1941), p. 4.

14. Trevor-Roper, 'Scottish Enlightenment', p. 1639.

15. Hume and Robertson represent the Scottish Enlightenment in J. B. Black, *The Art of History: A Study of Four Great Historians of the Eighteenth Century* (London, 1926). This merely followed the Victorian orthodoxy, exemplified by Sir Leslie Stephen who found Hume, Robertson, and Gibbon 'the triumvirate of great historians' and their works 'amongst the most characteristic products of the times', *English Thought in the Eighteenth Century*, 2 vols (London, 1876), I, 446. For a slightly wider selection, see D. B. Horn, 'Some Scottish Writers of History in the Eighteenth Century', *Scottish Historical Review*, 40 (1961), 1–18.

16. C. Camic, *Experience and Enlightenment: Socialization for Cultural Change in Eighteenth-Century Scotland* (Edinburgh, 1983), usefully condensed, but no more convincing, as 'Experience and Ideas: Education for Universalism in Eighteenth-Century Scotland', *Comparative Studies in Society and History*, 25 (1983), 52–82.

17. J. D. Hoeveler, *James McCosh and the Scottish Intellectual Tradition* (Princeton, NJ, 1981), p. 27.

18. J. Lough, 'Reflections on Enlightenment and Lumières', *British Journal of Eighteenth Century Studies*, 8 (1985), 9. Another variation on this well-worn theme is to regard the Enlightenment itself simply as a set of authors, thus: 'that remarkable group of philosophers, moralists, and social scientists sometimes referred to as the Scottish Enlightenment', A. O. Hirschmann, *The Passions and the Interests: Political Arguments for Capitalism Before its Triumph* (Princeton, NJ, 1977), p. 70.

19. J. Robertson, *The Scottish Enlightenment and the Militia Issue* (London, 1985), p. 8.

20. Original and informative studies of this kind include A. C. Chitnis, *The Scottish Enlightenment*

and Early Victorian English Society (London, 1986), and J. Rendall, 'Scottish Orientalism: from Robertson to James Mill', *Historical Journal*, 25 (1982), 43–69. One of the finest has been S. Collini, D. Winch and J. Burrow, *That Noble Science of Politics: A Study in Nineteenth-Century Intellectual History* (Cambridge, 1983). Also more recently, M. Kuehn, *Scottish Common Sense in Germany, 1768–1800: A Contribution to the History of Critical Philosophy* (Kingston, Ont., 1987) and D. W. Howe, 'Why the Scottish Enlightenment was Useful to the Framers of the American Constitution', *Comparative Studies in Society and History*, 31 (1989), 572–87, studies which continue a tradition earlier represented by A. Seth [Pringle-Pattison], *Scottish Philosophy: A Comparison of the Scottish and German Answers to Hume*, 2nd edn, (Edinburgh, 1890), and D. S. Sloan, *The Scottish Enlightenment and the American College Ideal* (New York, 1971).

21. The definitive examination of the relationship between Scottish and Marxist political economy, with specific reference to the origins of the labour theory of value and the materialist classification of society, is R. L. Meek, 'The Scottish Contribution to Marxist Sociology', in J. Saville (ed.), *Democracy and the Labour Movement* (London, 1954), pp. 84–102. Meek's conclusions are questioned in A. S. Skinner, 'Economics and History – The Scottish Enlightenment', *Scottish Journal of Political Economy*, 12 (1965), 1–22, and more directly in his subsequent 'A Scottish Contribution to Marxist Sociology?', in I. Bradley and M. Howard (eds), *Classical and Marxian Political Economy: Essays in Honour of Ronald L. Meek* (London, 1982), pp. 79–107. An assessment of the Scottish Enlightenment by a modern sociologist is A. Swingewood, 'Origins of Sociology: The Case of the Scottish Enlightenment', *British Journal of Sociology*, 21 (1970), 164–80.

22. Denina, *Essay*, p. 274.

23. N. T. Phillipson, 'Politics, Politeness, and the Anglicisation of Early Eighteenth-Century Scottish Culture', in R. A. Mason (ed.), *Scotland and England: 1286–1815* (Edinburgh, 1987), p. 228.

24. R. L. Meek, *Social Science and the Ignoble Savage* (Cambridge, 1976). Also U. P. Burke, 'Scottish Historians and the Feudal System: The Conceptualisation of Social Change' (1978), an unpublished paper for the use of which I must thank Mr Burke. In particular, the influence of the French *physiocrats* has been traced in Smith, on which see R. L. Meek, 'Smith, Turgot, and the "Four Stages" Theory', in his *Smith, Marx, and After: Ten Essays in the Development of Economic Thought* (London, 1977), pp. 18–32. An emphasis upon foreign influences goes back at least to the Victorian era. The undoubted significance of Port-Royal logic and of Pufendorf for the explication of Scottish philosophy drew the attention of J. Veitch, 'Philosophy in the Scottish Universities', *Mind*, 2 (1877), esp. 209, though once again Dugald Stewart is perhaps the ultimate source for such an account.

25. I. Hont and M. Ignatieff (eds), *Wealth and Virtue: The Shaping of Political Economy in the Scottish Enlightenment* (Cambridge, 1983).

26. The argument that natural jurisprudence and its influence on Stair and subsequent Scots lawyers, shaped Enlightenment discussions, here enunciated by Forbes, had earlier been outlined in P. Stein, 'Law and Society in Eighteenth-Century Scottish Thought', in N. T. Phillipson and R. Mitchison (eds), *Scotland in the Age of Improvement* (Edinburgh, 1970), pp. 148–68. This has more recently been extensively analysed in K. Haakonssen, *The Science of a Legislator: The Natural Jurisprudence of David Hume and Adam Smith* (Cambridge, 1981), and in L. Bauer and H. Matis, 'From Moral Philosophy to Political Economy: The Genesis of Social Science', *History of European Ideas*, 9 (1988), 123–43.

27. The somewhat tortuous evolution of a specifically 'civic' virtue before its translation into a Scottish context, by way of classical Athens, republican Rome, Renaissance Florence, and Puritan England, is charted in the monumental J. G. A. Pocock, *The Machiavellian Moment: Florentine Political Thought and the Atlantic Republican Tradition* (Princeton, NJ, 1975). For a critical overview of the whole unresolved debate, see C. J. Berry, 'The Nature of Wealth and the Origins of Virtue', *History of European Ideas*, 7 (1986), 85–99.

28. Ochtertyre, for example, was a notable spokesman for the view that the Union with England, and the contemporary arrival of English polite culture had themselves been responsible for the Scottish Enlightenment, arguing that it was 'the appearance of *Tatlers, Spectators*, and *Guardians* in the reign of Queen Anne' which had turned the hitherto barbarous Scotsman into 'a polite scholar', *Scotland and Scotsmen in the Eighteenth Century* (ed.), A. Allardyce, 2 vols (Edinburgh, 1888), I, 6–7.

29. This view is exemplified for recent times in N. T. Phillipson, 'Culture and Society in the Eighteenth-Century Provinces', in L. Stone (ed.), *The University in Society*, 2 vols (Princeton, NJ, 1975), I, 407–48. The possibility of considering Scotland as a definitively provincial culture was earlier explored in J. Clive and B. Bailyn, 'England's Cultural Provinces: Scotland and America', *William and Mary Quarterly*, 11 (1954), 200–13.

30. For example, T. M. Devine, 'The Scottish Merchant Community, 1680–1740', in R. H. Campbell and A. S. Skinner (eds), *The Origins and Nature of the Scottish Enlightenment* (Edinburgh, 1982), pp. 26–41; J. Clive, 'The Social Background of the Scottish Renaissance', in Phillipson and Mitchison (eds), *Scotland in the Age of Improvement*, pp. 225–44; and J. Patrick, *Scotland: The Age of Achievement* (London, 1972). The argument that Scottish political economy in particular originated as a matter of obvious concern to this group is found in R. Pascal, 'Property and Society: The Scottish Historical School of the Eighteenth Century', *Modern Quarterly*, 2 (1938), 167–79. Habitual recourse in historical explanation to a conveniently ever-rising middle class is roundly and quite properly condemned in J. C. D. Clark, *Revolution and Rebellion. State and Society in England in the Seventeenth and Eighteenth Centuries* (Cambridge, 1986), p. 166. However, the claims for Scotland in this respect are at least normally based on a thorough study of what was always a compact and readily identifiable urban community in Lowland Scotland.

31. N. T. Phillipson, 'Lawyers, Landowners, and the Civic Leadership of Post-Union Scotland', *Juridical Review* (1976), p. 107.

32. This, again, is not a new idea. H. G. Graham claimed in 1901 that 'If we wish to seek out the beginnings of Scottish literature, we shall find it in the clubs of gentlemen that met in dingy taverns, in dark wynds of Edinburgh', *Men of Letters*, p. 7. Henry Laurie, meanwhile, believed that in Scotland before the Union the 'troubled condition of the realm was unfriendly to learning or speculation'. Yet the Union, 'which closed a period in the national history, was the signal for a new departure ... the arts began to flourish, science progressed, and literature and philosophy entered on their Augustan age', *Scottish Philosophy in its National Development* (Glasgow, 1902), pp. 1–4. This view still survives in Neil McCallum's suggestion that in the 1720s the 'warm winds of Augustan England blew northwards to aerate the mustiness of Edinburgh and Glasgow, and help to liberate the Scot from the shackles of his theology', *A Small Country. Scotland 1700–1830* (Edinburgh, 1983), p. 57. Its connection with the republican paradigm is elucidated in N. T. Phillipson, 'Virtue, Commerce, and the Science of Man', *Studies on Voltaire and the Eighteenth Century*, 190 (1980), 750–2, and the pursuit of virtue in a depoliticised society is examined in his 'The Scottish Enlightenment', in R. Porter and M. Teich (eds), *The Enlightenment in National Context* (Cambridge, 1981), pp. 19–40.

33. The thorny problem of national identity, as it was moulded in the hands of the Scottish élite, is explored by R. Mitchison, 'Patriotism and National Identity in Eighteenth-Century Scotland', in T. W. Moody (ed.), *Nationality and the Pursuit of National Independence* (London, 1978), pp. 73–95, and by T. C. Smout in 'Problems of Nationalism, Identity, and Improvement in Later Eighteenth-Century Scotland', in T. M. Devine (ed.), *Improvement and Enlightenment* (Edinburgh, 1989), pp. 1–21. See also N. T. Phillipson, 'Nationalism and Ideology', in J. Wolfe (ed.), *Government and Nationalism in Scotland* (Edinburgh, 1969), pp. 167–88.

34. N. T. Phillipson, *Hume* (London, 1989), p. 6. The Union is similarly given greatest emphasis in J. Rendall, *The Origins of the Scottish Enlightenment* (London, 1978), and in D. Daiches, *The Paradox of Scottish Culture: The Eighteenth-Century Experience* (London, 1964). This opinion likewise had a nineteenth-century pedigree, as when Lord Cockburn, the distinguished former pupil of Dugald Stewart, reflected in the 1820s upon his having witnessed the completion of 'the change from ancient to modern manners' and the post-Union development of 'enlarged intercourse with England and the world', *Memorials of His Time* (ed.), W. F. Gray, (Edinburgh, 1946), p. 23. The view that Scottish intellectual life was in fact 'reactivated' after the Glorious Revolution is represented by G. E. Davie, *The Scottish Enlightenment* (London, 1981).

35. See, for example, D. B. Horn, *A Short History of the University of Edinburgh*, 1556–1889 (Edinburgh, 1967), esp. pp. 36–94. Also, J. D. Mackie, *The University of Glasgow*, 1451–1951 (Glasgow, 1954), esp. pp. 215–42. Bagehot had tried to explain why Scotland over the preceding century had produced so many learned writers like those responsible for the second

Edinburgh Review: 'as a preparation for the writing of various articles, the system of Edinburgh', he claimed, 'is enormously superior to that of Cambridge. The particular, compact, exclusive learning of England is inferior in this respect to the general, diversified, omnipresent information of the north; and what is more, the speculative, dubious nature of metaphysical and such like pursuits tends, in a really strong mind, to cultivate habits of independent thought and original discussion', *Collected Works* (ed.), N. St John-Stevas, 6 vols (London, 1965), I, 328–9. Even during the eighteenth century, the Scottish universities had been recognised as of exceptional intellectual significance: 'go to Edinburgh to learn the art of life', advised one Hungarian observer, 'for the exact sciences, Edinburgh is worth more than Oxford and Cambridge together', quoted in Mackenzie, *Scotland*, p. 27.

36.   Curricular reform is examined in R. L. Emerson, 'Scottish Universities in the Eighteenth Century, 1690–1800', *Studies on Voltaire and the Eighteenth Century*, 167 (1977), 453–74, and R. G. Cant, 'Origins of the Enlightenment in Scotland: The Universities', in Campbell and Skinner (eds), *Origins and Nature of the Scottish Enlightenment*, pp. 42–64. The most detailed study of an enlightened university is, however, the excellent R. L. Emerson, *Professors, Patronage and Politics: The Aberdeen Universities in the Eighteenth Century* (Aberdeen, 1992).

37.   P. Jones, 'The Polite Academy and the Presbyterians, 1729–1770', in J. Dwyer and A. Murdoch (eds), *New Perspectives on the Politics and Culture of Early Modern Scotland* (Edinburgh, 1982), pp. 156–78, and his 'The Scottish Professoriate and the Polite Academy, 1720–46', in Hont and Ignatieff (eds), *Wealth and Virtue*, pp. 89–117. Also, if in a slightly less familiar idiom, see O. M. Griffiths, *Religion and Learning: A Study in English Presbyterian Thought* (Cambridge, 1935), pp. 68–76.

38.   G. E. Davie, *The Democratic Intellect: Scotland and Her Universities in the Nineteenth Century* (Edinburgh, 1961). See also A. Law, *Education in Edinburgh in the Eighteenth Century* (London, 1965).

39.   R. G. Cant, 'The Scottish Universities and Scottish Society in the Eighteenth Century', *Studies on Voltaire and the Eighteenth Century*, 58 (1967), 1953–66. The relationship between the great Scottish university and high Enlightenment science is explained in J. B. Morrell, 'The University of Edinburgh in the Late Eighteenth Century: Its Scientific Eminence and Academic Structure', *Isis* 62 (1971), 158–71. See also R. V. Jones, 'Physical Science in the Eighteenth Century', *British Journal of Eighteenth Century Studies*, 2 (1978), 73–88, and S. Shapin, 'The Audience for Science in Eighteenth-Century Edinburgh', *History of Science*, 12 (1974), 95–121, which stress the popularisation of scientific knowledge both in the universities and society. Reasons for seeing scientific achievements beyond the Central Lowlands are advanced in P. Wood, 'Science and the Aberdeen Enlightenment', in P. Jones (ed.), *Philosophy and Science in the Scottish Enlightenment* (Edinburgh, 1988), pp. 39–66.

40.   The volume of work on Scottish clubs and societies has proliferated in the wake of the initial survey of D. D. McElroy, 'The Literary Clubs and Societies of Eighteenth-Century Scotland' (unpublished Ph.D. dissertation, University of Edinburgh, 1952), and his later *Scotland's Age of Improvement* (Washington, DC, 1969). Several of the most illuminating papers have been by Emerson, such as 'The Social Composition of Enlightened Scotland: the "Select Society of Edinburgh", 1754–1764', *Studies on Voltaire and the Eighteenth Century*, 114 (1973), 291–330, and his 'The Edinburgh Society for the Importation of Foreign Seeds and Plants, 1764–1773', *Eighteenth Century Life*, 7 (1982), 73–95, which deal respectively with the most distinguished and one of the most functional of enlightened societies. The one about which most is known, again thanks to Dr Emerson, is the subject of four detailed papers: 'The Philosophical Society of Edinburgh, 1737–1747', *British Journal for the History of Science*, 12 (1979), 154–91; 'The Philosophical Society of Edinburgh, 1748–1768', *ibid.*, 14 (1981), 133–76; 'The Philosophical Society of Edinburgh, 1768–1783', *ibid.*, 18 (1985), 255–303; and 'The Scottish Enlightenment and the End of the Philosophical Society of Edinburgh', *ibid.*, 21 (1988), 33–66. A valuable recent addition to the field has been S. A. Conrad's 1980 Harvard University Ph.D. dissertation, published as *Citizenship and Common Sense: The Problem of Authority in the Social Background and Social Philosophy of the Wise Club of Aberdeen* (New York, 1987).

41.   For example, in 1983 McCallum suggested that the Enlightenment had been a clean cultural break: 'Scotland's old literary tradition had been destroyed, and a new one had still to be created', *Small Country*, p. 63.

42.   A. J. Youngson, *The Making of Classical Edinburgh* (Edinburgh, 1966), p. v.

43. Focusing on the enlightened experiences of the capital city, see M. Joyce, *Edinburgh: The Golden Age*, 1769–1832 (London, 1951); D. Young (ed.), *Edinburgh in the Age of Reason* (Edinburgh, 1967); and his 'Scotland and Edinburgh in the Eighteenth Century', *Studies on Voltaire and the Eighteenth Century*, 58 (1967), 1967–90. Perhaps the most penetrating study relating enlightened principles to neo-classical architecture remains T. A. Markus (ed.), *Order in Space and Society: Architectural Form and its Context in the Scottish Enlightenment* (Edinburgh, 1982).

44. An early and plaintive plea on behalf of the late seventeenth century is H. W. Meikle, *Some Aspects of Later Seventeenth-Century Scotland* (Glasgow, 1947). As David Stevenson has aptly remarked, the general impression of a seventeenth century 'with few friends', of an age 'marked by cultural failure, religious fanaticism, economic decay, political violence, and corruption', owes much more to a lack of serious historical research in this field than to sober historical fact. See his and other recent counter-blasts to orthodoxy in R. Mitchison (ed.), *Why Scottish History Matters* (Edinburgh, 1991), esp. pp. 37–47.

45. G. Donaldson, 'Stair's Scotland: The Intellectual Heritage', *Juridical Review* (1981), p. 145. David Daiches, for one, has recently identified a belated tendency 'to look further back, into the seventeenth century, to see the roots of the movement and to see the Scottish Enlightenment as a natural development of an earlier phase of Scottish culture', D. Daiches, P. Jones and J. Jones (eds), *A Hotbed of Genius: The Scottish Enlightenment*, 1730–1790 (Edinburgh, 1986), p. 5. But Roger Emerson rightly still asserts the need for sweeping revisionism, as all too many recent studies, though having 'sited the Scottish Enlightenment in interesting social, political, and economic contexts, even in religious ones, ... have spent little ink analysing its native sources, its extra-Scottish dimensions, or the intellectual forces which impelled its development', R. L. Emerson, 'Science and the Origins and Concerns of the Scottish Enlightenment', *History of Science*, 26 (1988), 333. Such continuing deficiencies, when subjected to the even more intense scrutiny of Nationalist criticism, have been seen as mere craven acquiescence in what many die-hards claim is Scotland's deep-seated and self-inflicted cultural 'inferiorism'. See A. C. Chitnis, 'The 18th Century Intellectual Enquiry', *Cencrastus*, 25 (1987), 9–11.

46. The medical and scientific origins of the Scottish Enlightenment are surveyed in J. R. R. Christie, 'The Origins and Development of the Scottish Scientific Community, 1680–1760', *History of Science*, 7 (1974), 122–41. A convincing argument for such a community existing by the end of the seventeenth century is R. L. Emerson, 'Natural Philosophy and the Problem of the Scottish Enlightenment', *Studies on Voltaire and the Eighteenth Century*, 242 (1986), 243–92. The cohesion and direction of this group of 'virtuosi' is examined in his 'Sir Robert Sibbald, Kt., the Royal Society of Scotland and the Origins of the Scottish Enlightenment', *Annals of Science*, 45 (1988), 41–72. I am grateful to Dr Emerson for an early copy of this illuminating paper.

47. See I. G. Brown, *The Clerks of Penicuik: Portraits of Taste and Talent* (Edinburgh, 1987) and his 'Critick in Antiquity: Sir John Clerk of Penicuik', *Antiquity*, 51 (1977), 201–10.

48. A. Broadie, *The Tradition of Scottish Philosophy* (Edinburgh, 1990).

49. See e.g. D. Beales, 'Christians and *philosophes*: The Case of the Austrian Enlightenment', in his and G. Best (eds), *History, Society, and the Churches: Essays in Honour of Owen Chadwick* (Cambridge, 1985), pp. 169–94, and T. C. W. Blanning, 'The Enlightenment in Catholic Germany', in Porter and Teich (eds), *The Enlightenment*, pp. 118–26, both of which substantiate older suspicions about the claim that being 'enlightened' also entailed being sceptical of religion in general.

50. The 'evil odour' of Moderatism and its close relationship with the ideas of a putatively rationalist, secular, not to say amoral Enlightenment philosophy, intimately involved in the ostensibly secular view of a man like Hector Macpherson, also had a central role in an authentic Free Kirk historiography well into the present century. See e.g. J. MacLeod, *Scottish Theology* (Edinburgh, 1943), in which it seems that even the reconciliation in the Scottish communion in 1929 cannot unseat the Moderates from their focal position in the Evangelical demonology.

51. A. C. Chitnis, 'The Eighteenth-Century Scottish Intellectual Inquiry: Context and Continuity versus Civic Humanism', in Carter and Pittock (eds), *Aberdeen and the Enlightenment*, p. 79.

52. The definitive study of skilful Moderate manipulation remains I. D. L. Clark, 'Moderatism

and the Moderate Party in the Church of Scotland, 1752–1805' (unpublished Ph.D. dissertation, University of Cambridge, 1963), which was substantially restated in his 'From Protest to Reaction: the Moderate Regime in the Church of Scotland, 1752–1805', in Phillipson and Mitchison (eds), *Scotland in the Age of Improvement*, pp. 200–24.

53. D. C. Lachman, *The Marrow Controversy* (Edinburgh, 1988). See also J. K. Cameron, 'Theological Controversy: A Factor in the Origins of the Scottish Enlightenment', in Campbell and Skinner (eds), *The Origins and Nature of the Scottish Enlightenment*, pp. 116–30, and J. K. Cameron, 'The Church of Scotland in the Age of Reason', *Studies on Voltaire and the Eighteenth Century*, 58; (1967), 1939–51. For a broader survey, see A. L. Drummond and J. Bulloch, *The Scottish Church, 1688–1843: The Age of the Moderates* (Edinburgh, 1973), which emphasises the eirenical role of tolerance in general, and the Moderates in particular, in allowing polite culture to develop.

54. The most illuminating and detailed study of these twin pillars of the Moderate campaign is R. Sher, *Church and University in the Scottish Enlightenment* (Princeton, NJ, 1985).

55. J. Dwyer, 'The Heavenly City of the Eighteenth-Century Moderate Divines', in his and A. Murdoch (eds), *New Perspectives*, pp. 291–318. Becker claimed for the French Enlightenment that 'the *philosophes* were nearer the Middle Ages, less emancipated from the preconceptions of medieval Christian thought, than they quite realised or we have commonly supposed', *The Heavenly City of the Eighteenth-Century Philosophers* (New Haven, Conn., 1932), p. 29. An equally clear call for a fairer appraisal, likewise largely ignored in the Buckle-Gay tradition, was that of Ernst Cassirer, who questioned the 'declarations by its champions and spokesmen' that the Enlightenment was 'an age basically irreligious and inimical to religion', *The Philosophy of the Enlightenment* (Princeton, NJ, 1951), p. 135. As we shall later see, the testimony of contemporary self-publicists and propagandists, in particular, calls for the most meticulous cross-examination.

56. Thomas Somerville, *My Own Life and Times* (Edinburgh, 1861), p. 385.

57. It has recently been pointed out, for example, that whilst the tolerant and rational Hill opposed humanitarian movements, the fiery presbyterian Thomas Chalmers supported them: the enlightened improver and the Calvinist evangelical, it seems, actually had much in common. See J. M. Simpson, 'Scottish Enlightenment Studies: Three Routes Through a Busy Place', *Scottish Journal of Political Economy*, 34 (1987), 101. But the clearest statement on behalf of a possible 'Evangelical Enlightenment' is N. C. Landsman, 'Witherspoon and the Problem of Provincial Identity in Scottish Evangelical Culture', in R. Sher and J. R. Smitten (eds), *Scotland and America in the Age of the Enlightenment* (Edinburgh, 1990), pp. 29–45.

58. Macqueen has recently asserted that the 'Scottish Enlightenment was the natural, almost the inevitable, outcome of several centuries of Scottish and European intellectual history', J. MacQueen, *The Enlightenment and Scottish Literature: Progress and Poetry* (Edinburgh, 1982), p. 5. Perhaps it is significant, however, that the author is a student of Scottish literature rather than specifically of eighteenth-century ideas, thus finding it much easier to locate the Enlightenment within a longer tradition of local writing. Indeed, the most recent and spirited challenge to 'the Whig interpretation of cultural history' in early modern Scotland has likewise come from scholars whose interests and remit are initially literary rather than historical or intellectual. The *History of Scottish Literature*, (gen. ed.), C. Craig, 4 vols (Aberdeen, 1987), however, will remain an invaluable reference guide for the historian of ideas, and a deliberately powerful antidote to the recurrent view that Scottish thought jolted violently and inexorably from, 'say, the barbarism of the seventeenth century to the enlightenment of the eighteenth', *ibid.*, II, 1.

59. On Scott as a reader and copyist of Enlightenment historical literature see J. Anderson, *Sir Walter Scott and History* (Edinburgh, 1981). Yet Anderson, rightly as we shall see, also stresses Scott's familiarity with and inspiration by a great morass of Scottish printed and MS. histories from the sixteenth and seventeenth centuries.

60. Hume's famous claim to know of eight historical works then in progress in Scotland comes in a letter to William Strahan, *Letters of David Hume* (ed.), G. Birkbeck-Hill (Oxford, 1888), p. 155. One implication of this study may be that the reference to 'the historical Nation' reflects not just contemporary productivity but also an awareness of a much longer tradition of historical writing in Scotland, a possibility which, for all the recognition that 'Eighteenth-century Scotland was in fact obsessed with history', Daiches, Jones and Jones (eds), *Hotbed*

of Genius, p. 9, has almost always been ignored. The 'historical nation', John MacQueen most recently notes, was in fact 'what it had always been', *The Enlightenment and Scottish Literature: The Rise of the Historical Novel* (Edinburgh, 1989), p. 8.

61. See G. W. Stocking, 'Scotland as the Model of Mankind: Lord Kames' Philosophical View of Civilization', in T. H. H. Thoresen (ed.), *Toward a Science of Man: Essays in the History of Anthropology* (The Hague, 1975), pp. 65–89. Also A. S. Skinner, 'Natural History in the Age of Adam Smith', *Political Studies*, 12 (1967), 32–48. All of these treatments look back to A. W. Small, *Adam Smith and Modern Sociology* (Chicago, 1907); W. C. Lehmann, *Adam Ferguson and the Beginnings of Modern Sociology* (New York, 1930); and, more recently, to W. C. Lehmann, *John Millar of Glasgow, 1735–1801. His Life and Thought and His Contributions to Sociological Analysis* (Cambridge, 1960), each of which, as some of the titles immediately suggest, emphasises the alleged social scientific credentials of its respective enlightened scholar.

62. An influential work, though dangerously misleading in this respect, is G. Bryson, *Man and Society: The Scottish Enquiry of the Eighteenth Century* (Princeton, NJ, 1945). For Schneider, too, the implication is that we study ideas 'that today we would unhesitatingly call "sociological"', *The Scottish Moralists on Human Nature and Society* (Chicago, 1967), pp. xi, xv. Such attributions of intention or avoidance of contemporary intellectual significance, as we shall see, risk profoundly distorting the very meaning and function of enlightened scholarship in its own time.

63. The failure sufficiently to stress the significance of Scottish 'moral theory' in the formulation both of classical political economy and the historical tradition has been pointed out in Berry, 'Nature of Wealth', p. 86. Most recently, R. F. Teichgraeber has presented a study with the extremely promising title '*Free Trade*' and Moral Philosophy: Rethinking the Sources of Adam Smith's Wealth of Nations* (Durham, NC, 1986), which goes some way towards fulfilling this obligation, though again with no reference to a Scottish context before Hutcheson. Nicholas Phillipson has portrayed two leading figures as moralists in 'Adam Smith as Civic Moralist', in Hont and Ignatieff (eds), *Wealth and Virtue*, pp. 179–202, and 'Hume as Moralist: A Social Historian's Perspective', in S. Brown (ed.), *Philosophers of the Enlightenment* (Hassocks, Sussex, 1979), pp. 140–61.

64. J. Dwyer, *Virtuous Discourse: Sensibility and Community in Late Eighteenth-Century Scotland* (Edinburgh, 1987), p. 4.

65. A noteworthy and belated exception, bringing Enlightenment studies to the provincial Scottish scene, is the contribution of J. Strawhorn, 'Ayrshire in the Enlightenment', in G. Cruikshank (ed.), *A Sense of Place. Studies in Scottish Local History* (Edinburgh, 1988), pp. 188–99. That Enlightenment everywhere meant 'improvement', and that far from being a 'social phenomenon ... restricted to Edinburgh or to the universities' it was 'something whose influence made itself felt through a wider area', begins to seem more than likely. More widely, an attack on the notion that the Enlightenment was confined to 'high culture' has come in the form of R. Sher and A. Murdoch, 'Literary and Learned Culture', in T. M. Devine and R. Mitchison (eds), *People and Society in Scotland*, 3 vols (Edinburgh, 1988), I, 127–42.

66. In Graham's words, for example, the eighteenth century 'opens in Scotland to find the country almost devoid of literature. Men of letters there were none; of making books there seems to have been an end ... ', *Men of Letters*, pp. 1–2. The logical extension of this line of thinking is the attempt to install select individuals as the Augustan *fons et origo* of serious Scottish scholarship. One favoured candidate for the honour of having begun 'true historical scholarship in Scotland' is Thomas Innes, who flourished in the 1720s, H. R. Trevor-Roper, 'George Buchanan and the Ancient Scottish Constitution', *English Historical Review*, Suppl. 3 (1966), 1.

67. A similar short-sightedness has long afflicted the history of England in the same era, as specialist periodizations imported wholesale from political and religious history have been transposed onto the cultural and intellectual continuum. This tendency has only recently begun to be corrected, most obviously by Joseph Levine, whose remarks make instructive reading for the historian about to embark upon a study of early modern Scotland: 'the years between 1500 and 1800 can be seen as forming a single period, harboring at least one common set of assumptions and habit of mind which acted continuously upon the thought of the time ... The outlook of the age of Burke and Pitt and Fox, of Samuel Johnson and Edward Gibbon,

was in some respects the natural culmination of a movement begun three centuries before', *Humanism and History: Origins of Modern English Historiography* (Ithaca, NY, 1987), p. 10. We have in fact, says Alex Broadie, been guilty of nothing less than 'a systematic misrepresentation of the Scottish cultural scene', a view forcefully expressed in the significantly-titled 'Continuity of Scottish Philosophy', *Cencrastus*, 25, (1987), 6–7.

68. Lewis's suggestion is that by 1600 we 'enter a period in which historians of Scotch literature can fill their chapters only by dwelling upon writers who in happier lands and ages would hardly secure a mention', *English Literature in the Sixteenth Century* (Oxford, 1954), p. 113. Lewis's use of the provocative archaism 'Scotch' perhaps sufficiently indicates his unreliability as a judge of significant Scottish literature. Nevertheless, Lewis is by no means alone in his error: as George Davie observes, by the later nineteenth century 'an all-embracing oblivion [had] engulfed the heroes of Scottish learning since Renaissance-Reformation times', *Democratic Intellect*, p. 337.

69. Williamson's *Scottish National Consciousness in the Age of James VI: The Apocalypse, the Union, and the Shaping of Scotland's Public Culture* (Edinburgh, 1979), is the definitive study of the sixteenth-century controversialists writing in a historical idiom. Other valuable contributions in this area include R. A. Mason, 'Scotching the Brut: History and National Myth in Sixteenth-Century Scotland', in his (ed.), *Scotland and England*, pp. 60–84, and W. Matthews, 'The Egyptians in Scotland: Political History of a Myth', *Viator*, 1 (1970), 289–306. An important earlier treatment, for example, is V. V. Bransford, 'Scotland's Patriotic Historians', *Macmillans Magazine*, 76 (1897), 268–78.

70. The seventeenth-century scholars have at least recently been discussed in the excellent M. Lynch, *Scotland: A New History* (London, 1991), ch. 15.

71. Kelley explains: 'In general, history is not something which, like poetry, is recollected in tranquility. On the contrary, it is precisely in times of crisis, in times of self-doubt and self-searching, that men begin most intensively to question their antecedents and to seek the reasons for their plight', *Foundations of Modern Historical Scholarship. Language, Law, and History in the French Renaissance* (Columbia, NY, 1970), p. 11.

72. *Essais*, (ed. and transl.), J. Florio (New York, 1907), p. 343. This axiom was of obvious comfort to prospective enlightened scholars like John Home, clergyman, aspiring tragedian and the leader of Edinburgh's resistance to the Jacobite army in 1745. His own work explicitly relied for its authority upon Home's personal familiarity with the subject in hand. See *The History of the Rebellion in the Year 1745* (London, 1802), p. vi. Home also cites Xenophon as well as Wishart's *Montrose* in order to prove Montaigne's point. Many were thus, like James Graham of Freuchie in the 1650s, writing frenetically of events as 'an Eye and Ear Witness to all that passed from first to last', *An Account of the Expedition of William Earl of Glencairn, etc.* (Glasgow, University Library, MSS Gen. 372), Title.

73. The celebrated text runs 'I cannot praise a fugitive and cloister'd virtue, unexercis'd and unbreath'd, that never sallies out and sees her adversary, but slinks out of the race, where that immortal garland is to be run for, not without heat and dust', John Milton, 'Areopagitica', in *Prose Works: 1641–1650*, 3 vols (Menston, England, 1967), II, 12. As we shall see, it is almost possible to imagine Adam Ferguson mouthing the words.

74. Certain aspects of the Enlightenment discussion of causality have of course received consideration. Of late there has been some attempt to understand why, for example, Adam Smith still apparently conceived of an 'all-wise Author of Nature', whose "invisible hand" had shaped the design', P. Stein, 'From Pufendorf to Adam Smith: The Natural Law Tradition in Scotland", in N. Horn, (ed.), *Europäisches Rechtsdenken in Geschichte und Gegenwart*, 2 vols (Munich, 1982), I, 679. On a different tack, Roger Emerson has followed up the suggestions made in his own earlier paper 'Peter Gay and the Heavenly City', *Journal of the History of Ideas*, 28 (1967), 383–402, and offered an account of enlightened historical progress cognate with the scriptural and classical traditions found 'a generation before' in Scotland, 'Conjectural Historians and the Scottish Philosophers', *Canadian Historical Association Historical Papers* (1984), p. 63–90. The New Right, too, have reclaimed the Scottish fascination with causality for the defence of classical liberalism, as in F. A. Hayek, 'The Use of Knowledge in Society', in his *Individualism and the Economic Order* (London, 1949), pp. 77–91, and A. Flew, 'From ... The Virtue of Selfishness to the Invisible Hand', *Focus*, 1 (1980), 21–30. But the relocating of enlightened historical causality in its longer Scottish context has yet to be attempted.

75. R. Hamowy, *The Scottish Enlightenment and the Theory of Spontaneous Order* (Carbondale, Ill., 1987). As its preface by Iain Ross notes, however, this contribution retains many of the traditional defects, leaving unanswered some very important questions: '*How* did the Scots come to adopt this theory so pervasively in the eighteenth century, and perhaps more importantly, *why* did they do so?' These are among the major issues to which we will later address ourselves.

76. It is, for example, unlikely that Adam Ferguson, moral philosopher and presbyterian minister, intended writing anything which would lead D. G. Macrae to include him in T. Raison, (ed.), *The Founding Fathers of Social Science* (Harmondsworth, 1963), pp. 17–26, at least in the sense in which 'social science' is imputed to him by modern scholars. Perhaps Ferguson's surprise in reading this modern assessment would be tempered by his amusement at his author's slick but unconvincing claim that history is merely 'sociology with the brains taken out', Arthur Marwick, *The Nature of History* (London, 1981), p. 288.

77. See Q. Skinner, *The Foundations of Modern Political Thought*, 2 vols (Cambridge, 1978), I, xiii. What, in retrospect, it might be said that authors in fact turned out to have *done*, and what, at the time, they understood themselves to be *doing*, is a distinction to be grasped by all historians. The latter, broadly co-terminus with what J. L. Austin's speech-act theory identifies as the 'illocutionary act', is arguably the more important consideration for those seeking to understand the meaning and origins of a discussion in its historical context. As a premise, this has been challenged, notably by K. Minogue, 'Method in Intellectual History: Quentin Skinner's *Foundations*', *Philosophy*, 56 (1981), 533–52, and, with the aid of Gramsci, by J. V. Fermia, 'An Historicist Critique of "Revisionist" Methods for Studying the History of Ideas', in J. Tully (ed.), *Meaning and Context: Quentin Skinner and His Critics* (Oxford, 1988), pp. 156–75. But Skinner himself worked out the finer philosophical points of this elaborate argument in a series of influential early papers, most notably and iconoclastically in 'Meaning and Understanding in the History of Ideas', *History and Theory*, 8 (1969), 3–53.

78. Adam Ferguson, *Essay on the History of Civil Society* (Edinburgh, 1767), p. 188.

79. The hermeneutic approach developed by Skinner and Pocock, though clearly now the prevailing methodology for the history of ideas, stands in conscious opposition to an older convention deriving from Karl Mannheim and sociological theory, which held that thought and utterance are unconsciously determined by social environment – a view which itself has affinities with the most perniciously ahistorical aspects of modern critical deconstruction, as well as with the Marxism which, in a less profound form, we have seen has so shaped our current impressions of the Scottish Enlightenment. For the historian, however, as John Dunn makes clear, meaning and intention are the essential objects of study, 'The Identity of the History of Ideas', *Philosophy*, 43 (1968), 85–104. The whole debate is reviewed in M. Goldie, 'Obligations, Utopias, and their Historical Context', *Historical Journal*, 26 (1983), 727–46.

80. J. G. A. Pocock, 'Texts as Events: Reflections on the History of Political Thought', in K. Sharpe and S. N. Zwicker (eds), *Politics of Discourse: The Literature and History of Seventeenth-Century England* (Berkeley, Calif., 1987), pp. 28–9.

81. In arriving at my understanding of 'discourse' as the body of questions formulated and answers offered by a wide community of participants over time, but for a necessary antidote to the dehumanised, and consequently dehistoricised, usage preferred by the disciples of Foucault, I have found the most helpful discussion to be D. A. Hollinger, 'Historians and the Discourse of Intellectuals', in J. Higham and P. K. Conkin (eds), *New Directions in American Intellectual History* (Baltimore, Md., 1979), pp. 42–63. Foucault's approach, when applied to enlightened Scotland, has, for example, offered us the unedifying prospect of a 'discourse that is deliberately universalizing, thoroughly secular, and strenuously ahistorical', J. Christensen, *Practicing Enlightenment: Hume and the Formation of a Literary Career* (Madison, Wisconsin, 1987), p. 15. As my own argument thus far should make clear, any credible discussion of enlightened discourse in Scotland (including Hume) has to be sensitive both to the religious and to the historical.

82. Widely recognised since the distinction established by Saussure between *langue* and *parole*, the problem is this: if the meaning of words as understood by the author determines his usage, and yet it is his contextual employment of them which imbues them with meaning, how can the historian of ideas know how precisely to interpret a term in any single given text? In particular, how do we initially sense a delicate but crucial shift in the meaning attached to

a key term in an individual utterance? The circle can only be broken, it seems, by careful comparison and contrast between a wide number of texts and usages. Pocock, *Virtue, Commerce, and History: Essays on Political Thought Chiefly in the Eighteenth Century* (Cambridge, 1985), p. 4. As Pocock goes on to reaffirm, quantity is the most visible way around the obstacle provided by the ambiguous status of language as both 'speech act and context', *ibid.*, p. 11.

PART ONE

Early Modern Scholarship
1550–1740

CHAPTER ONE

'Mighty Heroes in Learning'

Calvinism and the Humanist Historian

SCOTLAND HAD POSSESSED a talented community of historians since at least the fourteenth century. This was the firm belief of most early modern Scottish historians. It was also one which was apparently without respect to the spirit of bigotry and dissension which otherwise seems to have scarred the acrimonious scholarship of the sixteenth and seventeenth centuries. Not until the middle years of the eighteenth century, and even then not completely, was the glory of this older Scottish tradition of historical writing finally obscured by the triumphal modernism and polished sensibilities of what presented itself as a self-consciously new and enlightened age. Hitherto, it had been clear to Scottish historians of all affiliations that they were collectively the inheritors of a proud and distinguished national tradition of scholarship. This had begun as early as 1370 with John Fordun and his *Scotichronicon*. It had been sustained by a lineal succession of historians like Hector Boece, John Major and George Buchanan, unsurpassed, it was invariably claimed, in the field of European letters. In the eyes of William Nicolson, a perceptive and widely read Bishop of Carlisle writing at the beginning of the eighteenth century, it seemed 'very strange and unaccountable' that 'such mighty Heroes in Learning, to whom the old *Romans* or *Athenians* would have erected Altars, should want even the cheap Acknowledgments of a Paper-Monument'.[1] Likewise, George Mackenzie, his contemporary and a voracious student of his own nation's literary heritage, lamented that Scotsmen had been 'so unjust to their Memories and to our Posterity'.[2] These wistful reflections, however, seem to have been only a more devious attempt to win wider recognition for Scotland's literary achievements; or else, perhaps, a crude device to stir up public enthusiasm for their own bibliographical activities. There is in fact no sign that Scottish authors themselves, at least until the middle of the eighteenth century, were at all reticent in lavishing praise on their scholarly forebears. Indeed the pompous Earl of Cromarty was probably typical with his defiant claim in 1695 that 'our Scots Writers' were of outstanding quality, and 'justly placed in the first Rank'.[3] Equally, Henry Maule of Melgum was adamant in the *History of the Picts* (1706) that even measured by the demanding yardstick of antiquity the long line of Scottish historians who had preceded him were 'nothing inferiour to them in beauty and profit'.[4] Sir Robert Sibbald, meanwhile, expended herculean efforts around the turn of the eighteenth century in producing what is still an invaluable manuscript survey of the considerable corpus of extant historical materials in Scotland then visible to his eclectic gaze.[5] So confident, in fact, were such historical authors of the weight and credit attaching to their Scottish predecessors that Samuel Rutherford, the erudite presbyterian radical responsible for the infamous *Lex Rex* (1644), had been able proudly to reel off the conventional litany of Scottish historians whom he took to have anticipated his own claims: '*Fordun, Major, Boethius*' and '*Buchanan*', to the seventeenth-century Scottish controversialist, clearly remained the obvious authorities for the support of any decent historical argument.[6]

The real source of this confidence, however, was the widespread under-standing that Scottish historical scholarship had risen to unprecedented heights in the sixteenth century.[7] At the heart of this perceptible transition in early modern scholarship had been a reinvigoration of the inherited or 'traditionary' account of Scotland's history by striking political and religious arguments which were themselves greatly indebted both to Calvinism and humanism.[8] A modern perspective reveals even more clearly how the religious upheavals begun in the sixteenth century and the continuing political problems which beset the Stuart state until the late seventeenth brought about the literal disintegration of Scottish historical writing. In effect, the broad medieval canon was rapidly torn apart. It was thereafter reassembled by diligent humanist scholars and eager Calvinist propagandists, each in search of a credible defence for his own highly polemical position. Yet the influence of radical exponents like George Buchanan and John Knox on the subsequent course of Scottish scholarship was ultimately to be fruitful, because, rather than in spite of, their tendentious use of historical techniques. So engaging and topical were their arguments, and so indisputably effective their historical methods, that all later Scottish authors were obliged at least to encounter and negotiate with their legacies. This was an aggressive colonisation of historical writing for the most violently partisan purposes. But it ensured that cultural values and assumptions integral to Calvinism and humanism were accommodated into the very structure of historical scholarship itself. This determined that Scottish historical writing would remain a strikingly combative and argumentative medium for the remainder of this period. It also forced upon subsequent Scottish historians an intensive questioning and forceful reassertion of their own role as scholars. Most particularly, it seems to have equipped them with an eloquent rhetoric for articulating within their texts a brilliantly clear sense of historical mission. This, significantly, was an aspect of their discourse which was to survive in Scotland until at least the emergence of ostensibly 'enlightened' texts in the fifth and sixth decades of the eighteenth century.

In this chapter I shall seek to demonstrate how from the later sixteenth until the early eighteenth centuries this vigorous tradition of polemical scholarship had developed among Scotland's historians. We will touch necessarily upon George Buchanan's problematical humanist vision of political society. It will also oblige us to look more closely at his equally radical humanist revision of the older debate focused upon Scotland's historic struggle for liberty, one which was to influence scholars of all persuasions. These issues should immediately emphasise to us the extent to which historical discourse in Scotland by 1600 was maturing as a humanist, and particularly as a Ciceronian medium. The works of John Knox and his reformist colleagues, however, simultaneously imposed upon Scottish historians involvement in a continuing debate on a well-defined agenda of unresolved ecclesiological issues. This development was accompanied by the emergence among Scotland's scholars of what soon became their national propensity for the grimly apocalyptic interpretation of history. For both these reasons Calvinism too came effectively to exercise a stranglehold over the historical discussions of later Scottish authors – including, to some degree, of men who were not themselves subscribers to the presbyterian cause. Yet this chapter will in no sense be an attempt simply to recount the switchbacks of Scottish political and ecclesiastical history in the succeeding two centuries: such narratives are only too familiar, and may be found at great length elsewhere. On the contrary, its second purpose will be to move on to show how an excessive focus on this unquestionably beguiling religious and political polemic would actually lead us to overlook some of the most important developments occurring in this broad historical tradition. We will therefore seek out instead some of the more profound effects of Calvinism and humanism upon the evolution of Scottish discourse. These were effects which were partially obscured, which have largely been overlooked because they lay hidden beneath the more colourful and eye-catching strata occupied by cataclysmic political and religious disagreement. In particular there will be a need to understand the participation of virtually all Scottish historians in a convention of self-justification. This turns out to have used to the full a historical rhetoric of scholarly intention drawing directly upon the discourses of Calvinism and humanism. I will argue that the impressively sophisticated arguments within this tradition actually point to the wider existence of a very deep sense of moral and social purpose running through early modern scholarship in Scotland. It is precisely this self-conscious reiteration of his purpose, indeed, which will allow us to go on to identify the vital contemporary tasks which the historian believed himself to be performing – tasks which, I shall argue, were later to prove such a major influence upon the meaning and function of Enlightenment scholarship in its own time. As we will see in much more detail in the next chapter, the ascription by scholars of a particular moral meaning to their own practice of history in fact led them on to nothing less than a continuous re-examination of the central ideas in what we would now recognise as their social theory. But as for the Scottish scholars of the sixteenth century, it is with their political use and abuse of humanism in historical writing that this story really begins.

1: HUMANISM AND RADICAL POLITICAL ARGUMENT

The emergence of Scottish humanism as an integral part of the northern Renaissance is now recognised as an important phase in the intellectual history of Scotland. Yet the humanist transformation of Scottish historical writing, it also seems certain, was a very slow process, and one which the most recent research only confirms was not properly to begin until the sixteenth century.[9] There had been a distinguished line of 'Makars' or poets, and there were also a number of other royal and ecclesiastical functionaries who had made conspicuous contributions to the cause of Scottish poetry and letters. Men such as these had been encouraged in their literary productivity and Latin scholarship by a happy succession of interested Stewart kings as well as by the growing Scottish connection with the French and Italian universities. Only William Elphinstone, however, the learned Bishop of Aberdeen, Principal and founder in 1494 of Scotland's third university, could be offered by the most ambitious early modern commentators as a reputable fifteenth-century Scottish historian.[10] As a result it was not until the early sixteenth century when a later Principal of King's College, Hector Boece, and the celebrated Parisian scholar John Major wrote their very different chronicles, that a new age in historical scholarship finally dawned in Scotland. These publications ushered in a phase in Scotland's cultural development which bore several of the hallmarks later to be seen as characteristic of a sophisticated Renaissance civilisation. There emerged in a growing number of Scottish scholars a new self-confidence in their own literature. There was as well an increasing familiarity with the literary culture of antiquity. This was accompanied by an open admiration for the classical example, alongside ready and felicitous reference to the works of more recent European scholars, men such as Petrarch, Erasmus, and Machiavelli.[11] One consequence was a growing and immensely productive attachment in Scotland to the cult of Cicero in particular. To this indelible mark of humanist culture was added the important practical conviction that historical study itself would provide an improved perspective upon and an informed insight into modern problems. The latter development was especially important. It ensured that in the successive political crises which convulsed Scotland after 1560 its ideologues and party apologists would turn with increasing assurance to the writing of history. Their use of history certainly built upon the civic humanism and moral vision of Boece's *Scotorum Historiae* (1527).[12] It also made less obvious use of the remarkably cosmopolitan air and forward-looking social perspective found in John Major's *Historia Majoris Britanniae* (1521).[13] Indeed, we shall later see that there were other senses in which all historical scholarship in Scotland from the early sixteenth century came to acquire at least the very strong tincture of the humanist tradition. Yet it was with George Buchanan alone that modern Scottish scholarship was thought by his successors to have come of age. Buchanan was an individual whose application of history to contemporary issues would have a continuing influence and an eternally controversial nature. He was also best to illustrate the fundamental importance of an overtly political and Ciceronian humanism throughout the evolution of later Scottish discourse.[14]

It would, of course, be churlish to suggest at the outset that Buchanan was the only sixteenth-century Scottish historian tapping into some form of Renaissance thought. He shared with several others in Scotland the fundamental humanist assumption that history provided crucial moral and political lessons to the contemporary world and its leaders. For example, John Bellenden, the definitive translator of Boece, had also been responsible on James V's direct instructions for the partial translation of Livy's *Ab Urbe Condita*, the classic Roman model for all humanist historians. As John MacQueen rightly suggests, Livy himself came to acquire a disproportionate influence among Scottish scholars for whom humanism was always, first and foremost, an influence upon historical writing.[15] More ironically, perhaps, Buchanan's Catholic opponent John Lesley, Bishop of Ross, was at no less pains to stress his own immediate humanist inspiration. Pausing only to heap excessive praise on both Cato and Cicero, Lesley's *History of Scotland* (1578) began by expressing a characteristically humanist desire to impart political instruction, *pace* Livy, Quintus Curtius and the historian of Conrad III.[16] Throughout the sixteenth century, meanwhile, a growing number of scholars were also found to be embracing other aspects of the same humanist enterprise. These included, for example, Sir Thomas Craig of Riccarton, whose *Jus Feudale* (1603) brought a 'historical approach' for the first time to the rationalization of the complex Scots law.[17] But most admired and most reviled was always to be the disturbingly radical turn to Buchanan's humanism. His frank indebtedness to the political philosophy of Cicero and the Stoics produced a distinctive theory of government which was singularly to reverberate through the work of successive generations of Scottish historians.

Buchanan's dangerous political cutting-edge was in fact achieved by the misleadingly simple device of locating the origins of human society within a fundamentally historical context. By this means he was able to deny in *De Jure Regni Apud Scotos* (1579) that passive obedience to the constituted political authorities had ever been a natural obligation on the subject. Buchanan argued, in a conjectural history of society borrowed from Cicero, that there had actually been a historical time when 'men did dwell in cottages, yea and in caves, and as strangers did wander to and fro without Lawes, or certain dwelling places'.[18] It seemed certain to Buchanan, in fact, that political society itself had emerged within the bounds of historical time, when men 'did Assemble together as their fond humours did lead them, or as some comodity and comon utility did allure them'. If political organisation was thus the product of previous human decisions, Buchanan continued, then it could not rightly be said to be of divine ordination. And if this was so, then government owed its very legitimacy to the fallible preferences of individual men. Buchanan now found himself with only one conclusion available: 'the people have the power to conferre the Government', he proclaimed, 'on whom they please'.[19] Men, it was clear, and even when acting as individuals – the individuals from whom society had first been formed – were sovereign. Indeed, they might actually have an obligation directly to resist a government which acted 'not for their Countrey's good, but for their own self interests, and have no regard to the publick utility'.[20] These carefully-worded principles were of course enunciated in a kingdom already struggling painfully with the political legacy of Mary's deposition, as well as with a monarchy that in any case had always been congenitally unstable. As such they were probably bound to attract criticism from some of Buchanan's less abrasive successors, who like Thomas Innes would rue the way in which he had so provocatively 'meddled with politicks'.[21] But Buchanan's statements were also to infuse later Scottish scholars with an insatiable desire to enter humanist discourse and engage in the same arguments through the practice of history. His works were certainly to remain profoundly influential in the social theory constructed by early modern historians. They deliberately elevated 'publick utility' above 'self interest', a humanist nostrum so redolent of the classical maxim *salus populi lex suprema*.[22] This depended at source upon the Ciceronian assertion that the public good had been the fundamental historical basis of all legitimate political authority. Let loose in an early modern society which was to be perpetually wracked by controversy over the burning questions of sovereignty, legitimacy, and resistance, Buchanan's claims successfully established an agenda to be addressed perforce by most serious Scottish historians.

That this radical strain in historical scholarship was traceable directly back to Scottish humanist usage was recognised at an early date by the clear-sighted William Nicolson. The Bishop of Carlisle also realised that Buchanan was less the 'First Parent and Founder' than the skilful elaborator of the 'imperfect Notions of Popular Government' found earlier in '*Hector Boethius* and others'.[23] Other Scotsmen, and perhaps most strikingly those who were themselves committed to the espousal of a radical presbyterian politics, went further. They openly acknowledged the influence of those humanist and neo-scholastic arguments deployed by inventive medieval churchmen in order to counter the imperial aspirations of the Papal monarchy.[24] Here the strictures of John Major acquired a special significance in the eyes of his Scottish successors, even though by J. H. Burns's intriguing reckoning Major had been by no means the first Scot to develop radical arguments for use against the prevailing Church regime.[25] Major's attacks on Papal secular authority, for example, were enthusiastically seized upon by the great Covenanting historian, Alexander Petrie. The author of *The Compendious History of the Catholic Church* (1662), Petrie used Major's claims as evidence in support of the presbyterian assertion that the Catholic Church had merely fabricated its powers rather than been created with them.[26] But more startling still is the apparent comfort with which Samuel Rutherford, St Andrews' divine and perhaps second only to Buchanan in his uncompromisingly political approach to scholarship, recorded his debt to Suarez and other neo-scholastic theologians, as well as to Major and Buchanan. Rutherford, like Buchanan, employed history to devastating effect in advancing the proposition that government proceeded 'from *God* by mediation of the consent of a Communitie, which resigneth their power to one or moe Rulers'.[27] Rutherford, it has recently been said, thus 'proved the truth of the Ciceronian maxim *salus populi, suprema lex*'.[28] This was carried out through a historical description of the principle in action. Rutherford was also utterly unembarrassed by his inheritance from those who he rather familiarly grouped together as the '*Parisian Doctors*',[29] as well as from a long line of humanists. He was therefore able to identify, with Buchanan, '*the good of the Subjects*' as the principal end of legitimate political authority.[30] To Rutherford, as to Buchanan, civil society rested ultimately on a natural though entirely voluntary contract between individual rational creatures in history. Buchanan's doctrine of resistance was also presumed unavoidably to apply, for if 'civill societie' was 'naturall', then so was it 'voluntary, *in modo*, in the manner of coalescing'.[31] Rutherford was of course addressing himself pertinently, and with entirely characteristic ferocity, to a contemporary political controversy. The immediate need was to offer a sound justification for the rebellion against Charles I then underway among that king's long-suffering Scottish subjects. But in his historical treatment of political government, and especially in the radical deployment of a Stoic conjectural history borrowed from Cicero, Rutherford's tract simply confirms the extent to which Buchanan had lent a potent humanist aspect to the subsequent discussion of Scotland's problematic civil history.

The sheer pervasiveness of Buchanan's influence may be seen by following the rampant progress of this classical analysis of politics in wider historical scholarship in Scotland. It certainly ensured that such scholarship would remain capable of adaptation for polemical use in what for long remained a most acrimonious northern world. In the work of the younger Robert Fleming, for example, the same perplexing Ciceronian vision of political history was to be fused effectively with elements drawn from the newer radical ideologies of the early eighteenth century. Once again this imbued an ostensibly historical discussion with dangerously humanist resonances. As an ardent Scottish opponent of the 'British Jacobites', Fleming used the *History of Hereditary-Right* (1711) to undermine the theories of divine right deployed by his enemies. He proceeded by ostensible reference to the 'Revolution Principles' of Mosaic law, then a popular stratagem among Whigs for countering tenacious absolutist claims.[32] But the lessons to be drawn from Biblical history were put to a more familiar and much older purpose by Fleming. This was simply 'to promote the Grand and Final end of all Government, *viz.* the *Salus Populi* the good of the Community. So that God and Man agreed then, that this was *Suprema Lex*, the Fundamental Maxim of all Government'.[33] From this it followed for Fleming, no less than for Buchanan or Rutherford, that 'a true Governour' was to be known in virtue of his 'reaching and securing the End of all Governement, *viz. The Good of the Community*'.[34] He was legitimated, in short, only by his '*Goodness* and *Aptitude* for promoting the *Publick Good*'.[35]

This same deeply humanist analysis of government also informed many another presbyterian historian. These included the irascible Covenanter Alexander Shields in the late seventeenth century, committed to the defence of the Kirk and its Faith. Shields found himself requiring a convincing justification for political resistance to a repressive Stuart state. As a result he tied himself explicitly to the coat-tails of Knox and Buchanan, amongst others, in the violently combative *Hind Let Loose* (1681). Here Shields argued forcefully that 'it is evident, that the Government is nothing else but a mutual stipulation between Kings & People ... ',[36] a contractarian argument which again displayed the continuing vivacity and relevance of the Calvinist and humanist radical tradition. To Shields the 'stipulation' arose historically out of 'the unviolated tenor of the Ancient Law, since the beginning of the Scottish Government ... engraven in the minds of men from the first original, and approved by the mutual consent of all Nations'.[37] For William Jameson, meanwhile, the blind presbyterian controversialist and Professor of History at the University of Glasgow who flourished at the same time as Shields, a *History of the Wisdom, Valour, and Liberty of the Ancient Albion-Scotish Nation* became the natural occasion for a vitriolic attack on those scholars who sought to prove that 'all men ... and Chiefly Scotsmen, are from the womb to the Grave bound Slaves'. To those who wanted to believe that 'Kings are so despotick and absolute be they ever so Tyrannical' or that 'the people may in no Case move in their own Defence', Jameson had a ready and familiar answer: there was in fact an 'Antient way of Governing' in historical time, a form of politics in which 'Chiefs were obliged to Consult'. In now predictable terms, Jameson concluded that in these 'Early Days' every 'Clan or Tribe made a state or Commonwealth'.[38] Once more, then, a conjectural history suggested by humanism led almost infallibly among the successors of Buchanan to a critique of absolutist theories of political obligation. This was of course an analysis which was known in crucial respects to look back to a distinguished line of Continental humanists and Scottish churchmen. But it was one which after Buchanan also came to be manipulated by an appropriately broad section of the scholarly community in early modern Scotland.

Buchanan had in addition applied his radical Stoic analysis to a closer inspection of Scottish constitutional history. In doing so he had made creative use of the scanty evidence for deliberative government and elective monarchy in Scotland. Again this was a devious humanist application of the conventional materials of history for the most partisan of purposes. Yet a tacit acceptance of those alleged institutions, first sketched out by Boece and so luridly illustrated by Buchanan, subsequently surfaces in some rather unlikely places. This suggests once more the extent to which the development of humanist politics bound together even some of the less sympathetic Scottish historians who succeeded Buchanan. In John Monipennie's *Scots Chronicles* (1612), for example, an otherwise sanitary piece of Jacobean court propaganda displays suspicious signs of contamination by Buchanan's humanism. This was so not least, perhaps, because of the early association of James' public culture with the popular ideologists both of the 1567 revolution and the Protestant movement.[39] Fergus I, Monipennie noted, was confirmed as King of Scotland only after 'the nobles and subjects condescended and agreed'.[40] Moreover, the rules of royal succession were very far from being the immutable artefact of divine decree. As Buchanan had suggested, they were arrived at historically, and only, according to Monipennie, after 'a long disputation and reasoning' when they were specifically 'concluded by plain consent of parliament, and enacted'.[41] Clearly Buchanan had been successful in defining the terms of an 'ancient Scottish constitution'. In committing his successors to a recognisably classical critique of Stuart government, however, he had also ensured that humanism would long retain an iron grip over historical discourse in Scotland.

Humanism of a rather more general sort, still richly suffused with classical learning and historical perspective but actually employed in the service of much more conservative political principles, was also to emerge strongly in Scottish historical scholarship after Buchanan. But here too it was often forced at the same time to confront the implications of the virulent Stoic analysis of political society let loose by Buchanan. Alexander Ross, for example, was a Scottish beneficiary of Laud's patronage and a great Aberdonian classicist, as well as the fleeting victim of Samuel Butler's immortalising satire.[42] Ross spent a disappointed retirement in the composition of several deeply embittered works, in which he frequently referred to the authority of Juvenal, Ovid, the Stoics and Machiavelli. During this time, and having witnessed the overthrow of his royal master by parties ideologically inspired by Buchanan, Ross seems to have allowed the Renaissance scholar to prey unhealthily on his own troubled mind: kings were not in fact constrained by ordinary historical and human law, his *Marrow of Historie* (1650) protested, for 'Princes are subject to the directive, not coactive power of the Law'. Indeed, in his attempt to despatch Buchanan's hovering presence Ross argued violently that 'The Prince is so much above the Laws, as soul and body united, is above a dead and sensless carkass'.[43] But even during Buchanan's own lifetime it is possible to find worried Scottish historians of this timid disposition desperately trying to apply their own classical learning to the demolition of classical politics. An example would be the skilful employment of traditionary material by John Lesley, a man who we have already seen was adept at brandishing his own humanist authorities. Lesley had tried to deal with precisely the claim that Boece had once implied and Buchanan was in his own time suggesting. History, Lesley's *Treatise* (1571) proclaimed, with perhaps greater accuracy than his radical humanist opponents, showed that the people 'these many thousand years hath embraced succession by blood, rather than election':[44] in short, history, that fundamental ground of humanist argument, actually offered up evidence to Lesley that people did *not* freely choose their monarchs. Resistance, as a result, *was* immoral and unnatural. Clearly, then, all kinds of Scottish historians shared an awareness of a politicised and sometimes radical humanist scholarship. Its use of history was of course especially provocative in an age when the established medieval orthodoxies, habitually defended as divine, immutable, and unchallengeable, were coming under sustained attack. Some contemporaries, however, were driven to borrow these same persuasive historicising techniques only in a doomed attempt to muzzle their more seditious political implications. But others, following the inspirational example of George Buchanan, had begun with increasing confidence to employ humanism and history in the construction of a recognisably modern political discourse.

Humanist scholarship as exemplified by George Buchanan, however, also brought to Scottish historical writing a second and related mode of political analysis. This involved a subtle reworking of the assertions of Scotland's martial and libertarian heritage which we know had so typified the traditionary account.[45] The propagandist origins of Scotland's medieval historical scholarship remained plain to see. But this was another area of early modern discourse over which Buchanan's troublesome presence was now continually to brood. John Fordun's *Scotichronicon* (1372), the definitive medieval history, had been a product of the same fervently nationalistic atmosphere which had also inspired later medieval Scottish poetical works like Blind Harry's *Acts and Deeds of Sir William Wallace* (*c.*1475) and John Barbour's *The Brus* (1375).[46] Like them it had sought to remove the nation from the dreaded sphere of English domination and to establish indisputably the credentials of the Scots as an ancient and independent people. Mythical origins aside, this had produced a traditionary history which hung sometimes menacingly, always with fierce pride, upon the valorous military defence of national liberties. These were articulated essentially in terms of Scotland's eternal political autonomy.[47] What Buchanan's virulent humanism now did, however, was to transform this consensual and intensely nationalistic definition of liberty into a much sharper and radical assertion of popular or presbyterian values.[48] First and most fundamentally, the application of the classical humanist models to the Scottish historical tradition successfully detached the original premise for liberty and increasingly replaced it with another. Scottish independence ceased to be the invariable crux of the argument, a development finally possible in an age of religious alliances and then of dynastic union with England. Constitutional government and a participatory political 'commonweal' took its place. Secondly, the meaning of 'liberty', and the very concept of the patriotic subject itself, acquired much stronger Stoic and civic nuances. This was a development traceable in part to Boece's account and to John Major's critique of chivalry.[49] But it was one which again achieved political maturity and lasting influence only in Buchanan's majestic *History of Scotland*, the unrivalled testament of the presbyterian and Jacobean revolutionaries. Henceforth, Scottish military glory would be the work of active citizens, at least as wary of domestic tyranny as of English encroachments. Scotland's heroes would now possess public virtues which smacked of the Roman republic rather more than of the Scottish feudal baronage. Of course, by no means did this mean that the Scottish aristocracy or monarchy were completely dismissed. Rather, it meant, as we will later see at greater length, that they were expected to exhibit values and perform functions cognate with this increasingly classical analysis. The consensus in the medieval discussion of liberty in Scotland had largely come to an end. The ever-watchful and irreproachable Cato rather than the perfervid and meteoric Wallace was the new role-model for Scottish patriots portrayed by many enthusiastic post-Reformation historians.[50]

The most noticeable consequence of this development, betraying *inter alia* the influence of Florentine humanism in late sixteenth-century Scotland, was the emergence of historical arguments in favour of participatory citizen armies. These were to be preferred, it seems, not simply on military but on moral and political grounds. They were advocated in particular at the expense of the morally-unsound mercenary forces employed by an unscrupulous and increasingly distrusted royal government.[51] Buchanan himself lingered with undisguised relish over what he believed was historical evidence for the moral superiority of the disciplined and vigorous Scottish citizen armies. The good King Donaldus, it seems, had noticed that his soldiers were 'wanton and idle, and spoiled by Luxury'. So according to Buchanan he had mustered a fresh army of volunteers from amongst his people. He had then 'so accustomed them to Training and Exercising their Arms, and Military Discipline, that, in a short time, the new-listed Tyroe's did equal the Valour of the Veterans, and old Souldiers'.[52] Even more pointedly, however, Buchanan portrayed the Scottish people as having offered only their steadfast resistance to the military plans of the tyrannical Guise regime. The Scots had protested their preparedness to fight and die for the privileges of free citizenship: 'they were willing to lay down their Lives and Fortunes for the Good of their Country, if need required. And as for the levying of Mercenary Auxiliaries, that t'was a matter full of danger', Buchanan warned, 'to commit the state of *Scotland* to Men, without either Lands or Hopes, but who would do any thing for Mony'.[53] Clearly, military participation was in humanist terms the mark of the citizen. A willingness voluntarily to resist the domestic aggression of an oppressive faction – indelibly signified by its dependence upon aliens, mercenaries or baronial warlords – also increasingly became the mark of the true Scottish patriot.

This was in essence a critique of absolute royal power for its acting contrary to the participatory rights of the citizen. Though reminiscent of classic humanist models like Livy, Machiavelli and Rinuccini, it was to survive through the next century and break the surface of Scottish political discourse again in the debates preceding the Act of Union at the beginning of the eighteenth century.[54] Then, as before, it was voiced with greatest fluency in the medium of historical discourse which during the sixteenth century had first introduced it to Scotland. The moral consequences of an indolent and spineless citizenry were colourfully illustrated by Augustan scholars at each and every historical opportunity. An excellent example is provided by George Ridpath, the controversial Whig journalist and sometime historian. Author of the *Historical Account of the Parliament of Scotland* (1703), Ridpath argued persuasively 'that it was a thing of most dangerous consequence, to trust the Safety of the Nation to mercenary

Soldiers, Men of no Substance or Expectation'. As an observation possessing clear syntactical similarities with contemporary translations of Buchanan's description of the Guise episode, this may even indicate that Ridpath was paraphrasing his great countryman.[55] Either way, however, it is significant evidence of the continuing availability of this humanist political argument within the early modern historical tradition in Scotland. It is also confirmation not least of its pertinence to a man who had been imprisoned for his Whig opinions and whose career in London, as John Robertson reminds us, had consisted in writing scurrilous anti-government pamphlets.[56]

Most notoriously, though, it was of course to be Andrew Fletcher of Salton who deployed a libertarian rhetoric in defence of citizen armies to greatest declamatory effect. Tenaciously clinging to classical and Florentine assumptions, Fletcher held that nothing was 'so essential to the Liberties of the People, as that which placed the Sword in the hands of the Subject'.[57] Once again Fletcher's analysis in the *Discourse Concerning Militias* (1697) was deeply historical in perspective. It followed George Buchanan in its continuing humanist faith in the 'excellent Rules of Government which the Antients have left us'.[58] Fletcher was eager, like Boece and Buchanan before him, to imbue the citizen with the spirit of the Roman republican patriot. To this greatest and most violent opponent of the centralising British state, then, recent history only confirmed, if people would but see it, how the commercial nexus and an army of expensive and disloyal mercenaries necessarily dragged a people 'into all the Corruptions which those great Enemies of Vertue want'.[59] Indeed, all those 'many remarkable Examples of History' so beloved of Buchanan were summoned up again to demonstrate for an English audience what was by now a deeply familiar point in Scottish discourse: liberty had been lost only during the entirely historical 'Alteration of Government ... about the Year 1500', a development which to a successor of Buchanan only highlighted the alternative case for political participation.[60] It was also undoubtedly this historical discussion of English liberty which allowed Fletcher to go on in the *Discourse of Government* (1698) to widen the focus to include his native Scotland, and to move boldly towards a positive programme of militia proposals. In a political climate such as Ridpath and Fletcher encountered around the turn of the eighteenth century, the powerful civic element built into Scottish historical discourse after Buchanan could clearly still propel a political argument with awesome force.

More broadly, however, and away from the advocacy specifically of a militia system for Scotland, the humanist revision of conventional martial libertarianism allowed early modern historians to make the sharpest of political points. For example, it allowed some to convey their continuing distaste for the centralised paraphernalia of the Stuart state which Buchanan had once so seminally assailed for its non-participatory character. One instance of this would be its employment by the late seventeenth-century presbyterian author Alexander Shields. Shields scoffed bitterly in 1687 at the professed motives of

James VII's hired 'forces and publick Officiers', who then threatened to overwhelm the voluntarist sects in the seeming interests of France, Rome, and Anti-Christ: 'What are they employed about, but to promote the Dragon's designs, and serve his drudgerie?', he asked. 'Shall these guard the Nation, who together with Religion tread upon the poor remaining shadow of Liberty?'[61] Instead, Shields set out to record the brave exploits of those heroes of the domestic struggle for civic liberty. These were the 'noble & vertuous Patriots' now retrospectively canonized by Shields and the new Calvinist and humanist order, Scotsmen who had chosen to fight against the 'rigorous & raging Tyrants' within the Scottish state.[62] This powerful use of civic rhetoric in the defence of denominational beliefs was badly needed by the upholders of a perenially insecure and necessarily militant Calvinist revolution. But it was one which was almost invited by the humanist notion of the voluntary and patriotic defence of a participatory liberty against an array of internal enemies.[63] It is possible to find similar echoes elsewhere of this distaste for the moral consequences of a professional soldiery, now built into the very language of Scottish historical polemic. This may, for example, explain Alexander Ross's impassioned royalist declamation against the turmoil of the recent civil wars. History had so clearly taught us, the melancholic exile lamented, that 'a Town or Country which breeds armed souldiers within them, are at last destroyed by them'.[64] A criticism which had been tainted by its association with a radical ideologue like George Buchanan, however, would always most readily appeal to a long line of embattled presbyterian historians. These were men like Robert Wodrow, minister of Eastwood in the early eighteenth century, who still openly saw Scottish history as an account of the handing-down of specifically civic liberties 'through so much blood and suffering' within the same bitterly divided post-Reformation national community.[65] Yet even examples such as these do not exhaust the evidence of the various ways in which radical humanist arguments for political liberty affected the evolution of historical discourse among successive generations of Scottish historians.

The vigorous and highly contentious use of militant libertarianism certainly attracts the modern reader of seventeenth-century historical texts. But there long survived in Scotland, and especially among its historians, something of the older tendency to exalt for broader nationalistic purposes 'the Noble Spirit of Liberty our Ancestors were possessed with'.[66] Even here, however, the humanist nuances of Buchanan's language of freedom probably proved inescapable for later practitioners. Opportunities for blatant Anglophobia of course still periodically presented themselves to Scotsmen. These were properly reflected in a historical tradition which was nothing if it was not topical. From the late seventeenth century, for example, we have the powerful invective of the anonymous Breadalbane MS, *Defence of the Independence of the Antient Kingdom and Church of Scotland*, developing historical evidence 'from Antient and unquestionable writters and Records against the Cavills of some Late writters'.[67] Such writing not only survived but positively flourished in the superficially different climate of the Augustan age. Another anonymous scholar around 1714 urged his fellow Scotsmen to look back to 'the glorious and heroick Actions of their Progenitors', and sought to excite in them a desire for freedom, 'a generous Resolution of recovering what was so valiantly defended and maintained by their Predecessors'.[68] The Jacobite historian David Scott likewise used the *History of Scotland* (1727) to vent his considerable spleen against the Act of Union. It was still entirely possible for an author like Scott, a Jacobite lawyer from Haddington who was imprisoned for his views, to lament at great length with his eighteenth-century fellow-countrymen 'the loss of those Liberties and Privileges which their Ancestors had preserv'd and defended for many Ages'.[69] Scott, in other words, preferred still to associate his nation's freedom with a collective resistance to foreign – English – attacks. Of course, in the immediate aftermath of the Union, and before the promised benefits had begun to materialise, this recrudescence of nationalist venom was especially possible. The language of Fordun and Barbour remained in occasional currency for use by authors like David Scott or William Wright who needed to evoke Scottish liberty as it had been conceived by later medieval historians.[70]

Yet, the employment of libertarian rhetoric for traditional purposes was any time after the sixteenth century patently a dangerous affair for the Scottish historian. David Hume of Godscroft, the historian of the Douglases, makes an excellent example of this difficulty. Godscroft appears to have erred too much towards implicit radicalism simply by virtue of his eagerness to emphasise Scottish heroism and liberty to the utmost degree. The *History of the Houses of Douglas and Angus*, which recapitulated accounts of medieval warfare in order to cast glorious reflections upon the family, was almost certainly written before 1625. But the concern that its tactless harping upon Scotland's libertarian tendencies might offend delicate political sensibilities seems to have prevented its actual appearance until as late as 1644, when undiplomatic histories had become the least of the establishment's problems.[71] A generation later it was Mackenzie of Rosehaugh, a man of otherwise impeccable loyalty to the Stuarts, who trod on equally uncertain ground. He may even unwittingly have aided the radical cause by his unguarded publication in 1680 of the *Declaration of Arbroath*, the Nicene creed of modern nationalism.[72] Mackenzie presumably regarded its references to an ancient line of Scottish kings as just so much admirable Stuart propaganda; and his own production of the document as a typically humanist contribution to the recovery of the national history. He certainly appears to have been blissfully unaware that it might just as easily be reflected in that other humanist mirror, the one originally fashioned by Boece and Buchanan. Then, as it was to be in the pamphlet editions of 1680 and 1703, its implicit references to elective monarchy and libertarian valour would acquire a dangerous new dimension, associated with rebelliousness and sedition rather than with deference and loyalty. So influential was the account of Scottish history offered in a humanist idiom by George Buchanan and his successors that all the conventional arguments and materials which he had touched thereafter remained tarnished with his views.

There was thus for those not in sympathy with his political tastes a very real danger simply of underwriting the radical implications of Buchanan's critique of royal government. This risk could in the final analysis only be reduced by the most scrupulous attention to rhetorical detail. Yet, as the Orcadian scholar James Wallace put it in his *History of Scotland* (1724), the elevation by some means of national reputation and dignity remained 'a Duty incumbent on all Scots Men', and not least upon historians:[73] many thought this obligation still worth the risk. To some it seemed possible to include the monarchy in the rhetoric of national virility and so to gloss over the problematic question of participatory civic liberties. Viscount Stair, for example, seems to have preferred to discharge this particular patriotic duty by not dwelling long on the historical 'Antiquity and Integrity' of the Scots as one of the 'kingdoms of the Earth', and thus keeping his influential *Institutions of the Law of Scotland* (1681) largely out of potential controversy.[74] Another, Sir James Dalrymple, the distinguished antiquary and Clerk to the Court of Session, seems to have found it equally prudent to begin the *Collections Concerning the Scottish History* (1705) in tactful vein. Dalrymple concentrated his readers' minds instead on the eminently respectable assertion that the Scots had historically been a brave and warlike race, 'under the Conduct', he strongly underlined, 'of a more numerous Race of Brave and Warlike Princes'.[75] Yet he was also writing in the more congenial climate of Queen Anne's reign. So Dalrymple was able to go on to make greater use of the historical reference to liberty, carefully picked out of the humanist vocabulary. After all, the Whig revolution of 1688–9 and the Protestant succession were developments which meant that the state could now cautiously be apostrophised rather than assailed by means of the same libertarian arguments. Liberty, his preface thus advised, was most obviously threatened by the 'growing Usurpations of the Church of Rome'. Consequently its greatest guardian and upholder was the Protestant monarchy, which alone ensured the citizen his inalienable rights of political and religious participation against enemies both at home and overseas.[76] But by either route historians who did not wish to imply the classical radicalism of Buchanan clearly found it awkward to deal with the conventional language of civic liberty and martial vigour. This had been adapted and nuanced after the later sixteenth century by a contentious form of humanist political argument. Only the most strenuous manœuvring could save the Scottish scholar from coming to occupy a highly uncomfortable position.

Thus the legacy of political humanism within early modern Scottish historical writing was unusually complex. And it managed not only to affect the many notable authors in Scotland who the sardonic Prior of St Pieremont, Richard Hay, was later to gather together as 'Buchanan and his Confederates'.[77] Buchanan's controversial Stoic analysis of government acquired a dangerous prominence. But the humanist transformation of a hitherto rabied and somewhat parochial Scottish libertarianism into a vigorous historical argument seems also to have been deliberately utilised by many historians, and perhaps inadvertently employed by others. These humanist components had either wholeheartedly to be embraced, or else deliberately and carefully expunged from the very core of any modern historical account. As radical political arguments they came to a surprising degree, not simply to engage, but to unite the works of a diverse range of Scottish authors. Scotland from the later sixteenth until at least the early eighteenth century should as a result be seen as a nation in which historians were obliged again and again to reinterpret their own political experience in the variable light cast by a distinctively humanist analysis of history. More broadly, their Ciceronian humanism now always entailed a historical perspective and a desire for ample classical support. Thus we might actually agree with Richard Hay that all Scotsmen who wrote history in the early modern period were in one sense or another, and however grudgingly, the 'confederates' of Buchanan. We have already had to allude on several occasions to the existence of a specifically presbyterian history. This had operated alongside, and sometimes within, the utterly pervasive secular humanism of Buchanan's successors. We must now move on to consider the influence of the Calvinist revolution upon the early modern historical tradition. There is a need to examine, in particular, both the ecclesiological polemic and the violently apocalyptic perspective which it was to contribute to the development of historical discourse in Scotland.

II : KNOX AND THE PRESBYTERIAN IDIOM

During the same period in which Buchanan was fragmenting as well as considerably reinvigorating the Scottish line of traditionary history, another of John Major's most able pupils, the thunderous John Knox, was laying the foundations for even more violence to be done to the hitherto unexceptional story of Scotland's ecclesiastical history. Knox was the man who the admiring seventeenth-century historian and minister of Carnock, John Row, recognised as God's 'principall mean and instrument' in the Reformation.[78] He set about justifying his own role in events with such trenchancy and verve that no later Scottish account of church history was to seem complete without in some way addressing Knox's quite extravagant claims. The definitive statement of his position was delivered with characteristic force in *The Historie of the Reformation of the Church of Scotland*, first published in 1587 but largely unknown and incomplete until the 1644 edition. This was much more than simply the personal apologia of a leading participant in events. Rather, and building upon some of his own earlier works, Knox took up some of the more controversial arguments which had been employed by its proponents during the tempestuous passage of the Reformation in Scotland and elsewhere. The *Historie* espoused views of scholarly history and of historical time which encapsulated the attitude of the great Calvinist reformers towards their own prodigious achievements. Two things are worthy of particular consideration in tracing the course of early modern historical discourse in Scotland. Both were essentially hermeneutic devices adopted by Knox in order to dictate an interpretation of the Reformation which saw it in what its adherents believed to be its true historical context. Both of them, moreover, were firmly rooted in the sort of deeply learned and humanistic Calvinism which had propelled the Reformation and which, as recent scholarship has begun to recognise, was greatly to affect the subsequent development of religious life in Scotland.[79] One suggested that history itself, within a sweeping Calvinist vision of the past, needed to be read as a record of the millenarian conflict between Christ and Anti-Christ. This apocalyptic perspective on their scholarship will deserve more comment shortly, for it gave rise not least to some intriguing methodological presumptions within Scotland's incestuous scholarly community which acquired even greater prominence as the seventeenth century progressed. But more immediately, Knox portrayed the actual history of the Scottish Kirk as though it had been an unfolding sequence of symbolic episodes. Each of these had hinged on the very ecclesiological issues over which the Reformation itself had eventually been fought.[80] This device certainly helped serve Knox's partisan aim of using history to substantiate the fundamental claims of the Calvinist revolution in Scotland. But it was also more widely to oblige subsequent Scottish historians of all persuasions to recognise a derivative agenda as the only relevant framework within which they could offer worthwhile contributions to the continuing debate.

It was significant that Knox began his personal account of the Reformation with the persecution of the Lollards in Scotland. The portentousness he attached to this episode was not simply a product of the convention (accepted by more recent historical scholarship) that the Lollards held beliefs which had prefigured Protestant doctrine.[81] Instead, it seems that the Lollards' principal significance to Knox and the reformers had been their open rebelliousness towards the prevailing church hierarchy. Indeed, the reformers' own argument in rejecting Papal sovereignty and establishing their own non-episcopal church government was itself usually expressed in terms of a reinstatement of the putative religious prerogatives of an ancient Scottish church. Any evidence of an ancient line of resistance to ecclesiastical domination by Rome was therefore invaluable.[82] John Spotswood, the Jacobean Archbishop of Glasgow, was merely one of several Scottish scholars who observed how much the Scottish Reformation had been justified from its very beginning by 'examples drawn forth of *Scottish* Histories'.[83] Moreover, this ability to historicise the origins and authority of what claimed to be an immutable Catholic hierarchy in Europe had been one of the foremost debts owed by all the Lutheran and Calvinist reformers to the humanist scholarship of the Renaissance.[84] So Knox's treatment of the Lollards, echoed by scholars like Sir Thomas Craig who believed that the Scots 'were the first to impugn the tyrannical dogmas of Rome and to resist them stoutly', was an attempt to present historical evidence for a continuing struggle to reassert Scotland's inherent ecclesiological integrity.[85] This integrity was one which its proponents alleged had been usurped within historical memory by an illegitimate and indefensible Roman hierarchy. Further weight was lent to this purpose by the contention that the Lollards had actually handed down these truths by a line of rebellious succession unbroken up to the time of the Reformation: hence perhaps Knox's shrill claim that in spite of the Scottish prelates' cruel suppression of the Lollards their 'wicked practice did not greatly advance their Kingdom of darkness, neither yet was it able utterly to extinguish the Trueth'.[86] The plans of the satanic episcopacy had inevitably been thwarted. The testimony of the Lollards was seen to have possessed the necessary Scottish pedigree. And it had been transmitted, only enhanced by their sufferings and by those of other intermediaries like Patrick Hamilton and George Wishart (naturally also the subjects of Knox's sympathetic pen), to the victorious reformers of the sixteenth century.

Such recognition of a broadly humanist and historical approach to the justification of the Calvinist position seems to have moved many committed Scotsmen to follow Knox's example in the writing of history. Among these was certainly the Earl of Cromarty in the early eighteenth century, who set out trenchantly in 1713 'to vindicate that primary Reformation ... A Work worthy of many and the best concerned, and too heavy for a few'.[87] This meant, most obviously, a concentration of historical discussion around the earliest Scottish Christians and subsequent bishops and kings. These were groups upon whose precise historical status and character the whole precarious edifice of reformist ecclesiology in Scotland since Knox had come to depend. Apart from the Lollards, the most salient ancient Scottish believers had been the Culdees, a shadowy order within the primitive Celtic church whose legitimate authority the Papal hierarchy of bishops had supposedly usurped.[88] It was clear to George Buchanan, for example, a vociferous early critic of the Roman hierarchy, that the Culdees were distinct from and superior to the monastic and clerical orders who had supplanted them. For 'these last were as far inferiour to the former, in Learning and Piety', he insisted, 'as they did exceed them in Wealth, in Ceremonies, and in Pomp'.[89] Among later presbyterian historians the Culdees thus assumed an exaggerated historical importance. David Buchanan, author in 1644 of an influential preface to Knox's *Historie*, is an excellent example of this point. He claimed nothing less than that the Culdees were in fact true presbyterians, and went on to argue that they had chosen 'out of themselves some eminent men, in piety, knowledge, and wisedome, to oversee the rest'.[90] Other historians, as late as the eighteenth century, including Matthew Crawford, were drawn to use the Culdees or equivalent historical groups in the bold assertion of ancient Scottish religious integrity and authority.[91] In an earlier case of this kind the episcopalian John Spotswood had given eloquent voice to a highly flattering account of the ancient druids in Scotland. To the Bishop of Glasgow they were 'well learned in all natural Philosophy, men of moral conversation, and for Religion not so grossly ignorant and superstitious, as other heathen Priests'.[92] Interestingly, this eulogistic passage derived from Caesar's *De bello Gallico* and was itself later borrowed and placed in a specifically Glaswegian context by the early eighteenth-century presbyterian author and civic archivist, John MacUre, who was able to employ them in much the same way as both George and David Buchanan had the Culdees.[93] It would seem that it mattered little to such authors whether any Scottish druids had in reality been pagan. More important was the fact that they could illustrate for the early modern historian of any denomination the moral and intellectual virtues which after Knox were claimed for Scotland's indigenous religious heritage, untainted by the later corruptions of Rome.[94]

Yet there were at least two more important historical pillars supporting Calvinist ecclesiology in Scotland, both of which featured prominently even before the belated publication of Knox's version of events. These were the vital matters of the origins of the Scottish episcopacy and the subsequent relationship between an imposed church organisation and the royal line.[95] For the presbyterians in particular it was essential to demonstrate that Christianity had prospered in Scotland prior to the belated arrival of the Roman hierarchy. David Buchanan, for example, made this point very clearly. And he did so with a pointed reference to the putative historical consensus on this question, a device which again underlines the fundamental importance to the Calvinist case of the appeal to history. It was certain, Buchanan insisted, laying down the premise upon which this argument would always be founded, that the Scots 'are acknowledged to be among the first who embraced the Faith of Christ'.[96] Others in later times, like Sir James Dalrymple in the *Collections Concerning the Scottish History* (1705), set themselves the same task. Dalrymple offered a study with 'an Account given of the Antiquity and Purity of the Scottish-British Church, and the Noveltie of Popery in this Kingdom'.[97] An anonymous early eighteenth-century chronicler had the same vision of primitive religiosity in Scotland. Compared to England, he claimed, Scotland had 'had 36 christian Kings ere that Nation took the Faith, & has kept it undefiled'.[98] The whole tenor of this line of historical argument had never been more clearly revealed, however, than in the words of Alexander Petrie, minister to the Scottish community in Rotterdam after the Restoration. Petrie, be it noted, was again typical in referring to an (entirely spurious) historical consensus: 'All who have written the History of Scotland, do testifie', he disingenuously assured the readers of the *Compendious History*, 'that the Church was governed without Bishops' until the time of Pope Gregory VII.[99] It was simply essential to such authors, as it had been at the time of the Reformation, to prove that episcopacy was of historic rather than divine origin. As an institution it was shown by historians to have been unacceptable in Scotland because of its intimate association with Papal jurisdiction.[100] Clearly between presbyterian and episcopalian authors this would always be a considerable bone of contention. It was also predictably a debate which intensified amid the religious acrimony which marked the second half of the seventeenth century. Indeed at this time a whole genre of tracts emerged in Scotland specifically to address the question of the origins and legitimacy of the episcopacy, a complex problem which the 'Killing Times' had so conspicuously failed to resolve by more direct means.

From the episcopalian side came historical contributions like the *Apology for the Clergy of Scotland* (1692) by Alexander Monro, St Andrews' divine and pre-Revolution Principal at Edinburgh. Monro argued, once again with a significant glance at an alleged accumulation of historical evidence, that the 'famous and remarkable Instances of Ecclesiastical History' illustrated the innovative and pernicious character of the presbyterian system.[101] A generation later the Catholic historian Thomas Innes would review the same historical evidence as Monro and come to a conclusion in similar bold refutation of the Calvinist orthodoxy: there was in fact, Innes insisted, no 'pretended primitive Church government without bishops'.[102] A little earlier, in a manuscript history of 'The First Introducing of Christianity into Scotland', Richard Hay of Drumboote was likewise to condemn 'Mr George Buchanan, one of the most accurat Writers of his adge', as well as the scarcely less eminent Hector Boece, for propagating the spurious notion that the Faith had arrived early in Scotland, and in an unepiscopal form.[103] But fittingly speaking in the argumentative register of the original Calvinist apologists of the Reformation, were always to be found Whig presbyterians like Thomas Forrester, author of *The Hierarchical Bishops* (1699), as well as Gilbert Rule, distinguished minister of Greyfriars' Kirk and Principal of the University of Edinburgh after 1690.[104] Rule is perhaps especially representative of the Scottish Calvinist historical tradition. His stress in the *Vindication of the Church of Scotland* (1691) is upon past histories as a source of authority, focusing particularly on the primitive state of the Kirk. The 'Christian Church of *Scotland*', Rule adjudged, 'was governed by the *Culdees*, who are sometimes called *Priests*, sometimes *Monks*, sometimes *Bishops*'.[105] Moreover, it was emphatically 'evident from our Church Histories', he announced, that the 'Protestant Church of *Scotland*' had always strenuously opposed prelacy.[106] In a sense, therefore, one might say that these ferocious intellectual battles of the later seventeenth century between episcopalians and presbyterians were fought over the decisive control of fundamentally historical arguments. These again, on Knox's compelling evidence, were ones which had first emerged in Scotland in the initial defence of the Calvinist revolution.

The continuing imperative of upholding the integrity of ancient Scottish Christianity and examining the origins of the episcopacy therefore was traceable to Knox's influence and the claims of the original Calvinist reformers. But the role of the Scottish monarchy in religious life also long remained a prominent concern of those addressing this radically historicised post-Reformation agenda. Here, the characteristically Calvinist concern for the exaltation of the godly prince coincided productively for Scotland's scholars with the extremely delicate local matter of a national history during which royal policy towards the Kirk had always been controversial. As Roger Mason's work has recently shown, the moral and religious character of the monarchy had already been the perennial obsession of medieval historians in Scotland.[107] So when many post-Reformation authors also perceived an intense obligation either to entrench or to overthrow the presbyterian revolution of the sixteenth century, the historical religiosity of the Scottish monarchy took on an even greater significance. The defence of the Reformation, indeed, came to rely upon the authoritative dismissal of those kings of Scotland who had allowed themselves to be dominated by their monastic and clerical servants, or who had given too great a secular rein to their churchmen. To supporters of the Calvinist cause, such kings were to be charged with nothing less than moral responsibility for the historic inroads which good presbyterians believed had been made by superstition and luxury in the Scottish church. Modern monarchs were accordingly to be warned by their anxious scholars of the disastrous consequences which resulted from unwise patronage of the Kirk.

King David, for example, once idolised as a paragon of pious medieval virtue, was now influentially condemned in George Buchanan's *History* for having practised only craven appeasement in the face of clerical avarice. By this means, it seems, David had been guilty of ensuring the decline of virtue and the unrestrained growth of false doctrine: 'The study of Learning was extinct', Buchanan wailed with unashamed exaggeration, 'Piety degenerated into Superstition, and the Seeds of all Vices sprung up in them, as in an unplowed Field'.[108] In such analyses, of course, the compulsive Calvinist urge to dissect in grisly detail the sordid personal affairs of the king was to some extent integrated into the conventional narrative structure inherited from Fordun and Boece. This allowed the concerned historian to examine, in turn, the moral conduct and vicious inclinations of the familiar chronological succession of monarchs. David Symson, for example, then Historiographer Royal for Scotland, wrote in glowing terms in 1712 of Walter the Steward, still seen as the progenitor of the Stuart royal line, that he was 'an illustrions Example of Piety and Vertue', one of a small number of eminent Scotsmen distinguished by their prudent and devout religiosity.[109] More recently, however, James V had been rather less praiseworthy in his dealings with the Kirk. Indeed, he had carelessly bestowed on undeserving churchmen all the corrupting blandishments of wealth and influence. According to Robert Lindsay of Pitscottie, a vehement scholarly critic active during the Reformation, James had chosen to follow the advice of a flatulent train of 'familiar Servants, and certain Kirk-Men, as, Bishops, Abbots, Priors, Canons, Monks, and Friars', a ringing chorus comprising all the essential criminals of Roman ecclesiology in the eyes of the enthusiastic Calvinist historian.[110] His demise therefore stood as a stark lesson to 'all Kings, Princes, or Governours', that they ought instead to heed the exhortations of the Calvinist preachers and become more godly. In short, according to Lindsay, they 'must cause preach the Word of God truly to the People, and cause an Ecclesiastical Discipline to be used by the ministers thereof'.[111]

James VI, however, was much more the model of the Protestant prince. Consequently, Stuart historical propagandists like the unctuous Robert Johnston were able to turn this intensified post-Reformation focus upon the religious character of the monarchy into a powerful ideological prop for the

Jacobean regime. Johnston was able to reject out-of-hand the excesses of Knox, that 'imitator of the Vandalls devastations'.[112] Instead he directed his readers' attention towards the dutiful royal performance of those princely responsibilities identified by Calvinist polemic in great exemplars like Edward VI of England, who Knox himself had with unaccustomed diplomacy seen as a 'most godly and most vertuous king'.[113] James, therefore, was claimed by Johnston to have forced the Scottish clergy to keep 'a strict discipline to follow vertue and obedience'.[114] This was of course precisely the obligation laid upon the godly king by Lindsay at the time of the Reformation. No less sycophantic was John Gordon, briefly Bishop of Galloway and author of *The Union of Great Britaine* (1604). Gordon sought to idealize the religious character of mythical and historical kings in order to flatter James VI as the worthy descendant of a line of proto-Calvinist monarchs. Lucius, a legendary Scottish king, he claimed had been notable because 'of a King, he became a Preacher (as some Histories say)'.[115] James VI, Gordon also argued, should take only the godly to be his advisors, admitting like Constantius none but those 'such as are knowne to be well grounded in the true Christian religion'.[116] Equally, the moral and spiritual conduct of the sovereign had always been important in determining the contemporary state of church government. So royal propagandists like John Spotswood hailed James VI as 'the *Salomon* of this age', a king noted especially for 'his patience and piety (which shined above all his other virtues, and is witnessed in the learned works he left to posterity)'.[117] The religious character of monarchs thus occupied an even more prominent position in the Scottish historical tradition after the Reformation than it had enjoyed in the medieval period. It was an essential part of a reinvigorating and broadening of the historical discussion in Scotland that was taken up by scholars of all persuasions once the Calvinist reformers had made history a matter of incomparable significance. But this intense and continuing concern for the resolution of inherited ecclesiological issues was by no means all that the Calvinist revolution brought to Scottish discourse. It is arguable that the apocalypticism which it also introduced was to be even more important for the future of Scottish thought. This induced characteristic conceptions of the historical process and the narrative art which were to have far-reaching implications for scholarship in Scotland. These were fundamentally to affect subsequent generations of Scottish thinkers, even if within the historical tradition itself they seem to have become especially significant only once the great ecclesiastical histories had at last begun to appear, after the middle of the seventeenth century. We can, however, no longer delay a discussion of the apocalyptic as it infused the writings of Scottish scholars in the early modern period.

The Calvinist obsession with the apocalypse, exemplified in Knox's *Historie* which was eventually published complete in 1644, was expressed most directly in the historian's vivid identification of evil and spiritual conflict at large in the human world.[118] It is surely significant in this respect that Knox's own narrative technique when writing history so clearly attempted to subdue the intrusive

authorial voice, and to do so in favour of a compelling and cumulatively over-
whelming sequence of quotations and excerpts from documentary sources. This
empiricism, it seems, may have been precisely calculated by Knox. It certainly
served to evoke for the sensitive reader something of the spiritual proximity and
impending violence perceived by those participants in the Reformation who
believed it literally to be part of a titanic clash between opposing and
transcendent spiritual forces.[119] For example, Knox and his reforming
colleagues had undoubtedly sensed that in the era of the Reformation, 'Idolatry
is maintained, and Christ Jesus his true Religion despised, while idle bellies, and
bloody tyrants the Bishops are maintained, and Christs true Messengers
persecuted'.[120] But Knox chose to convey this impression of impending conflict
by means of a direct quotation from the evocative declaration issued by the
Scottish nobility in 1559. This succeeded by presenting the impressionable
reader with lurid first-hand testimony from people who had themselves been
both witnesses to and participants in that millenial struggle. The same technique
of almost unadulterated documentary quotation, moreover, was to be followed
by several of Knox's most significant successors. As these certainly included the
Covenanting die-hard David Calderwood, the Lanark minister James Kirkton
and the early eighteenth-century hagiographer Robert Wodrow, this is once
again a continuity which suggests the unremitting influence of basic Calvinist
assumptions upon the later course of Scottish scholarship.[121] Most Calvinists of
this sort not only believed that God attached a peculiar importance to the
creation and dissemination of an accurate historical account. They believed that
history itself was in some sense a special formulation of the Divine Word.
Indeed, they were convinced that historical time was marked, or even motivated,
by providential occurrences, and that history was therefore capable of being a
prophetic medium second in authority only to scripture. This was again a most
significant intellectual development attributable to the influence of the
Reformation. Yet only during the 'Killing Times' after the Restoration, the
bloody attempt by the last Stuart kings to suppress the presbyterians and to
overturn more than a century of Calvinist religious and political achievement in
Scotland, did the great Calvinist histories emerge. And only then did the great
Scottish scholars begin to stake the boldest claims on behalf of their craft.[122]

The apocalypse in historical scholarship, and so the prophetic allusion which
it invited, came to acquire great prominence in Scottish thought. But even in the
later seventeenth century it was not confined to presbyterian historians. As in
contemporary England, where recent scholarship has tended wisely to close the
gap once presumed to divide Calvinist from other intellectual life, Scotsmen of
most persuasions were gradually enveloped in an all-embracing apocalpytic and
providential vision of history, from which escape was neither possible nor
desirable.[123] It is likely for example that Gilbert Burnet, the doyen of
episcopalian scholars, was gesturing specifically at the potentially prophetic
character of historical study. He certainly asserted in 1677 that 'nothing does
more clear the Prospect of what is before us, than a strict Review of what is

past'.[124] Nor is it the case that such a vision was unanticipated in Scotland: indeed Burnet had equally conservative Scottish antecedents who had long been moving towards this view of their own scholarship. John Gordon, for example, had insisted as early as 1604 that in 'the order of Histories', it was possible to identify unmistakable evidence of what would come to pass. This was the case, Gordon argued, because events 'hath beene long before foreseene by the divine providence'.[125] Equally Jenny Wormald is correct to observe that throughout the *Plaine Discovery of the Whole Revelation* (1593) John Napier of Merchiston had probably regarded the 'historical approach' as intimately associated with prophecy.[126] Yet, the full extent of the connection in the Calvinist mind between history and prophecy was to be revealed with greatest clarity only at a later date, in the second half of the seventeenth century. One example from 1701 would be Robert Fleming with the richly apocalyptic *Epistolary Discourse*. If 'history, in the *general notion* of it, be *an account or relation of the actions of men in the world*', Fleming argued, '*prophecy* is no less a *species* of this … '. For if history 'is a relation of things past, prophecy is an account of things to come'.[127] His father the elder Robert, minister at Cambuslang and another Dutch exile likewise readily associated prophecy with history on the grounds that all events tended towards 'the *accomplishment of the Scripture*'. This unerringly teleological purpose he saw starkly in 1681 as 'that great business' clearly outstanding amid the 'various changes and revolutions which are here within time'.[128]

History was thus, in the eyes of later seventeenth-century historical thinkers such as these, quite explicitly the record of the substantiation of the prophetic texts. On this reasoning the analysis of history could even be regarded as a tool for use in the more accurate exegesis of the prophetic passages of traditional scripture. James Durham, the Glaswegian divine and a notable seventeenth-century student of the Book of Revelation, was one who made this logical connection. The purpose of scriptural analysis, he suggested in the *Commentarie Upon the Book of the Revelation* (1680), was simply to make 'agreeable to the nature of, and matter contained in, these prophecies, to History, in what is past, and to reason … '.[129] Inherent in the Scottish Calvinist's apocalyptic view of history there had always lain the notion that it represented a detailed record of the accomplishment of divine prophecy. History therefore was an incomparable stock of knowledge to which devout minds could turn with some hopes at least of an imperfect understanding of God's Will. This was a notion to some extent implicit in Knox's own highly teleological history of the Scottish Kirk. But it was also one which was to be most fully expressed only after the Restoration. This timing is something which we will later see is highly significant for an understanding of the profound changes which were occurring simultaneously in the social theory of early modern historical discourse. Even without a full-blown theory of historical prophecy, however, it is not difficult to account for the extreme ferocity with which successive generations of post-Reformation authors in Scotland had always fought for control of the nation's historical tradition. The uncommon authoritative weight which we have already seen that Scottish scholars attached to the evidence of history in the defence of the presbyterian revolution is explanation enough for the vigour with which they struggled.

The latent idea of prophetic history was surely a concomitant of the violent apocalypticism which was to be found growing out of the Reformation. But it also explains the typical Scottish attitude towards historical evidence as it grew to maturity during the seventeenth century. The progress of the millenarian conflict, after all, was believed to be manifested in terms of historical human events – the Reformation itself being the most obvious example. Those historical events could themselves be regarded as a prophetic illumination of things still to come. The history of the church, for example, as Spotswood argued, revealed the direction of the future. This was because, 'To know the success and event of every course, there needs onely the knowledge of things past, and a fit comparing of them with the present'.[130] History, moreover, as David Symson saw it in 1712, could be regarded as susceptible of reduction to certain broadly true rules. This understanding, rendered in a more secular idiom, led Symson to talk of deducing such 'natural Inferences as are not inconsistent with the Laws of History, and in no ways can be refuted'.[131] A direct consequence of such views was that the study of history could be seen as a devotional performance in its own right. It brought the audience into the closest possible contact with immediate prophetic evidence for the most valuable of spiritual truths. This understanding of course paralleled the well-known Calvinist preference for first-hand scriptural study rather than the mediating distractions of the Roman liturgy.[132] Knox, and one must presume Calderwood and his many imitators, conceived of historical evidence as a physical testimony of the apocalyptic struggle within which, as Calvinists, they believed themselves to be acting out their worldly parts. Their task as historians, as the Earl of Cromarty and others later agreed with gusto, was simply to gather together such testimony, and to offer spiritual, moral, and prophetic instruction amongst the true believers. It was, in this aristocrat's preferred visceral idiom, to rip up 'the Intrails of Antiquity for discovering the putrified Corruptions of Persons, Actors of publick Mischiefs'. This might even allow the historian 'to discover, prevent, and cure, the Maladies and Distempers, which did cut them off'.[133]

Evidence and not narrative, testimony and not interpolation, were as a result to provide the very backbone of the canonical Calvinist histories. This was an empirical assumption traceable directly to the theology of the Reformation. It was one which also dictated the strongly empirical preferences of authors from Knox in the mid-sixteenth to Robert Wodrow in the early eighteenth century. History was not, on this reading, the poor relation of scripture. On the contrary, it was the true continuation of orthodox scripture, just as the prophetic allusion implied: many historians in the early modern period were in any case also accomplished scriptural scholars.[134] There was a further corollary of this logical connection. This was that historical evidence was itself maintained deliberately by divine providence so as to implore the construction by the empirical scholar of an inspirational and instructive record. It is one which seems neither to have escaped Knox nor his various successors. To return once again to the paradigm case of the Lollards, Knox for example regarded the survival of judicial indictments against the heretics as far from coincidental. Instead, Knox claimed that 'God of his mercifull providence caused the enemies of his truth to keep [them] in their registers'.[135] Similarly Sir James Dalrymple, a pillar of early eighteenth-century Calvinist respectability, later claimed that 'by the Providence and Goodness of God, such Vestiges remain'd as do clear that the pure Christian Religion was establish'd' in ancient Scotland.[136] But equally Thomas Innes, the Catholic historian of the same period, seems to have had no less highly developed a belief in the divine provenance of those tangible fragments of historical evidence likely to be most conducive to faith. In the case of manuscripts attesting the deeds of St Columba, for example, it seemed obvious to Innes that there had been seen the 'special care' of providence, acting 'to preserve and bring down to posterity this ancient monument'.[137] The publisher of John Spotswood's manuscript *History* in 1655 likewise indicated that he recognised the work of a divine hand in ensuring the unlikely survival of this episcopalian testimony: 'Providence had so disposed of it', he claimed, that a copy arrived in 'more Ingenuous and Noble hands' than it would otherwise have found.[138] In James Anderson's polemical *Historical Essay* (1705), meanwhile, it was even considered beyond dispute that 'Providence, which favours injur'd Innocence' had 'preserved and discover'd' a single charter as evidence of Edward I's malevolence towards the Scottish nation.[139] And the Earl of Cromarty asserted without equivocation that providential intervention had ensured the durability of criminal evidence, so that historians could produce narratives like his own *Historical Account* (1713), devoted to the fulsome pursuit of 'Truth and Justice'.[140] Such different scholars were apparently as one in their conviction that history served as a record of concrete human interactions with a spiritual drama of cosmic proportions. Developments in that conflict, they believed, were relayed to the human sphere and recorded in the form of indisputable historical evidence. We therefore have grounds again for concluding that a specifically Calvinist form of humanism, introduced under the influence of John Knox and greatly elaborated by his many learned successors, had become a dominant feature of early modern Scottish historical scholarship.

On this reading, and taken alongside what we have already seen was the factionalization of an increasingly radical humanist history after Buchanan, something of the purpose of historical works in early modern Scotland has clearly begun to emerge. It was in part about the eloquent and decisive assertion of political and religious arguments which had an overpowering contemporary significance for their authors. No doubt for modern tastes this seems all too often to have produced discourse in which the historian is heard dimly above the incessant crackle of hell-fire and the pained cries of tortured souls. But it is important to ask whether this was all that such a surprisingly large community of historians were striving to do when writing history. Certainly it might seem the end of the story if we were to allow the hubbub of revolutionary polemic and religious fervour merely to drown out all other worthwhile sounds. Yet I would now like to shift the focus of our attention elsewhere, to a consideration of the rhetoric utilised by the historians in explaining their purpose. In other words, I want to suggest what might be missing from the more familiar account in which Scottish historical writing is taken simply as a lurid reflection of political and denominational strife. In fact, it will become apparent that the authorial rhetoric also spoke to the reader in a strikingly Calvinist and humanist idiom. This argued that history itself had a crucial role to play in three areas of concern within what we might now call Scottish social theory: the education of a social leadership, the propagation of virtue and the explanation of historical change. The historians who we have so far examined hereafter begin to seem extraordinarily self-conscious and highly motivated practitioners of their art. They possessed a Calvinist and humanist vision of their function. This was remarkable both for its clarity and its consistency, and it drew Scotland's scholars unwittingly together seemingly irrespective of their ideological or confessional allegiances. It is therefore to their propensity for compulsive and articulate self-explanation that we should now turn.

III: RHETORIC AND THE PURPOSE OF HISTORY

There was a common conviction among those early eighteenth-century Scotsmen who wrote the sort of history which we have so far been examining. This was that they were contributing to a profoundly instructive and educational medium. History was, as William Duncan of Dundee saw it in 1722, 'of great Use to improve our Minds in Knowledge'.[141] It brought knowledge and wisdom to the diligent reader. It also equipped him better to face the challenges of the future. As an unusually optimistic Alexander Ross had figuratively expressed it in 1652, 'that which makes a man truly wise and double-faced with Janus is History of things past ... [it] makes men ripe and aged in knowledge, though they be children in Years'.[142] Likewise to Henry Maule in the *History of the Picts* (1706), it still seemed clear that 'history is the theatre of man's life, whereby all may learn one common lesson by the goodly examples she represents'.[143] In particular such authors believed that the reading of a historical text peculiarly imparted the blessings of accumulated experience. These, as David Reid has recently argued, were assumed by most Scotsmen throughout this period to include the improvement of moral conduct and the honing of sound judgement.[144] Maule, for example, was unusually explicit in sketching the versatile performances of which history was presumed uniquely capable by virtue of her embodiment of past experience: 'Experience verifying the testimonies which wise antiquity doth offer', Maule wrote, 'she [History] is the mistriss of man's life, the testimony of truth, the recorder of justice, the resplendent beams of virtue, the register of honour, the trumpet of fame, examiner of actions, comptroller of the times, the rendezvous of diverse events, the soul of good and evil, and the soveraigne judge of all men and all exploits'.[145] Similarly, though with rather less prolixity, John Spotswood had given similar assurances to his audience in the *History of the Church of Scotland*, written early in the seventeenth century. Spotswood insisted that 'There is not amongst men a greater help for the attaining unto wisedome, then is the reading of History'. This was undoubtedly true, Spotswood went on, because 'it teacheth us at other mens cost, and carrieth this advantage more, that in a few hours reading, a man may gather moe Instructions out of the same, then twenty men living successively one after another, can possibly learn by their own experience'.[146]

It should not be thought, however, that this was an attitude common only amongst the historians of the seventeenth and early eighteenth century. The expressions of an earlier generation of Scottish authors provide a useful corrective. They help emphasise that the function of historical scholarship as it was understood by Maule and Spotswood was also abundantly clear to their earliest post-Reformation predecessors in Scotland. Indeed from at least the time of the Reformation – and possibly earlier if the poets of such medieval texts as the anonymous *Liber Pluscardensis* poem 'Rycht as all stryngis ar rewlyt in a harpe' (*c.*1461) are any guide – Scottish scholars seem to have been developing a keen humanist sense of the vital instructional role of their work, and an equal determination to broadcast this in self-justification to their potential audience. For example, when offering the study of history to his readers, Bellenden, the early sixteenth-century translator of Livy and Boece, was in his humanist confidence precociously illustrative of subsequent Scottish thought. Bellenden was Archdeacon of Moray and therefore well used to ministering to men's souls. But he insisted that he found no 'exercitionis' more fitting or 'profitable to thame, than frequent reading of thir and othir historyis'.[147] Quoting that eminent Christian humanist source, 'Erasmus Roterodamus, in his buke, namit The Institution of Cristin Kings', Bellenden emphasised that it was beyond dispute that 'na thing be sa fruteful to dant the commoun errouris of pepill, as honest and virtewis life of kingis' which were to be found in the works of historians.[148] That such a conception of a useful and edificatory humanist history was reinforced and popularised by the spiritual priorities of the Reformation era could amply be demonstrated. But no one would now suggest that the heightened moralistic and educative spirit of the sixteenth and seventeenth centuries was confined to the religious revolutionaries. Jesuits, neo-Thomists, and ingenious Tridentine theologians, not to say the learned episcopalians and bookish Catholic scholars of Scotland, all shared in the intensified desire to edify and instruct their fellow men.[149] It would accordingly be simplistic to assume that there was ever a uniquely presbyterian formulation of historical purpose. Expressions of faith in the instructive power of history were in Scotland sometimes deeply obligated to the Calvinist notion of historical prophecy which we have already encountered. Yet theorizations even of the most vehement presbyterian historians failed, at least in this crucial respect, to distinguish themselves from the more broadly humanist position. This stance was one which identified a constituency of Scottish authors as often tainted with Catholic apologetic as Reformation zeal.

The positions adopted by splenetic authors like William Lithgow, writing in the 1630s, moreover, suggest not only that the humanist vision of history, particularly in its compelling association with the aim of moral and intellectual improvement, had subscribers throughout the Scottish historical community. They also suggest that it was the instinctive exculpatory defence for those fending off the expected arrows of critics, those 'clownish Carpers, Critticks, Calumniators, and distracted Censurers' so strongly rebuffed by a defiant Lithgow.[150] Another author who was painfully aware of the same need to justify the production of historical works was his contemporary David Hume of Godscroft. Godscroft was an eloquent though idiosyncratic humanist, a loyal secretary to the 8th Earl of Angus who came to fame as the controversial historian of the Douglases. In the 1620s he addressed the accusation that history was educationally vacuous, or even pernicious, a claim which was in fact rarely made but which many practitioners sought to pre-empt. Godscroft countered with a forthright assertion. In it 'we see men, and our selves in them, our vertues or vices ... this leads us also to God'. If the critics say 'that History maketh men profane', he insisted, 'and leadeth them to profanitie and atheisme; then certainly we may justly say, that it is nothing less'.[151] In precisely the same idiom, John Lesley, the Catholic historian of the Reformation, had seventy years earlier defended man's study of history. Lesley straightforwardly justified such scholarship on the grounds that it served 'to direct his liefe to the plesour of God, embrasing and following vertew, and declining fra vyce and syn'.[152] Historians in Scotland, even beyond the frontiers of the Protestant community, thus seem to have wielded a classic humanist defence of historical scholarship. They argued vehemently that their work instructed by the provision of exemplary moral and spiritual models, from whose experience the reader would receive unparalleled edification. As Walter Scott of Satchells, a far-from-eminent genealogical versifier put it in 1688 when defending the purpose underlying his own rather laboured account of the Wars of Religion: 'Let their example be a spur to you,| That you their worthy vertues may pursue'.[153] Referring to the classical sources dear to all humanists, Scott urged the same didactic function upon his fellow historians: 'this task's most fit for learned men', he glowed, 'For Homer, Ovid, or for Virgil's pen'.[154] An anonymous scholar of the later seventeenth century, possibly William Dunlop, the celebrated Principal of the University of Edinburgh, also spent considerable time in laboriously compiling a manuscript listing the histories of all the major Scottish dynasties: here again was a Scotsman who believed without reservation in the unquestionable moral benefits of simple genealogy.[155] Perhaps anticipating the proliferation of such dubious and vulnerable work in Scotland, we even find the same issues addressed by William Drummond of Hawthornden, that eloquent and much-revered man of letters. Drummond defended the contemporary fashion for genealogy in strongly edificatory terms, arguing as a humanist that it was 'a matter so far from contempt, that it deserveth highest praise'. Indeed, he pronounced, 'Herein consisteth a part of the knowledge of a mans own self'.[156]

History, as these statements show, was believed by its early modern Scottish practitioners principally to be an educational medium. It deployed the lessons of experience in order to cultivate the rational and moral faculties of man; that is, it served to 'improve their judgment in Civil Wisdom, and the necessary conduct of Life', as the Jacobean courtier Sir James Melville put it in his own historical *Memoires*.[157] As in Continental humanism, however, this bestowed upon Scottish historical writing a very special role in the theory of civil government. This was a development which saw its most explicit embodiment in Scotland, as elsewhere during the Renaissance, in the emergence of the 'mirror for princes' genre.[158] In this form, Scottish authors openly assumed the position of teachers and counsellors to statesmen and aristocrats. They set out, like Castiglione, directly to tackle the ethical problems of leadership and office encountered by this eminent audience.[159] Undoubtedly the most striking Scottish example of the genre remains James VI's own *Basilikon Doron* (1599). In this homily the self-professed royal scholar set out to fulfill the acknowledged obligation of being 'carefull' for his son's 'godlie and vertuous education'.[160] James significantly advised the prospective ruler to be 'well versed in authenticke histories', for these were where 'ye shall learne experience by Theoricke, applying the by-past things to the present estate'[161] : the humanist mirror thus reflected the historical experience of antiquity onto the nascent leaders of the future. The other outstanding case of the deliberate historical education of a prince was of course George Buchanan's *History*, specifically though not exclusively intended for the moral and intellectual instruction of the young James VI. In it the great humanist grandiloquently claimed to be sending the prince 'Faithful Counsellors from History, that you might make use of their Advice in Your Deliberations'. After all, history was unhesitatingly described by Buchanan as 'that sort of Writing, which tends to the Information of the Mind', and which 'would best supply the want of my Attendance'.[162] History, it seems, could in early modern Scotland offer the eminent reader not only the most erudite advisers of the past. With consequences which we shall later examine in much greater detail, it also offered a narrative which promised to perform the moralistic functions of the Calvinist preacher as well as the part of the practical and knowledgeable humanist courtier.

Such a posture, with the historian rhetorically adopting the stance of a counsellor, seems to have become almost instinctive for post-Reformation Scottish authors. In short, and in a world in which books increasingly vied with sermons and pamphlets as the primary modes of formal communication, Scotsmen regarded their historical texts as edificatory and didactic utterances directed not least to those in the positions of highest influence.[163] Even an author as unlikely as the mercenary soldier Robert Monro, therefore, writing an elaborate historical defence of his military exploits in the Continental wars of the

1630s, was wholly enveloped by this Renaissance convention. Monro openly echoed Buchanan's humanist view of prudent historical counsel when he dedicated his work to the Prince Elector Palatine of Rhine. He had 'beene bold', the gnarled veteran humbly confessed, 'to send unto your Highnesse at this time, worthy Counsellors, whose counsell your Highnesse may be bold to follow'.[164] The rhetorical orientation of the historical text towards the education of the influential achieved such currency in early modern Scotland, moreover, that it was entirely subsumed within the convention of obligatory claims made by most practising historians: historical scholarship, in effect, was the means which extended the untold benefits of the edificatory humanist mirror to a much wider Scottish audience. This would seem to have been an opportunity which few Calvinists and humanists from the time of Hector Boece would scorn.[165] If, as we have seen, history and prophecy began increasingly to be conflated after the Reformation, it should be no surprise that Napier of Merchiston, a notable seer at the close of the sixteenth century, was also bound up in the same literary conventions. Napier had expressly claimed the same privilege for his own discipline, arguing that as an amalgam of prophecy and history it followed directly in the tradition of prophets who had unashamedly addressed themselves 'generally to kings, princes, and governours'.[166] With similar thoughts in mind, early modern historians ostentatiously presented their texts to all kinds of distinguished men. Lord Seaforth, for example, was the recipient of George Mackenzie's historical review in 1708, a gift made with the intention of exhorting the aristocrat to the full performance of his public duties. A man's worth, according to Mackenzie, was assumed to consist in 'Imitating the Actions of those *Illustrious Heroes*'. Accordingly the author edified and instructed by serving up for a patron 'the *Lives* and *Characters*' of those historical models.[167] Indeed, in more than one case a Scottish scholar was to be found offering an historical tract which linked the general purpose of advising 'princes and counsellors' with more specific tasks; as, for example, in the case of one who sought to educate his own son 'by my faults'.[168] Here Sir James Melville, clearly had in mind the essential importance of history as an educational and often severely practical conveyor of experience to the future leader: 'I willingly opened these things to thee', Melville candidly admitted in the prologue, 'that thou mayst as well know what is usually done, as what ought to be'.[169]

In the light of its perceived educative function in Scotland, it was also necessary for history to follow still further the established precedent of Renaissance humanism. This involved making a special claim to authenticity and historical accuracy. Since Thucydides had first called into question the methodology and accuracy of his one known predecessor, Herodotus, it had been necessary for most serious Western historians to seek credibility by the assiduous distancing of their own work from that of supposedly less reliable earlier colleagues.[170] The claim to truthfulness was therefore an integral feature of the Scottish historians' justificatory rhetoric. Truth was apostrophised very fittingly, for example, by the Edinburgh lawyer and antiquarian James Anderson in 1727. Anderson saw it unquestionably as 'the Life and chief Ornament of History'.[171] Gilbert Burnet, too, was invariably an eloquent mouthpiece for the rhetoric of historical purpose, and on the subject of truthfulness he was especially faithful to the convention. 'History', Burnet advised the readers of the *Reflections on Mr Varillas' History* (1686), 'ought to relate things as we find they really were designed and transacted; and not as we imagine they ought or might have been'.[172] James Anderson, it seems, simply echoed Burnet in stressing the utmost necessity of factual accuracy. The historian 'ought in Matters of Fact', he warned, 'to lay aside all partial Regard to Religion, Country, Interest, Prepossessions, Parties, or other Views'.[173] His contemporary, the Jacobite lawyer David Scott also argued in much the same vein. Writing in 1727 he railed against historians becoming simply 'party tools and parasites'.[174] To this extent, then, early modern Scottish historians, had accustomed themselves to the humanist notion that critical scrupulousness – at least in the sense of avoiding known falsehood – was an important duty incumbent upon the conscientious scholar.

However, Hume of Godscroft provides an excellent instance of a historian who still managed to display a studied ambivalence towards what the modern author would recognise as the more complete ideal of empirical scholarship. Godscroft not only insisted in the *History of the Houses of Douglas and Angus* that 'the truth be stuck unto'. He also suggested, more problematically, that there actually remained some place for 'partiality and labouring to please' in the writing of history.[175] Even Gilbert Burnet, on closer inspection, turns out elsewhere to have qualified in this way what might initially have seemed an absolute commitment to impartiality. In fact, Burnet claimed that partiality in the historian was as forgivable as it was potentially troublesome: 'it lessens the credit of an author', Burnet considered, 'yet it does not blacken him'.[176] Evidently the absolute standard of accuracy necessary for the construction of history was crucially different from that of impartiality as conceived in early modern eyes. The expression of a polemical position, the imperative of moral instruction, or even the inevitably servile demeanour of loyal dynastic historians, it seems, could each justify some concessions to open commitment. Such commitment was not only unavoidable. It was also desirable, whilst never denying the need to uphold the strict principle of factual scrupulousness. In simple matters of fact and on questions of evidence the opinion of Sir Robert Gordon of Gordonstoun was probably typical. A Jacobean courtier and genealogist educated at St Andrews, Edinburgh and in France, Gordon was apparently comfortable with what would appear as an awkward humanist ambivalence towards truthfulness. He demanded a kind of truthfulness which stood apart from what he saw as the necessarily partisan claims of the committed historian. He thought it 'aneugh in histories (as ane old writer sayeth), iff maters be rehearsed plainlie as they are done, and recorded without any lie, and that there be nothing related without apparence of truth, or aganiest commoun sense or reasons'.[177] The scholar, he concluded, should certainly rely only upon 'old records, charters, manuscripts, registers, histories, and monuments'. All things according to Gordon should at least be 'grounded upon evident probabilities'.[178] But about partiality or special pleading, Scotsmen like these passed over in embarrassed silence. Or else, like Hume or Burnet, they dared to prevaricate, to defend it as a practice which was essential to the author's successful involvement in an edificatory humanist medium. Again, then, it was precisely because of an essentially humanist understanding which they had of their own function as scholars that the parallel requirements of factual accuracy and moral or political commitment had to co-exist in the rhetoric of history widely voiced by early modern Scottish writers.

What is quite clear, therefore, as we have seen so far, is that they possessed a habitual desire to explain the profoundly meaningful purpose of their historical works. In satisfying this urge, Scottish authors of the post-Reformation era used a rhetoric founded essentially in a humanist view of their work as an edificatory, instructive and necessarily accurate medium. And the intention was explicitly to practise history in order to further the incomparable cause of virtue. None in fact saw this ultimate purpose more clearly than Sir Robert Gordon, erstwhile opponent of inaccuracy and deception. Gordon wrote the *History of the Earldom of Sutherland* with the very specific intention of 'discovering and disclaiming against vyce wheresoever I find it predominant; and praising vertue wher I doe perceave it to shyne cleirlie'.[179] Drummond of Hawthornden, too, the most famous and lyrical Scottish author of the seventeenth century, likewise justified a deeply committed history in terms of its being 'a great spur to virtue to look back on the worth of our line'.[180] Others too, even those personally indebted to apparently very different ideological perspectives, nevertheless signalled that they had similarly virtuous purposes in mind when they turned to the creation of historical works. Patrick Abercromby, for example, the Catholic physician and historian, was certain that his *Martial Atchievements* (1711–15) would help substantiate the valuable classical maxim attributed to Cato, that 'Vertue never fails of being rewarded sooner or later'.[181] Writing as 'late' as 1729 in a history which drew very heavily upon the humanist Guicciardini, 'the Prince of all the Italian historians', we find the capable antiquarian Alexander Gordon taking a similar line. Yet another distinguished Aberdonian classical scholar, Gordon was no less concerned to stress that his work would succeed in its task of stimulating virtue by presenting vice in its many guises: 'the more Villainy is exposed to the Eyes of the World', he advised, 'the more is an Abhorrence of it establish'd in virtuous and good Minds'.[182] This was indeed the authentic voice of the Scottish historian, of the quintessential Scottish humanist scholar alive and well after two centuries of continuous dynamic evolution. More than a century earlier, for example, the shadowy Patrick Gordon of Ruthven had regarded it as his 'natural duty' in writing the *Famous History* (1615) to immortalise 'the never-enough-praised Virtues' of men like the Bruce.[183] Even at the very start of the modern period of Scottish scholarship John Lesley had seen himself in the *History of Scotland* as engaged in the encouragement of the 'embrasing and following vertew'.[184] And his religious opponent Buchanan had likewise regarded this educational medium as serving directly to provide the Scottish mind with 'good instructions' and to encourage it in its 'endeavours by vertue to attain to true glory'.[185]

True history, then, was in Scottish eyes surely as Robert Johnston's *Historie of Scotland* (1646) claimed. It necessarily sought to excite its 'readers minds to embrace vertue, honesty, and wisdome'.[186] This was an unashamedly moralistic function which bound in authors of all political and religious persuasions in early modern Scotland – and which also justified, indeed probably required, the partiality with which most scholars instinctively wrote. Few could seriously have quibbled with Peter Rae, the Hanoverian historian of Dumfries, who considered that there was simply no 'civilised Nation, where there may not be found some Accounts of the Heroick Actions of their Noble and Valiant Ancestors; whose brave Example hath provok'd them to an Imitation of their eminent Vertues'.[187] According to Hume of Godscroft, moreover, that great defender of his craft, history was, 'as it were, the ABC. of this Method, and the beautiful Picture; by looking on which, our desire of honour is kindled, and so of vertue, which onely brings true honour with it'.[188] Historians taking this view asserted with both clarity and consistency that they wrote in order to encourage virtuous forms of conduct, notwithstanding the obligations to be both accurate and candid. There is thus only one sensible way to interpret claims like Abercromby's, in *The History of the Campagnes of* 1548 *and* 1549, written in the year of the Act of Union, to make 'the Vertues shine in their full lustre' whilst 'elsewhere Vice is set out in its Natural Dress'.[189] They were the universal sentiments of scholars deeply influenced by those inherited Calvinist and humanist preoccupations with which we began this chapter. The fascinating character of the virtues as conceived by these historians will also form an important part of our own subsequent inquiries. But it seems clear, so far, that the expressed purpose of early modern historians in Scotland was indeed to provide the impressionable reader in some real sense with an accurate but deeply committed 'spur to virtue'.[190]

They had argued that historical writing peculiarly strove to educate and instruct. They had also insisted that it operated intentionally and absolutely unequivocally in pursuit of virtue. But Scottish historians were commonly obliged to recognise a third responsibility. Any coherent historical vision would at this time, as for Dilthey and Hegel in the nineteenth century, still have required a suitable grasp of causality and change: few were yet sympathetic to the positivist view today associated with Karl Popper, which holds that historical accounts are ontologically separable from and hence incommensurable with scientific interpretations.[191] A form of literature directed specifically at the influential, however, would also need to provide an explanation as to how leaders might bring about wider developments over time. Andrew Fletcher's *Discourse* (1697) provides an example of this task as it was conceived in the context of one of the most famous historical polemics produced in early modern Scotland. The author expressed quite simply his determination to 'deduce from their Original the Causes, Occasions, and the Complication of those many unforeseen Accidents' which history presented to the reader.[192] But this clarion call for the exploration and demonstration of causal mechanisms had long been heeded by his Scottish predecessors. Gilbert Burnet, for example, had considered it absolutely essential to his task that the historian publish material useful 'for opening up the secretest Causes and Beginnings of great Changes or Revolutions'. It was clear, Burnet wrote in 1677, that this obligation was absolutely unavoidable, 'this being the chief Instruction that men receive from History'.[193] The same convention of self-explanation had also driven George Scott of Pitlochie, Melville's grandson and editor, to argue in 1683 that historians 'discover those hidden Springs of Affairs, which give motion to all the vast Machines and stupendous Revolutions of Princes and Kingdoms'.[194] But in providing this causal analysis in their histories, and as we shall discover more fully in the next chapter, Scottish authors of the early modern period had more than one formal explanation of their task to offer.

One argument for the study of causality derived from the Calvinist conception of history as an account of providential activity, to which we have already alluded. This led some to lay particular stress upon the historical elucidation of divine causality in human affairs. David Buchanan, for example, Knox's first editor, emphasised the need to examine 'the strong Reasons, and necessary Causes that moved these men ... through the help and assistance of God, who by them, mean Instruments, brought things to passe'.[195] Clearly Buchanan envisaged history as an analysis of human agency and providential intervention. This was, of course, a classic dichotomy in the historical discussion of causality, one which often led many devout Scotsmen to have recourse to an interpretative vocabulary borrowed straight from the Calvinist doctrine of instruments.[196] Another, the typically defensive Hume of Godscroft, was himself convinced of the self-evident spiritual importance of understanding causality in history. For 'in it we see and behold', he advised, 'as in a Glasse, Gods Providence guiding and ruling the World'[197] : the humanist mirror therefore reflected more than simply the mundane faces of princes and statesmen. John Spotswood was a more confident episcopalian of the early seventeenth century who seems to have preferred a less transcendental idiom than Hume. But his ecclesiastical history still eloquently maintained the theological need for a specific examination of causality. To his mind, this seemed essential to any meaningful historical analysis, 'For take away from the story the causes whereupon, the manner how, and the purpose wherefore things were done, that which remaineth is more like a Fable than a History', Spotswood argued, 'delighting the Reader, it may be, for the present; but giving little or no instruction at all'.[198] Instruction, and a proper causal analysis, thus went hand in hand with the post-Reformation mind. In a more spiritual register, indeed, the elder Robert Fleming in 1681 pointed to the ancient histories in order to highlight 'a very convincing appearance of a divine hand' and 'an extraordinary providence which we cannot but see when we read them'.[199] Significantly, his son also directly addressed the question of historical causality in his *Epistolary Discourse*. For the younger Fleming history was again that medium wherein 'we may observe the various, and yet uniform steps of divine Providence in governing the world'.[200] To the anonymous Edinburgh author in 1716 responsible for the curious *Short History of the Late Rebellion*, it likewise seemed appropriate that because 'GOD discovers himself by his *Works*, as well as by his *Word*, by his *Providences*, as well as in his *Ordinances*', it was 'certainly every Christian's Business *to regard the Work of the LORD, and the Operation of his Hands*'.[201] Evidently a providential causality was an important aspect of the ontological argument for post-Reformation writers. But it was also widely regarded as an essential element in the instructive and educative focus of the cogent and purposeful historical text.

Causality was also, of course, a traditional humanist preoccupation, and it was one whose pertinence in early modern Scotland can only have been enhanced by the concurrent significance of this Calvinist ontological argument. Gilbert Burnet, for example, displayed the most pragmatically humanist approach to this question in one of his clearest observations on the role of history. This was that 'those who have had much practice in humane Affairs see that the conduct of the World is not so steady and so regular a thing'. From this mundane realisation, tinged with a wistful humanist appreciation of change and mutability, it followed by Burnet's reasoning that those readers seeking practical advice had to pay particular regard to other significant causal mechanisms in history, such as 'unlookt for Accidents, the caprices of some Tempers', and 'the secrets of Amours and Jealousies', which were 'the true sources of almost all that is transacted in the World'.[202] More succinctly, Abercromby's *Martial Atchievements* (1711–15) claimed in similar vein to rely upon an analysis of 'Causes and Effects', a focus that was deemed to be essential to an educative account which 'must needs comprehend the whole'.[203] Equally, Robert Monro had in 1637 regarded just such a humanist rhetorical purpose as most useful for justifying his own bloodthirsty recollections. Any man seeking to become 'circumspect and prudent', the old soldier had advised, needed 'to observe the varieties of chances incident unto all estates, from the Crowne to the lowest Cottage', in order that 'he may learne to better himselfe, and become wise in his profession'.[204] Thus a strand of historical rhetoric, noisily concerned to uncover what Sir Robert Gordon called 'the infallible rule of the changes and alterations which wee sie incident to mankynd',[205] seems to have condensed very rapidly in post-Reformation Scotland and remained prominent throughout the early modern period. It served to express the humanist fascination with mutability, and the obsession of individuals like Abercromby for that which 'gives Kingdoms and takes them away, depresses and raises Families, distracts and re-settles Nations'.[206] It served equally to ascribe to history the closest identification with the providential interests of the post-Reformation presby-terian scholar. As Gilbert Burnet perhaps most eloquently pleaded, and the rhetoric of his compatriots insistently claimed, the causality of historical development was a crucial component in instruction, and therefore a major purpose of any meaningful historical explanation: 'There is no part of History better receiv'd', Burnet observed, 'than the account of great Changes and Revolutions of States and Governments, in which the Variety of unlookt-for Accidents and Events, both entertains the Reader, and improves him'.[207]

IV

The early modern Scottish historians, I have argued, shared an eloquent and broadly humanist theorization of historical purpose. They would have agreed, like the Catholic bishop John Lesley in 1578, with what 'Cicero in fewe wordes hes comprehendit, saying, Historie is the witnes of time, the licht of truth, the life of memorie, maistress of life, and messenger of antiquite'.[208] Certainly, and as we have also seen at some length, they engaged in historical writing more immediately for what were antagonistic reasons. They used Calvinist and humanist resources to modify a powerful and adaptable tradition of history in order to defend highly partisan, and sometimes even revolutionary, positions. To this extent a more orthodox view, namely that Scottish historical writing discourse evolved within the familiar co-ordinates of an intensive religious and political dialogue, would have a sound basis. But having begun the practice of history as a Calvinist and humanist discourse, very many Scottish authors of this period would have found that their chosen medium also claimed to serve other valuable purposes. These purposes, it transpires, were just as relevant to scholars within the cultural and intellectual context in which they lived and wrote. It is of course just possible that the humanist inspiration for their work, or perhaps even the sheer vulnerability of literary scholars in a dangerous post-Reformation climate, may simply have compelled Scottish authors to voice these claims. Maybe they were simply part of an inherited and obligatory rhetoric, one which appeared to lay down an agenda of which individual historians were in reality only peripherally aware. But we have already seen how early modern historians nevertheless expressed themselves cogently, and, it would seem, comfortably, in a discourse dominated by Calvinism and humanism. They made the most astute use of the explosive political and religious analyses which had formed the original basis of the Scottish use of Calvinism and humanism. I have suggested, moreover, that the Scottish historians, persistently and throughout this period, did isolate three other very clear areas of theoretical concern which they held to be of unconditional significance to their own discipline: the education of a social leadership, the definition and inculcation of virtue and the causal explanation of historical change. Each of these, we have now confirmed, loomed large in the eloquent self-appraisal of their own function as historians. This position, then, opens the way for a more detailed analysis of the purpose of early modern historical writing in Scotland. We need to ask how these more profound Calvinist and humanist claims for history, voiced in this resonant and highly cohesive rhetoric of intention, reflected, and were reflected in, an authorial practice.

NOTES

1. William Nicolson, *The Scottish Historical Library* (London, 1702), p. 254+.
2. George Mackenzie, *Lives and Characters of the Most Eminent Writers of the Scots Nation*, 3 vols (Edinburgh, 1708–22), I, i.
3. Earl of Cromarty, *A Vindication of Robert III King of Scotland* (Edinburgh, 1695), p. i.
4. Henry Maule, *The History of the Picts* (Glasgow, 1818), p. 2. This was originally published in 1706, and was long thought to be the work of the distinguished antiquarian and patron of Scottish letters, Sir James Balfour.
5. See the *General Historical MSS: Scotland* (Edinburgh, National Library of Scotland, Adv. MS 33.3.16 and 33.5.17–18). In a similar panoptic vein see also the bibliographical manuscripts gathered together by Robert Wodrow (National Library of Scotland, MS Wodr. Qu. LII). Both were seemingly aware that theirs had already long been 'the historical nation'.
6. Samuel Rutherford, *Lex Rex: The Law and the Prince* (London, 1644), p. 449.
7. That the sixteenth century was indeed a turning-point in the fortunes of Scottish scholarship was clear, for example, to Thomas Innes, writing in the early eighteenth century. Letters had revived, he thought, 'within these two last ages', *A Critical Essay on the Ancient Inhabitants of Scotland*, 2 vols (London, 1729), I, iv.
8. That these controversies reinvigorated rather than stifled Scottish scholarship and thought has by no means always been accepted. H. G. Graham, for example, writing in 1901, imagined that there had been 'a literary stagnation', caused by Scotland being 'hotly stirred by political and ecclesiastical questions ... These causes dulled intellectual interest ... ', *Men of Letters*, p. 2.
9. See e.g. J. MacQueen, 'Some Aspects of the Early Renaissance in Scotland', *Forum for Modern Language Studies*, 3 (1967), 201–22, and J. Durkan, 'The Beginnings of Humanism in Scotland', *Innes Review*, 4 (1953), 5–24. But by far the most penetrating and comprehensive study, also taking historical writing very often as its subject, is R. A. Mason, 'Kingship and Commonweal: Political Thought and Ideology in Reformation Scotland' (unpublished Ph.D. dissertation, University of Edinburgh, 1983). Much of Dr Mason's interpretation of pre-Reformation material is alluded to in the following study, and in general I am indebted to his work for confirming many of my own suspicions about Scottish scholarship after Knox and Buchanan.
10. To William Nicolson, for example, the bishop had 'spent *all the time he could spare from the publick Service, in writing the History of his Nation*', *Scottish Historical Library*, p. 97. This merely regurgitates a eulogy taken directly from the distinguished (and much plagiarised) episcopalian historian John Spotswood in his *History of the Church of Scotland* (London, 1655). To an anonymous eighteenth-century Aberdonian, meanwhile, Elphinstone remained simply 'the only Scots historian in the 15th Century', [ ], *Historical Notes of Scotland to 1757* (Aberdeen, University Library, MS 615), fo. i.
11. Machiavelli's works, in French translation, first appeared in Scotland in 1536. See J. Purves, 'First Knowledge of Machiavelli in Scotland', *La Rinascita*, 1 (1938), 139–42. A notable early translation was made by William Fowler, uncle to Drummond of Hawthornden and secretary to Anne of Denmark, James VI's queen. It has appeared as 'The Prince of Machiavelli', *Works* (ed.), H. W. Meikle, 3 vols (Edinburgh, 1914–36), II, 69–164, and neatly complements his output as an early Scottish translator and admirer of Petrarch's *Trionfi*. It is clear that before the Reformation there was 'a good deal of intellectual traffic between Scotland and the continent', D. Hay, 'Scotland and the Italian Renaissance', in I. B. Cowan and D. Shaw (eds), *The Renaissance and Reformation in Scotland* (Edinburgh, 1983), p. 120. But, like so much else in the humanist tradition within early modern Scotland, the departure of James VI to London did not terminate the fertile connections between Italy and Scottish men of letters, as is particularly clear from R. D. S. Jack, *The Italian Influence on Scottish Literature* (Edinburgh, 1972). Italy continued, for example, to exert a pull on the minds of Drummond and Urquhart, to whom we will be referring, whilst other foreign influences of the Reformation era are reviewed in J. Durkan, 'The Cultural Background in Sixteenth-Century Scotland', in D. MacRoberts (ed.), *Essays on the Scottish Reformation* (Glasgow, 1962), pp. 274–331.

12. Hector Boece, *Hystory and Croniklis of Scotland* (ed. and transl.), J. Bellenden, ([Edinburgh, 1542?]). Bellenden worked from the Latin text published at Paris in 1527, and did so at the personal behest of no less a patron than James V.

13. John Major, *Historia Majoris Britanniae* (Paris, 1521). A modern translation appeared as *A History of Greater Britain, as well England as Scotland* (ed. and transl.), A. Constable (Edinburgh, 1892), and it is from this that my quotations will be taken. Significantly, a later edition of the Latin text was produced in 1740, under the capable direction of Thomas Ruddiman. The distinguished names in the lengthy subscription list testify to the enlightened Scottish interest in the older historical tradition, in spite of the growing chorus of strident modernism. The outstanding treatment of Major (or 'Mair') as historian is R. A. Mason, 'Kingship, Nobility, and Anglo-Scottish Union: John Mair's *History of Greater Britain* (1521)', *Innes Review*, 41 (1990), 183–222.

14. That humanism as a mode of radical political argument achieved such a high profile in Scotland, whilst humanism *qua* 'literary creation in classically inspired styles' faded somewhat during the later sixteenth century, has plausibly been attributed to Flodden, religious controversy, and chronic political instability. This would have ensured, as Buchanan exemplified, that Scottish humanism 'emerged less in the form of intellectual dependence on ancient models than in that of freedom of conscience in politics and religion', A. M. Kinghorn, *The Chorus of History* 1485–1558: *Literary-Historical Relations in Renaissance Britain* (London, 1971), p. 221.

15. Indeed, 'Livy as an author is particularly important to Scots humanism, which was essentially Latin and historical ... the Scots were already the historical nation', J. MacQueen, 'Aspects of Humanism in Sixteenth and Seventeenth Century Literature', in his (ed.), *Humanism in Renaissance Scotland* (Edinburgh, 1990), p. 19.

16. John Lesley, *The History of Scotland* (Edinburgh, 1830), pp. 3–5. Originally published at Rome in 1578.

17. J. Wormald, *Court, Kirk, and Community: Scotland*, 1470–1625 (London, 1981), p. 178.

18. George Buchanan, *De Jure Regni Apud Scotos Dialogos*, (ed. and transl.), Philalethes ([ ], 1680), p. 11. For an explanation of the humanist rather than the scholastic origins of this account, see Skinner, *Foundations*, II, 340–1. Buchanan himself appears to have copied almost verbatim from Cicero, *De inventione*, I, ii, 2.

19. *ibid.*, p. 19.

20. *ibid.*, p. 69. This argument has led Quentin Skinner, for example, to judge Buchanan 'by far the most radical of all the Calvinist revolutionaries', *Foundations*, II, 341 n. But, although Skinner's account does not continue the story in Scotland, this dubious eminence did not, as we shall see, prevent Buchanan from remaining an influential political theorist for at least the next two centuries. Indeed, his political and historical work was still valuable enough at the beginning of the eighteenth century to warrant the final publication of Thomas Crauford's long-posthumous expository guide *Notes and Observations on Mr. George Buchanan's History of Scotland* (Edinburgh, 1708).

21. Innes, *Critical Essay*, I, 315.

22. Cicero, *De legibus*, III, iii, 8.

23. Nicolson, *Scottish Historical Library*, p. 114.

24. The indebtedness of early modern republican thought to scholastic and humanist predecessors alike, including Marsilius, Occam and Gerson, is emphasised by H. Baron, 'Calvinist Republicanism and its Historical Roots', *Church History*, 8 (1939), 30–42. The most recent detailed study of its medieval European origins is found in Skinner, *Foundations*, though for a distinctly Scottish account of the intellectual link see F. A. Oakley, 'On the Road from Constance to 1688: The Political Thought of John Major and George Buchanan', *Journal of British Studies*, 2 (1962), 1–31, which stresses the importance of later medieval Continental thought in forming sixteenth-century Scottish radical politics.

25. See J. H. Burns, 'The Conciliarist Tradition in Scotland', *Scottish Historical Review*, 42 (1963), 89–104.

26. Alexander Petrie, *A Compendious History of the Catholic Church*, 2 vols (The Hague, 1662), I, 23–4. Typically for a Scottish scholar of this time Petrie also cited the humanists Guicciardini, Erasmus, Vives, and, of course, Hector Boece, in further support of his attacks on the inflated claims of the Papacy.

27. Rutherford, *Lex Rex*, p. 5. It is perhaps worth noting in the context of a discussion tracing

the continuity of Scottish humanist radicalism that this work shared with Buchanan's *De Jure Regni* the unfortunate distinction of being publicly burned by the common hangman at the Market Cross in Edinburgh because, in part, of this dangerously historical approach to the 'divine' institution of government. Major, significantly, is cited at *ibid.*, pp. 50, 418, 449, but it is the spirit of Buchanan which pervades the text.

28. I. M. Smart, 'The Political Ideas of the Scottish Covenanters, 1638–88', *History of Political Thought*, I (1980), 176. For an earlier discussion of the same subject, see Hector Macpherson's illuminating 'Political Ideals of the Covenanters, 1660–88', *Records of the Scottish Church History Society*, 1 (1926), 224–32, in which the author's belief that it was the Calvinist dogmatists who were 'enlightened and democratic', *ibid.*, p. 232, locates him firmly within the Evangelical tradition which sees Enlightenment secularism as a vicious aberration in the otherwise glorious evolution of a robust yet radical Scottish theology.

29. Rutherford, *Lex Rex*, p. 78. His other cosmopolitan sources include Aristotle, Suarez and Grotius.

30. *ibid.*, p. 398.

31. *ibid.*, p. 2.

32. Robert Fleming, *The History of Hereditary-Right* (London, 1711), p. 28.

33. *ibid.*, p. 56.

34. *ibid.*, p. 28.

35. *ibid.*, p. 48.

36. Alexander Shields, *Hind Let Loose: or, an Historical Representation of the Testimonies of the Church of Scotland*, ([Amsterdam], 1687), p. 35. On Shields see H. Macpherson, 'Alexander Shields, 1660–1700', *Records of the Scottish Church History Society*, 3 (1929), 55–68. On Shields as 'a model for the continuity of radical discourse against the existing social order', see F. T. Gatter, 'On the Literary Value of Some Scottish Presbyterian Writings in the Context of the Scottish Enlightenment', in D. Strauss and H. Drescher (eds), *Scottish Language and Literature, Medieval and Renaissance* (Frankfurt, 1986), pp. 180–1.

37. Shields, *Hind Let Loose*, p. 35.

38. William Jameson, *The History of the Wisdom, Valour, and Liberty of the Ancient Albion-Scotish Nation* (Edinburgh, National Library of Scotland, MS Wodr. Qu. XCVII), pp. 1–3.

39. M. Merriman, 'James Henrisoun and "Great Britain": British Union and the Scottish Commonweal', in Mason (ed.), *Scotland and England*, pp. 85–112. On the complex question of Anglo-Scottish union in Jacobean Britain, see B. Galloway, *The Union of England and Scotland, 1603–1608* (Edinburgh, 1986).

40. John Monipennie, *The Abridgement or Summarie of the Scots Chronicles* (Glasgow, 1820), p. 18.

41. *ibid.*, p. 21.

42. 'There was an ancient sage *Philosopher*,| That had read *Alexander Ross* over', Samuel Butler, *Hudibras: The First Part* (London, 1663), II, 71.

43. Alexander Ross, *The Marrow of Historie* (London, 1650), p. 123.

44. John Lesley, *A Treatise Touching the Right of Marie, Queene of Scotland, to the Croune of England* ([ ], 1571), 3v. Mary's erudite supporter Adam Blackwood, a lawyer and political theorist educated at the universities of Paris and Toulouse, likewise turned history in 1587 to the specific refutation of Buchanan's assertion, as he put it, that 'the croune ought not to go by succession, but by election'. This claim Blackwood regarded as 'subvertinge all auncient politie of kingdomes and common wealthes in the chieffe fundamentall pointes, takinge awaie the force of the old customes and lawes so religiouslie obserwed from all antiquitie in all ages', *History of Mary Queen of Scots; A Fragment* (ed.), A. Macdonald (Edinburgh, 1834), pp. 56–7.

45. See Mason, 'Kingship and Commonweal', esp. pp. 59–97. More generally see J. Schwend, 'Nationalism in Scottish Medieval and Renaissance Literature', *Scottish Studies – Mainz*, VIII (1986), 29–42.

46. A surviving example of this traditional nationalistic militarism in scholarship, significantly in deliberate opposition to presbyterian and humanist interpretations, is found in 1594 in the work of a Scottish Jesuit, who contrasted the Catholic millenium when Scotland had possessed 'men of a physical courage which brought them fame at home and abroad for their military glory', with the modern Protestant age in which Scotsmen were instead reduced to 'civil wars … polluted with massacre and bloodshed … a perpetual shambles', George

Thomson, 'The Antiquity of the Christian Religion Among the Scots' (ed. and transl.), H. D. G. Law, *Miscellany of the Scottish History Society* (Edinburgh, 1904), II, 130–1.

47. Increasingly, however, the conventional view that Scottish identity emerged in the thirteenth and fourteenth centuries, in more or less direct response to English harrying, has been called into question. See e.g. E. J. Cowan, 'Myth and Identity in Early Medieval Scotland', *Scottish Historical Review*, 63 (1984), 111–35, which employs the ethnological theories of the anthropologist Claude Lévi-Strauss to argue that 'a shared identity, fostered by the myths of the past', characterised Scotland by 1200.

48. 'Liberty was one of the prominent aims of that many-sided movement which we call the Reformation', G. D. Henderson, 'Religion and Democracy', in his *The Burning Bush: Studies in Scottish Church History* (Edinburgh, 1957), p. 120.

49. See Major, *History of Greater Britain*, p. 48.

50. On the earlier discussion of liberty see G. W. S. Barrow, 'The Idea of Freedom in Late Medieval Scotland', *Innes Review*, 30 (1979), 16–34.

51. On Florentine humanism generally, see H. Baron, *In Search of Florentine Humanism*, 2 vols., (Princeton, NJ, 1988), and J. G. A. Pocock, *Machiavellian Moment*, pp. 83–271. More especially, for an example of the sort of Florentine conception of civic liberty which so influenced early modern Scottish thought, see the tract *De Libertate* by Alamanno Rinuccini, which construes freedom in radically participatory terms: 'In states where liberty exists ... there the citizens speak without subterfuge and give advice to the Republic based on their real convictions'. Indeed, 'the basic principle of all liberty is citizen equality', understood, of course, in civic rather than economic terms. Liberty, in sum, requires that offices, political and military, remain in the hands of the citizens: 'in free states, offices are filled by chance selection from certain lists ... all those who aid the Republic privately by payment of taxes are also given a chance to participate ... '. Translated and printed in R.N Watkins, *Humanism and Liberty. Writings on Freedom in Fifteenth-Century Florence* (Columbia, SC, 1978), pp. 193–223.

52. George Buchanan, *The History of Scotland* (ed. and transl.), J. Fraser (London, 1690), p. 117. This was republished in response to the avid demands of enlightened Edinburgh in 1762 and 1766, and of Glasgow in 1799, a further indication of continuing public interest in the Scottish historical tradition. Interestingly, the 1690 translation appeared just prior to the stormy English campaigns against the 'standing army', and a little before Fletcher of Salton reached his loquacious peak as a Scottish proponent of militias. Buchanan's analysis would surely have struck a chord with contemporary authors and readers.

53. *ibid.*, p. 117.

54. For a study of this type of argument as it caught light at the end of the seventeenth century and burned again intermittently during the eighteenth, see Robertson, *Scottish Enlightenment*. I would differ with Dr Robertson's account only in that I would wish to stress more strongly the preparations for Harrington's reception in late Stuart Scotland which were laid by Boece and Buchanan in an earlier age. In particular, the case of Buchanan makes it hard to accept the suggestion that it was only in 1697–8 that 'the experience of Scotland was at last brought into the debate, and subjected to analysis in the terms of the civic tradition', *ibid.*, p. 15. With Fletcher's strikingly pregnant vision located in the much longer Scottish humanist perspective, moreover, we might also find it easier to understand the urgency with which Hume and Smith subsequently set about reworking his resonant interpretation to suit a commercial and depoliticised society.

55. George Ridpath, *An Historical Account of the Antient Rights and Power of the Parliament of Scotland* (Edinburgh, 1703), p. 71. Consider especially Buchanan's contention, ostensibly that of the Scottish people in the mid-sixteenth century, 'that t'was a matter full of danger, to commit the state of *Scotland* to Men, without either Lands or Hopes', *History*, p. 117.

56. See J. Robertson, 'Andrew Fletcher's Vision of Union', in Mason (ed.), *Scotland and England*, p. 221 n.

57. Andrew Fletcher, *A Discourse Concerning Militia's and Standing Armies* (London, 1697), p. 6.

58. Fletcher, *Discourse*, p. 4. As Robertson remarks, the 'key to Fletcher's originality' lies in 'the unique historical perspective in which he sets the problem of military organisation. It was a perspective quite distinct from that adopted by either Trenchard or Defoe', English neo-Harringtonians of the same period, *Scottish Enlightenment*, p. 29. Again, it is necessary to

reiterate that the profoundly historical roots of Fletcher's later political proposals for a militia point to his inheritance from a Scottish humanist tradition stemming from Boece and especially Buchanan.

59. *ibid.*, p. 13.
60. *ibid.*, pp. 4–5.
61. Shields, *Hind Let Loose*, p. 724.
62. *ibid.*, p. 15.
63. As Williamson points out, David Hume of Godscroft is another whose presbyterian position entailed this deeply humanist political construction of national liberty: he 'saw the threat to the presbyterian polity as a threat to Scotland itself', *Scottish National Consciousness*, p. 89.
64. Alexander Ross, *The History of the World – The Second Part in Six Books* (London, 1652), p. 384. The author, after all, was closely attuned to the Scottish tradition of historical writing, and, as we shall later see, deployed a striking humanist moral analysis which links him to compatriots like Boece, Buchanan and, less uncomfortably, to James VI.
65. Robert Wodrow, *The History of the Sufferings of the Church of Scotland*, 4 vols (Glasgow, 1828), IV, 493. Originally written in 1721–2. On the author, see W. J. Couper, 'Robert Wodrow', *Records of the Scottish Church History Society*, 3 (1929), 112–34.
66. William Duncan, *The History of the Kings of Scotland* (Glasgow, 1722), p. iv.
67. [ ], *Defence of the Independence of the Antient Kingdom and Church of Scotland* (Glasgow, University Library, MS Gen. 1471), Sub-Title.
68. [ ], *Memoirs Concerning the Affairs of Scotland* (St Andrews, University Library, MS DA805.M2), III-IV.
69. David Scott, *The History of Scotland* (London, 1727), p. 736. Scott's evocation of medieval spirit in 1727 compares intriguingly with the determinedly pro-unionist use of libertarian rhetoric by Sir Thomas Craig of Riccarton, writing around 1605. Nimbly shifting between scripture and history as the basis of his arguments, a move which was almost reflexive to the Calvinist and humanist mind, Craig had portentously claimed that Britain was 'as it were a corporation', where, in radically participatory and openly Roman terms, and as Agrippa was summoned to instruct, it was 'every member's duty' to 'avert external danger from, to bend every nerve upon the security and well-being of the whole body corporate, and to work together to preserve and guard it', *De Unione Regnorum Britanniae Tractatus*, (ed. and transl.), C. Sanford Terry (Edinburgh, 1909), p. 233.
70. An example of the historical pamphlets, similar to Scott's larger work, in which the consequent sense of disappointment was reflected, is Wright's, *The Comical History of the Marriage Betwixt Fergusia and Heptarchus* (Edinburgh, 1717), in which it is aggressively, even somewhat atavistically proclaimed, that 'Liberty is the best of all Things, I'd rather have a Highland Plaid with Liberty, than the greatest Dainties, with a Hook in the Heart of it', *ibid.*, p. 23. Liberty, thus conceived, was of course associated with Scottish political autonomy and the traditional symbols of clannish nationhood rather than with the humanist critique of monarchical or non-participatory regimes.
71. See G. P. Johnston, 'The First Edition of Hume of Godscroft's History', *Papers of the Edinburgh Bibliographical Society*, 4 (1901), 149–71.
72. Sir George Mackenzie of Rosehaugh, *Observations upon the Laws and Customs of Nations* (Edinburgh, 1680), pp. 20–1. On Mackenzie's use of tainted materials in the attempt to flatter the Stuarts, see T. I. Rae, 'The Scottish Antiquarian Tradition', *Abertay Historical Society Publications*, 16 (1972), 18–19. For a modern translation of this resonant text, see H. Rothwell (ed.), *English Historical Documents 1189–1326* (London, 1959), pp. 541–3.
73. James Wallace, *The History of Scotland* (Dublin, 1724), C1r.
74. Viscount Stair, *Institutions of the Law of Scotland* (Edinburgh, 1681), A2v.
75. Sir James Dalrymple, *Collections Concerning the Scottish History* (Edinburgh, 1705), A1v. The integration of radical political history into the orthodox defence of the dynasty was finally to result in enlightened authors like Andrew Henderson lauding George III, somewhat improbably but with obvious conviction, as 'descended from the Lineage of the *Scots* Kings, who swayed a Sceptre with Glory thro' a longer Succession than any Monarchs upon the Earth can boast of', *Considerations On The Question Whether a Militia Ought to Extend to Scotland* (London, 1760), p. 46. A little earlier, probably in the 1720s, an anonymous Whig presbyterian was likewise to feel entirely safe in regurgitating the mythical descent of the Scots: see the *Chronicle of Scotland* (Edinburgh, University Library, MSS

Dc.4.12). Boece's kings, despite attacks on their historicity and doubts as to their ideological utility, had nevertheless survived to become thoroughly acceptable props to the Hanoverian regime.

76. Dalrymple, *Collections*, A1v.

77. Richard Hay, *A Vindication of Elizabeth More* (Edinburgh, 1723), p. iii. Interestingly, Hay was also responsible for an ill-fated project in 1719 which sought to reprint the *Scotichronicon*. The public proposal is reproduced in his *Genealogie of the Hayes of Tweeddale* (Edinburgh, 1835). As a Catholic historian, it is perhaps not surprising that Hay also turned his hands to the atavistically nationalist style of scholarship in his unpublished *Life of Sir William Wallace* (Edinburgh, National Library of Scotland, Adv. MS 33.4.18).

78. John Row, *The History of the Kirk of Scotland* (Edinburgh, 1842), p. 9. Originally composed around 1637, but surviving only in MS until its publication by the Wodrow Society.

79. See the discussion of the point that 'Protestantism had imbibed the individualism of humanism ... Calvinism played a decisive role in Scotland's educational programme, ensuring that that educational programme was fundamentally humanist', J. K. Cameron, 'Humanism and Religious Life', in MacQueen (ed.), *Humanism*, p. 175. See also M. Prestwich, 'The Changing Face of Calvinism', in her (ed.), *International Calvinism, 1541–1715* (Oxford, 1985), esp. p. 4.

80. On Knox's own elaboration of Calvinist ideas, see J. R. Gray, 'The Political Theory of John Knox', *Church History*, 8 (1939), 132–47.

81. See, for example, the orthodox narrative of J. T. MacNeill, who explains in what sense 'Protestantism in Scotland had its forerunners', *The History and Character of Calvinism* (New York, 1954), pp. 292–3. Also, Wormald, *Court, Kirk, and Community*, pp. 91–2.

82. An interesting insight into the importance of establishing the historicity of Scottish presbyterianism as 'late' as the eighteenth century may be obtained by examining the intentions of Matthew Crawford, minister of Eastwood in Glasgow, as he advertised them to his prospective subscribers. In particular, he claimed to offer 'A History of the Reformation, how carried on, and if by Presbyters or not?', and a study of the means by which 'Episcopacy was then abolished, and the Presbyterian Government re-established', *Proposals for Printing a General History of the Church of Scotland* ([ ], 1720?), p. 2. To the best of my knowledge Crawford's plans never in fact came to fruition.

83. Spotswood, *History*, p. 278. The episcopalian bishop Robert Keith, for example, cited a letter from Throckmorton to Queen Elizabeth, noting how the Scots employed 'Examples forth of their own Histories, grounded (as they said) upon their own Laws', and Spotswood may merely be echoing this comment, *History of the Affairs of Church and State in Scotland* (Edinburgh, 1734), p. 422. This was still the case during the Bishops' Wars which immediately preceded the Civil War. In recounting a disputation in 1638 as to the authority on which the Covenanters had unilaterally called an Assembly into existence, James Gordon of Rothiemay noted the protestations of the episcopalians that their own case was grounded fundamentally in precedents which 'wer obviouse in the church historye', *History of Scots Affairs from MDCXXXVII to MDCXLI* (eds.), J. Robertson and G. Grub, 3 vols (Aberdeen, 1841), I, 81.

84. This point is seminally argued in J. N. Figgis, *Studies of Political Thought: From Gerson to Grotius 1414–1625* (Cambridge, 1907). See also Skinner, *Foundations* and R. R. Bolgar, *The Classical Inheritance and its Beneficiaries* (Cambridge, 1973), esp. pp. 334–6. On Scotland, see Williamson, *Scottish National Consciousness*, pp. vii–viii. On Calvinism and humanism, see G. D. Henderson's discussion of Calvin as 'a staunch Humanist', *Presbyterianism* (Aberdeen, 1954), pp. 20–1.

85. Craig, *De Unione Regnorum*, p. 381.

86. John Knox, *The Historie of the Reformation of the Church of Scotland* (London, 1644), p. 2.

87. Earl of Cromarty, *An Historical Account of the Conspiracies of the Earls of Gowry and Robert Logan of Restalrig Against King James* (Edinburgh, 1713), pp. 15–16. John Pocock's view that English contemporaries seem to have been at home in historical argument, *The Ancient Constitution and the Feudal Law* (Cambridge, 1957), p. 89, may thus be capable of extension to seventeenth-century Scotsmen. Perhaps even in England it was humanism and the religious use of Foxe's *Acts and Monuments* as much as the legalism of Bracton and Fortescue which inured early modern controversialists to the use of historical argument.

88. The historical Culdees are discussed in J. A. Duke, *History of the Church of Scotland to the Reformation* (Edinburgh, 1937), pp. 67–70.
89. Buchanan, *History*, p. 125.
90. Knox, *Historie*, d2v. Clearly, although her work does much to remedy the recent neglect of pre-Enlightenment historical writing in Scotland, I cannot agree with Marinell Ash when she says that David Calderwood was 'perhaps the first' Scotsman to use the Culdees as an argument for early presbyterianism. *The Strange Death of Scottish History* (Edinburgh, 1980), p. 33. George Buchanan evidently did as much in his own version of events.
91. Crawford, for example, thought this aspect of his task especially worthy of advertising: 'Of the Constitution and Government of the famous *Culdees*, from their first footing here, to their Dissolution', *Proposals*, p. 2.
92. Spotswood, *History*, p. 3.
93. John MacUre, *A View of the City of Glasgow* (Glasgow, 1830), p. 3. Originally published in 1736. For a source see *De bello Gallico*, VI, 13–14.
94. The utility of the druids for an enthusiastic proponent of British religious integrity is perhaps unwittingly illustrated by a modern scholar who explains that 'The Christian bishop was meant to take the place of the Druid priests', Duke, *History of the Church*, p. 20.
95. Once more, Matthew Crawford's impression of the orthodox agenda for post-Reformation historians makes this very clear. It was essential, he believed, to establish 'When the Christian Faith was introduc'd into these Northern Parts of *Great Britain*, and by what Means', and then to note, after due consideration of the Culdees, 'the Succession of the Bishops, from the first Foundation of their respective Sees', *Proposals*, p. 2. David Reid has recently seen material on this subject as comprising 'a minor literature of genuine interest. It is taken up with the great affair of national life, the struggle about authority in church and state', *The Party-Coloured Mind: Prose Relating to the Conflict of Church and State in Seventeenth-Century Scotland* (Edinburgh, 1982), p. 3.
96. Knox, *Historie*, b1r. The same strident claims that 'the Scots adopted the faith about the year 185 AD', in sharp contrast to the English and other Europeans, found its way into Jacobean unionist polemic in the hands of Scotsmen like Craig: see *De Unione Regnorum*, pp. 369–70.
97. Dalrymple, *Collections*, Sub-title. That this wholly meretricious claim was made by a long line of Calvinist historians, almost equally opposed to episcopacy and to Rome, and who ran at least from George Buchanan to Dalrymple in his own day, was apparently clear to the perceptive Catholic historian Father Innes in *The Civil and Ecclesiastical History of Scotland AD80–818* (Aberdeen, 1853), p. 16. No more hesitant in his use of ancient Scottish Christianity was the anonymous 1579 chronicler who observed with pride how as early as 203 in the reign of the mythical Donaldus the king and nobility 'wes baptissit be certane leirnit personis that wes weill instructitt in the Catholick ffaithe', a faith, moreover, which they 'hes newer left', *A Chronicle of the Kings of Scotland, From Fergus the First to James the Sixth* (ed.), J. W. Mackenzie (Edinburgh, 1830), p. 20.
98. [ ], *Chronicle of the Kings of Scottis from Fergus Ferchard Till* 1346 (Aberdeen, University Library, MS 192), p. 3.
99. Petrie, *Compendious History*, p. 276.
100. Gilbert Burnet in 1682, for example, turned this historical deconstruction of episcopal claims to the advantage of royal patronage, noting how 'In the progress of the History we find, that some Bishops were made by the Arch-Bishops, and others by the king', *The History of the Rights of Princes in the Disposing of Ecclesiastical Benefices* (London, 1682), p. 138.
101. Alexander Monro, *An Apology for the Clergy of Scotland* (London, 1692), p. 17. An eloquent earlier example of the genre, also admirably illustrating its author's development from episcopalian polemicist to polished civil historian, is Gilbert Burnet's *A Vindication of the Authority, Constitution, and Laws of the Church and State of Scotland* (Glasgow, 1673).
102. Innes, *Civil and Ecclesiastical History*, p. 43.
103. Richard Hay, *Ane Account of the Most Renowned Churches, Bishopricks, Monasteries, etc.* (Edinburgh, National Library of Scotland, Adv. MS 34.1.8), pp. 1–3.
104. Thomas Forrester, *The Hierarchical Bishops Claim to a Divine Right* (Edinburgh, 1699). A specific refutation of Monro is paginated separately, as pp. 1–145.
105. Gilbert Rule, *A Vindication of the Church of Scotland* (Edinburgh, 1691), p. 5.
106. *ibid.*, p. 10. A little earlier, another presbyterian polemicist, William Rait, 'Minister of the Gospel at Dundie', had anticipated Rule's use of history to defend his own ecclesiological

position: 'It is known to such as are not ignorant of Church history', he confidently suggested, 'that when Christianity came first into this Ysle, they had nothing to do with Rome, for a long time they were strangers and adversaries to her soveraignty...', *A Vindication of the Reformed Religion: From the Reflections of a Romanist* (Aberdeen, 1671), d2r.

107. This emerges throughout Mason, 'Kingship and Commonweal'.

108. Buchanan, *History*, p. 223. Cf. 'David, that most excellent King of the Scots', Major, *History of Greater Britain*, pp. 133, 138–42. Once more, the sixteenth-century historians set the mould for early modern appraisals. Alexander Petrie, for example, wrote of David's benefactions that they had stifled wit, which 'did dayly decay, the study of learning failed, piety was turned into a formality and superstition, and as in untilled land, the seeds of all weeds and vices sprang up', *Compendious History*, p. 375. This is as clear an example of plagiarism as one could hope to find.

109. David Symson, *A Genealogical and Historical Account of the Illustrious Name of Stuart* (Edinburgh, 1712), p. 33.

110. Robert Lindsay, *The History of Scotland from 1436 to 1565* (ed.), R. Freebairn (Edinburgh, 1728), p. 162.

111. *ibid.*, p. 178. Not unlike Lindsay in tone, though a committed enthusiast of the Catholic Mary and a zealous early critic of George Buchanan's account, was John, 5th Lord Herries, author in the 1580s of the MS history later published by the Abbotsford Club as *Historical Memoirs of the Reign of Mary Queen of Scots and a Portion of the Reign of King James the Sixth* (ed.), R. Pitcairn (Edinburgh, 1836). Herries lamented that 'Heer..., in a corner of the wordle... prelats and bishops who should have governed the Church...turned lasie in spiritual exercises; priests and the inferior Clergie... loose and idle, and lascivious... ', *ibid.*, p. 14. The moral corruption of the sixteenth-century Scottish Kirk was a theme which attracted the comment of authors of all persuasions in later times.

112. Robert Johnston, 'The Historie of Scotland During the Minority of King James', *Scotia Rediviva*, 1 (1826), 374.

113. Knox, *Historie*, p. 97.

114. Johnston, 'Historie', p. 466.

115. John Gordon, *The Union of Great Britaine* (London, 1604), p. 24.

116. *ibid.*, p. 25.

117. Spotswood, *History*, p. 546.

118. See R. Kyle, 'John Knox's Concept of Divine Providence', *Albion*, 18 (1986), esp. 403–4.

119. See M. Cherno, 'John Knox as an Innovator in Historiographic Narration', *Clio*, 8 (1979), 389–403.

120. Knox, *Historie*, p. 190. On Knox as chiliast, see R. Kyle, 'John Knox's Concept of History: A Focus on the Providential and Apocalyptic Aspects of His Religious Faith', *Fides et Historia*, 18 (1986), 5–19.

121. See David Calderwood, *The True History of the Church of Scotland* ([ ], 1678). Also James Kirkton, *The Secret and True History of the Church of Scotland from the Restoration to the year 1678* (Edinburgh, 1817), written in the years after 1678, and the more famous Robert Wodrow, *History*, compiled in the 1720s.

122. There is thus a substantial case for considering the Reformation in fact to be a process which continued well into the seventeenth century. See e.g. W. M. Campbell, *The Triumph of Presbyterianism* (Edinburgh, 1958), and M. Lynch, 'Calvinism in Scotland, 1559–1638', in Prestwich (ed.), *International Calvinism*, pp. 225–55, both of which emphasise the extent to which the age of the Covenant marked the true completion of the project begun two generations earlier.

123. Thus 'royalist and Puritan providentialism shared instinctive and profound assumptions', B. Worden, 'Providence and Politics in Cromwellian England', *Past and Present*, 109 (1985), 59. Also 'Puritan providentialism was doctrinally indistinguishable from Anglican and Catholic', B. Donagan, 'Providence, Chance, and Explanation: Some Paradoxical Aspects of Puritan Views of Causation', *Journal of Religious History*, 11 (1981), 385.

124. Gilbert Burnet, *The Memoires of the Lives and Actions of James and William Dukes of Hamilton and Castleherald* (London, 1677), Dedication.

125. Gordon, *Great Britaine*, p. 5. To some extent, once more, Gordon is typical here of the providential, and so of the apocalyptic and prophetic mood, of those historical tracts most

intimately connected with the Jacobean British court. Indeed, providence was a crucial defence of the new constitutional arrangements, as Sir Thomas Craig bullishly proclaimed in 1605: 'none can fail to recognise and marvel', he suggested, 'at the hand of Providence in this union', *De Unione Regnorum*, p. 264. Yet providence was not to erupt most explosively on to the wider historical scene, nor was a prophetic history fully to emerge, until the middle of the seventeenth century.

126. Wormald, *Court, Kirk, and Community*, p. 180.
127. Robert Fleming, *An Epistolary Discourse Concerning the Rise and Fall of the Papacy* (Edinburgh, 1790), p. 110. Originally published in 1701. Even so, although his equation of prophecy and history took him some way beyond the position earlier taken by Knox, Fleming's view was tempered with a caution which reflected the doubts of the great reformer, doubts to which any early modern Calvinist critic of human reason would necessarily be prone. Though he allowed himself 'to conjecture with some just grounds of probability', Fleming explicitly disavowed positivism: 'I do industriously avoid the fatal rock of positiveness', he claimed, 'which so many apocalyptical men have suffered themselves to split upon', *ibid.*, p. 24. Perhaps here too, Calvinist anti-rationalism, deeply mistrustful of human percipience and elaborate systematisation, pointed towards later Scottish attacks upon the more extravagant claims on behalf of the unaided human intellect, an assault most effectively carried out by David Hume.
128. Robert Fleming, *The Fulfilling of the Scripture* ([ ], 1681), p. 6.
129. James Durham, *A Commentarie Upon the Book of the Revelation* (Glasgow, 1680), p. 282. Durham, moreover, was convinced that God made provisions to permit the *cognoscenti* to foresee important moral events: 'the Lord', he instructed his readers, 'may in particulars of the last kind sometimes reveal himself to some by foretelling events before they come', *ibid.*, p. 404. History was thus invaluable as an aid with which to interpret and rationalise such prophetic signs when they occurred in scripture. On the author, see G. Christie, 'James Durham as Courtier and Preacher', *Records of the Scottish Church History Society*, 4 (1932), 66–80.
130. Spotswood, *History*, a5r. The scriptural origin of this prophetic view of history is clear, for Spotswood's next comment was that 'there is no new thing under the Sun; what hath been, or is, the same also shall be, *saith the Preacher*'. For an equivalent humanist use of this allusion to *Ecclesiastes*, I, 8, see Coluccio Salutati's expression, quoted in Skinner, *Foundations*, I, 110. Similarly, one can find an echo of this key discursive assumption in Patrick Abercromby during the early eighteenth century, when he revealingly knitted together the humanist and the scriptural sources of this principle: 'under the Sun there's nothing new, and the *Machiavelian* Maxim did ever hold, *Si vis fallere plebem, finge Deum*', ('If you wish to fool the people, invent a God'), *The Martial Atchievements of the Scots Nation*, 2 vols (Edinburgh, 1711–15), I, 329.
131. Symson, *Genealogical Account*, p. 25.
132. See M. C. Bell, *Calvin and Scottish Theology* (Edinburgh, 1985), p. 42. Knox's biblicism is also examined in G. D. Henderson, 'John Knox and the Bible', *Records of the Scottish Church History Society*, 9 (1947), 97–110.
133. Cromarty, *Historical Account*, p. 1.
134. See G. Christie, 'Scriptural Exposition in Scotland in the Seventeenth Century', *Records of the Scottish Church History Society*, 1 (1926), 97–111.
135. Knox, *Historie*, p. 3.
136. Dalrymple, *Collections*, p. LI.
137. Innes, *Civil and Ecclesiastical History*, p. 145.
138. Spotswood, *History*, A3r.
139. James Anderson, *An Historical Essay Shewing that the Crown and Kingdom of Scotland is Imperial and Independent* (Edinburgh, 1705), p. 171. This effort, intended principally as a counter-blast to English slanders, earned the author the official gratitude of the Scottish Parliament.
140. Cromarty, *Historical Account*, p. 125.
141. Duncan, *History*, A4r.
142. Ross, *History*, a1r.
143. Maule, *History*, p. vii.
144. See Craig, *Scottish Literature*, II, 187.

145. Maule, *History*, p. 2. Such a litany of history's diverse accolades imitated, though it did not precisely follow, Cicero's famous apostrophe in *De oratione*, II, ix, 36, which underlay the humanist vision of an educative and edificatory form of literature. For another citation, see Ross, *History*, a4v, and, from across the religious divide, the writings around 1635 of the Dumfriesshire presbyterian minister Gavin Young, *A Mappe of Mutationes, etc.* (St Andrews, University Library, MS D18.Y7C35), p. 2.

146. Spotswood, *History*, a5r. The emphasis upon experience was, of course, a humanist common-place, though in its association with the lessons of history in particular, experience acquired a subsidiary function as an occasional Protestant tool for dishing the preposterous claims of eternal Rome. The early sixteenth-century suggestion, therefore, that 'Thou mayest see by Experience,| The Pope's princely Preeminence', Sir David Lindsay, 'A Dialogue of the Miserable Estate of the World Between Experience and the Courtier', *Works* (Edinburgh, 1709), p. 111, may have appealed to a burgeoning awareness of the polemical power of historical experience which the subsequent triumph of Calvinism and humanism simply confirmed.

147. Boece, *Hystory*, fo. CCXLIX r(2).

148. *ibid.*, fo. CCXLIX r(1).

149. For the work done by French jurists like Bodin and Baudoin in bringing historical techniques to bear in the analysis and teaching of law, thus intensifying the European post-Renaissance revival of edificatory historical scholarship, see J. H. Franklin, *Jean Bodin and the Sixteenth-Century Revolution in the Methodology of Law and History* (Columbia, NY, 1963), esp. pp. 83–4. There was in particular, throughout Europe, the 'growing interest of educators in the technique of teaching history to students', a concern which was most seminally expressed by the Spanish Jesuit scholar Juan Luis Vives in his *De tradentis disciplinis* (1531).

150. Lithgow's characteristically stern view was that they were tearing 'the Life of Vertue in pieces with their spightfull tongues', *A True and Experimentall Discourse Upon the Beginning, Proceeding, and Victorious Event of this Last Siege of Breda* (London, 1637), p. 51.

151. David Hume of Godscroft, *The History of the Houses of Douglas and Angus* (Edinburgh, 1644), Preface. Indeed, Godscroft piously argued that an attack on history was an attack on 'all humane learning & knowledge, all Arts and Sciences, which are the blessings of God, and in which *Moses* and *Paul* were trained up, and well seen'.

152. Lesley, *History*, p. 5. Perhaps Lesley and Godscroft shared the realistic appraisal of Sir Richard Maitland of Lethington, Mary's skilful courtier, and presumably one only too familiar with the actual disasters which befell even the most learned of minds. He had observed how one of the Lords Seton, 'Nochtwithstanding that this Lord George wes ane weill letterit and ane nobill man, yit he was sumpairt gevin to voluptie and plesour, quhilk was the caus of his truble in his lyf tyme, quhairthrow he hurt his heritage', *The History of the House of Seytoun* (ed.), J. Fullarton (Glasgow, 1829), p. 36. Recognising that scholarship was not necessarily of moral benefit, Maitland concluded that 'I would exhort all nobill men to forbeir this vice for the mekle mischeif that followis thairon'.

153. Walter Scott, *A True Historie of Several Honourable Families of the Name of Scot*, 2 pts (Edinburgh, 1776), I, 4. Originally written in 1688, by a veteran of the Earl of Buccleuch's campaigns in Holland.

154. *ibid.*, II, R2r.

155. [William Dunlop?], *Genealogies of the Nobility of Scotland* (Edinburgh, University Library, MSS Dc.1.64).

156. William Drummond, *The History of Scotland* (London, 1655), p. 245. Genealogy in particular was a genre which could be presented as providing models for emulation by modern successors. William Gordon, for example, explaining his purpose in 1726, claimed that his work would 'in some Measure ... contribute to raise in them a generous Emulation of their illustrious Ancestors', *The History of the Ancient, Noble, and Illustrious Family of Gordon*, 2 vols (Edinburgh, 1726–7), I, vi.

157. Sir James Melville, *Memoires* (ed.), G. Scott, (London, 1683), a2v.

158. See R. J. Lyall, 'Politics and Poetry in Fifteenth and Sixteenth-Century Scotland', *Scottish Literary Journal*, 3 (1976), 5–29.

159. The reformers' chronic distrust of immoral counsellors and corrupt courtiers could only have intensified the desire of the committed historian to appropriate these crucial roles to himself. Knox, for example, had identified (through history) the dangers of godly princes corrupted

by unscrupulous advisers, 'moste ungodlye, conjured enemies to goddes true religion, and traitours to their princes', *A Faythfull Admonition* ([Zürich], 1554), C5v. Equally, the anonymous 1579 chronicler condemned the mythical Lugathus for 'resisting alltogidder to those that gaiff him counsell to wse the adwyse of his nobillity and wyise subiectis', *Chronicle*, p. 17. During the next century, moreover, others were to follow in this moral and intellectual critique of those unfit persons to whom the royal ear seemed perpetually bent. Thus we find James Melville recalling the reliance of James VI on 'Courtiers, and some of the Ministers who were more loose & worldly minded', *A Short Relation of the State of the Kirk of Scotland* ([Edinburgh], 1638), A2v-A3r.

160. James VI, *Basilikon Doron* (London, 1603),)(4v. Determinedly working within the metaphorical conceit at the heart of the genre, he advised his son to look to 'the historical partes' of the scriptures, 'for there shall ye see your selfe, as in a mirror, in the catalogue either of the good or the evill kings' *ibid.*, p. 9. For a similar remark linking Scottish historical discourse to this humanist genre, see Sir James Balfour's comment that 'as in a Mirrour, they may see the Vicissitude of Human Affairs ... ', quoted in Nicolson, *Scottish Historical Library*, p. 155.

161. James VI, *Basilikon Doron*, pp. 92–3. Despite his out-of-hand rejection of the 'infamous Libels' of Knox and Buchanan, it seems that James was as deeply enmeshed in Calvinist and humanist thought as his erstwhile teacher and adviser. Consider, for example, his concluding exhortation to his son, to note 'that God is the author of all vertue, having imprinted in mens mindes by the very light of nature, the love of all morall vertues; as was seene by the vertuous lives of the olde Romaines', *ibid.*, p. 101.

162. Buchanan, *History*, b1v.

163. At a practical level, it seems likely that Scottish authors of the seventeenth century could expect to be read by a surprisingly large, varied and discerning public: 'the typical clients of [the] Edinburgh book-dealers were ministers, writers, regents, merchants, gentry, and noblemen', J. Bevan, 'Seventeenth-Century Students and their Books', in G. Donaldson (ed.), *Four Centuries: Edinburgh University Life, 1583–1983* (Edinburgh, 1984), p. 17.

164. Robert Monro, *Monro His Expedition With the Worthy Scots Regiment e.t.c.* (London, 1637),)(2v. Perhaps even more extraordinary in one so involved in the violence and hatred which it has been assumed stifled Scottish literary and intellectual life in the seventeenth century, Monro went on to 'dare be bold to affirme, that reading and discourse doth as much or rather more, to the furtherance of a perfect Souldier, than a few yeares practice without reading', *ibid.*,)(4r. Nor was Monro alone, for in the same year his countryman William Lithgow produced the almost equally colourful *True and Experimentall Discourse*, retailing his experiences as a witness to the siege of Breda. Historical scholarship in early modern Scotland, as in other humanist cultures, was widely assumed to have an important bearing upon military knowledge and the various arts of war, an assumption whose most enduring product was perhaps Machiavelli's *Arte della guerra* (1520). Machiavelli was a favourite author of the Jacobean secretary William Fowler, who is the reputed author of an early example of this genre, a *History of the Warrs Between Sweden and Poland*, published in London in 1656. See Lawrence Charters, *Catalogues of Scotish Writers* (ed.), J. Maidment (Edinburgh, 1833), p. 87. I can find no copy with which to substantiate Charters' claim. For certain cases in Scotland, see, for example, a practical attempt to provide insight for the British officers then besieging Vauban's fortifications at Tournai, John Macgregory's *The Geography and History of Tournay* (Edinburgh, 1709). Also David Kennedy's *The Late History of Europe* (Edinburgh, 1698), the work of a discharged officer seeking to feed an expectant public eager for accounts of the Continental wars.

165. Boece's translator, for example, writing in the early sixteenth century, clearly considered history as being cognate with the *speculum principis* tradition, insisting that 'the tale of our progenitors' was something 'Quhair we may cleir, as in a mirrour, see,| The furious end somtymes of tyranie,| Somtymes the gloir of prudent governours,| Ilk state apprysit in thair facultie', John Bellenden, 'Vertue and Vyce', in R. and A. Foulis (eds), *Two Antient Scots Allegorical Poems* (Glasgow, 1750), p. 20.

166. John Napier, *A Plaine Discovery of the Whole Revelation of St John* (Edinburgh, 1593), A3r.

167. Mackenzie, *Lives and Characters*, I, A1r. More specifically, Mackenzie explained that 'The Moral and Intellectual Conduct of Men's Lives, is, in a great Part, Owing to the Observations which they make, either upon the Vertues or Failures of Others; and accordingly as they

Imitate them, so they prove either Vicious or Vertuous', *ibid.*, I, i. In expanding upon this view of the moral function of historical examples still widely prevalent in early eighteenth-century Scotland, Mackenzie borrowed John Dryden's notable exposition of the principle that 'the Examples of Virtue, are of more Vigour when they are thus Contracted into Individuals', *Plutarch's Lives*, 5 vols (London, 1688), I, 57–8.

168. Melville, *Memoires*, b1r.

169. *ibid.*, b3v.

170. The point has been well made that medieval scholars like Caxton and Higden in England also knew of the distinction between fact and fiction. But humanism was characterised by its preparedness to allow this distinction actively to govern the inclusion or exclusion of evidence, as Valla, Talbot, and Leland showed, and Scotsmen like Major and Buchanan gradually copied. See Levine, *Humanism and History*, pp. 29–32.

171. James Anderson, *Collections Relating to the History of Mary Queen of Scotland*, 3 vols (Edinburgh, 1727), I, iii.

172. Gilbert Burnet, *Reflections on Mr Varillas' History* (Amsterdam, 1686), p. 61.

173. Anderson, *Collections*, I, lv.

174. Scott, *History*, p. vii.

175. Godscroft, *History*, Preface.

176. Burnet, *Reflections*, p. 8.

177. Sir Robert Gordon, *A Genealogical History of the Earldom of Sutherland* (Edinburgh, 1813), p. 13.

178. *ibid.*, p. 22. A similar position was taken by a later author who in 1712 insisted on the citation of manuscripts and documents in history: she should 'acknowledge them her Parent, and the great Law by which she ought to act and be determined', Symson, *Genealogical Account*, Preface. Again, writing in 1720, Matthew Crawford crowed that his work would be 'collected from the best and most ancient Authors, original Manuscripts and Records, and will contain a great many valuable Papers never before published, *viz.* Bonds, Associations, Declarations, Protestations, Letters, Speeches, Treaties', an assiduous commitment to literary sources which would not disgrace the modern Eltonian empiricist. *Proposals*, p. 2.

179. Gordon, *Genealogical History*, p. xii.

180. Drummond, *History*, p. 245.

181. Abercromby, *Martial Atchievements*, I, 315.

182. Alexander Gordon, *The Lives of Pope Alexander VI and Caesar Borgia* (London, 1729), b1v. The author was the original of Sandy Gordon in Scott's *The Antiquary*, and compiler of the *Itinerarium Septentrionale* (1726), a classic survey of Roman remains in Scotland. Among the earliest Scottish proponents of the view that factual accuracy allowed the audience more acutely to judge the morality of historical actions seems to have been Maitland of Lethington in 1560. Clearly slightly embarrassed by his relation of medieval religiosity in an age which was increasingly indifferent or even hostile to such display, he protested that 'gif I had nocht writtin the saidis werkis, haldin godlie for the tyme, sum wald, or micht, have reprevit me for omitting and forgetting sic thingis; as the lyk and semlable ar writtin in uther histories ... ', *History*, p. 40. It was better, it seems, to include everything and leave the evaluation to the reader.

183. Patrick Gordon, *The Famous History of Robert the Bruce* (Edinburgh, 1718), p. xi. Originally published at Dort in 1615.

184. Lesley, *History*, p. 5.

185. Buchanan, *De Jure Regni*, p. 61.

186. Johnston, 'Historie', p. 369.

187. Peter Rae, *The History of the Late Rebellion Rais'd Against His Majesty King George, by the Friends of the Popish Pretender* (Dumfries, 1718), p. v.

188. Godscroft, *History*, Preface.

189. Patrick Abercromby, *The History of the Campagnes of 1548 and 1549* ([ ], 1707), p. iv. Apart from the preface, this work comprises a translation from the notable French work, Jean Beaugué's *L'Histoire de la guerre d'Écosse* (1556), but now using Scotland's military heritage as a Jacobite statement against the Union.

190. One important consequence of this conception of history as a moralistic medium was that the virtuous could be regarded as the peculiar subjects of historical narrative. Such a privilege could be presented as an additional incentive for virtuous conduct, as in the observation that

'your Lives will become Patterns, and your Sentences Laws to Posterity; who shall enquire into your actions, not only that they may admire, but (which is more) that they may imitate you in them,' Sir George Mackenzie of Rosehaugh, *Moral Gallantry* (London, 1669), A5v. But again, the humanist antecedents of Rosehaugh, among them Sir Richard Maitland, writing his MS history in 1560, recognised that scholarly recognition was itself a spur to an active virtue: 'it will give thame occasion', he claimed in relation to the descendants of illustrious ancestors, 'to exerce thame selfis in vertu and honour, sua it may be writtin of thame as of thair gude predecessouris; that thair fame and name may leif and lest lang and mony yeires efter thair bodie be deid', *History*, p. xi.

191. See G. Leff, *History and Social Theory* (London, 1969), p. 97.
192. Fletcher, *Discourse*, p. 7.
193. Burnet, *Memoires*, a1v.
194. Melville, *Memoires*, a2r.
195. Knox, *Historie*, *3r.
196. For example, another saw Knox as 'that blessed instrument', the clear implication being that 'the contrivance of Providence' was the crucial causal influence, Kirkton, *Secret History*, p. 7.
197. Godscroft, *History*, Preface. He had also written that 'In History also we may see men, and our selves in them, our vertues or vices ... ', *ibid.*, Preface.
198. Spotswood, *History*, p. 1.
199. Fleming, *Fulfilling of the Scripture*, p. 264.
200. Fleming, *Epistolary Discourse*, p. 168.
201. [ ], *A Short History of the Late Rebellion, And of the Conduct of Divine Providence* (Edinburgh, [1716]), A1r.
202. Burnet, *Reflections*, p. 9.
203. Abercromby, *Martial Atchievements*, I, b1v.
204. Monro, *Monro His Expedition*, II, 155.
205. Gordon, *Genealogical History*, p. 85. This is a Scots rendition of a similar comment found in the works of the distinguished humanist and historian, Giovanni Ferrerio. Not only does this illustrate in general terms the importance of mainstream humanist sources for the discussion of mutability in seventeenth-century Scotland, but it implies the continuing Scottish influence of an Italian scholar who had been a courtier of James V, the Cistercian Abbot of Kinloss, and the continuator of Boece's *Hystory*. See J. Durkan, 'Giovanni Ferrerio and Religious Humanism in Sixteenth-Century Scotland', *Studies in Church History*, 17 (1981), 181–94.
206. Abercromby, *Martial Atchievements*, I, 339.
207. Burnet, *Historie*, I, b1r.
208. Lesley, *History*, p. 4. The reference again is to *De oratione*, II, ix, 36.

CHAPTER TWO

The 'Honest Science'
Reconstructing Virtue in an Historical Audience

THE PURPOSE OF HISTORY, according to Robert Fleming in the *Epistolary Discourse* (1701), was to instruct. It existed in short, he considered, to ensure that 'we have the best examples that can be, to be imitated by us, and an account of the worst also, that we may avoid such pernicious courses'.[1] An eminently practical view, this was widely shared amongst the otherwise diffuse Scottish community engaged in writing history during the later sixteenth and seventeenth centuries. It in no way deflected scholars like Buchanan and Lesley from violent conflict with one another. Yet their faith in the value of history was voiced in a rhetoric of historical intention possessing both growing currency and persuasive force. This fact alone must surely encourage us to take a closer look at early modern historical discourse before judging it, with the weight of conventional wisdom, the fractured and partisan record of a hopelessly intolerant debate. The resources of Calvinist and humanist thought, it is clear, were now giving rise in Scotland to a greatly enlivened, and sometimes disconcertingly radical, conversation between the most bitter opponents. The evidence of this we have already seen in abundance. But the same influences were also permitting *a fortiori* the development of a characteristic rhetoric. This pointed history itself towards the apparently vital questions of leadership, virtue, and historical causality. Their rhetoric may offer an insight into the purposes sought by historical scholars in the sixteenth and seventeenth centuries. It marks out, too, the routes of inquiry which the modern scholar would need to follow in the attempt to understand what social and intellectual role history was actually playing in Scotland in that crucial formative period from the Reformation to the Enlightenment.

We will begin this chapter by exploring some of the consequences which followed from the widespread belief among Scotland's scholars that history operated as a moralistic and edificatory medium. We shall look in particular at the implications of the view that the historian's function was analogous to those of the humanist orator and the Calvinist preacher. This entailed in the first instance a particularly important place in Scottish historical thought for the Ciceronian notion of *eloquentia*. But it also confronted the early modern historian with the difficult further obstacle of identifying an appropriate audience for his moralistic utterances. Scotland at this time was an unstable country, one which seemed to lack both a resident monarch and a reliable aristocracy. This unfortunate circumstance meant that the scholars' moralistic aims could only be achieved in Scotland by a momentous development in their conceptualisation of virtue. Leading historians, it seems, now tried increasingly to exhort their audience to the performance of moral responsibilities which themselves served to confer social legitimacy; in short, they sought to reconstruct Scotland's leadership in a more acceptable image. Humanist notions of public spirit were to be especially useful for this purpose. A Calvinist emphasis both upon self-control and personal piety was also invoked very widely for the same reasons. The harmonious fusion of republican and spiritual discourse thereby accomplished, however, was to be most remarkable in its implications for the future. The virtues of rational learning and wisdom were being apostrophised by means of arguments drawn from both traditions. These, it seems, sometimes came close even to elevating scholars themselves to the legitimate leadership of Scottish society. The possible significance of this in a country which in the eighteenth century would accord considerable status to its historians, scientists, and philosophers, is something about which we will necessarily have a great deal to say at a later stage. Yet the simultaneous evolution of Calvinist and humanist discourse, I shall argue, posed the most perplexing problems for Scottish historians, especially as the seventeenth century progressed. They had always needed to offer an account of causality which would underscore their dynamic social theory. The humanist vision, personified as capricious Fortune, as a result long predominated in Scotland. But the more rigid Calvinist and Stoic alternatives, often dismissive of human intentions and usually reliant upon God's eternal Providence, were ultimately to acquire the upper hand. This situation was to create increasing difficulties for the plausible assertion of a social theory of leadership in Scotland for which an active and effective virtue still seemed axiomatic – problems to which the eighteenth-century literati were of course the immediate heirs. Our historians' rhetoric consequently turns out to have set them a formidably awkward task in the performance of their scholarly responsibilities. In seeing how they coped with these very special obligations, we must begin with their treatment of oratory.

I: Oratory and the Virtuous Audience

In recognising their instructive and educational function, the historical authors of early modern Scotland were led to an obvious but deeply portentous conclusion by their Calvinist and humanist inspiration. The historian was to be the fount of advice and a credible instructor of his audience. So he would have to adopt the persona of the orator and preacher, a role which recent scholarship only confirms had familiar and highly sympathetic resonances both within humanist social thought and in the Calvinist vision of the moral community.[2] History itself, on the understanding of Renaissance scholars like Lorenzo Valla, was now conceived in Scotland as a medium ideally suited both for the training of rhetoricians and as the source of material for their subsequent oratory.[3] This crucial self-perception among the historians is signified for us by fleeting but suggestive references to their own technical rhetorical responsibilities. They frequently alluded to the rhetorical devices, to the significance of verbal mastery and the power of the spoken word, in ways which emphasise the extent to which they now understood history as being, first and foremost, a form of oratory. But we will also see that a second and much deeper insight into the living concept of an oratorical history is to be gained from appreciation of another feature of their work. This is their heavy emphasis upon actual examples of influential and inspirational oratory in the historical past. A sense of their own oratorical function conjured up in the Scottish historians' minds a morbid fascination with the use and abuse of that vital position by previous practitioners, as well as a concern for the techniques and stances which it was presumed to require. By looking at these characteristics of their scholarship it will be possible for us to see the adoption by Scotland's historians of a role thrust upon them by the urgent promptings of both Ciceronian and Calvinist discourse.

In the first instance the occasional remarks of Scottish authors suggest their growing awareness, like that of their English and Italian contemporaries, of the technical requirements of oratory, considered both as a conveyor of historical knowledge and as a medium reliant upon rhetorical skills.[4] Alexander Ross, for example, managed this despite what we have seen to be a considerable penchant for gloom and despondency. Ross had little doubt that the *History of the World* (1652) would be of especial value among 'Orators' and 'School-Masters'.[5] He seems in other words to have entertained the pleasing thought that his own endeavours would provide ideal historical subject-matter both for future rhetoricians and their instructors. That the Scottish historian might perceive his own function as oratorical was also somewhat ambivalently shown by that self-conscious Jacobite Patrick Abercromby in his *Martial Atchievements* (1711–15). Abercromby nodded at the perceived convention that an 'uncommon Genius ... . a discerning Judgement ... a refin'd Taste ... Purity of Language', were the skills required by 'History and Biography'.[6] Blushing with an ingenuous shame never uncommon among Scottish scholars, Abercromby, however, advised his own audience that they ought not to 'expect from me those modish Turns of Phrase, nor that exact Propriety of Words' properly associated with the art of history.[7] Some, though, did feel better equipped to live up to the expectation of rhetorical technique and of high literary style which clearly went along with their oratorical function: theatrical self-assurance was here again the characteristically immoderate Scottish alternative to chronic insecurity. Indeed, as John Leyden, the nineteenth-century editor of *The Complaynt of Scotland* correctly observed, it was usual for assertive Scottish authors at this time to affect 'a wider sphere of reputation, than their vernacular tongues afforded them a prospect of attaining'.[8] Hume of Godscroft, for example, writing in the 1620s, showed a deep sense of the special obligation to write history with both 'vertue and grace'.[9] Eschewing any attempt 'to speak English', he avoided 'the imputation of affectation', and employed instead the native Scots in his work. This Godscroft did precisely for the reason that he held it to be more eloquent than the English – which he acidically claimed was 'but a Dialect of our own, and that (perhaps) more corrupt'.[10] Nor was Godscroft alone in his brash assertion of Scottish eloquence. James Anderson was another of that breed of early modern authors who sought to redeem the sullied reputation of previous Scottish historians. He also chose to portray the style and elegance of earlier Scottish writing as a particular matter for celebration. The anonymous account of bishop Lesley's diplomatic missions for Queen Mary possessed, he claimed, a 'Language' which was 'better than what we find in the Writings of most Englishmen at that Time'.[11] For scholars like his contemporary Patrick Boyle, meanwhile, pre-eminently well-versed in Cicero but equally steeped in the classical historical texts of Herodotus, Thucydides and Xenophon, the desire to speak 'elegantly' was likewise an insatiable one.[12] A conceited allusion to the Scottish possession of *eloquentia*, conventionally associated by the Erasmian humanist with the orator and preacher, could therefore exalt both the historian and his nation. In spite of the gross communicative shortcomings of the Scots language, the confident remarks of Hume and Anderson actually cohere with the diffidence of Patrick Abercromby. They indicate that the Scottish author, after the mid-sixteenth century, was coming with increasing assurance to regard himself as the functional equivalent of that prolific Renaissance ideal.

There is more substantive evidence, however, of the assumption by Scottish historians of the orator's laurel. This is provided by their clear predilection for the elevation of the orator in the historical past. A colourful but neglected example of this can be found in Patrick Gordon's *Famous History of Robert the Bruce* (1615). This was ostensibly a poetical account of that central episode in the traditionary cycle, the fourteenth-century wars with England. But a careful reading reveals much more of interest. Gordon actually opens his verse with the highly rhetorical announcement that 'Of Martial Deeds, of dreadful Wars I sing',[13] a painfully self-conscious allusion to the *Aeneid* which itself suggests that Gordon saw himself as adopting the guise of the classical oral historian. The verse then develops into an expansive humanist commentary on the struggle between implacable Fortune and heroic Virtue. Above this conflict rise the pre-eminent characters of the Earl of Douglas and Robert the Bruce. Both, it turns out, are equipped with the oratorical capacities which implicitly identify the greatest historical figures. It is the Earl of Douglas who initially represents the continuity of Scotland's vital line of patriotic and influential public orators. He has returned from France where portentously, and not unlike the sixteenth-century historians Boece and Major, 'he both Arts and Eloquence obtains'.[14] He is skilled in the art of persuasion and imbued with the worldly learning which on the Scottish reading of Cicero this entailed. He therefore readily becomes the eloquent instructor and inspiration of the diffident and rather uncertain Bruce.[15] The future king hovers inactively on the fringe of events, lamenting his fortune as 'that luckless BRUCE whose hapless Name| Thou does so much exalt and magnify'.[16] But Douglas communes with the airy spirit of Scotland's glorious historical past, the ghost of King Fergus. Through his intimate relationship with history, Douglas, mindful of the prophetic element we have already seen within Scottish historical thought, employs his persuasive eloquence to instruct the Bruce to follow his revealed destiny: 'Where *Fergus* Ghost directs', he counsels, 'there must you go'.[17]

Subsequently the national fortunes are reinvigorated by Douglas's eloquent counsel and by the Bruce's belated leadership. Gordon's verse can certainly be considered for this reason as an elaboration of the dynamic virtues possessed by the Scottish patriot and orator. Yet, when the English forces are finally defeated, a further episode develops to underscore the earlier lesson that eloquence is of crucial importance. In the wake of his victory the Bruce falls ill. The Scottish armies simultaneously begin to melt away, re-awakening fears of an English counter-attack. It is at this moment that the Bruce recovers his strength and, more importantly, his speech. In a manner not dissimilar to Florentine humanists like Bruni and Guicciardini, who had employed the fictitious oration to embellish the character of their favoured subject, Gordon gives the king a rich and emotive peroration with which to bolster his faltering support. Leaving little room for the reader's misinterpretation, Gordon makes it quite clear that it is the Bruce's eloquent exhortations to patriotic duty and his incantation of historic victories which have been decisive: we are to note that 'his Speech doth all appease'.[18] By this means, Gordon's historical narrative managed to elevate Douglas and the Bruce into something approaching classic humanist exemplars. But it also strove to convey, more specifically, the importance of the oratorical function in rendering historical material of inspirational service to the national community. Like 'Demosthenes and Cicero', therefore, Scottish men of letters were implored by Gordon's enthusiastic successors like Robert Hepburn to 'turn their Eloquence ... to the Service and Advantage of their Country'.[19]

An equivalent concern for the proper use of Scottish eloquence is naturally to be found in the very *fons et origo* of modern Scottish historical writing, George Buchanan's *History of Scotland* (1582). Buchanan's own works were, of course, suitably couched in elegant and much-lauded Latin prose. But he also sought to extol the classical eloquence of the ancient orators, and to propagate a more recognisably humanist historical literature in Scotland. As a result he resorted to a blistering attack on an ethnic vernacular which he deemed especially inappropriate for the weighty purposes of an oratorical and edificatory national history. Accepting, as Hume of Godscroft was to do, that history required eloquence, he arrived, however, at a strikingly contrary assessment of the vernacular. The Gaelic language, in his view, came from men who were simply 'rude and impolite'.[20] It 'came forth harsh, rugged, and uncouth', a grave fault which Buchanan considered could be only slowly and imperfectly corrected. Because Gaelic remained inadequate in its 'natural Horror and Unpleasantness', the nation should replace it. This was a prospect which Buchanan welcomed. He thought that it would allow him to 'joyfully perceive those barbarous Sounds, by little and little, to vanish away', as Scottish letters as a whole passed 'from Rusticity and Barbarism, to Culture and Humanity'.[21] In short, Buchanan seems to have believed that the adoption of Greek and Latin would allow all scholars in Scotland to emulate ancient eloquence, and facilitate the production of an implicitly oratorical form of history. Here was a humanist urge for a reformed national language and literature, for a Renaissance in which history would of course play a central part. It necessitated a destructive critique of the crude and unrefined vernaculars still spoken by many of Buchanan's country-men. These languages, as we have seen Abercromby later bemoaning, were damnable most especially because they were thought to have hamstrung the Scottish scholar's aspirations to present to the rest of the civilised world a credible oratorical image.

We thus have a variety of arguments, all of which acted as reiterations of the instructive and edificatory power of an eloquent history. There is also to be weighed the accompanying insinuation that an elegant and persuasive literary style itself implied the classical and humanist credentials of the author. Together these facts suggest that early modern Scottish scholars had indeed acquired a profoundly Ciceronian sense of the importance of oratory and of their own particular need to aspire to it. This was a sense which studies of Italian preaching at this time in any case suggest was broadly characteristic of other post-Renaissance cultures.[22] From a slightly different angle, though to much the same purpose, it is possible to find a diversity of Scottish authors after the mid-sixteenth century imputing eloquence, and the associated humanist arts of wise counsel, to the most admirable historical figures. Those skills came to be considered in Scotland as the mark of the truly influential and prudent man. As early as 1565 in the work of Robert Lindsay, we find this treatment being given to Bishop Kennedy of St Andrews, a conventional exemplar of medieval Scottish learning. Kennedy was held up as a man able 'to give any wise Counsel, or any Answer, when the Time occurred'.[23] Thus he was seen by an early Protestant as a man who – perhaps like Lindsay himself – combined the skills and the moral responsibilities of humanist oratory. In the early eighteenth century, moreover, and in recognisably the same vein, Robert Wodrow's ecclesiastical history likewise still sought out notables such as Bishop Leighton. These were Scotsmen who seemed 'of an excellent utterance, and of a grave and abstracted conversation',[24] Calvinist ministerial qualities again worthy of particular comment to the aspiring historical orator. On the other hand Alexander Petrie writing at the Restoration regarded the sad fact that 'only Monks were noted to have some eloquence' as sufficient evidence of the moral degeneracy of the Popish ages.[25] For George Crawford, author of the flattering *Peerage of Scotland* (1716), meanwhile, it was obvious that a man like Lord Belhaven, who had 'made several learned and elaborate speeches' against the Act of Union, would be one whose actions 'Posterity will celebrate' as a 'Patriot of his Country'.[26] There was thus a general emphasis upon the role of eloquent, stylish, and prudent speech in the great moments of history. And in the light of the historians' underlying ambitions for recognition of their own *eloquentia*, this must only reinforce our suspicion, further augmented by the recent conclusions of David Reid, that key purposes behind the texts were their authors' attempts to present themselves as Ciceronian orators.[27] Even such grandiose claims as those of Napier in 1593 to mimic 'the whole Prophets of al ages'[28] might not have been without their oratorical pretensions, given the persuasive oral force normally associated with those Old Testament leaders. I shall later argue that this self-appointment by the author to the rank of national orator was to have deeply significant consequences in Scottish scholarship. It gave rise to a social theory of leadership which depended crucially upon a Calvinist and humanist remodelling of the concept of virtue itself. At this stage, however, let us simply pause to examine the way in which this assumption took Scotland's scholars along tracks once trod in their *Philippics* by Demosthenes and Cicero themselves. It led them in particular towards a heightened awareness of the salient problem of audience as it confronted early modern Scottish society.[29]

Many Scottish historians were able to think that they were themselves amongst the orators of the nation. They saw themselves performing the vital duties of eloquent and moralistic oratory developed by the humanist counsellor and subsequently elaborated by the Calvinist preacher. Yet there was somewhat less clarity in Scotland, as arguably there had been since the days of William Dunbar, when it came to the identity of those who might constitute their attentive audience.[30] Most post-Renaissance European scholars, like their classical models, predicated their work upon the existence of a natural and undisputed leadership in society. This may equally have been vested in an absolute prince, in a republican political class or in a Calvinist ephorate. But early modern Scotland, to some extent unlike other Calvinist societies in the same period, never in fact presented its historians with a clear-cut, reliable audience for their earnest directions and exhortations.[31] Both Calvinism and humanism, on the whole, assumed that a community would possess a clearly defined group of social leaders. These were the class of people from whom a political government would be drawn. Perhaps even more importantly, they were the elements upon which the moral health and direction of the community would depend. For Erasmus, in the *Institutio Principis Christiani* (1516), they were the Christian princes; in the *Convivium Religiosum* they were more broadly the educated and broad-minded lay professionals of northern Europe.[32] To John Calvin in search of a similar character in the *Institutionis Christianae Religionis* (1536), they were the pious city fathers of the Genevan republic. These were the magistrates engaged in 'a lawful calling approved by God', entirely prepared to support the output of the preachers and to propagate moral reformation in the community at large.[33] Active and exemplary groups of this kind, then, were the natural audience for the oratory of an intensely edificatory medium. They were the group through whom the humanist author or Calvinist preacher, like the anonymous scholar responsible for the *Scotch Presbyterian Eloquence* (1692), might best hope to influence the moral condition of Scottish society.[34] Yet as some of its cynical historians also openly lamented, this was far from being the case in Scotland. Here was in fact a society which, to judge from the wailings of a plethora of budding Scottish men of letters starved of patronage and recognition, was singularly ill-equipped to receive or comprehend lessons offered in this oratorical form. Scotland required, but lacked, its Maecenas.[35]

The Scottish monarchy, which during the later sixteenth century was a bone of considerable contention, in the seventeenth removed from Scotland altogether. This was an unprecedented constitutional development which the disoriented historians understandably viewed with consternation. William Drummond, for example, the greatest Scottish poet of the seventeenth century, gave elegiac voice to the instincts of many. Obviously troubled by the absence of the king, when James VI paid a brief visit to Edinburgh in 1617 Drummond wrote:

'Ah why should *Isis* only see thee shine?
Is not thy FORTH, as well as *Isis*, Thine?'[36]

James Crauford, moreover, author of *The History of the House of Este* (1681), later argued that the lack of a court in Scotland had had the most profound detrimental effects upon scholarship. It had led to Scottish men of learning 'having no more the great incitements, which a Court residing among us would afford'.[37] Clearly perturbed by the fact that a nominal monarchy had no ready focus for the instructive urges of its historical orators, Crauford was scarcely able to contain himself in a fulsome description of the virtuous learning sustained in his capital city by the very presence of Alphonsus, Duke of Este. Scholarship was encouraged there, Crauford claimed, for 'the whole City resembled a great University ... the very Monasteries and Nunneries turned Seminaries of Virtue'.[38] To William Lithgow, meanwhile, writing in 1637, it seemed disturbing indeed that '*Scotland* now a dayes hath no Historian, bravest Wits turne dull, Poets sing dumbe, Pen-men grow deafe, and best spirits slumber' – and all because 'there [was] no *Maecenas*'.[39] Likewise in the mind of Patrick Abercromby the lack of a Scottish court seemed inimical to the practice of true scholarship. Undoubtedly feeling vulnerable as a vernacular writer, he considered that with a Scottish monarch reinstalled in Edinburgh 'Scoticisms would become Fashionable'.[40] Robert Burton's celebrated observation that 'poets, rhetoricians, historians, philosophers, mathematicians, sophisters, etc.' were 'like grasshoppers, sing they must in summer, and pine in winter, for there is no preferment for them', thus seems to have been particularly apt as an evocation of early modern Scotland – the world of Boece, Major and Buchanan, each cited on numerous occasions throughout the *Anatomy of Melancholy*.[41] Evidently, the presence of a monarch in particular was thought to guarantee the cultural integrity and acknowledged eloquence of the Scottish literary community, not least by providing native historical scholarship with patronage and a sense of local oratorical direction. As a regretful Sir James Melville noted in his unashamedly pragmatic *Memoires* in the early seventeenth century, history had in any case amply demonstrated that Scotland had always been an unpropitious breeding-ground for reliable and estimable princes. It had, he observed, clearly had 'but few Wise, Vertuous, and Potent kings'.[42] Moreover, as an eighteenth-century editor also observed, Scotland had rarely in the last two centuries possessed a court which could justifiably inspire the virtuous man of letters. Even during the days when a monarch had actually been present in Edinburgh it had behoved responsible scholars like 'Sir David Lindsay, albeit a Courteour, and exercised about Matters of Estate ... to Enveigh most sharply, both against the Enormities of the Court, and the great Corruption of the Clergy'.[43] Scotland's court all too often had become a sink of immorality and viciousness. Despite some notable exceptions, including the singular George Buchanan, the bulk of its historians could not generally expect to seek out or to edify a responsive king. The mirror for princes in post-Reformation Scotland increasingly sought to capture the more agreeable reflections of others.

Nor were the Scottish aristocracy any closer to resembling the ideally receptive and cultivated focus for the oratory of Calvinist and humanist scholarship. They had been concerned to undermine the Crown, the nation and each other, in the headlong pursuit of dynastic advantage and political influence; or at least this was the decidedly unwholesome (if not entirely truthful) picture of its aristocracy which Scotland's scholars chose to paint.[44] Sir James Balfour, the Stuart antiquarian, poet and Lord Lyon, observed as much in his long-unpublished *Annales*. The Scottish nobility, he suggested, had often been men 'quoho studied warre more then peace, and ther aven particular, befor the publick good'.[45] Robert Johnston too noted how 'displaying the banner of publique good' they had striven only 'to advance their owne honour and potency'.[46] Certainly, as we saw in the previous chapter, many historians still expressed their gratitude to those aristocrats who were both their patrons and inspiration. Men like Hume of Godscroft and Scott of Satchells were obliged to address obsequious dedications to Scottish nobles, if only because the recipient had commissioned the work, or else his protection and material support were necessary for the vulnerable scholar in an age of political conflict and religious controversy. But the aggregate picture of Scotland's hereditary leadership offered by scornful historians increasingly attached to the moral values of Calvinism and humanism was in fact far from complimentary. As David Moysie, a burgess of Jacobean Edinburgh, observed in attempting to flatter the king with sharing the natural concerns of his more reflective subjects, James VI had noted the truculence of the nobility and had 'wished for nothing more than a perfect union and reconcilement among them in their hearts'.[47] Other Scotsmen, including Robert Rollock, Alexander Hume and Sir Richard Maitland, inveighed from the pulpit and with the pen against the lawlessness and ceaseless feuding which still often characterised early modern aristocratic life: with 'astonishing confidence in the Word of God', Keith Brown portrays to us men like these who issued 'fundamental challenges' made 'in a public manner about the very basis of a feuding society'.[48] For many historians the feuding and ambitious nobility, no less than the distinctly dubious Scottish monarchy, were simply beyond redemption. They had mimicked Cesare Borgia rather than Cato and the corrupt Alexander VI rather than the virtuous Calvinist fathers of Geneva. Consequently the Scottish aristocracy had rendered themselves unsuitable as a class for their once automatic role as social leaders.

This conclusion meant that steadily from the later sixteenth century onwards, and even more strongly and widely during the early seventeenth, Scottish historians disengaged themselves from the medieval model predicated upon the dominance and reliability of a hereditary social leadership. This was a model to which they could no longer, as proponents of a Calvinist and humanist scholarship, offer their unqualified intellectual assent. Like Robert Burton in England in the 1620s, Scotsmen looked around them at the 'vile buffoons, ignoramuses, wandering in the twilight of learning, ghosts of clergymen, itinerant quacks, dolts, clods, asses, mere cattle' who held positions of influence and eminence, and professed to understand with the melancholy Student of Christ Church why 'the Muses are in mourning'.[49] To a disenchantment with an absent and frequently controversial monarchy we have seen was coupled a deepening sense that the moral calibre of the Scottish nobility left much to be desired. The received assumptions were therefore ripe for replacement by a new social theory of leadership which would only further hasten the rejection of the old. In this situation, the searching and constructive turn of mind characteristic of the Scottish historians led them increasingly to focus their attention upon the possibility of cultivating in Scotland what scholars like William Gordon in the early eighteenth century were still choosing to call the truly 'great man'.[50] He would not be identified straightforwardly by his splendid royal titles or by the fortunate accident of his birth. He would be distinguished or would stand or fall instead according to the strictly ethical criteria of Calvinism and humanism. History itself would become the means to defining and identifying the characteristics of the model social leader.

Alexander Ross, for example, provides a preface to his *History* which is most illuminating in this respect. Its insight into the deficiencies of an orthodox model of social hierarchy which had been based on the rash belief that noble or royal birth necessarily implied good leadership was probably typical of the historians' approach as it had matured by the middle of the seventeenth century. 'In Histories', Ross warned, 'great Men will find what uncertainty and vanity there is in outward splendour'.[51] Here already Ross was limbering up for a direct challenge to the notion that the finery and elegance associated with nobility necessarily indicated any moral superiority on the part of their possessors. The implication was that the opposite was all too often the case. How much this simply reflected the disenchantment of a defeated episcopalian, bitterly contemplating the contrast between erstwhile courtly gaity and more recent humiliating royalist incompetence and duplicity, is open to question. But, in developing this sentiment further, Ross showed a great debt to the humanist analysis of social leadership. He displayed also an addiction to the Calvinist disdain for worldly confidence, a disdain consistent with the scornful reproaches of many other early modern authors in Scotland. He alleged that history would teach 'what it is that makes true and genuine Nobility, and discriminates it from that which is suppositious and adulterate'.[52] In other words Ross expected scholarship to identify a true qualification for social eminence, a qualification which would replace the tired and inadequate definition inherited from a less enlightened and less perceptive medieval past. Finally Ross concluded with a provocative indication of his line of thinking. History, he argued, should ensure that 'they are incited to vertuous actions', a frank suggestion that moral activity rather than inherited rank was the criterion for the leadership who would form his own preferred audience.[53] This perception was again deeply rooted both in humanist and Calvinist presuppositions stressing the absolute imperative of an active virtue. It applied particularly to those who were to lead and inspire others. It was also a conviction about 'activity' which was to inform generations of humanist historians from John Bellenden to Robert Freebairn as they sought to construct in Scotland a more suitable audience for their oratory.[54]

The notion thus emerged in Scotland, and spread with startling rapidity after the sixteenth century, of a history focused on a new audience of active 'great men', a circle of disciples and attentive listeners now apparently unconstrained by the strict traditional requirements of high birth and aristocratic demeanour. As a guiding principle of authorship this was clearly to motivate a considerable number of Scottish scholars in the early modern period. Some, as we will shortly see, reconstructed virtue in such a manner as to hint that a particular kind of person, most obviously the Scottish clergymen, already possessed many of the qualities upon which such greatness depended. Clearly in a predominantly Calvinist community the ministers of the Kirk would inevitably be prime candidates for the leadership of society. But Alexander Monro's well-turned argument in 1692 that history served less specifically 'to preserve the memory of the *greatest* men, the *greatest* Conquests, or the most remarkable Actions', was perhaps more typical.[55] This is the case both in its insinuation that action rather than title was the crucial mark of the 'great man' and in its stubborn refusal to identify by means of history any single contemporary group to whom the historian envisaged the leadership definitively falling. Sir James Melville, too, suggested a recognisably post-Renaissance but usefully unspecific conception of greatness, with his exhortation to the young James VI to cultivate only 'Great and Active Men'.[56] But there also emerge even more striking and provocative elaborations of Ross's position, indicative in some cases of the wide currency of this humanist analysis of leadership in the Scottish historical community. One such was offered by Robert Fleming, the presbyterian polemicist. It was clear from scriptural history, Fleming argued, that God had enshrined '*Priority* of *Virtue* and *Worth*, instead of *Priority* of *Birth*, at the Bottom of all Government'. This was itself 'the Essential Property of a true Governour'.[57] As Ross had implied, worth and greatness were in Fleming's view to be founded on virtue rather than heredity, to be identified by moral conduct rather than by inherited status. This was a method for reckoning a man's standing which in Fleming's eyes had been ordained by God and which was of particular importance in the evaluation of a specifically political leadership. Fleming's use of the familiar humanist critique of government, however, carried with it serious implications for the broader issue of Scotland's social leadership: the virtuosity necessary for political legitimacy was merely a special and radical case of what was equally necessary in a social leadership. Following on from these humanist claims therefore came an almost instinctive attachment among historians to Juvenal's timeless Stoic maxim that virtue was the sole and single qualification for true nobility in society.[58] As 'late' as 1728, indeed, Robert Freebairn, Lindsay's editor, still felt it appropriate to preface his work with the bold assertion, '*virtus est sola & unica Nobilitas*'.[59] In similar high-flown style, Walter Scott, author of the *True History* (1688), tried to impress this lesson upon his audience. Scott alluded to classical antiquity in order to illustrate that it was through virtue alone that a truly honourable character could be acquired. In Rome, he related,

'Two stately temples there erected was,

Where none might into honour's temple come,

But first through vertue's temple they must pass.'[60]

The moral character of hereditary nobility had been so demonstrably undermined by the Scottish experience that a new picture of social leadership simply had to be developed by sixteenth- and seventeenth-century authors. This made it even more necessary for scholars like Walter Scott to argue that in the exercise of any public office 'men by vertue must true honour win'.[61]

Alexander Ross was of course equipped to be a perceptive critic of aristocratic misconduct. His classical training and encyclopaedic knowledge made him the natural enemy of all that was most parochial and mean-minded in the Scotland of his day. But he was also very well aware, as a royalist and episcopalian, of the dangers inherent in the humanist approach to the important question of social leadership. In *The Marrow of Historie* (1650), some time before putting together his more destructive comments on aristocratic deportment, we can find strong signs of Ross's essential ambivalence. On the one hand, Ross expressed a view of nobility which was strikingly reliant upon the possession of virtue. 'Hee is truly and intirely Noble', he insisted, 'who maketh a singular profession of publick Virtue'.[62] According to this formulation, clearly again a development of Juvenal's dictum, it was by committed and public-spirited leadership alone that virtue was proven and nobility thus identified. It was, in short, by 'serving his Prince and Countrie', Ross argued, that a man attained to virtue, and hence to acceptance as a truly legitimate leader.[63] Yet, on the other hand, Ross was not prepared, surely because of his own deeply conservative commitments, to turn this undoubted disillusionment with the mildewed Scottish nobility into a full-blown rejection of hereditary social or political right. Instead,, he advised that there was more involved than simply demonstrating one's 'publick Virtue'. The truly noble man should also be 'descended of Parents and Ancestors that have don the like'.[64] In short, Ross came close to suggesting the heritability of precisely those Calvinist and humanist virtues which were only proven in the final analysis by the most militant personal activity. In a similar fashion, moreover, Sir Robert Gordon's *Genealogical History* recorded the virtuous deeds and activities of his own 'worthie ancestors'.[65] This Aberdonian was no more willing than Ross to imperil the social standing of the Earls of Sutherland by too brash an assertion of the humanist case. Instead the crafty Gordon offered to his readers the men who 'for many ages have ben eminent among the nobilite of this kingdom' as examples for future generations.[66] They were men, said Gordon, 'whose vertues and heroicall actions, I wish you may surpasse, or at least equalize'.[67] Gordon seems to have regarded his own noble ancestors in the same ambivalent way as Ross did those of his royalist colleagues. Genuinely noble forebears were the men who had successfully legitimated their inheritance by virtuous actions. High social status could be retained in subsequent generations by others who were prepared to make the same active moral commitments. This was of course a devious and clearly very risky argument. But it allowed historians like Ross and Gordon to cohere with a Calvinist and humanist account of leadership without having to risk undermining the established social standing of valuable patrons and favourite feudal dynasties.

Such a hedged conclusion, it would also be true to say, was favoured even by some of their less provocative presbyterian contemporaries, led perhaps by the professor of philosophy and mathematics at Glasgow, George Sinclair, a notorious Calvinist demonologist who nevertheless saw the Earls of Winton properly 'imitating their Noble Ancestors' as 'notable examples of Love and Piety towards their Soveraigne'.[68] David Hume of Godscroft, by no means the most uncontroversial student of the existing order, was another. Godscroft was certainly prepared to claim with Juvenal, and perhaps more significantly with John Major, that history was the tool by which 'honour is kindled, and so of vertue, which onely brings true honour with it'.[69] But in an extended encomium on the illustrious Douglases, Godscroft was forced to compromise in broadly the same manner as Alexander Ross. The laudable actions of the family were recounted at such flattering length that they served effectively to underpin their implicit claim to perpetual nobility. Yet a rather stronger insistence on the sole position of virtue as the definition of honour, and so of legitimate social standing, was still on occasion to emerge in Scottish historical writing for at least the next century. Even the conservative Mackenzie of Rosehaugh, for example, seems to have agreed with the Stoical instructions of Seneca and Juvenal. These were literally to be heeded by modern men for 'nothing but virtue', the sage lawyer repeated, 'deserves the name of Nobility'.[70] Passing through such different minds as those of Walter Scott and Robert Fleming, this remarkable assertion – necessarily hedged by radicals yet also stridently proclaimed by the conservative – was continually delivered to the audience of this Calvinist and humanist historical tradition. It even emerged once more on the eve of the Enlightenment in the unusual context of an *Account of the Royal Family* (1739), the work of the Jacobite minister at Blair Atholl, Duncan Stewart. This

impeccably conservative minister nevertheless opened his discussion with the
Roman satirist's now-familiar assurance. 'It is only Virtue, or a clear
Conscience', Stewart claimed, 'that makes any Man Noble, for that derives
even from Heaven itself'.[71] Quite clearly, Scotland's historians could show due
deference to the traditional status of particular dynasties and monarchs. But
equally they advocated ceaselessly in Scotland after the sixteenth century the
Stoic argument that an active and humanist virtue alone should be recognised
as the true mark of the legitimate social leader.

   The great majority of historians were characterised, as we have seen, by a
Calvinist and humanist emphasis upon a virtuous social leadership. This in
crucial respects was to remain central to the complex historical discourse of early
modern Scotland. But it also points us for the moment towards a number of
further questions which must surely be addressed in the search for a firmer grasp
of what post-Reformation Scottish scholars actually understood themselves to
be asking for when telling their audience to practise 'virtue'. Virtue clearly had
become the unimpeachable mark of the legitimate Scottish leader. And the
precise nature of this quality was a matter of the utmost concern to scholars
charged with identifying those Scotsmen who could assume the vital role of
social leadership. One line of inquiry is obviously open. It certainly seems that
the classical and humanist roots of their historical analysis might have led
historians to advocate a practice of virtue which was resoundingly public in
character. What we will now see of the prospering of this humanist strain of
moral thought in Calvinist Scotland gives the lie to the old historiographical
myth, increasingly under threat from scholars like Arthur Williamson, that
Knox and his presbyterian colleagues had propagated an individualistic spiritual
morality which was straightforwardly inimical to the pursuit of the classical
public virtues.[72] Nevertheless, we will then move on to another tack. This will
be to see that there did indeed develop alongside this classical republican theme
a recognisably theological formulation of virtue. Here we will find that much of
the supposed tension between private and public virtue derives from the
inappropriate heuristics of modern scholarship rather than from problematical
contradictions present within early modern minds. The elevation both of the
individual spirit and of the public 'commonweal' we shall see was effected with
little intellectual discomfort. Indeed, because of the sheer dominance of
Calvinism and humanism in Scotland there was to emerge a formidable
confluence of civic and spiritual ethics which allowed historians persistently to
locate learning itself among the most esteemed virtues. To a limited extent this
elevation of rational virtue, I shall argue, even promised to confer social and
moral legitimacy upon Scotland's scholars themselves – though as a possibility
this was still beset with immense practical and theoretical problems. The latent
potential within their highly-complex thought, therefore, can be approached at
this stage only as a natural extension of their own profoundly humanist emphasis
upon public spirit. It is to the intimate relationship between virtue and public
spirit in Scotland that we should therefore now turn.

II: VIRTUE AND PUBLIC SPIRIT

Scottish historians by the later sixteenth century were managing successfully to undermine an archaic social theory of leadership. It had become dispensable because it was predicated on the availability of reigning monarchs and the high calibre of a hereditary aristocracy. These were happy but unlikely eventualities which had long since ceased to obtain in Scotland. In rejecting the old certainties I have argued that historians employed an invocation of virtue which epitomised the widespread adoption in post-Reformation Scotland of a Stoic and humanist definition of nobility and honour. This still patently required a much fuller explanation as to what it actually *meant* to be virtuous. In answering this need they claimed with one voice that public spirit or public orientation was the very essence of virtue. Hence it was a primary qualification for legitimate leadership in society. Such a claim of course came naturally to the Scottish historical orator, moving easily as he did within a fundamentally humanist discourse. As we have already seen, and even before the Reformation, historical writing in Scotland had been motivated by strongly humanist political imperatives. This was most obviously manifested in a line of openly republican discourse exemplified by Hector Boece, George Buchanan and the Flemings. But Scottish scholars also came much more widely by the end of the sixteenth century to flaunt their admiration for the civic humanist values of patriotism and public spirit. Authors like Bishop John Lesley, contemporary with but deeply hostile towards the Reformation, were among them. Lesley, for example, determinedly upheld the Stoical example of Cato, the Roman statesman who had 'travaillit so earnestlie in the common wealthe of his countrey'.[73] Their embodiment of the public interest clearly endeared historical figures like Cato to a long and eloquent succession of Scottish writers in search of moral exemplars for their expectant audience. To Alexander Ross in 1652, for example, it was 'onely Cato with a few others' who could be said to have 'preferred the publick good to their owne private interests'.[74] Here was a compelling orientation of minds towards the public community. It was a stance already steeped in political nuance and ideally suited for presentation as the precondition of legitimate social leadership. It therefore became, I will argue, synonymous with virtue for most historical authors in Scotland from the mid-sixteenth century onwards. Bishop Lesley himself had argued this point, time and again urging the pursuit of virtue through the committed practice of patriotism and public spirit. 'Men are most bound to the preservation of their Countrey ... ', he waxed, 'to do good therein, to his Prince, his Countrey, and to the common Weale'.[75] If virtue was truly the natural object of the good man, Lesley reasoned, then he would devote himself instinctively to the public interest.

This was an understanding which can readily be illustrated from the historical writings of Robert Johnston, the tame Jacobean propagandist responsible for the highly orthodox *Historie of Scotland* (1646). Observing the conduct of the Earl of Morton, for example, it seemed clear to Johnston that the

Regent had in fact been virtuous. In spite of the habitual corruption and self-seeking which were known to be characteristic of the Scottish aristocrat faced with the temptations of power, Morton had in fact sometimes been remarkably scrupulous in his adherence to virtue. He had according to Johnston often 'honoured justice and piety', those juxtaposed virtues of the classical governor and the Calvinist magistrate. These things he manifestly had 'performed for the publick good'.[76] However, in building a balanced and accurate picture of the disgraced Regent Johnston felt it only fair to add that 'other things were enacted as private malice dictated which made demurres in his magnificent performances'.[77] Johnston implied that the satisfaction of personal ambition at the expense of the public interest was itself the height of immorality: in short, again, that virtue was to be equated with the public good. For a quiescent Stuart apologist like Johnston there was little doubt that the public interest could be identified directly with the maintenance of good order. It was therefore fitting that in exhorting the recalcitrant Scottish clergy to preach 'vertue and obedience' James VI could be said to have demanded acceptance of 'a strict discipline'.[78] Discipline and obedience were the prerequisites of the public good in the mind of a conformist historian like Johnston. This necessarily tinctured them with the unmistakable quality of a virtue. In Johnston's case, his particular understanding of virtue may actually be considered a reflection of his own propagandist and conservative position. But in more general terms the equation of virtue and the furtherance of the public good was an authentic echo of classical humanist discourse, loudly reverberating through the works of most of his contemporary Scottish colleagues.

Hume of Godscroft, we have seen, showed an understandable hesitancy in following the Calvinist and humanist model of leadership to its logical conclusions. But he seems also to have been unable not to lend his eloquent support to the claim that virtue itself was attained principally through public-oriented activity. Godscroft began the *History of the Houses of Douglas and Angus* with an interesting assertion. Of the five different kinds of 'nobility' ('Vertue', 'Degree', 'Offices and imployment', 'Blood', and 'Fame'), he claimed that virtue was clearly the most crucial.[79] He needed, however, to understate the humanist argument that virtue was alone the mark of nobility. So the tactful servant softened the point by substituting a more acceptable classical epigram for the Juvenalian maxim which he might otherwise most readily have employed: '*virtus nobilitat*', the assertion merely that virtue ennobles, usefully failed to claim to be an exclusive definition and left open the way for his necessary boast that the Douglas' continuous virtues had always legitimated their noble status.[80] But in his subsequent historical narrative, Godscroft's adherence to a humanist public virtue was undiminished. The medieval Scottish nobility had been truly worthy of applause, he argued, only when they 'had regarded Justice, or the good of the Common-wealth'.[81] When attaining virtue and justifying their social status as the nobility, individual men had necessarily had to seek the public interest. The need for such prominent and patriotic men was also strikingly clear to this author. He vigorously refuted the allegation that the aristocracy were merely an unnecessary danger to the monarchy and the kingdom, a suggestion for which we have seen that increasing numbers of his scholarly colleagues were to blame. Godscroft claimed instead that 'it is certain that, without great Subjects, there can be no great service'.[82] In this view the great man was essentially he who was capable of virtue. That quality was always expressed most characteristically and beneficially in the service of the kingdom. So the need was self-evident. To the Scottish historian analysing social leadership according to a strongly humanist set of values, greatness and virtue were clearly indistinguishable. Virtue had to be evinced in Scotland by a sincere and committed orientation towards the service of the public interest.

Johnston and Hume, the royalist propagandist and the carping presbyterian, seem in this respect to represent only two sides of the same coin. They eloquently testify to the extent to which a broad matrix of Calvinist and humanist concerns and values had been embraced by the broadest community of early modern Scottish historians. The first harboured deep political reservations about the tradition consolidated by George Buchanan. The second served an aristocratic interest with consummate tact. Yet both succumbed, almost unthinkingly, to participation in a discourse which was seeking to remodel the social leadership of Scotland in the striking image of the humanist public virtues. As the early eighteenth-century genealogist William Gordon went out of his way to explain, in his own view 'Among the many species of *Virtue*, there's none more glaring, nor makes a great Man more conspicuous, than *Piety* towards his *Country*', and 'Christians do not differ from the Heathen in their Esteem of this Virtue ... '.[83] Nor were ready conflations of public spirit and virtue of this kind simply confined to the works of well-connected humanists like William Drummond, determined to excoriate the moral complexion of the unscrupulous individual who 'Removed from publick imployments ... giveth himself to study private revenge'.[84] In post-Reformation Scotland, as they assumed it had been in classical antiquity, it seemed to be true to all kinds of authors before the Enlightenment that 'a publick Spirit' was the 'courted Character'. There was truly in Scotland, as the Aberdonian classicist Thomas Blackwell later maintained, 'a Necessity for those Virtues'.[85]

Even literary editors sometimes sought to present their texts as sermons specifically on the utility and moral imperative of public spirit, or else as expressions of a similar orientation on their own part. Robert Freebairn, for example, was the editor of Lindsay's *History of Scotland* (1728). He sought openly to elevate 'those great and good Qualities' which 'ought to be imployed in the publick Service'.[86] James Wallace, the son and literary executor of the author of *A Description of the Isles of Orkney* (1693), followed suit. Wallace announced that his father had, in his scholarship, striven simply 'to improve the Talents GOD bountifullie bestowed upon him, for the good of the Publick'.[87] In exalting the public over the exclusively private interest, early modern scholars like these were also prepared vividly to illustrate the greatest virtues by reference to the historical examples set by other public-spirited individuals. The antiquarian Sir Robert Sibbald, for example, used this polarity to impugn the example of the ancient Britons. They were to be condemned, he judged, for 'minding only what was necessary for their private Subsistence, and little concerned for the Publick Good'.[88] Ecclesiastical historians, too, upheld the reputations of public-spirited individuals from the past. Robert Wodrow, the early eighteenth-century presbyterian author, eagerly tried to canonise John Anderson. The minister of Dumbarton had been one of 'the public spirited individuals in Scotland, who, in times of peculiar difficulty, distinguished themselves by their steady and noble minded adherence to the cause of religious truth and civil liberty'.[89] Noticeably in this instance we see something of the more radical political bent which I have argued was typical of presbyterian authors from Knox and Buchanan onwards. Here, however, it simply allowed Wodrow more forthrightly to associate the nobility of Scotland with the virtuous pursuit of the public good. Even to Gilbert Burnet, writing from a less vehemently Calvinist perspective, virtue and a commitment to the public condition of Scotland had nevertheless become inseparable. The Earl of Arran was to the erstwhile minister of Salton a historical pillar of virtue precisely because he had 'set nothing before his eyes but the Publick Good'.[90] Nor did even this exhaust the polemical uses to which public spirit could productively be put. Within the raging torrent that was Scottish presbyterian martyrology, in other respects so different from the calmer waters of humanist scholarly discourse, no less concern for a classical virtue was often to be found.

Alexander Shields provides perhaps the most powerful and revealing insight into the continuing humanist public obsessions of the authentic Calvinist mind. But his was also a fervently millenarian exposition of the scriptural message to the Scottish people. God's soldiers, Shields advised his seventeenth-century audience, 'Discovering a Gallant greatness & generosity of a Publick Spirit, having their designs & desires not limited to their own interests, even Spiritual', should take comfort. They should aim 'at no less than Christs's Publick Glory, the Churches publick good, the Saints publick Comfort, having a publick Concern for all Christs Interests, Publick Sympathie for all Christs Friends, and a publick declared Opposition to all Christs Enemies'.[91] This was a searing image of commitment to the public welfare as well as to private spirituality. Here Shields was speaking in the voice of Cato as well as of Calvin, boldly affirming for Scotsmen that they 'that make a prey of the Common-wealth, are not joined to us by any civil bond or tye of humanity, but should be accounted the most Capital enemies of God and of all men'.[92] This explicit reference to the vicious and tyrannical attacks on the public interest represented by Sharp's archiepiscopate, moreover, was interestingly compared with Caligula's imperial usurpation of the Roman state. To Shields this clearly allowed the lesson to be drawn from classical history that such enemies to the public welfare in Scotland constituted *ipso facto* a religious justification for patriotic resistance. In conclusion Shields warned his flock that these people were 'not to be counted as within humane societie, but transgressors of the limits thereof', and should be identified and confronted forthwith.[93] The virtuous duties incumbent on the pious and the godly were thus neatly encapsulated for a violent Covenanting controversialist in the classical theme of public orientation. The service of God's cause entailed the defence of the Scottish public as His proper arena. To employ public offices in the service of private interest was accordingly conceived of both as ungodly and, which amounted to the same thing, vicious. As Shields had earlier argued, history showed many Scotsmen in particular to have been virtuous in this specifically public sense: 'how generously zealous these noble Patriots were for the countries good', the preacher reflected, 'against Tyrannie, thô they were ignorant of Religion'.[94] The compelling Calvinist and humanist account had clearly led even this most furious and polemical of presbyterian Covenanters, truly one of the 'most wild and violent of the Hill-men',[95] to equate virtue with the stolid defence of the public interest. Men were exhorted to be virtuous, if necessary, at the risk of waiving liturgical performances and private devotions. Should they be sufficiently active and righteous in the defence of the public domain, they might even be virtuous in the utter ignorance of theological doctrine itself.

The association of virtue with a committed pursuit of the public interest could thus be as consistent with the newer Calvinist religious priorities introduced to Scotland by John Knox as it was richly evocative of its ancient humanist lineage. The intelligent use by Knox's successors of humanist libertarian arguments in defence of his Calvinist revolution had manifestly succeeded. They had reduced even further the distance between the languages of the spiritual and the public in Scotland. Exclamations like that of Sir James Dalrymple in 1705 were able to extol the recent circumstances by which 'our Civil and Religious Interests came to be so closely United and Incorporated together'[96] in the Protestant monarchy. Such an argument was possible only because of the deeply rooted sense drawn from Calvinism and humanism that a concern for the moral and spiritual state of the public community was now essential to the proper discharge of an individual's godly responsibilities. Even religious faith, on this reading, had a distinctively public dimension. This line of thinking was integrated from an early time into the humanist discussion of public orientation as it was propounded by Erasmian scholars in Scotland. These were men like Sir Richard Maitland of Lethington – lawyer, historian, and politician under Mary Queen of Scots – who around 1560 had requested men both to behave 'towart Almychty God ar hewinlie father as becummis the dewitie of ane gude and faithfull cristin man' and to do 'no thing' in respect of prince and country 'that may [be] skaythfull or dampnable thairto or contrair to the common weill thairof'.[97] Nevertheless, and as the case of Maitland would simply confirm, it would be rash to ignore at this stage these private and devotional nuances of virtue. They continued to resound through the historical works of post-Reformation Scotland, indeed providing an eloquent counterpoint to enlightened emphases in the apparently quite different eighteenth-century world inhabited by Lord Kames and William Robertson. Spiritual piety and moral self-restraint were foremost among the virtuous qualities urged upon their Scottish audience by a host of early modern scholars. Each formed an important focus for discussion in their analysis of historical examples. Each proved indispensable as they attempted to construct in Scotland a coherent model of the truly virtuous social leader. We should turn now to see how this attitude towards the cultivation of private virtue so often led the Scottish historian of the sixteenth and seventeenth centuries on towards an emphasis upon the moral potency of learning and scholarship itself.

III: PIETY, REASON AND SCHOLARSHIP

Scholarly enthusiasm for the propagation of individual piety was nothing new. It had been displayed in Scotland from the very beginning of this formative period in the development of modern historical writing. John Bellenden, for example, had observed approvingly as early as 1542 in his great translation of Boece how there 'risis every day new fervent devotioun to the ornament of cristin faith'. This seemed an overdue rejuvenation of piety in Scotland. In his view it suitably complemented those other 'auld virtewis usit sum tyme amang our eldaris'.[98] This sense of the immense importance and proximity of spiritual improvement was, however, intensified still further by the Scottish Reformation. It thus seems to have been essential to the instructional and moralistic content of historical writing throughout the early modern period that it sought to encourage its readers to perform their 'godly' responsibilities. George Buchanan, for example, was keen to point out one of the few redeeming features of Scottish monks at the time of Charlemagne. This had been their reputation for 'Piety, the antient Discipline being then not quite extinguished'.[99] In the same pious vein Buchanan also held up to his audience the rare example of King Kenneth III. Kenneth had realised the necessity of reforming the spirituality of his immediate household as the prerequisite to national reformation. He had wisely recognised a maxim which was underscored by the Calvinist and humanist emphasis on militant activity: he must simply 'express in *Deeds*, what he commanded in *Words*'.[100] This position, one of advocating individual or familial piety as an important and immediate expression of virtue, coloured the historical approach of many post-Reformation Scottish authors, and not only of those personally committed to the Calvinist revolution. Alexander Ross, in this as in so much else, is perhaps typical. His forthright assertion was that deeply religious qualities marked out the truly virtuous social leader. Addressing his exhortation to 'Magistrates, and such as would bring rude and barbarous people to civilitie and of stones to make them men',[101] Ross attempted to outline some of the personal characteristics most necessary for those who wished to take the lead. In short, he claimed with genuine ardour, they 'must have the perfections of *Deucalion*', the classical Noah, and display 'prudence, religion, justice, &c.'.[102] This clear reference to the classical Stoic virtues, allied to the crucial virtue of religious devotion, seems to have encapsulated for the Calvinist or humanist scholar the qualities of men who, like Deucalion, would provide leadership and an example to their people in difficult times. Men of influence and importance, the Scottish historians insisted with John Gordon, should be those 'such as are knowne to be well grounded in the true Christian religion'.[103] Leaders, as the Jacobean episcopalian John Monipennie similarly averred, ought to be like King Donaldus, one of his choice exemplars: a 'valiant prince, and godly'.[104] The result was a perennial stress by historians upon godliness and piety in the individual social leader. His virtue was expressible by personal devotion to his God no less than by his ostentatious commitment to the public interest.[105]

Nor is it difficult to see how this insistent historical emphasis upon the virtues of personal godliness and piety served the more immediate purposes of post-Reformation religious polemic. These were, after all, purposes for which I have already suggested that much of Calvinist and humanist history in Scotland had originally condensed. It was not just godly princes, as we saw earlier, who were the stock object of historical eulogy because of their virtuous 'diligence' in religious observances.[106] In the later seventeenth century, in particular, the issues of historical godliness and a virtuous piety were also summoned to the defence of deeply entrenched ecclesiological positions. Loaded reference was made on many occasions to the individual spirituality of the respective adherents of the episcopalian and presbyterian governments.[107] Here, for example, was to be found Thomas Forrester, the presbyterian arch-controversialist. Forrester tried vigorously to refute the charges levelled at the presbyterian regime by opponents like Alexander Monro. 'His Conscience can tell him, yea, its known to all Men, who know *Scotland*', the minister fulminated, 'that since our Reformation, there hath been, and are Hundreds therein, not only of Ministers, but others of most Considerable Note and Character, Men of Conscience and Learning, who adhere to the *Presbyterian* Government'.[108] The significance of learning in this defiant assertion of presbyterian virtue is something which we will shortly have to examine in more detail. It gave to Scottish scholarship a most powerful case to argue in the reconstruction of a broader social leadership, a project which ultimately transcended the narrower question of ecclesiological legitimacy. But it must be clear for the moment that its production of 'Men of Conscience' was also central to the moral validity of any system of church government which had successfully produced them. Spiritual conscientiousness was outstanding among the personal virtues identified by those Scottish scholars concerned, like Forrester, to stress the legitimacy of individuals as religious leaders. The individual conscience led men to piety and godliness, they argued. Adherence to its righteous dictates therefore qualified a man for prominence and moral leadership in society.

Yet personal virtue as envisaged in the Calvinist register seems even more importantly to have involved self-control and moral discipline. This was a Calvinist concern which simply reinforced the severe republican morality favoured by so many Scottish humanists. Like Philip of Macedon, the classical figure aptly chosen by Alexander Ross to exemplify the greatest leaders, the Scotsman was encouraged by his historians always to be 'master of his affections'.[109] Abstemiousness and self-restraint – typically Calvinist antidotes for the tempting excesses offered to the animal passions by a luxurious world – were widely thought to be the essence of moral virtue and therefore crucial qualifications for the model leadership of society.[110] Small wonder, then, that Ross utilised the timeless myth of the Lotus-Eaters in his *Mystagogus Pedagogus* (1647) to illustrate the personal characteristics of unsuitable men. They had demonstrated the dire moral consequences awaiting those who failed to foster and engage virtue in controlling their salacious desires and appetites.[111] Ross's contention was simply that 'whosoever shall neglect the remedies by virtue and pietie prepared, putteth himself altogether under the power of his sensual appetite'.[112] As Bellenden had also argued at the very outset of the Scottish Reformation, history clearly taught that 'Our eldaris howbeit thay wer rycht virtewis baith in weir and peace) wer maist exercit with temperance'.[113] This was as crucial to the early Scottish humanist as it was to his Calvinist successors because temperance was assuredly 'the fontane of all virtew'.[114] It was in the same vein, moreover, that his own author, Hector Boece, had gone on to examine the moral policies of successive Scottish kings, in so far as they had impinged upon the individual practice of virtue. This was of course a focus for comment which linked Boece himself to a medieval tradition in Scotland which, as Roger Mason has shown, had long regarded the monarch as pivotal to the moral condition of the *communitas*.[115] Ewin, in order 'to stabil his realme in virtew', had wisely displayed an awareness of the importance of personal self-control.[116] He had, Boece said, 'commandit the young children … to be regularly exercit in swift rinning and wersling … and ordainit thaim, to abstene fra all thing that micht make thaim soft or effeminat'.[117] This Spartan regime had been designed by the monarch to inculcate individual self-control in each of his impressionable younger subjects. It also marked out Ewin to Hector Boece as a king agreeably familiar with what was to become the standard exhortation of the Calvinist and humanist scholar in search of prescriptions to assure personal moral well-being.[118]

This concern for the specific individual value of temperance and abstemiousness was clearly shared throughout the early modern historical community. Nor was it in fact uncommon elsewhere, for in England Robert Burton was at this time busily prescribing his own idiosyncratic antidotes to melancholy and the 'gross humours of an idle body'.[119] In Scotland John Spotswood, for example, represented King Constantine to his Jacobean audience as having been a monarch who 'did banish all riot and luxury, and in a short time brought the kingdom again to a flourishing estate'.[120] And Patrick Boyle a century later was to laud the virtuous customs of Italy where frugality was displayed 'almost to excess' and there was, Boyle confidently supposed, great sobriety 'both as to eating and drinking'.[121] Thus far, then, a Calvinist emphasis upon public morality was consistent with the classical republican remedy of corrective sumptuary legislation. So whilst Scottish Calvinists were fully capable of expressing their wholehearted support for the public virtues, neither did this preclude a highly focused concern on their part for the exercise of the private spiritual virtues. More often with Calvinist and humanist scholarship in Scotland, indeed, moral discipline was thought to be imposed better by the will of the self-controlling individual than by the sovereign will of the state: freely to choose virtue was morally preferable in Christian terms to the mere bending to external compulsion. In John Lesley's blindingly simple view, history implored men to excel in 'embrasing and following vertew, and declining fra vyce and syn'.[122] Embracing virtue meant electing to discipline one's own passions and instincts. This was a choice only reinforced by the historians' edifying focus upon individuals who had actually possessed exemplary self-control. Patrick Gordon's portrait of the Earl of Douglas, for example, has already been considered as a fine case of the Scottish pre-occupation with oratory. But it is perhaps equally significant for our present considerations that Douglas was said to have experienced 'A Strife betwixt the Passions of the *Mind* and *Reason*'.[123] This was a conflict emblematic of the psychological dichotomy underlying the work of so many of Scotland's historical orators. Naturally Douglas overcame temptation (in the alluring form of an Arran maiden) by the exercise of his own unbending rational will. But in doing so he had also underscored his fitness to be the virtuous leader of a national campaign for Scottish independence.

Sir James Melville, that pragmatic critic of so many previous Scottish kings, had also observed – perhaps with a disapproving eye on the sumptuous Jacobean court – how the state flourished only when princes 'have by Wisdom and Vertue conquered their own passion, opinions, and desires'. This victory was the moral prerequisite to ravishing 'the hearts of the most and best part of the Subjects, to assist them with heart and hand to suppress the Rebels, and to punish the Offenders'.[124] It would seem, therefore, that a fundamentally rational self-control was among the most important definitions of virtue imposed upon the minds of scholars by the influence of Calvinism and humanism in early modern Scotland. It elevated a man to virtuousness, they were brought to believe, because it offered a means to hampering the disorderly exercise of the vicious passions. As Mackenzie of Rosehaugh, the elegant moral essayist, insisted, luxury might most effectively be resisted by the retired or the secluded: in the philosopher, for example, it could be remedied by 'Contemplation and Thinking, or else in the practice of Virtue'.[125] Conversely, it was sometimes held, and particularly by those most stridently concerned to excoriate luxury and immorality, that material excess and sensual gratification would themselves tend to blunt the keen edge of the rational intellect. Hence, for example, we find Boece's translator again fulminating with an entirely characteristic bellicosity as early as 1542 against the Scottish taste for exotic imports. This was specifically because 'throw this immoderat glutony our wit and reason ar sa blindit within the presoun of the body', he complained, 'that it may have no knowlege of hevynly thyngis'.[126] Others were even more committed to the specific questions of state. They were easily led from this understanding to regard the learned king or statesman himself as the individual in whom the rational control of desire was especially noteworthy. Thus James I of Scotland, a much-admired royal figure, had his self-discipline highlighted by those historians who wished to defend his reputation for virtue. To William Drummond, for example, he had 'a good command over his Passions, his desires never being above his reason'.[127] Such a man, it seemed, whose 'favour was mastered by equity, Ambition by Virtue',[128] possessed one of the crucial requirements for moral legitimacy in the Calvinist and humanist social leader.

The evidence of Mackenzie and Drummond, then, is clear. Building upon a tradition of thought and literary composition which in Scotland looked back perhaps even as far as William Dunbar, Calvinism and humanism were now compelling Scottish scholars to continue to dwell upon the possible social functions of eloquence and learning.[129] That reason controlled the desires, and, as we have seen, that those whom Thomas Forrester elevated as 'Men of Conscience and Learning'[130] could themselves be seen as necessarily among the most virtuous because of their sincere and informed piety, made it possible for the Scottish historian to announce that learning was itself a virtuous activity. Some scholars, it seems, were not above presenting their own literary efforts and eloquent ratiocinations in the guise of public-spirited educational offerings to the commonwealth, thereby acquiring for themselves even more the un- mistakable character of a humanist virtue. To James Wallace's claim in 1693 which we have already discussed, one might for instance add Robert Fleming's disingenuous suggestion in 1711 that, by his writing, he had 'labour'd to do all, on my part, that a private and obscure Man in my circumstances, could possibly do for the publick interest'.[131] It is, however, necessary to stress at this point that the elevation of a learned virtue was not intended at this stage to advance the historian or his fellow scholars to the social leadership, even though in Scotland the poet and the scholar – as the case of Dunbar underlines – had long enjoyed a genuine and peculiar eminence. Scottish society from the Reformation until the early eighteenth century remained in practice ill-suited for leadership by its small and fractious community of scholars. Yet nor was it tolerable for scholars to allow its continued domination by a vicious and unreliable hereditary leadership. So they instead advanced a more plausible claim, a compromise between a purely intellectual and a flagrantly aristocratic leadership. This was that learning should at least be included among the crucial qualities of the serious candidate for leadership, whether he be minister, gentleman or aristocrat. The result was a historical tradition in Scotland which displayed an inordinate interest in developing the equation of virtue and learning. It achieved this very largely and very successfully without claiming that only the learned professions themselves had a reasonable claim upon leadership. In fact, Scottish historical discourse for the moment contented itself simply with recalling historical exemplars with outstanding intellectual and scholarly credentials. These qualities had seemed to ensure for their possessors in their own time recognition of a virtue. This, in turn, had legitimated their undoubted social prominence.

James Durham, for example, the Glaswegian divine and author of the posthumous *Commentary Upon the Book of the Revelation* (1680), was particularly deliberate in his argument that scholarship was uniquely beneficial to men in responsible positions. It is clear enough too that Durham actually stopped short of suggesting that the presbyterian ministry themselves were alone destined for the leadership of Scottish society. His claims, however, nevertheless do demonstrate a continuing link between a historical defence of learning and the well-attested Calvinist campaign for an educated and knowledgeable ministry. Durham began with the very typical instruction that 'the knowledge of humane learning, and the studying thereof', must embrace the specific disciplines of 'tongues, sciences, historie, &c.'.[132] He accepted that those learned qualities, including history itself, could not be regarded as 'essential, and simplie necessary for the being of every Minister, so as none could be a Minister without them'.[133] Clearly, such matters as personal piety and moral discipline, as we have seen, were at least as necessary for the exemplary and instructive office of the minister in particular. They were also more obviously the required virtues for a Scottish clergyman. Yet speaking for all Calvinist and humanist theoreticians, Durham still insisted of the learned virtues that 'we conceive them useful exceedingly to all, and necessary for the Church', providing that they were 'used in a right subordination, to the great end of edification'.[134] It was, as I have persistently argued, self-evident to contemporaries that the proper purpose of early modern scholarship and its associated skills was one of edification and moral instruction. Durham was therefore able very comfortably to include this kind of learning among the most important qualifications at least of the specifically religious social leader. Of course, this was a focus on the learned clergyman, in which he was far from alone. His contemporary Thomas Crauford, for example, the Edinburgh professor of mathematics and natural philosophy, shared this view. In 1646 Crauford had readily identified the complementary 'pietie, learning, and wisedome' of Robert Rollock as his most significant ministerial qualifications, in a strenuous assertion of the importance of scholarly virtues in the cleric who had assumed a position of social leadership.[135] These remarks by seventeenth-century presbyterians clearly imply that learning was viewed as a virtuous, public-spirited activity, and that the powers of reason which it refined were instrumental in cultivating moral self-restraint. As a general understanding of the moral value of learning this also clearly transcended the narrower question of fitness for the ministerial office addressed by Durham and Crauford, and was available for use by the widest community of Scottish authors.[136] Here was a clear supposition that what John Napier had once called the 'honest science' of learning was indeed a widely applicable quality as well as an activity of the utmost moral gravity.[137] It was possible for later scholars like Durham to focus confidently upon the role of this ubiquitous reason and versatile scholarship in the exercise of duty specifically by the Scottish minister. But this was still a considerable distance from any suggestion that the clergy as a group were themselves necessarily and exclusively suited to the social leadership of Scotland.

In developing this persuasive argument for the moral value of learning, meanwhile, James Durham also drew upon a characteristically Calvinist suspicion for the unconditional exaltation of pure learning. This remained an error which, to the Calvinist anti-rationalist in Scotland, was principally associated with the medieval scholastics.[138] But Durham was by no means alone in still seeing the esoteric and redundant skills of the Aristotelian metaphysicians as a warning to be heeded. In the distinguished company of Montaigne, James VI and William Lithgow before him, Durham saw the scholastics as proving merely that 'He is not the most learned and skilful Lawyer, Schoolmaster, &c., who knoweth most speculatively'.[139] Rather the most learned man, Durham argued, was actually 'he who can reduce it best to practice, as the nature of his Calling doth require'. This use of the Calvinist doctrine of calling occurs in a way which of course only makes clearer the theological dimension of this view of moral learning. 'Art thou a King? Art thou a Councillor? Art thou a Minister?' the Edinburgh preacher and academic Robert Rollock had likewise asked his audience almost a century before: 'Gif I see not gude deidis in thy awin calling, al thy wordis is bot winde'.[140] Many Scotsmen since the Reformation had believed with great fervour that a man should use his learning most profitably in the prosecution of whatever divinely ordained business or calling he took up. The case for learning naturally concentrated on that knowledge and those intellectual skills of immediate moral use to the practitioner. But again the references by both Rollock and Durham to the secular professions indicate even here a softening of the focus upon the clergy themselves. Scotsmen at this time, in the absence of a clear social leadership, were becoming concerned more widely to foster the scholarly arts among all men who were potential leaders.[141]

Interestingly James Durham also offers in the same discussion a further echo of the Scottish scholar's self-reflective fascination with the communicative and rhetorical skills. The practically minded theologian considered that the truly learned minister was in fact 'he who can inform, convince, or edifie others with most dexteritie ... though, it may be, the lesse knowing man'.[142] Clearly Durham envisaged the legitimate candidate for the ministry as being equipped with the edificatory and instructive skills derived from his practical training in 'humane learning'. It seems from the equivalent case of James Melville in 1638, moreover, that much the same kind of learned but essentially practical clergyman had been envisaged by Calvinist polemicists even before the Bishops' Wars and the signing of the National Covenant. To be fit for clerical office, Melville had written, they ought quite simply to 'be qualified both for life, learning, and skilfull government'.[143] Men drawn directly from the Scottish clergy were foremost among the possessors of learning and rational virtue. So Durham and

Melville may indeed have been arguing for recognition of the presbyterian clergy among the legitimate leaders of Scottish society. But they also clearly had ample precedent and broad support for their commitment to the social use of scholarship. They were drawing upon what had become an axiomatic and almost universal presumption that learning, a moral virtue in its own right, was an important qualification for anyone in Scotland seeking social recognition.[144] Even when the ministers were not themselves the specific men in question, this was a view of social leadership widely shared among Scottish historians from the Reformation at least until the early eighteenth century. And it was one which led sixteenth- and seventeenth-century scholars to identify what John Spotswood appropriately yoked together as 'knowledge and virtue' in all those men – of whatever profession or office – to whom they wished to impute a legitimate social and moral pre-eminence.[145]

George Wishart, for example, the episcopalian Bishop of Edinburgh and immortalising biographer of the Marquis of Montrose, could scarcely be accused of complicity in the deliberate aggrandisement of an over-assertive presbyterian clergy. But he seems to have shared their high regard for humane learning as an attribute which greatly strengthened the claims of a historical subject to be viewed, at least, with admiration and approval. Lord Kilpontin was lauded by Wishart as 'a good Philosopher, a good Divine, a good Lawyer', as well as (which seemed then to follow) 'a good Souldier, a good Subject, and a good man'.[146] The Napiers, too, and we can assume that John Napier would have revelled in the suggestion, were 'Philosophers and Mathematicians famous through all the world'.[147] Similarly, Sir Robert Spotswood was deemed remarkable by Wishart for having been 'a man admirable for his knowledge of things Divine and Humane'.[148] His place in the national history was assumed by Wishart to depend upon a just appraisal of his learned achievements. This was notwithstanding his claims as Lord of Session, Lord President, and a leading supporter of Montrose. Perhaps Wishart calculated that, in a Calvinist and humanist assessment to which any historical personage could reasonably be expected to be subjected in the early modern period, Spotswood's confessional and political entitlements to fame and eminence would be secondary to his undoubted scholarly capacities. These were things which educated men of all persuasions in Scotland could safely be relied upon to recognise. It was 'his Skill in the tongues, *Hebrew, Chaldee, Syriack, Arabick*, besides the Westerne Languages', and 'his knowledge in History, Law, and Politiques', which now caught the attention. They represented a combination of cosmopolitan eloquence and historical learning, one which ultimately rendered Sir Robert Spotswood deservedly 'the Honour and Ornament of his Country and our Age'.[149]

From the Reformation onwards learning of this kind was clearly a crucial indicator of an individual's moral and social legitimacy. As such, it was perhaps inevitably an important focus for disagreement in the sort of partisan discussion to which Scottish scholars were so often given. When casting around for a caricature of his opponents, for example, the episcopalian Alexander Monro in the 1690s looked no further for his insult than this very point: 'A *Presbyterian* had rather be accused of *Adultery*, *Sodomy* or *Incest*', he scoffed, 'than be thought *Ignorant*'.[150] In a sense, this was very true. There were few presbyterians in Scotland who were prepared to accept the allegations levelled at them by their detractors (like the author of the *Scotch Presbyterian Eloquence*) that they lacked or were somehow inimical to learning.[151] Thomas Forrester, for example, strenuously defended his presbyterian colleagues at the same time precisely in terms of their being 'Men of Conscience and Learning'.[152] Yet that one side or another conspicuously spurned humanistic learning was always regarded as a telling indication of their essential moral inadequacy. To Gordon of Rothiemay, surveying King's College, Aberdeen, in the 1640s after the forcible expulsion by the presbyterians of the episcopalian 'doctors', it had been most useful to be able to allege that 'learning beganne to be discountenanced'. Indeed, Gordon claimed that 'such as wer knowing in antiqwitye and in the wryttings of the fathers, were had in suspitione as men who smelled of poperye'.[153] Here the concern for learning may have been amplified by the always ambiguous urge for a hierocratic society in Scotland, over the future control of which the wrangles of men like Forrester, Gordon and Monro were to some extent conducted. But historical discourse, following the example set not least by Erasmus, had effectively broadened this focus upon learning into a lingering emphasis upon anyone who could be shown to have possessed the requisite qualities for social leadership.[154] The possession or absence of learning as a result was of concern in groups and individuals far removed in time and preoccupations from the seventeenth-century clergy. It also provided in addition a sharp cutting edge for the opinions of a host of weighty Scottish secular polemicists from the sixteenth century onwards.

Buchanan, for example, was no friend of the ancient Scottish bards. He had dismissed their pretensions to leadership and to an instructive role on precisely the ground that they were deficient in learning. It seemed plain to this prodigious Calvinist and humanist that 'having no Learning at all', the bards should stand condemned: 'let any Man judge', he mocked, 'what credit is to be given to them'.[155] Buchanan was of course only the first and most eloquent advocate of a Scottish classical revival. It was necessary for him to campaign for an improvement in learning. This obligation to learning and scholarship he thrust upon Scotsmen apparently without respect to profession or office. All who were morally and intellectually qualified, Buchanan believed, should in future rise to the task both of propagating and preserving Scottish learning. Men 'should therefore go on with vigour to illustrat learning', he demanded, 'and to commend themselves and those of their nation to the memory of after ages, & posterity'.[156] The most damaging aspersions to be cast upon a nation were, on this understanding, not those of cowardice, indigence, or impiety. They were instead those which questioned the capacity of its diverse social leaders to participate in these most important of moral activities. Buchanan's response to such suggestions was characteristically unwavering. It was nothing less than a national duty, he argued, to establish the moral integrity of Scotland. This was to be done, he instructed, by disproving conclusively the ludicrous notion 'that men in the cold regions of the world, are at as great distance from learning, humanity, & all endowments of the mind, as they are distant from the Sun'.[157] This sonorous call for patriotic scholarly endeavour was sufficiently in keeping with the broad thrust of Calvinist and humanist ideas that it was later to be heeded literally and with suitable energy by scholars like James Watson and Allan Ramsay, at the dawning of the Scottish Enlightenment.[158]

Both Calvinism and humanism, as Buchanan's influential formulation clearly demonstrates, suggested to Scotsmen that learning was of pre-eminent importance to the broader image of their society. Its status at a given time was even held to provide an unfailing index of the state of public morality. As Alexander Gordon put it in 1729, a 'Nation's Courage, Politeness, and Love of Liberty may justly be reckon'd greater or lesser, in Proportion as their Esteem or Disregard for Learning prevails'.[159] Only this widespread belief in the equation of learning and morality can sufficiently account for the almost embarrassing adoration lavished upon previous generations of Scottish scholars by their fawning successors.[160] The detailed arguments of Wishart and Durham, which we have taken as representative of Scottish thought at this time, meanwhile, provide a moral context which helps explain this habitual tendency of historians to impute learning to a catalogue of unlikely and extremely varied historical figures. Richard Hay, for example, in 1712 flattered his patron the Earl of Stair who, he claimed, had 'always distinguished [himself] by a more than ordinary knowledge of every Thing that's curious'.[161] Similarly the Angus minister and poet Alexander Tyler had addressed the Earl of Perth a generation earlier as one whose 'admirable *Progress* in all the *Parts* of Universal *Learning*', was allied to his most laudable 'brave, radiant *Virtues*'.[162] For Robert Monro, moreover, it was clear that 'wisdome and vertue were the best Guards of safety'. The King Of Denmark was praised by Monro for having been 'learned in the liberall sciences' and one who 'understands well the Mathematicks and the practice of fortifications, as a souldier studied in the Lawes, joyning Armes with Justice, two great helpes for the government of a Princely dignity'.[163] From Patrick Abercromby, meanwhile, came a fatuously optimistic claim in 1711 on behalf of the Scottish aristocracy and gentry. Abercromby held that they were 'Men in all ages accustom'd to improve the Education they receive at Home by their after-Studies and Travels Abroad'.[164] Furthermore, they were 'by the politer and more judicious Part of the World, acknowledg'd to be generally knowing and well-bred'. Indeed, Abercromby insisted, 'Among the other qualifications they acquire, that of being acquainted with ancient and foreign History, is none of the least'.[165]

Such implausible claims indicate the extent to which Calvinist and humanist thinking on the moral importance of learning had come to inform even the most blinkered and deluded early modern mind. This is, it is important to remember, a discursive theme which stands in extremely sharp and agreeable contrast to the later predilections of post-Enlightenment authors in Scotland like Sir Walter Scott. Nineteenth-century scholars in particular were later to be guilty of wilfully understating these same elements of 'sense and prudence' in the archetype of the sixteenth- and seventeenth-century man, qualities whose profound moral significance had been understood only too well by Scottish contemporaries.[166] History, unsurprisingly in view of its advocates' occupation, had certainly been numbered in early modern Scotland amongst the most apposite forms of learning. It was widely taken on humanist assumptions to be peculiarly adapted to the education of a leader, helping to ensure that he would possess the required qualities of 'virtue and learning'. The study of history would enable a man like the bishop, poet, and classical scholar Gavin Douglas, in the view of John Spotswood, to emerge clearly as a 'Vertuous and Learned Person' and as a man entirely worthy of his position in the Scottish pantheon.[167] Learning more generally was regarded as an activity which at its best could impart useful knowledge. It could improve the communicative skills and turn men towards public affairs. It played a crucial role in developing the strict disciplinary powers of the moral intellect over the wild and unruly passions. It came to seem to Scottish scholars of all persuasions that learning was a distinguished and virtuous attribute, one that was more than worth the acquisition. It confirmed its historical possessors, like King James I of Scotland, and by extension at least the more responsive part of the historical orator's audience, as legitimate leaders of society.[168]

The Calvinist and humanist tradition of historical writing, then, had encouraged its practitioners to identify and instruct suitable social leaders in Scotland. In doing so it had recast the necessary virtues in its own deeply scholarly image. As I have suggested, the classical imperative of patriotic commitment had been retained and reinforced in historical usage. This had the effect of producing a vital public dimension for emulation by the aspiring social leader. Alongside this humanist influence, however, the effect of the Reformation was to emphasise to Scotsmen the importance of the individual virtues of godliness and moral self-restraint. Both of these elements were also embraced as historians discussed the complex character of the model social leader. To a man otherwise as untypical and extreme as Alexander Shields, ostentatious public orientation and sincere personal piety were now to seem entirely compatible qualities in the discussion of the Scottish social leader. Yet there is more impressive and more important evidence of coherence in this tradition of Scottish moral thought. It lies in the pre-eminent status accorded to learning, which emerged in this period as a virtue in its own right. This development coincided with and was rendered more concrete by the actual revival of letters in Scotland and by the prominence of a growing throng of erudite ministers and laymen, including our authors themselves, after the sixteenth century. The Renaissance and Reformation, as Scotsmen were quick to realise, were in fact related and productive influences over the dawning of modernity in Scotland, each reinforcing and amplifying as much as negating the influence of the other.[169] Like Robert Baillie, perhaps the greatest spokesman for civil war presbyterianism, Scotsmen of all persuasions were now grateful if they had acquired all the overlapping social graces 'of piety, of good letters, and of moral vertue'.[170] Like Alexander Ross's preferred audience, they now strove energetically to become the 'Gentlemen and Schollars' which modern Scotland was increasingly assumed to require.[171] These attainments did not elevate the scholarly community itself to social leadership – an elevation which Scottish society would not yet realistically sustain. But nor were its members confined to discussions merely of the character or legitimacy of Scotland's perpetually warring clerical factions. Learning was advertised by historians as the moral attribute which would equally become the minister or the layman. It was seen as the quality serving above all others to confirm his status as a credible and legitimate social leader. In early modern Scotland legitimate standing now required clear evidence of virtue. This was shown, not least among the other public and private traits dear to Scottish scholars as worldly and wise as Robert Monro, by the conspicuous possession of learning: 'A Souldier without Letters', Monro prudently warned his mentor the heroic Elector Palatine, had come to seem 'like a ship without a Rudder, or like a bird without Feathers'.[172]

IV: FORTUNE, STOICISM AND THE LEGACY OF JOHN KNOX

So far we have seen how the intellectual resources of Calvinism and humanism to some extent coalesced with, or at least complemented, each other. On more than one occasion it has even been appropriate – if still perhaps a little shocking to some – to refer expansively to the development of 'Calvinist humanist discourse' in Scotland. These two influences, I have argued, produced a convincing and unitary account of historical purpose. They also lay behind a consequent practice which both defined a social leadership in Scotland and instructed it enthusiastically in the particular ways of virtue. When turning to the question of historical causality, however, there are immediate problems. An interpretation which regarded 'Calvinist humanism' as an individual and consistently coherent body of thought would begin to encounter considerable difficulty. It is clear, in fact, that the discussions of causality suggested to Scotsmen by their Calvinist and humanist sources were frequently different and in some respects even incompatible. This was because Calvinist causality, in essence, relied upon a resolute faith in providential determinism. Teetering dangerously on the brink of fatalism, it left little room for manœuvre for a creative human direction of affairs. It was a scheme unashamedly for ascribing both virtue and action to an omnipotent God, leaving man in possession of little more than the guilt. The classical causality espoused by most ancient and Renaissance humanists, however, had always reserved a much clearer role both for human actions and constructive intention in the explanation of events. Fully justifying the more impious connotations of the humanist tradition, it concurred with Hamlet's apparently boundless faith in the human capacity as 'the beauty of the world, the paragon of animals'.[173] I shall argue that in Scotland, to a considerable extent, most historians from the Reformation onwards still preferred to propose a variation on this optimistic interpretation. They largely forsook the constricting historical causality offered by a strictly predestinarian Calvinist theology. And they favoured instead a permissive account of events which was more obviously conducive to the picture of the dynamic, purposeful, virtuous, rational, and necessarily influential human agent insistently drawn by their social theory of leadership. The dominance of this humanist account, nevertheless, was noticeably waning after the middle of the seventeenth century. An increasing number of scholars in Scotland by the end of the civil wars can be identified as having turned uneasily to Stoicism and, in many cases, to outright divine providentialism. This development was itself to have a profound impact on the discussion of causality as it was eventually taken up by Enlightenment scholarship in Scotland. Explanations for this momentous sea-change will only be offered in the most tentative way, however, in deference to the meagre understanding which we still possess of intellectual life in seventeenth-century Scotland. At least for the substantial period from the Scottish Reformation until the middle of the seventeenth century, it seems to have been the orthodox classical account of causality which in any case dominated historical scholarship in Scotland. It is this interpretation of events which should obviously concern us first.

To understand the attractions of the humanist account of historical causality as it captured the Scottish scholarly tradition after the mid-sixteenth century, a grasp of George Buchanan's attitude is, as ever, of paramount importance.[174] Like Guicciardini and Hector Boece before him, Buchanan possessed a characteristically dynamic vision of the sometimes malign forces against which human agents were obliged to struggle, and of the misfortunes which mankind would invariably suffer.[175] Speaking of the migrant ancient Scots, for example, he observed that it was 'no great Wonder among the Wise, if Men, having long conflicted with adverse Fortune', should eventually invade a distant country.[176] Similarly, and displaying a widespread tendency to diminish the pagan connotations by the use of Christian terms, Buchanan commented that the sympathy of the Irish for the Scots derived simply from the fact that 'they pitied the common Miseries of Mankind, and were particularly affected with their Condition, whom Divine Providence had so grievously affected'.[177] In both cases, Buchanan was of course portraying an unseen and irresistable force at large in the world. He was able to emphasise its obvious uncontrollability, moreover, by describing it in a Christian vocabulary. Yet, crucially, in neither case was the actual irrelevance of human or contingent causes at all suggested. Here, indeed, lay the basic attraction of Roman or Machiavellian causality to Buchanan and his successors, even in their more pessimistic moments. Fortune, it appears, could either display its unashamedly pagan character or adopt the useful disguise of Christian Providence. It could most certainly pose problems and erect considerable obstacles to human action. But ultimately it could either be conspired with or confronted as men imposed themselves triumphantly upon a fundamentally malleable destiny.

More importantly still, however, a confrontation with classical Fortune carried with it no vicious implication of impiety, immorality or *hubris*. On the contrary, to tilt with one's apparent fate was in humanist terms an indication of the highest virtuousness and moral character. Scottish historians like Buchanan could still attribute suitably condign outcomes to the interposition of judicious external forces. But at the same time they were at least as enthusiastic in ascribing to the virtuous themselves a prodigious capacity to shape events. Thus, for example, in praising the tranquillity brought to Scotland by James IV, Buchanan was able to present the king as a paragon of humanist virtue, not least for having confronted and successfully overcome the apparent destiny of Scottish kings to suffer amid civil strife and bloody conflict. It seemed to the humanist, 'yea, as if Fortune had submitted her self to be an Handmaid to the king's Virtues'.[178] But although Buchanan and others sometimes made use of a more rigidly deterministic view of man's condition, perhaps encouraged by Calvinist theology, this merely underscored the pessimistic resonances already present in the humanist account. In this sense Scotsmen can be seen to have adopted on occasion the more demanding perspectives of Savonarola and Guicciardini rather than the opportunistic permissiveness of Machiavelli.[179] With John Bellenden, for example, they thought it hard to outwit the 'chance of misfortunitie' in a world in which the 'cursid weird yet ithandly enduris'.[180] However, like Bellenden's personification of Virtue, over which 'nae influence of starns can eir prevail' or 'rigne owre [us] with infortunitie', wisdom and virtue held out the hope of taming destiny and shaping a better future.[181] Once the possibility of a human causal power over outcomes had at least been conceded in this way, the scholar was committed to tracing history within what was a humanist rather than a strictly Calvinist framework. He would sometimes still employ the vocabulary of Providence, with all its suitably pious connotations. But he was also keen to present opposition to Fortune and its undesirable directives as the characteristic of the truly virtuous. Buchanan in particular had accepted that events could indeed ultimately be influenced in this way by the sheer force of character of the virtuous man. He therefore tied himself, and the greater number of Scottish scholars in the sixteenth and seventeenth centuries, to the humanist causality of his own Roman and Florentine predecessors.

This delicately balanced and broadly humanist account of causality seems to have maintained its dominance in Scottish historical writing in the generations after Buchanan. Certainly there is little sign of its early dissipation. Patrick Gordon, for example, obscure author of the *Famous History of Robert the Bruce* (1615), was in this respect probably a typical humanist of the Jacobean era. He was nothing short of energetic in his attempts to present his eponymous hero as a man who had overcome the adverse Fortune which had hitherto confronted him. Like Buchanan, of course, Gordon displayed a keen humanist awareness of 'Fortune's Wheel that still is roll'd'.[182] This provided adequately for a retributive force intruding with great solemnity and power in the human sphere. In his view, events seemed simply to prove 'that Heav'n and Fortune had control'd| The Fates'.[183] The Bruce's mishaps and disappointments were readily attributable in this scheme to a potent combination of malign Fortune and his own weak spirit. However, with the Douglas' aid, Gordon suggested, there still arose hopes that the Bruce would respond constructively. He would act virtuously in order to acquire 'Fate's Favour, Fortune's Constancie',[184] and thus legitimate the extravagant earlier claim that he could become 'Fortune's Champion'.[185] The Bruce of course protests like any true humanist against the ravages of countervailing Fortune. But he adopts the necessary qualification, as acceptable to the humanist as to the Calvinist, that recognition of the considerable power of destiny at least helps prevent too hubristic a faith in the inevitable success of 'Man's subtil Plots and Wits'.[186] Such recognition, the Bruce adds, also accounts conveniently for those undeserved defeats in which virtuous men sometimes nevertheless yield 'to Fortune, not to Valour true'.[187] However, in spite of the initial opposition of the fates, the Bruce's pre-eminent virtue triumphs, his proven eloquence and demonstrable public orientation predictably to the fore. These eventually conspire successfully with 'Heav'ns fierce Destiny'[188] to inflict a decisive defeat on Balliol and the English. Apparently it was indeed the virtuous leader, and in particular the Bruce's singular capacity to impose himself upon circumstances inherently unfavourable to his purposes, which Fortune had ultimately favoured. In short, she was seemingly convinced and tamed. Perhaps Fortune had even been seduced, as a playful Machiavelli had once claimed, by the moral strength and irresistible virtues of the great individual.[189]

The application of this fundamentally permissive interpretation to the familiar events of Scottish history allowed early modern authors to sketch the sort of world in which an active and virtuous audience might prosper. They set out vividly to portray key individuals, and by extension the model social leader, as men bowing to Fortune in their disappointments whilst successfully courting her favour in their triumphs. Like the Jacobean courtier Simione Grahame, author of the *Anatomie of Humors* (1609), they perceived a highly unstable and unpredictable world where 'Forton blinde playes to a poltrous chance [and] makes deceat in glittring robs to dance'.[190] But this was also a world in which 'the strange alterations of Time, and the inconstant wavering of ever-changing Fortune' seemed to the same historian to offer not inconsiderable hopes of reward for the strong and resourceful man of virtue.[191] To John Monipennie, meanwhile, Grahame's contemporary and the author of the propagandist *Scots Chronicles* (1612), this belief offered an opportunity to portray the exemplary James I of Scotland in the guise of the virtuous humanist statesman. The king had been buffeted initially by 'the gusts of adversitie, and flawnes of hard fortune'.[192] But his virtue had finally imposed itself and he had wooed Fortune's favour. No detail or analysis was apparently necessary for Monipennie. The humanist orator's audience could safely be assumed to have an immediate apprehension of the moral lesson being offered. A similar and equally concise account commended itself to Robert Johnston in 1646, who pictured James as 'tossed by the strivings of fortune',[193] but ultimately able to overcome unpropitious external circumstances by force of virtue. Johnston, too, shared with Castiglione and others the humanist foreboding at the fickleness of a decidedly feminine Fortune, 'whose recreation is to humble the highest stones lowest'.[194] But he still believed that virtue could enforce a change in Fortune's disposition. Sir William Kirkcaldy of Grange, for example, seemed to Johnston an individual who had eventually prospered 'by the sodaine change of fortunes wheele'[195] induced by his virtues. Relinquishing high office for a period of disgrace and close confinement, Grange had then overcome this loss to recover his former eminence. Such a remarkable catalogue of change was truly a case, as Johnston averred, of 'Fortune delighting to play the chamelions part'.[196] As for most of his Scottish colleagues, Fortune for Robert Johnston was clearly something which was to be suffered heroically in adversity. Yet it was also to be embraced confidently when by dogged perseverance and the relentless pursuit of virtue it was finally rendered benign.

The implication of the humanist analysis of causality, then, was that intentional human action had a continuing and by no means subsidiary role to play in the direction of events. Transcendent forces, it seems, were capable of being won over by sheer virtuousness, even though they frequently imposed results at variance with human wishes. In response to the latter eventuality, Hume of Godscroft in the 1620s was entirely typical of the humanist tradition in Scotland in counselling men simply to 'bear with patience, and hear with calmnesse, either what he is now, or what he was before'.[197] This was a dictum whose forbearance, if not whose resilient activism, anticipated the Stoic solution which began to be adopted by some of his compatriots after the civil wars. It implied that whilst viciousness might sometimes enjoy fleeting success, it would still ultimately reap only its deserved punishment at the hands of judicious Fortune. Virtue would suffer set-backs. It might even be tested to its furthest human limits by mercurial Fortune. Yet it would always receive its just reward in this world, and if not in the next. With this in mind, authors like Sir James Balfour attributed a man's successes, not to the will of Fortune, but directly to his virtuous and intellectual subjection of her. In the case of Charles the Bold, for example, Balfour recounted that 'quhatever formerlie neglecte or eivell fortune had lost or omitted, by his wisdome he providently forsaw and recovered'.[198] To Maitland of Lethington, meanwhile, Sir John Seton of Garletoun was indeed 'a vertuous man' and 'much given to policie' who had therefore successfully been 'ane improver of his fortune'.[199] One of the most striking results of this ubiquitous classical scheme, of course, was that Scottish authors possessed in defence of activity and worldly commitment a much more persuasive and convincing argument than could be offered by a deterministic, predestinarian account. This rendered it especially suitable to underlie the Calvinist and humanist social theory which we have already examined. Virtue could realistically hope to effect desirable outcomes. So the malignant aspect of Fortune could be no excuse for inactivity or idleness, a lesson which we have seen many frenetically activist Scottish authors were desperate to underline. Even Alexander Ross, who we will shortly see was by no means the most committed to a straightforward humanist vision of causality, still insisted that he 'naturally hated Idleness, the Mother of mischiefe'.[200] Most others, too, followed the editor and publisher Robert Freebairn in insisting that, despite some disappointment and difficulty, they would prefer to 'tread those rugged Paths of Virtue'.[201] The Scottish humanist naturally accepted the limitations on immediate or complete success. These were clearly imposed by the constraints of human frailty and a restless and mercurial Fortune. But he vehemently denied, along with influential theorists like Cicero and Sir Thomas More, that these could ever constitute grounds for abdicating the inescapable moral responsibilities of a virtuous and active leadership.[202]

One of the most eloquent pronouncements on the absolute imperative of exercising such an active virtue in the face of Fortune was one which was explicitly tied to humanist foundations. This was delivered with some aplomb by James VI himself in the *Basilikon Doron* (1599). It was 'not enough', the king argued, ' that ye have and retaine (as prisoners) within your selfe never so many good qualities and vertues'.[203] It would not do, he demanded, to plead that the vicissitudes of Fortune required the virtuous man to quarantine himself, away from the active scenes of life. Virtues, he believed, existed principally that they might be used. There was a reasonable expectation that Fortune would actually be transformed by persistence and noble endurance. It could finally be compelled to serve rather than to thwart one's better desires. Accordingly James advised his son that he should perpetually seek to utilise his precious virtues. One should tirelessly 'employ them, and set them on a worke, for the weale of them that are committed to your charge: *Virtutis enim laus omnis in actione consistit*'.[204] With a pointedly Ciceronian flourish, the royal scholar thus commended fortitude and active perseverance to the virtuous leader faced by the apparently insuperable opposition of Fortune. Precisely this posture, moreover, commended itself to the ebullient Robert Monro in the 1630s, the original of Scott's perfervid Dugald Dalgetty. As an assessment of causality it was adopted by another Protestant prince, Gustavus Adolphus, in his 'wisedome' and 'discretion'. Indeed, 'according to the time, and circumstances', observed Monro with obvious approval, Adolphus had chosen 'sometimes to try Fortune, as well by pursuing, as by defending'.[205] This active employment of virtue was a profound counterbalance to Fortune. And as we have already seen, it was not only consistent with, but absolutely central to, a humanist conception of the legitimate social leader.

A virtuous determination directly to confront Fortune similarly informed Sir James Melville, as ever, all too frank in admitting his doubts as to the feasibility of virtuous activity in the face of adverse circumstances. 'My *daft opinion* was that I might stand by *Honesty* and *Vertue*, which I find now', he confessed, 'to be but a Vain Imagination, and a Scholasticall Discourse, unmeet to bring Men to any profitable *Preferment*'.[206] Yet as a Jacobean humanist Melville was nevertheless obliged still to commend virtue. There was quite simply no defensible alternative: 'my mind will not suffer me to proceed by any other means', he affected to complain.[207] Sir Thomas Urquhart, moreover, that contradictory and colourful translator of Rabelais, regarded Seaton, the early seventeenth-century Scottish professor at Louvain, as a man who though 'at the lowest ebb of his fortune' had made use of his virtuous 'learning, and incomparable facility, in expressing any thing'. As a result he had managed eventually to raise 'himself to the dignity of being possessed with the chair of Lipsius'.[208] William Drummond's opinions, too, in the *History of Scotland* (1655), seem to have been similarly marked by an assurance that Fortune, or a substantially humanist force tactfully taking the name of Providence, could be made to respond to virtue. In his dedication to the Earl of Traquair, for example, Drummond's humanist compliment was that 'How ever fortune turn her Wheel I finde you still your self, and still so ballasted with your own worth, that ye may out-dare any Storm'.[209] In the same vein Drummond also criticised James III for having 'to much of the *Stoical* virtues, little of the *Heroical*', and for seeming 'too much to have delighted in retiredness, and to have been a hater of business'.[210] The king apparently had been seduced by what Drummond took to be a typically Stoic passivity in the face of Fortune. In short, he had eschewed the self-evident obligations of a virtuous leadership which was resoundingly active in character. What this tells us about how Stoic attitudes towards Fortune and destiny were beginning to be used in seventeenth-century Scotland is something to which we must now turn. For it seems plain from Drummond's anxiety in particular that Scottish scholars in the later sixteenth and seventeenth centuries were only too aware that there existed worrying alternatives to the prevailing humanist approach to causality.

In search of a historian markedly less hostile towards other interpretations of historical causality, and to the specifically Stoic option so disliked by Drummond, it turns out that we need look no further than Alexander Ross, the brooding and anxious episcopalian of the civil war period.[211] Ross offered, as we have seen, his qualified assent to Calvinist and humanist social theory. Yet his conception of Fortune possessed a sternness and rigidity rarely found amongst his fellow Scottish authors at this time. Most writers hitherto had tended to follow a humanist account of permissive Fortune, sometimes prudently tempered by the vocabulary of Providence. But Ross appears to have presented to his audience a prospect of stern and unbending providentialism, only slightly weakened by his tendency to use a classical Stoic terminology. In effect, whilst attempting to distinguish Providence from Fortune, Ross began decisively to tilt the delicate balance in favour of determinism. All events and outcomes were in this view determined and underwritten by a mysterious and fearsome God, a deity 'who hath set bounds to the Sea, and to its proud waves, who holdeth the wind in his fist'.[212] Ross, indeed, openly chastised those who, like Mohammed, proceeded only by 'scoffing at providence, and acknowledging no other deitie but good luck'.[213] This was a slur which, as we shall see, was also frequently aimed at their humanist contemporaries by the stricter Calvinist polemicists. From this position followed a characteristically erudite attempt by Ross in *Mystagogus Pedagogus* (1647) to defend the strictly private pursuit of learning. His argument was redolent of that elusive classical ideal *otium cum dignitate*. But it was also frankly subversive of the emphatically activist virtues espoused in succession by Boece, Buchanan, James VI, Monro and Drummond. Ross in fact claimed nothing less than that it was 'not the least happinesse to hide ones selfe in *Parnassus* amongst the Muses, for a Scholar to spend his time privately and quietly in his study'.[214] This, he provocatively claimed, would assuredly protect his own virtue whilst 'the tumultuous floods of troubles and crosses prevaile abroad in the world'.[215] This was not a recipe for idleness, he blithely argued, but simply a call for moral integrity acquired through solitude in a world of truly uncontrollable forces and manifest evil. They 'that will live chast', Ross pruriently cautioned, 'must with *Diana* live on hills and woods, and use continuall exercise: for idlenesse and great Cities are enemies to virginitie'.[216] The sylvan dells and rolling plains of Arcady, for Ross as for an equally misty-eyed John Milton, were thus summoned up in the 1640s as a striking alternative to the world of affairs and of corruption which so affronted the classical moralists' vision.[217] Of course, it would be tempting to dismiss this simply as the singularly self-conscious and intensely personal justification of a marginalised royalist. Perhaps it would even be possible to see Ross as simply retreating into the scholarly cloister in a vain attempt to avoid soiling by an increasingly radical world. But it would probably also be mistaken. Ross was in all other respects clearly a mainstream humanist. He certainly made articulate and constructive use of a humanist theorization of learning which we have seen was central to historical discourse in Scotland. It is also clear that Ross in fact drew upon a strikingly classical body of learning, and a recognisably humanist vocabulary borrowed from Stoicism, to explain his own apparently different and more deterministic causality. Certainly in admonishing Sir Walter Raleigh he sought instead to equate Stoic Fortune more strongly with 'God's Providence', attributing thereby the deserved 'effects of virtue to Fortune' and so to the Almighty.[218] For Ross Stoicism apparently suggested that Fortune was a manifestation of the divine, a veritable agent of the all-seeing, all-knowing God. It was, in short, an embodiment of Providence. This Stoic elevation of private seclusion, then, offered a position from which the anxious Scottish scholar could hope to retain something of a Calvinist and humanist virtue whilst moving at the same time inexorably towards a more deterministic, even fatalistic system of causality.[219]

Nor, it seems, was Alexander Ross the only Scotsman at this time with these shocking but nevertheless appealing proclivities. Other seventeenth-century

Scotsmen were drawn to profess a determinist causality in conjunction with a redolently Stoical seclusion. Among them was Sir George Mackenzie of Rosehaugh, a scholar who for all his many peculiarities and obsessions stands out clearly as one of the most unashamed and thoroughgoing. His several essays on moral questions were written largely during the 1660s and contain what amounts to an extremely elaborate development of the determinist view. This turns out to be strikingly consistent with the sort of residual classical scheme we have just seen in Ross's interpretation of Stoicism. His claims may perhaps have been conceived in the tradition of humanist mock-argument, with Mackenzie mischievously advancing a case with which he was by no means as comfortable as he seemed. But the background of the civil war and religious feuding also ensured that the consoling Stoic introspection of his *Moral Essay* (1665) caught for Scotsmen something of the changing mood of the times.[220] 'The world', Mackenzie observed to his audience, 'is a Comedy where every man acts that part which providence hath assigned him'.[221] Worldly eminence and even virtue, he argued, were no defence against the ravages of unbridled Fortune. Observing the unhappy existence of man, for example, Mackenzie admitted that 'seeing these are only the misfortunes of men in Employment, I see not why Employment should be so desirable by men who fear misfortunes'.[222] Nor could he 'see how greatness can be defended against misfortunes; for ordinarily these arise from such unexpected beginnings, that none see in (or apprehend the least danger by) them'.[223] He concluded therefore with an anti-rationalist echo of Calvinists like Knox and Durham, judging that 'all the world is not able by conjecture to fall upon that *medium* by which providence intends to infer their ruine'.[224] Mackenzie's controversial solution to the contrariness and un-accountability of affairs under the unchallengeable control of Providence, and especially in the active scenes of life, was later to be found in the *Moral History of Frugality* (1691). This made pious reference to 'that just and equal Oeconomy, whereby God governs the World'.[225] It also vested the naturalistic determinism of the Stoics with a degree of Christian respectability. As a personal remedy, however, a virtuous and intensely private scholarship now seemed to Mackenzie the best answer. The philosopher, he had already reasoned elsewhere, did not found 'his happinesse upon what is subject to the Empire of fate'. Consequently 'capricious Fortune cannot make him miserable'.[226] As a result Mackenzie could emphasise to his readers the advantages of the passive and resigned aspect of a distinctly intellectual Stoicism. The '*Stoiks*', after all, 'were in all probability a Tribe of *John* Baptists' and Socrates himself had been 'the Deity's *proto martyr*'.[227] Thus blending notions of Christian Providence with the vocabulary of a specifically Stoic and deterministic Fortune, another Scottish scholar was able to produce a disturbingly persuasive case for virtuous solitude.

It would be wrong, however, to imply from this that the purveyors of historical writing in Scotland had suddenly or completely lost their earlier faith in the humanist account of causality. Nor should we say that Scotsmen in touch with fashionable thinking hereafter always gave themselves over to an almost heretical rejection of the public and active virtues. As I have already suggested, the situation was much more complex than these simplistic conclusions would allow. Ross and Mackenzie actually represent in their very different ways an intermediate and highly convoluted phase in the evolution of Scottish discourse. Neither was quite prepared to abandon the familiar and sympathetic vocabulary of humanist Fortune, to which their classical learning and social theory had accustomed them. But neither were they willing to endorse any longer the brazen diminution by Renaissance humanists of the absolute causal power of Providence, an historical actor whose omnipotence they increasingly took to be axiomatic. Ross fully accepted the compromise of the Stoic position as the creed by which to live. Mackenzie meanwhile, though embracing it ostensibly in a scholarly debate, also understood its considerable attractions in the uncertain world in which he found himself. Each as a result accepted a classical terminology in order to describe a much harsher Fortune. This entity also began increasingly to perform a function more in keeping with Calvinist doctrines of predestination. This development did not of course stop them from continuing to advocate many aspects of the Calvinist and humanist social theory of leadership. But their pagan vocabulary ensured budding Scottish Stoics as unfriendly a reception from the Calvinist purists and fiery Augustinians who succeeded Knox as we have seen that their alleged indolence and passivity had always received from more thoroughgoing and sanguine humanists like William Drummond.[228] They offended the Calvinist because they specifically high-lighted the embarrassing similarities between classical fatalism and modern providentialism. They simultaneously infuriated the humanist when they seemed to suggest that the best attitude towards Fortune was one of resigned and contemplative passivity. Stoicism in mid-seventeenth-century Scotland is of course something about which far too little is yet known. But it may yet turn out to have been the almost inevitable position of men enmeshed in a waning post-Renaissance culture. These were men who were now inclined to accept determinism as the most convincing account of physical causality. But they were still too committed in the final analysis to the pervasive Calvinist and humanist faith in individual rational virtue. Like the bibliographer George Mackenzie at the turn of the eighteenth century, they were ultimately unable finally to relinquish hold of their intellectual past. This had been marked above all in Scotland by the compelling – and, for scholars, self-justifying – vocabulary of humanist morality.[229]

In this kaleidoscopic light it would not be surprising to find individual historians into the eighteenth century still prepared in their work to utilise an unreconstructed humanist causal scheme. Gilbert Burnet, it seems, was one, even at the end of the seventeenth century being fully capable of appearing a confident and vocal humanist in his presentation of Fortune. Cardinal Wolsey, for example, was criticised by Burnet for being a man 'having no ballast within himself, but being wholly guided by things without him, he was lifted up, or cast down, as the Scales of Fortune turned'.[230] In short, the Cardinal had lacked the virtue necessary to impose himself decisively upon Fortune – a characteristically humanist possibility which to the episcopalian historian apparently remained open. The Duke of Hamilton, too, though of course more favourably painted, was one 'who apprehended himself under some inauspicious Star, that crossed all his attempts'.[231] Again the hint of a pagan undertone was evidently not disagreeable to Burnet. As for the unfortunate Lady Jane Grey, moreover, the Scottish historian was equally sure that her 'great Parts, and greater Vertues' ought properly to have brought her 'a great Fortune'.[232] Once more this was a restatement of the classic humanist juxtaposition of moral character and conflicting destiny. Burnet – and he was by no means alone – had thus not simply jettisoned the humanist account in order to embrace a renewed providentialism.[233] It remained possible, indeed necessary, for all historians to assert the continuing value of the Calvinist and humanist virtues. It was also possible for some to suggest that a man endowed with the classical virtues might actually impress himself upon events. But by 1700 Scottish historical discourse had nevertheless become more providentialist in its causality. This was a development whose remarkable evolution should surely be traced back to the very beginning of modern Scottish scholarship at the time of the Reformation. It was, after all, widely accepted even in the later seventeenth and eighteenth centuries that something of a sea-change had swept across the intellectual landscape of Scotland after 1650. Bedfellows as unlikely as James Crauford and Dr Samuel Johnson were later to be found agreeing that something of great consequence had happened to Scotland's humanist culture after the middle of the seventeenth century.[234] The apocalypse and prophecy were, I have already argued, important parts of the Calvinist and humanist inheritance for Scottish scholars. These parts were manifestly experiencing a recrudescence at precisely that time. Providential causality, no less indebted to the conceptual resources made available in Scotland by the Reformation, may have been another aspect of the same gradual movement towards a post-humanist intellectual culture. We need in any case to understand the nature of this problematic rival account of causality, for it utterly subverted the intellectual hegemony once enjoyed in Scottish discourse by a pervasive humanist belief in Fortune. It therefore seems inevitable that we should return once again to the reasons for which the presbyterian apologists of the religious revolution in Scotland had first begun to practise historical scholarship.

John Knox, of course, had been only too clear that predestinarian theology was the spiritual essence of the Reformation message. It was also equally in his view the main hermeneutic tool for the interpretation of events in the human sphere. He claimed nothing less than 'that the doctrine of God's eternal Predestination is so necessarie to the Church of God, that, without the same, can Faith neither be truly taught, nether surely established'.[235] It stood, he proclaimed, 'in such firmitie that it cannot be overthrown, nether by the raging stormes of the world, nor by the assaultes of Sathan'.[236] A knowledge of predestinarian principles was deemed by Knox to be crucial to the inculcation of humility. It promised an awareness of man's weaknesses which was itself 'the mother of all vertue' and 'the root of all godlynes'.[237] Yet displaying his own impressively wide reading and a deep understanding of parallel intellectual currents, Knox seems to have realised the pressing need to bolster the more vulnerable and unappealing aspects of his own dogmatic account of moral causality, which challenged the Renaissance vision and rooted all events in the will of God. Significantly, in seeking to do this he singled out the Stoics for special consideration. Perhaps Knox was aware that their doctrines were especially seductive to those affrighted souls who would otherwise be ripe for conversion to the Calvinist cause. Stoicism certainly provided the most natural haven for the Scottish classical scholar or natural lawyer now wary, like Knox himself, of the more common and latitudinarian forms of humanist causality. Citing Calvin as his source, Knox therefore launched into a savage assault on Stoicism. He noted how what he called 'the doubtful and hard opinion of the Stoiks' had widely and justly been criticised. They were to be condemned out of hand, he insisted, because they had claimed that 'all things chanced and come to passe by fatall or mere necessitie'. Then Knox's grudge became plain. The Stoics had unashamedly embraced a blind and heartless fatalism. No one, he fulminated, should in good faith either 'admit ... nor receave the term which the Stoiks used in Latyn, called *Fatum*'.[238]

Knox's most acute problem with the classical determinists, however, appears not to have been that they were associated with a stern causality. Rather it was that they had introduced confusion into what Knox regarded as the pivotal question of metaphysics by leading a perfectly defensible determinism to carry the most awkward pagan connotations. As well as flirting with the dangerous language of fatalism, then, the Stoics had attributed ultimate causality in their necessitarian system to a hypostasised 'Nature'. They had also claimed to discern a worryingly impious 'perpetual conjunction of natural causes' behind events in the human world.[239] Some Stoics may still have identified the correct deterministic mechanism. But Knox considered that all had erred fatally in not ascribing causality strictly to God. They threatened as a result to undermine the whole logical thrust of the Calvinist argument by which an iron determinism, linked by a predestinarian theology, was tied securely to the Creator. The suspicion that Knox was merely trying furiously to deny the obvious similarities between his own Calvinist causality and the Stoic scheme is only heightened by his irritable rebuke to potential critics: 'How dull and ignorant you are', he snapped, 'if ye can not make difference betwixt God's will and that Necessitie which the Stoiks maintained'.[240] The difference, however, seems to have been only that one ascribed determinism to God whilst the second attributed the same influence to the *logos*: as the leverage brought to bear by eighteenth-century scepticism allowed an amused Montesquieu to discern, God's providential determinism only supposed 'Laws as invariable as the fatality of the Atheists', a correspondence which was indeed 'a very great absurdity'.[241] Knox held firm to a radical interpretation of predestination, a system which he later unguardedly chose to call 'necessitie without man'.[242] This position in turn entailed the providential account of causality which underpinned his *Historie*. It suggested both to Knox and his many later disciples in Scotland a determinist account of history in which human virtue and human causes theoretically had little directive role.

Knox's severe Calvinist reading of historical causality was clearly the natural consequence of his own all-embracing predestinarian theology. In the Scottish tradition of scholarship which he began, this resulted in a characteristic form of narrative which gave to Providence the leading role in historical events.[243] Alexander Petrie, for example, was one of those who wrote in this narrow tradition of ecclesiastical history. He seems to have been especially aware of the peculiar importance of predestinarian teachings to the interpretation of history. In the *Compendious History* (1662), Petrie devoted inordinate space to discussions of the evolution of what seemed an especially significant branch of theology. He related Angelom's explanation of predestination at considerable length, and dismissed Hincmar's impious reassertion of human free will. It was only natural for Petrie to conclude his history convinced that there had indeed been a direct divine influence at work throughout the course of Scottish church history: one should 'mark the speciall providence of God' throughout its evolution, he claimed.[244] Similarly Alexander Shields busied himself in 1687 with a deceptively neat systematisation of the different manifestations of Providence. He divided them into God's decisions 'by the order of His Counsel or Providential will', which 'orders all actions even sinful', and those 'ordained by order of His Word & Preceptive Will', which determine 'only that which is good & acceptable in the sight of God'.[245] These, he thought, offered to explain all historical human actions as reflections of 'the Providence of Heaven, overruling all things for the accomplishment of the Divine purpose',[246] in accordance with Shields's own strict Covenanting beliefs. Yet another ecclesiastical historian, moreover, this time John Row, tells us how in 1583 the Assembly of the Kirk had even ordered that 'masters instruct their schollars in the falshood of these tenets', which included 'Casus et fortuna locum habent in rebus naturalibus et humanis': that 'chance and fortune have a place in natural and human affairs'.[247] In other words, the early Calvinist dogmatists and their legislators had actually attempted to silence any echoes of the rival pagan causalities. This they had done by denying the possibility that chance or Fortune had any role to play in the moral or physical worlds. Of course, the Kirk long remained thwarted in this ambitious project: loquacious and combative humanists such as Buchanan, Monro and Godscroft could not so easily or so immediately be muzzled. But by the middle of the seventeenth century a growing number of Scottish historians, especially churchmen like Petrie and Shields, were nevertheless beginning to bow to the logic of an exclusive predestinarian theology. This new generation of historians was at last to impose a strictly divine determinism, as well as an apocalyptic vision and prophetic function, upon the theory and practice of Scottish scholarship.

A minority of presbyterian scholars writing ecclesiastical history in the seventeenth century, whilst never in fact abandoning the Renaissance social theory of leadership, had of course always sought to oppose the humanist causality which gave it real credibility. They had tried, like the Assembly of the Kirk in the 1580s, to suppress the fact that there might be alternatives to predestinarian theological orthodoxy. Their opposition was implacable, whether to malleable humanist Fortune or the ostensibly more favourable naturalistic determinism of the Stoics. Petrie, Shields, Row, and even Knox in an earlier age, wished to undermine the dominant humanist causality of the Scottish historical tradition. Calvinism and humanism, it seems, had produced in Scotland a necessarily eclectic historical discourse. The consensual nature at least of the social theory of leadership was demonstrated by the support, as we have seen, that it continued to attract among Scottish scholars of all persuasions. The philosophical problems of upholding the palatable ideal of virtuous activity whilst advocating at the same time a causality which bordered on the fatalistic, however, likewise stemmed from the very nature of Calvinist theology. These contradictions were embodied, for example, in the disorderly careers of the Cameronians of the later seventeenth century, anarchic and unruly sectarians who believed themselves to be so favoured by God and so blessed by Providence that no human laws or social obligations could bind them. The same philosophical crux provided Robert Burns at the end of the eighteenth century with his satirical victim 'Holy Willie', the pious presbyterian elder so convinced of his own unalterable providential favour in God's grace that the public virtues of sympathy and generosity could be flouted.[248] In nineteenth-century Scotland, meanwhile, James Hogg later explored the same logical antinomian extremes of doctrinal Calvinism in the disturbing characterisation of Robert Wringhim.[249] In Wringhim the certainties of Providence and divine fatalism are shown by Hogg to offer the ultimate justification for odious misanthropy and criminal self-possession. These startling contradictions, with the reiterated obligations of virtue seemingly neutralised by the glittering prospect of a predestined judgement, should loom no less large to the modern reader of many seventeenth and early eighteenth-century works in the Scottish tradition. Far from being submerged and lost beneath the consistency and obvious convenience of what had by the end of the sixteenth century become a pervasive humanist causality, the Calvinist account rapidly overwhelmed Scottish scholarship after the time of Mackenzie and Ross. Providence subsequently emerged in Scotland, just as in contemporary America, as the brooding and unaccountable presence dominating the greater swathe of her considerable historical stage.[250]

Accounting for this transformation is still problematical. It is possible that within Scotland it had affinities with the contemporary emergence of a mechanistic natural philosophy in the universities. Certainly at this time the Cartesian and then Newtonian cosmologies were coming to redefine men's views of the physical universe in which they lived.[251] Political events, too, as Jonathan Clark has recently argued, may have played their part in inducing the rapid development of Whig doctrines of providential intervention, before and especially after 1688. They could certainly have led men to explain the startling earthly reversals of the late seventeenth century overtly in terms of direct divine intervention: providentialism offered Hanoverian Whigs a potent ideological counter to Tory arguments based on 'indefeasible hereditary right', and a loaded vocabulary tailor-made for claiming political legitimacy.[252] But whatever its relationship to secular developments, it is certain that the movement towards providentialism in late seventeenth-century Scotland had the most profound consequences in cultural terms for the historians of the day. One of the most visible early results, not dissimilar to the developments we have seen were associated with the emergence of Stoicism in Scotland, was that Providence and Fortune were sometimes tentatively equated with each other. By this means men who were both Calvinists and humanists increasingly struggled to reconcile a rigid post-Reformation metaphysics with their abiding commitment to the humanist social theory, which both defined and justified their intellectual activities as scholars. There are certainly indications that they were increasingly concerned by the mounting accusations of impiety. One of the first to display nervousness was actually David Hume of Godscroft, who with great alacrity had followed George Buchanan's lead in speculatively identifying the pagan with the Christian concept. Caesar's Fortune, the anxious scholar suggested, 'we know to be Providence... which turnes the wheel of humane affairs beyond, and sometimes contrary to their expectation'.[253] Alexander Ross, too, in making his lonely progress towards outright Stoicism, had in 1647 suggested that 'the wiser sort by Fortune understood God's will or Providence'.[254] Mackenzie of Rosehaugh, meanwhile, tried a different approach. The ancient '*Fortune*', he dissembled, was not meant to take the place of Providence: it merely connoted 'free will', fickle, inconstant, mercurial, human. Only 'fate', he pleaded, the version recognised and submitted to by Stoic and Christian alike, was meant to refer to Providence.[255] The artful matter-of-fact tone adopted in these apologetics of course only partially masks the devious and dangerous games actually being played with the problematic language of causality. Semantic gymnastics of this kind, however, became less and less tenable as the century progressed. Nimble prevarication gave way ultimately to the untrammelled assertion of divine Providence. Such certainty was all the more comforting and attractive to vulnerable Calvinists like Alexander Shields and the martyrologists of the turbulent later seventeenth century. Like the apocalypse in the minds of the Flemings and prophecy in such hands as those of the Glaswegian divine James Durham, a providential causality after 1650 underscored the wider triumph of a robustly Calvinist attitude towards scholarship. These changes occurred at exactly the time at which many practitioners were being called upon to re-evaluate their strongest personal convictions and their own relationship with God's providential Faith. Some were even required to testify with their lives in the final acts of Scotland's long-running religious revolution. Within fifty years of William Drummond's death and sixty of the eventual publication of Knox's *Historie*, these religious developments in the main had allowed a Calvinist causality finally to capture the historical mainstream. 'GOD over-rules the World', wrote Robert Keith in 1734, with no sense of embarrassment or exaggeration.[256] This deeply consoling but essentially limiting view of causality in human affairs, then, had not only survived. Contrary to some influential recent accounts of European culture in this period, providentialism was actually flourishing anew in the emerging age of polite letters and scientific advancement which ushered in the Scottish Enlightenment.[257]

By the early eighteenth century we may say that the advocacy of overwhelming providentialism was found very widely in mainstream historical writing in Scotland. No longer was it largely confined to the narrower strands of ecclesiastical chronicle or polemical hagiography which had nurtured it since the Reformation. It was instead finding a congenial home even in the orthodox political histories of Augustan Scotland. Providence had always been the natural point of reference for presbyterian historians. From the time of Gilbert Burnet, however, it acquired in addition a central role in the development of a mature and self-confident Whig ideology. Here providentialism showed its extreme usefulness for defending and justifying unexpected political change. It possessed a versatility which won it authority in apparently the least auspicious Catholic and Jacobite circles. One example of this striking process of dissemination was Patrick Abercromby's *Martial Atchievements* (1711–15), all the more remarkable as the work of a disaffected Jacobite whom one would not automatically associate with the strenuous reassertion of the Reformation world-view.[258] Looking at the rise and fall of the Roman empire, Abercromby was certain that he could see irrefutable evidence of an over-arching providential causality at work. This, he believed, underlay all aspects of human existence and forced men, 'when at the Height of humane Grandeur, to stoop below Men, they could scarcely allow to be of the same Nature or kind with themselves'.[259] Hence, and perhaps mindful of the continuing attractions of the humanist account, Abercromby advised his audience against 'whatever vain Debauchees, or emptier Wits, may talk of an unactive Providence, or of a lazy unconcern'd Deity'. Indeed, ''Tis still true, there's a designing and over-ruling Power', he assured them, 'who at last brings Order from Confusion, Light from Darkness, and Good from Evil'.[260] Abercromby's faith in 'that unsearchable Providence that over-rules the Projects and Efforts of Men' came from a man who often, as we have seen, expresssed a considerable faith in the capacity of human individuals to choose virtuous conduct and thereby to shape events.[261] But these other commitments seem not to have hampered in any way his explicit espousal of a strongly providentialist and consequently determinist causality. Similarly, Gilbert Burnet had had a noticeably heightened sense of providential control. This was in spite of his enthusiasm for the Calvinist and humanist model of the social leader and a tendency still sometimes to drop into the polarised vocabulary of Fortune and virtue. In fact the bishop manifested on occasion, and in line with many other Restoration Anglicans, a considerable preference for the doctrine of instruments in historical explanation.[262] This tied Burnet firmly into the advocacy of providential agency in the tradition of Knox, as well as into an emergent Whig historiography in which Providence had become the very underwriter of a liberal constitution.[263] Moreover in the case of the Bishop of Salisbury, the pious judgement that *'the enquiring into these seemingly unequal steps of God's Governing the World*, is a Vanity' may also reveal the beginnings of his sheer exasperation with the presumptuous (and, on recent events, misplaced) confidence of the humanist account.[264] This was now finally being buried beneath the crushing weight of its remorselessly anti-rational Calvinist alternative.

Scottish historians by the turn of the eighteenth century were disposed like Burnet in his more pessimistic moments to agree with the splenetic William Paterson, author of *An Enquiry into the State of the Union* (1717). Paterson it was who launched into the most explicit and violent rejection of the vocabulary of humanist causality to emerge from any Scotsman in the early eighteenth century. 'The Word *Chance* is an ungodly Word', he claimed.[265] Paterson then proceeded to draw deeply upon the Calvinist reformers' distaste for the perceived vagueries of the humanist account. Like Knox, Paterson claimed that any suggestion of 'Chance' was pernicious because, in fact, 'every thing really proceeds from divine Providence'.[266] This, he insisted categorically, 'is in, through, and infinitely over all'.[267] Paterson was still of course amongst the foremost proponents of the view that men should display virtuous 'publick Spirits' and thereby effect 'the Amendment of things Amiss'.[268] But he was no less adamant that a deterministic, providential causality underlay all events. Even if 'the *Lot* from the Lap, or from the Wheel (as they have done of late) may seem to us a *Chance*', he reminded any remaining humanist doubters, 'yet the disposing thereof is of the Lord'.[269] Like the Earl of Clarendon in the 1660s, torn between the humanism of Livy and Machiavelli on the one hand and the pre-eminence of Providence in history and contemporary politics on the other, an increasing number of Scotsmen like William Paterson still devoted 'all their energies to changing the course of history'. This commitment implied and presupposed the confidence in autonomous and effective human action which humanism alone could offer. But at the same time their works show that they believed paradoxically, but with Clarendon's conspicuous conviction, in 'the inexorability of Providence'.[270]

Authors like Paterson and Burnet thus continued to indicate their commitment to the humanist account of social leadership. They presented models of virtuous conduct and human activity which arguably presupposed a capacity freely to originate historical change. So it is all the more remarkable how successful was Calvinist Providence in insinuating itself, through the works of these and similar authors, on to the wider historical stage in Scotland. By James Wallace in 1693, for example, Providence was seen as determining even the most minor incidents in recent Orkney history. These ranged improbably from drownings to miraculous escapes. All of these were held to prove, though only in so far as they referred to divine Providence, '*Quod est inevitabile fatum*'.[271] Peter Rae, moreover, claimed in 1718 that the 'Conduct of Divine Providence' had been especially visible in the events in Dumfries during the recent rebellion, another conspicuous example of providentialism invoked as a political tool in the hands of a Whig scholar.[272] Similarly in the view of the ecclesiastical historian Robert Wodrow the revolution of 1688 had been effected under the controlling and directive influence of Providence. In it, he claimed, 'we observed a wonderfull chain of interpossalls of Divine Providence in our deliverances'. Indeed, the Revolution itself 'was next to a miracle, and had a continoued chain of wonders in it, as hath been observed above, and by many'.[273] The subsequent naval victory over the French at La Hogue in 1692, meanwhile, had 'wanted not very plain signatures of Providence'. And in the failure of the 1715 Jacobite rebellion, Wodrow discovered the same inexorable divine determinism at work: the timely demise of Louis XIV of France had apparently been the work of 'the Lord, in Providence', who worked 'by timing the deaths of great persons at junctures when, had they not been taken away, vast hurt had followed to the Revolution'.[274] Local occurrences and individual events of political significance could be attributed in this way to what the Calvinist had always known as 'special providences'. At the same time 'general providence' was taken to refer to the ultimate design of divine control, to which end the former made regular and exemplary adjustments. As the elder Robert Fleming insisted in 1681, in a striking proclamation of general providence, 'all things even which would seem most contradictory, run within that straight channel of the word, and cannot go without these bounds'.[275]

Assertions of both kinds of providential causality were widespread in Scottish scholarship by the early eighteenth century. They became so intense that their advocates were apparently unembarrassed by the logical extremes to which such arguments could be carried. The elder Fleming, for example, argued without equivocation that 'amidst the various emergents, and hazards of men's life, may not experience tell that surely things contingent are not abandoned to fortune'. On the contrary, he insisted, 'there is a providence which doth number our haires, without which they cannot fall to the ground'.[276] Here, for the same reasons that both Knox and Paterson had assiduously sought to suppress the humanist causal vocabulary in view of its pagan tinge and its implication of random chance, Fleming now felt obliged to deny Fortune any place in his own account of causality. Similar intellectual faith in a more deterministic order was to be found in Augustan Scotland. It led, for example, Sir James Dalrymple in 1705 to avow 'the Dependence we ought to have upon Divine Providence'.[277] Identical convictions brought the Earl or Cromarty in 1713 to present the evil perpetrators of the Gowrie conspiracy as men inevitably 'always defeated by Divine Providence'.[278] These scholars were of course even more committed to providentialism because of its ideological utility in the defence of a Whig revolution of which both were keen supporters. Others may have failed to elaborate on their providentialist beliefs in quite the same unflinching way as

Fleming, or with quite the same partisan gusto as Dalrymple or Cromarty. But ultimately most Scottish scholars of the early eighteenth century shared in the heightened sense that the human agent moved only within an unseen and immutable framework of divine determinism. This conclusion might be awkward to integrate into some of the more grandiose presumptions about the 'modernisation' of early eighteenth-century Scotland which have afflicted Enlightenment studies until very recently. But the advance of causal determinism across a broad front in late seventeenth-century historical scholarship in Scotland is patently too important to be ignored.

Why this transformation may have occurred is a matter which must await conclusive judgement until such time as Scottish Stoicism and the intellectual impact of the civil wars and 'Killing Times' on historical scholarship have been properly considered by modern students. Much of the intellectual history of early modern Scotland of course remains unwritten. Or it is at best thickly clouded with suppositious beliefs and deeply ingrained prejudices regarding the alleged absence of worthwhile scholarly activity. Any conclusions offered by this study must necessarily be considered as highly provisional. Certainly the grip of a highly permissive Renaissance scheme of causality, ultimately traceable to Boece and George Buchanan, held in Scotland until at least the middle of the seventeenth century. This scholarly consensus was challenged first by Stoicism, but secondly, and decisively, by the strenuous reassertion of Calvinist providentialism. The dangerous religious climate of the second half of the century was surely the most important factor disposing men to take this course. The presbyterian victory in 1689 helped further entrench and legitimate the very providentialism which over the previous thirty years had been born of persecution, exile and, not infrequent, martyrdom. The simultaneous influence of a mechanistic natural philosophy and the political significance of a Whig theory of resistance could also have played their part in effecting that profound shift by which Scottish historical scholarship was transported from the dynamic opportunism of Machiavellian causality back to the unfathomable but comforting certainties of the Knoxian world-view. Stronger conclusions than these, however, probably cannot be offered. Instead, we have identified a tension between a social theory of leadership and a resurgent determinist causality which lay problematically at the very heart of Scottish scholarship by the early eighteenth century. We should now conclude this exploration of Calvinist and humanist discourse and take stock of what we have so far discovered about the intentions and function of historical scholarship as they were understood and acted upon in Scotland in the sixteenth and seventeenth centuries.

v

In this chapter we have seen that the authors contributing to the early modern Scottish historical tradition justified, to a considerable extent, their own rhetorical claims. They wrote in order to instruct a social leadership in virtuous conduct and they sought to advance an explanation of historical causality. In doing so, they also instinctively adopted the oratorical posture suggested by their Calvinist and humanist sources, a stance which itself entailed their unending search for the most suitable and receptive audience. This, on the understanding of their own social theory, had ultimately to be created afresh in the vivid image of the Calvinist and humanist virtues. It led to the elevation of the rational man of learning as a pre-eminently suitable candidate for legitimate social leadership. At the same time a suitably conducive humanist causality had predominated for most of this period, with its allowance of an appropriate scope for intentional and influential human virtue. But precisely the same post-Reformation intellectual milieu in which the historical tradition had been dynamised also seems to have bequeathed to Scottish scholars a theological requirement for a more deterministic causality, one suggested by predestinarian doctrine itself. This potential, moreover, always realised within the confined regions of historical discourse exemplified by the writings of John Knox, was more widely actualised in Scotland after the middle of the seventeenth century. Sometimes this took the form of Stoic naturalistic determinism. More often and more enduringly it emerged as unbridled and unremitting Calvinist providentialism. Neither strategy actually seems significantly to have weakened the desire or the need among Scottish historians for the insistent exposition of the model social leader to their audience. Yet it nevertheless raises serious philosophical questions for the modern student. In particular, it makes more than doubtful the long-term viability in Scotland of a humanist theory of active and rational leadership in the teeth of what looks to have been an advancing anti-rationalist and determinist revolution: as the perceptive Mackenzie of Rosehaugh understood only too clearly, predestination and divine determinism were potentially catastrophic for the cause of virtue because they might seem to 'have man to play the mere spectator in his own Salvation'.[279] It is time, however, to consider the case of the Scottish Enlightenment as the immediate inheritor of this dynamic and rumbustious discourse. I want to argue that an understanding of this crucial relationship will allow us to place the historical achievements of the eighteenth century at last in a distinctively Scottish intellectual context.

NOTES

1. Fleming, *Epistolary Discourse*, p. 168.
2. For the argument that humanism and rhetoric are virtually synonymous, see H. H. Gray, 'Renaissance Humanism: The Pursuit of Eloquence', *Journal of the History of Ideas*, 24 (1963), 497–514, and Bolgar, *Classical Inheritance*, esp. pp. 266–75. One of the best studies of the significance of eloquence and preaching in a Calvinist society is the classic authority, G. D. Henderson, 'The Scottish Pulpit in the Seventeenth Century', in his *Religious Life in Seventeenth-Century Scotland* (Cambridge, 1937), pp. 190–219. More recently, R. M. Healey, 'The Preaching Ministry in Scotland's *First Book of Discipline*', *Church History*, lviii (1989), 339–53. The most interesting contemporary account, to which we shall have occasion to refer, was the anonymous *Scotch Presbyterian Eloquence* (1693), an episcopalian satire wickedly caricaturing the homely and occasionally bizarre oratory of men we have already met as historians, like Rutherford and Shields. The argument of this tract is examined more closely in R. H. Carnie, 'Scottish Presbyterian Eloquence and *Old Mortality*', *Scottish*

Literary Journal, 3 (1976), 51–61, and in T. Maxwell, 'The Scotch Presbyterian Eloquence: A Post-Revolution Pamphlet', *Records of the Scottish Church History Society*, 8 (1944), 225–53.

3. See Valla's reference to '... conditores oratoriae artis, quae historiae mater est' (' ... the practitioners of the arts of oratory, which is the mother of history'), *De Rebus a Ferdinando Aragoniae Rege Gestis Libri Tres* (Rome, 1520), Preface, f. a iii.

4. Equivalent tendencies among sixteenth- and seventeenth-century English historians included the recurrent use of the idiomatic phrases 'You have heard ... ' and 'Hear the words ... ' in order to invoke for the reader a sense of being part of an orator's audience. For a particularly tiresome repetition of 'ye sall heir ... ', see [John Colville], *The Historie and Life of King James the Sext*, (ed.), T. Thomson, (Edinburgh, 1825), pp. 24, 208, 271, *et seq.*, originally composed in MS around 1596 by Colville, a St Andrews graduate and minister-turned-politician.

5. Ross, *History*, b2r.

6. Abercromby, *Martial Atchievements*, I, c1r.

7. *ibid.*, I, c1r. Similarly in 1724 James Wallace had hoped that his 'Judicious Reader will excuse it's Want of the Recommending Ornaments of Rhetorick', *History*, C1v. Much the same bashfulness, however, had found poetic voice in the MS genealogy of an anonymous Jacobean a century earlier. 'Their langwage has a harse pronunciation', simpered the metrical poet, apologising for his countrymen's unsugared tongue: 'Fitter for martialists commande in war,| Then for to melt in throw a ladies ear ... '. As a result, in reciting the names of Scotland's heroes, 'Fewe woels heir or liquids shall you fynd,| On mutes and crakeing consonants they end', *Surgundo*, (ed.), C. K. Sharpe (Edinburgh, 1837), p. 3.

8. [Robert Wedderburn], *The Complaynt of Scotland* (ed.), J. Leyden (Edinburgh, 1801), p. 26.

9. Godscroft, *History*, Preface.

10. *ibid.*, Preface. A century later, Allan Ramsay was to agree that there was 'nothing can be heard more silly than one's expressing his Ignorance of his native Language'. Despite the affectatious use of French and Italian, some Scotsmen remained scornful of their own eloquent vernacular: 'shew them the most elegant Thoughts in a Scots Dress', he bemoaned, and 'they as disdainfully as stupidly condemn it as barbarous', *The Ever Green, Being a Collection of Scots Poems Wrote By the Ingenious Before* 1600, 2 vols (Edinburgh, 1724), I, x–xi.

11. Anderson, *Collections*, II, v.

12. Patrick Boyle, *Notes on History* (Glasgow, University Library, MS Murray 304), e.g. fo. 19 (r).

13. Gordon, *Famous History*, p. 1.

14. *ibid.*, p. 2.

15. On the close relationship between philosophical knowledge and humanist rhetoric in the mainstream Ciceronian and Petrarchan traditions, see the classic study of J. E. Seigel, *Rhetoric and Philosophy in Renaissance Humanism* (Princeton, NJ, 1968). Also E. Grassi, *Rhetoric as Philosophy: The Humanist Tradition* (London, 1980).

16. Gordon, *Famous History*, p. 9.

17. *ibid.*, p. 35. Later, Douglas is shown his own family's future by an English wizard, and the relationship between history and prophecy is further underlined by reference to 'This History, by Heav'n long since divin'd', *ibid.*, p. 95.

18. *ibid.*, p. 137. For earlier interest in the Bruce's stirring verbal skills, see Major, *History of Greater Britain*, pp. 247–8.

19. Robert Hepburn, *A Discourse Concerning the Character of a Man of Genius* (Edinburgh, 1715), p. 7. The orator 'is as much superior to the rest of Mankind by the Force of this admirable Talent', the Dutch-educated Haddingtonshire lawyer proclaimed, 'as Man is to the Brutes, in Reason and Speech', *ibid.*, p. 11.

20. Buchanan, *History*, p. 6.

21. *ibid.*, p. 6.

22. See J. W. O'Malley, 'Content and Rhetorical Forms in Sixteenth-Century Treatises on Preaching', in J. J. Murphy (ed.), *Renaissance Eloquence. Studies in the Theory and Practice of Renaissance Rhetoric* (Berkeley, Calif., 1983), pp. 238–52.

23. Lindsay, *History*, p. 70.

24. Wodrow, *History*, I, 238. On the historical Leighton see H. R. Trevor-Roper, 'Scotland and the Puritan Revolution', in his *Religion, the Reformation, and Social Change* (London, 1967),

pp. 392–444. An episcopalian critique of presbyterian rhetoric meanwhile informed James Gordon of Rothiemay, minister and cartographer, when writing his MS history after the Restoration. Referring to their verbosity, and insinuating that it concealed a lack of intellectual substance, he noted how at Aberdeen 'ther rethoricke drew off non but Dr. Guild, a man of little learning in comparison of most of the rest', *Scots Affairs*, I, 83.

25. Petrie, *Compendious History*, p. 210.

26. George Crawford, *The Peerage of Scotland* (Edinburgh, 1716), p. 36. Scott later saw him likewise as a 'patriot' and, with the wording again significant, as 'the energetic and eloquent friend of freedom', in 'Guy Mannering', *The Waverley Novels*, 12 vols (Edinburgh, 1819), II, 335.

27. Reid notes that during the late sixteenth and seventeenth centuries in Scotland, 'many unpretentious writers worked up an ornate, often Ciceronian, paragraph when rhetorical occasion demanded', even though 'plainness' was the norm, Craig, *Scottish Literature*, I, 186. As one contemporary recalled of his boyhood in the 1670s, 'I listened with a greedy ear to all the Traditions, and poems of my Countrymen, of which they had a vast many, and very ornate, full of the Flowers and the Elegancies of the Ancient Greeks and Romans ... ', Alexander Campbell, 'The Genealogical and Historicall Account of the Family of Craiginsh' (ed.), H. Campbell, *Miscellany of the Scottish History Society* (Edinburgh, 1926), IV, 187.

28. Napier, *Plaine Discovery*, A3r.

29. Renaissance scholars and their successors, including the early modern Scottish historians, were 'acutely conscious of rhetoric's moral and cognitive powers', they 'frequently worried about abusing those powers for morally undesirable ends', and they sought directly to address and improve an audience, W. J. Kennedy, *Rhetorical Norms in Renaissance Literature* (New Haven, Conn., 1978), pp. 1–19. In short, as another observes, 'The aim of Ciceronian rhetoric is always the task in hand, centering upon a specific audience at a certain time and place', T. O. Sloane, *Donne, Milton, and the End of Humanist Rhetoric* (Berkeley, Calif., 1985), p. 93.

30. It is remarkable that, even among late medieval Scottish poets like Dunbar, moreover, there had been an unusually strong emphasis upon an 'hye stile of eloquence' and a 'sense of being part of a community of writers'. See G. Kratzmann, *Anglo-Scottish Literary Relations, 1430–1550* (Cambridge, 1980), p. 259.

31. A society seemingly less troubled by the problem of audience was to be found in colonial New England, where a relatively undifferentiated and cohesive Calvinist community received a cacophony of preaching and spiritual exhortation. See H. S. Stout, *The New England Soul: Preaching and Religious Culture in Colonial New England* (Oxford, 1986).

32. Erasmus began the *Institutio*, for example, with a discussion of the 'qualities, education, and significance of the Christian prince', *The Education of the Christian Prince* (ed. and transl.), L. K. Born (New York, 1936), p. 139. The *Convivium Religiosum* or 'Godly Feast' is one of the central testaments of Christian humanism, and is found in *The Colloquies of Erasmus* (ed. and transl.), C. R. Thompson (Chicago, 1965), pp. 46–78. That Erasmus specifically had his educational and moral programme in mind for secular men is made very clear, *ibid.*, p. 628.

33. John Calvin, *Institutes of the Christian Religion*, (ed. and transl.), F. L. Battles, revised edn, (London, 1986), p. 209.

34. As the anonymous episcopalian was to put it in 1693, 'the End of Preaching, should be the Edification of the Hearers; the Design of it being to perswade Men to Piety towards God, and Charity towards one another', [Gilbert Crockat?], *Scotch Presbyterian Eloquence Display'd: Or, The Folly of their Teaching Discover'd* (Rotterdam, 1738), p. 1. Such virtues were self-evidently best transmitted through an exemplary social leadership.

35. Certainly, the view that Scottish letters lacked the necessary infrastructural support was being expressed even before James VI's departure to London, as in 1593 when John Napier feared that they would 'be buried with aeternall silence' without 'some mightie Maecenas to incourage them', *Plaine Discovery*, A4v–A5r. An undated allegorical poem from roughly the same period likewise sympathised with the lonely Scottish poet, cheated of his natural audience: 'Yet could thou but aspye amongest the crewe| Of Gold breid mortales, one Mecenas furth,| To cherish thee, and to mantaine the worth,| Of Poecie, then might thou boldly singe', *Surgundo*, p. 2. Simione Grahame, too, noted that in his own day 'learning hath no Mecaenas', *The Anatomie of Humors and the Passionate Sparke of a Relenting Minde*, (ed.), R. Jameson (Edinburgh, 1830), F3r.

36. William Drummond, 'Forth Feasting. A Panegyricke to the King's Most Excellent Majesty', in *The Poetical Works of William Drummond of Hawthornden* (ed.), L. E. Kastner, 2 vols (London, 1913), I, 141–53.

37. James Crauford, *The History of the House of Este* (London, 1681), a2v. Whether any real decline in Scottish historical scholarship can in fact be attributed to this development is debatable. The suspicion must be, as this study tangibly illustrates, that this abyss was largely a spectre summoned up by the disoriented oratorical posturing and humanist assumptions of early modern scholarship, desperately seeking a cohesive and responsive local audience. Scottish scholars wrote with greater rather than declining frequency. Indeed, as Marinell Ash has commented, national myths and history were, if anything, revived as a 'reaction against the gradual anglicization of the crown and the threat posed to Scottish life, politics and religion by the union of the crowns in 1603', *Scottish History*, p. 30.

38. Crauford, *History*, p. 246.

39. Lithgow, *True and Experimentall Discourse*, p. 51.

40. Abercromby, *Martial Atchievements*, I, c1r.

41. Robert Burton, *The Anatomy of Melancholy* (ed.), H. Jackson, (London, 1932), I, 307.

42. Melville, *Memoires*, p. 188.

43. Lindsay, 'Dialogue', A1v. See also the ire of Simione Grahame in 1609 directed against the 'hellish Court where cut-throat flattrie dwels', *Anatomie of Humors*, D3r.

44. This, at least, was the strident assertion of censorious Scottish historians from John Major onwards. In reality, however, we now know much more about the late medieval aristocracy in Scotland, and can exonerate them very largely from the conventional accusation that they were especially 'overmighty'. See J. M. Brown, 'Taming the Magnates?', in Menzies (ed.), *Scottish Nation*, pp. 46–59, and A. H. Grant, 'Earls and Earldoms in Late Medieval Scotland, *c*.1310–1460', in J. Bossy and P. Jupp (eds), *Essays Presented to Michael Roberts* (Belfast, 1976), pp. 24–40. Also, Keith Brown, *Bloodfeud in Scotland, 1573–1625: Violence, Justice and Politics in an Early Modern Society* (Edinburgh, 1986).

45. Sir James Balfour, *Historical Works*, 4 vols (Edinburgh, 1825), I, 124. John Colville's MS history from the 1590s uses similar words in making the point that the Scottish nobility always seemed to proceed 'rather for advancement of their awin particulers than for any gude zeal that thay bure to the commonweill', *Historie*, p. 188. This critique had earlier been used by Major, who remarked that the Scottish aristocracy not only, when living near to each other, resorted to 'quarrels and even shedding of blood', but also, and even more worrying for the scholar, were learned 'neither in letters nor morals', *History of Greater Britain*, p. 48. Major, indeed, was incensed by the fact that they did not 'search out men learned in history, upright in character'.

46. Johnston, 'Historie', p. 375.

47. David Moysie, *Memoirs of the Affairs of Scotland* (Edinburgh, 1755), p. 125.

48. Brown, *Bloodfeud*, esp. pp. 186–92. They were 'not interested in social upheaval, but they wanted social and moral change, and they wanted the nobility to lead the way towards it by fulfilling their God-appointed role in society, a role which the ministers had interpreted and were determined to encourage'.

49. Burton, *Anatomy*, I, 327–30.

50. Gordon, *History*, II, v.

51. Ross, *History*, a1v.

52. *ibid.*, a1v.

53. *ibid.*, a1v.

54. As Robert Freebairn put it in 1728, when picturing the patriotic virtues of the Earls of Crawford, they had preferred 'a life of Toil and Hazard, to inglorious Ease, and unmanly Quiet', Lindsay, *History*, p. iv. Even earlier, moreover, Bellenden had spoken warmly of the ancient Scots, because, in spite of achieving peace, 'thay sufferit nocht their bodyis to be corrupit with sleuth, bot wer exercit othir in continewall hunting', Boece, *Hystory*, Di (r).

55. Monro, *Apology*, p. 54.

56. Melville, *Memoires*, p. 144. Similarly, see Alexander Tyler's insistence on referring to John Sobieski as 'this great MAN', *Memoires of the Life and Actions of Johne King of Poland* (Edinburgh, 1685), p. 6.

57. Fleming, *Hereditary-Right*, p. 28.

58. Juvenal, *Satires*, viii, 20.

59. Lindsay, *History*, p. vii.
60. Scott, *True History*, II, 6. That equally incorrigible versifier, Alexander Tyler, used almost the same figure in 1685 to describe the heroism of the Poles: 'Transcendant *Merit*, here oft bears the *Van*,| Where *Honours Temple's* reacht throw *Virtues Fane*', *Memoires*, p. 7.
61. Scott, *True History*, II, 6.
62. Ross, *Marrow of Historie*, p. 82.
63. *ibid.*, p. 82.
64. *ibid.*, p. 82.
65. Gordon, *Genealogical History*, p. xii.
66. *ibid.*, p. xii.
67. *ibid.*, p. xii.
68. George Sinclair, *Satan's Invisible World Discovered* (Edinburgh, 1685), *5v.
69. Godscroft, *History*, Preface. Even before Godscroft, this issue had vexed the scholastic divine John Major, leading him to offer in his *In Quartum Sententiarum* a detailed consideration of modern nobility. This appears in translation as an appendix to Constable's edition of the *History of Greater Britain*, pp. 397–400.
70. Mackenzie of Rosehaugh, *Moral Gallantry*, pp. 8–9.
71. Duncan Stewart, *A Short Historical and Genealogical Account of the Royal Family of Scotland* (Edinburgh, 1739), p. iv. See also the view of the Grahams that they had been 'famous in succeeding generations' for having imitated 'the virtue of their Ancestors', George Wishart, *The History of the Kings Majesties Affaires in Scotland* ([ ], 1649), A2r.
72. Williamson rightly points out that 'The belief that a presbyterian humanism would constitute a contradiction in terms' has 'contributed to the *a priori* conclusion that the Renaissance in Scotland could not have amounted to very much'. Yet clearly, 'important elements within the presbyterian party made the most striking use of humanist insights', as we have already confirmed. See *Scottish National Consciousness*, p. 87. This claim, palpably untrue in the light of much that we have already seen, was advanced by contemporaries who alleged of the presbyterians that 'All true and solid Learning, particularly Antiquity, is decry'd by them, because in it there is no Vestige, no not so much as any Shadow of *Presbytery* to be found', [Crockat?], *Scotch Presbyterian Eloquence*, p. 22. One surviving student of the 'scholasticism of orthodox Calvinism', as represented by Ramist logicians like John Cameron and Andrew Melville who discarded the older Aristotelian methods, is B. Armstrong, *Calvinism and the Amyraut Heresy: Protestant Scholasticism and Humanism in Seventeenth-Century France* (Madison, Wisc., 1969), p. 44. An even less plausible and belatedly Weberian attempt to associate Calvinist morality with the venerable spectre of economic individualism in early modern Scotland is G. Marshall, *Presbyteries and Profits: Calvinism and the Development of Capitalism in Scotland, 1560–1707* (Oxford, 1980).
73. Lesley, *History*, p. 3.
74. Ross, *History*, p. 21.
75. Lesley, *Treatise*, 2v.
76. Johnston, 'Historie', p. 405.
77. *ibid.*, p. 405.
78. *ibid.*, p. 466.
79. Godscroft, *History*, A2v.
80. *ibid.*, A2v.
81. *ibid.*, p. 152.
82. *ibid.*, p. 208.
83. Gordon, *History*, I, xii–xiii. Gordon was therefore presumably aware of the suggestion that Christianity and the humanist virtues were antithetical.
84. Drummond, *History*, p. 52.
85. Thomas Blackwell, *An Enquiry into the Life and Writings of Homer* (London, 1735), p. 53. A more immediate exposition of the perceived need for men of public spirit in difficult times was William Paterson's impassioned plea that perhaps 'some Men in Places should likewise happen to have publick Spirits, and thereby incline to the Amendment of things amiss', *An Enquiry into the State of the Union of Great Britain* (London, 1717), p. 22.
86. Lindsay, *History*, p. viii.
87. James Wallace, *A Description of the Isles of Orkney* (Edinburgh, 1693), A3r.

88. Sir Robert Sibbald, *Historical Inquiries Concerning the Roman Monuments and Antiquities of Scotland* (Edinburgh, 1707), p. 2.
89. Wodrow, *History*, II, 360 n. Anderson's true character is the subject of J. Campbell, 'John Anderson, Minister of Dumbarton, and of the Ramshorn Kirk, Glasgow, 1698–1721', *Records of the Scottish Church History Society*, 9 (1947), 155–65.
90. Burnet, *Memoires*, a2v.
91. Shields, *Hind Let Loose*, p. 554.
92. *ibid.*, p. 660.
93. *ibid.*, p. 660.
94. *ibid.*, p. 16.
95. [Crockat?], *Scotch Presbyterian Eloquence*, p. 27. Even this anonymous critic was obliged to admit that Shields was indeed 'one of their honestest and best Writers', *ibid.*, p. 34.
96. Dalrymple, *Collections*, A2v.
97. Maitland, *History*, pp. ix–x. By a curious coincidence, George Sinclair's epistle in 1685 to a later Lord Seton displayed much the same fusion of virtues, reminding Seton of his discoveries in mining technology which as it redounded privately 'to your self, so does it to the publick Advantage of the countrie', *Satan's Invisible World*, *7r.
98. Boece, *Hystory*, D iii (r).
99. Buchanan, *History*, p. 165.
100. *ibid.*, p. 188.
101. Alexander Ross, *Mystagogus Pedagogus, or The Muses Interpreter*, 2nd edn (London, 1648), p. 94.
102. *ibid.*, p. 94.
103. Gordon, *Great Britaine*, p. 25.
104. Monipennie, *Scots Chronicles*, p. 67. Again, the Gordon poet only added to the chorus of Jacobean flattery, remarking that James was a man 'whose holines, whose pious sanctitie,| Whose wertue and whose learneing did agrie...', *Surgundo*, p. 45. Reason and religion went hand-in-hand, indeed, for it was 'the flood of God's admyred trueth' which 'Glyds smothly furth with undiscovered growth | In reasones bankes...', *ibid.*, p. 20.
105. For example, Walter the Steward, a pivotal figure in Stuart hagiography, was described as 'an illustrions Example of Piety and Vertue', Symson, *Genealogical Account*, p. 33. Mis-spelling original.
106. Petrie, *Compendious History*, p. 210, gives an example from the tenth century, noting how 'diligence decaieth, and every vertue fainteth through want of established Princes'.
107. As Gilbert Burnet put it, a church was most worthy of support when its 'Church-men were adorned with the Vertues that became their Profession', *Rights of Princes*, p. 194.
108. Forrester, *Hierarchical Bishops*, p. 83.
109. Ross, *Marrow of Historie*, p. 326. This injunction was a significant common-place in early modern literature, exemplified by the continuing popularity of the legend of the Seven Wise Masters in Scotland. As an English editor related, a man was to be given 'Cunning and Wisdom' and taught 'to be his own Governour, and to master his own affections', [ ], *The History of the Seven Wise Masters of Rome* (London, 1684), A4r. It should therefore be no surprise that the earliest Scottish version of this particular myth should be *The Sevin Seages* (Edinburgh, 1578), 'Translatit out of prois in Scottis meter be Johne Rolland in Dalkeith', at the time when Calvinist and humanist scholarship was condensing in its characteristic early modern form and in the very year in which George Buchanan so perplexed contemporaries with his *De Jure Regni*.
110. See J. Sekora, *Luxury: The Concept in Western Thought, Eden to Smollett* (Baltimore, Md., 1977).
111. Those who leave 'the wayes of vertue' soon 'begin to tast of libertie, and youthfull pleasures'. Ross, *Mystagogus Pedagogus*, p. 239.
112. Ross, *Marrow of Historie*, p. 11.
113. Boece, *Hystory*, C vi (v).
114. *ibid.*, C vi (v).
115. Mason, 'Kingship and Commonweal', which discusses the tendency to address the person of the king at the heart of a 'polity of manners'. Gilbert Haye's *The Buke of the Governaunce of Princis* (1456) is taken as an earlier example of this evolving Scottish genre, and Mason concludes that Haye's emphasis upon 'the classical at the expense of the theological virtues

was, perhaps, an augury of a future more receptive to humanist influences. For, in increasingly secular guise, this form of sententious moralising was to survive (indeed, to thrive) in Scotland, as it did elsewhere in Europe, well into the early modern period', *ibid.*, p. 33.

116. Boece, *Hystory*, fo. xx v (1).

117. *ibid.*, fo. xx v (1).

118. Although early modern Scotland predictably forms no significant part of the classic study of Spartanism in the Western tradition, which restricts itself to a fleeting reference to Buchanan, men like Boece, Ross and Fletcher in particular, point to the continuing importance of this component in Scottish moral thought. As late as the 1720s, indeed, the younger James Wallace of Kirkwall was still somewhat monotonously repeating a Boecian litany of fictional kings, observing with unashamed approval how Donaldus had enjoyed the Spartan exercise of hunting 'and besides the Mind did Suck in the purest Pleasures there from, and was greatly Strengthened thereby against Covetousness, Luxury, and other vices ... ', *History*, p. 7. For a general survey of the immense influence of Spartanism in Europe as a whole, nothing betters E. Rawson, *The Spartan Tradition in European Thought* (Oxford, 1969).

119. Burton, *Anatomy*, I, 243.

120. Spotswood, *History*, p. 25.

121. Boyle, *Notes*, fo. 47 (v).

122. Lesley, *History*, p. 5.

123. Gordon, *Famous History*, p. 69 n.

124. Melville, *Memoires*, p. 188.

125. Sir George Mackenzie of Rosehaugh, *The Moral History of Frugality and its Opposite Vices* (London, 1691), p. 87.

126. Boece, *Hystory*, D ii (v). Given the intensity of such feelings in Scottish moral discourse, it should be no surprise that, more than a century later, Gilbert Burnet would review the state of the Eastern Orthodox church, and conclude that 'Wealth and Ambition' had there corrupted, in particular, 'the Minds of Church-men', *Rights of Princes*, p. 75. The urbane Burnet was of course no less concerned with imposing reason upon the vicious 'Appetites and Passions, that are apt to rise up in our Minds, against its Dictates', *The Historie of the Reformation of the Church of England*, 3 vols (London, 1681–1715), III, xviii. So strong was the coincidence of republican and Reformation thought on this question that Scottish authors of all persuasions were bound by its stern moral vision.

127. Drummond, *History*, pp. 31–2.

128. *ibid.*, p. 32.

129. See e.g. Dunbar's 'Lament for the Makaris', found in *Poems* (ed.), W. M. Mackenzie (Edinburgh, 1932), pp. 20–3. Dunbar directly addressed the nascent humanist discussion of mutability through a lingering focus upon previous literary figures in Britain. His haunting refrain, '*Timor mortis conturbat me*' ('The fear of death afrights me') is therefore to be understood as an elegy on the passing influence of particular men of letters, a theme which was later to recurr in Buchanan and George Mackenzie, as well as David Hume and Adam Smith. Interestingly, when in 1724 Allan Ramsay reprinted this poem, he added his own Postscript which professed to foresee that 'Aftir twa centries pas, sall he,| Revive our Fame and Memorie', *Ever Green*, I, 135. The Enlightenment itself thus got underway not with the new but with a self-conscious revival of the old: the Scottish works, claimed Ramsay, 'sall nevir die', *ibid.*, I, 136.

130. Forrester, *Hierarchical Bishops*, p. 83.

131. Wallace, *Description*, A3r, and Fleming, *Hereditary-Right*, p. 151.

132. Durham, *Commentarie*, p. 172. The imperative of learning in a Calvinist clergy continued to be emphasised by later ecclesiastical historians, as by Robert Keith, who recorded that in 1588 were convened 'all the *Ecclesiasticks* of the Kingdom, that were known to be Men of Learning and Capacity', *History*, p. 81.

133. Durham, *Commentarie*, p. 172.

134. *ibid.*, p. 173.

135. Thomas Crauford, *History of the University of Edinburgh from 1580 to 1646* (Edinburgh, 1808), p. 23. Written in 1646.

136. For example, Alexander Ross pungently expressed the claim that 'men that delight in learning, scorn fleshly lusts, which prevaile most in ignorant idle men', *Mystagogus*

Pedagogus, p. 298. Equally, one finds Robert Ferguson, the radical presbyterian and polemicist, defining virtue itself as an adherence to the dictates of reason, apparently *pace* Seneca and Apuleius: virtue is a quality 'which because of its conformity to Reason is *Morally* good', *A Sober Inquiry into the Nature, Measure, and Principle of Moral Virtue* (London, 1673), p. 14.

137. Napier, *Plaine Discovery*, A4v-A5r.

138. A similar concern had informed George Buchanan on the subject of James I's eminence as a scholar. The historian was at considerable pains to point out the usefulness of the king's poetic and other works: 'But, perhaps, some will say, These are but the Flowers of his Studies, where is the Fruit? These are more for Ornament, than Instruction or Use, to strengthen a Man for doing of business: Know then, that, after he had learn'd other Parts of Philosophy, he was also skill'd in *Politicks*, concerning the Regulation of Kingdoms, and of Mens Manners', *History*, p. 357. This 'wise and learned soveraigne', who devoted himself to 'the improvement of religion, learning, and arts', received the praise in the 1730s of John Drummond of Balhaldy in his anonymous *Memoirs of Sir Ewen Cameron of Locheil* (ed.), J. MacKnight (Edinburgh, 1842), p. 20, and of James Wallace in the 1720s, *History*, p. 89, who found him 'not Ignorant of any Science worthy the knowledge of a Person of a fine Genius'.

139. Durham, *Commentarie*, p. 173. See e.g. James VI's cutting claim to express his ideas better 'then any simple schoole-man, that onely knowes matters of kingdomes by contemplation', *Basilikon Doron*, B1v. Montaigne vigorously protested that he would rather see 'wisdom, judgment, civil customs, and modest behaviour, than bare and mere literal learning', *Essais*, p. 126. William Lithgow in the 1630s likewise condemned those callow youths of his own time who were 'over-master'd with Art, not Masters of it; having their shallow braines loaden with the empty apprehension of bottomless Syllogismes, rotten ragges of Heathnish Philosophy, and clouted phrases of Paganisme Authors', *True and Experimentall Discourse*, p. 52, though here, noticeably, Calvinist piety led to a suspicion of too carefree an attention to humanist authorities and rhetorical verbosity.

140. Quoted in Brown, *Bloodfeud*, p. 191.

141. This highly specific enthusiasm for the practical use of learning points towards a Scottish tradition of anti-rationalism, founded on a deep mistrust of amoral knowledge and a sometimes hysterical fear of human vanity: 'Remember that you are men, and so may erre', warned Henry Leslie, the Scottish Bishop of Down and Connor; 'that better men have erred, & have thought no shame to acknowledge the same ... ', *A Treatise of the Authority of the Church* (Dublin, 1637), p. 107.

142. Durham, *Commentarie*, p. 173.

143. Melville, *A Short Relation*, A2r.

144. Another argument based on this general presumption, and again unrelated to the specific discussion of ministerial qualifications, was voiced by the author, traveller and translator, Sir Thomas Urquhart in 1652, wholly apposite in view of the fact that it was he who first gave the world the amazing story of that *locus classicus* of the learned Scottish man of the world, the Admirable Crichtoun. Accepting that 'the intellectual faculties have their vertues as well as the moral; and that learning in some measure is no less commendable then fortitude', he thought it especially noteworthy that individual Scotsmen had achieved 'great renown for their exquisite abilities in all kind of literature': *Tracts*, (ed.), G. Paton (Edinburgh, 1774), p. 108. Once it was established that learning did indeed give a virtuous dimension to the character of a man, recognition and social eminence would be fully justified, regardless of his formal occupation.

145. Spotswood, *History*, p. 160.

146. Wishart, *History*, pp. 46–7.

147. *ibid.*, p. 155.

148. *ibid.*, p. 173. Drummond of Balhaldy in the 1730s remained suitably impressed by this man's intellectual and, significantly, his oratorical skills. Even his enemies, like the Earl of Argyll, had recognised Spotswood as 'a subtile lawyer, and very learned and eloquent', and as a man 'capable to deduce his wicked maxims and dangerous principales in such an artfull and insinuating manner, as would be apt to fix the attention of the people, and to impose upon their understanding'. In short, of course, he was indisputably a 'great man', *Memoirs*, pp. 81–2.

149. Wishart, *History*, p. 173.

150. Monro, *Apology*, p. 31.
151. See e.g. *Scotch Presbyterian Eloquence*, p. 22.
152. Forrester, *Hierarchical Bishops*, p. 83.
153. Gordon, *Scots Affairs*, III, 243–4.
154. Erasmus had wished to introduce the educated laity to the performance of the moral and intellectual responsibilities hitherto reserved for the priests, e.g. *Colloquies*, p. 628.
155. Buchanan, *History*, p. 39. Of course, to one who had a much higher opinion of the 'Bards & Shenaichies', their historical and intellectual qualifications seemed on the contrary to justify their social eminence. Their task was 'to hand down to posterity the valorous actions, Conquests, battles, skirmishes', a function which they performed among Highland clansmen until the 'Printing of Hysterie' became 'more frequent', Campbell 'Genealogical Account', p. 190. Indeed, because of these oral annalists 'no people have their History so exactly keept by Tradition as the Highlanders', *ibid.*, p. 193.
156. Buchanan, *De Jure Regni*, p. 2.
157. *ibid.*, p. 2.
158. Watson, for example, praised his fellow publishers, who 'for the Glory of our Country ... have retrieved the Art of PRINTING', *The History of the Art of Printing* (Edinburgh, 1713), p. 6. For Watson, this took the form of gathering together and reprinting verse from the Scottish Renaissance, in *A Choice Collection of Comic and Serious Scots Poems Both Ancient and Modern*, 3 vols (Edinburgh, 1706–11). Buchanan, meanwhile, would doubtless have been gratified to hear that, in explaining the flowering of the Scottish Enlightenment nearly two centuries later, the Italian critic Carlo Denina praised Francis Hutcheson and the Duke of Argyll precisely for having been able to 'bring to maturity, in the cold regions of the north, what had heretofore been foolishly supposed incapable of taking root but in the warmer climes of ASIA MINOR, GREECE, and ITALY', *Essay*, p. 276.
159. Gordon, *Lives*, Book II, Dedication. Urquhart, too, had enjoined all the educated and professional classes of the Cromwellian period to abandon 'dishonesty, and disrespect of learning', as, quite simply, the 'negatives of vertue, and (at best) but the *ultimum non esse* of vice', as well as detrimental to the 'good fame' and 'positive integrity' of the nation, *Tracts*, pp. 48–9. See also Crauford, *History*, a3r, for similar views of national virility measured in terms of learning.
160. Hence, for example, the claim that if 'It is well known that the Scots made a greater figure abroad than any other nation in Europe .... 'tis entirely owing to the fineness of their education', MacUre, *View of Glasgow*, p. 277.
161. Richard Hay, *An Essay on the Origine of the Royal Family of the Stewarts* (Edinburgh, 1722), Dedication.
162. Tyler, *Memoires*, A5r–A5v.
163. Monro, *Monro His Expedition*, pp. 42–3.
164. Abercromby, *Martial Atchievements*, I, b1r. Cf. the anonymous claim in 1714 that 'The Scots Gentry so far exceed those of England so that in the one you shall find all the Accomplishments of well bred Gentlemen, and in your country, English Squires, all the Barbarity imaginable', [ ], *Memoirs of Scotland*, p. 175.
165. *ibid.*, I, b1r. Despite Abercromby's unreasonable vehemence, the occasional Scottish scholar was actually prepared to admit that an admirable historical subject had nevertheless been something less than a paragon of learned virtue. William Baird of Auchmedden, for example, conceded of Thomas Baird that 'he writes in his letters to his father that he was not of a hard "ingyne" as to learning, and incapable of any of the sciences'. But even so, and if the purely academic skills were beyond the ken of this unfortunate youth, the audience were still assured that 'he had an excellent turn to mechanics' and the practical arts, *Genealogical Collections Concerning the Sir-Name of Baird* (ed.), W. N. Fraser (London, 1870), p. 21. Originally composed in MS by Baird, an obscure but gifted Banffshire Jacobite born in 1701.
166. Scott's characterisation of Dugald Dalgetty, for example, famously modelled on Robert Monro who we have already seen to be adept both as a theoretician and an exponent of humanist scholarship, is highly illuminating in this respect. Though Dalgetty is at least permitted to introduce himself as 'a person of sense and prudence, one imbued with humane letters in his early youth', *Tales of My Landlord*, 3rd ser. (Edinburgh, 1819), p. 172, his inappropriate classical allusions and tiresome references to his education at 'Mareschal College of Aberdeen' are used to suggest an incorrigibly headstrong buffoon, thoroughly

steeped in gore, and given to vaguely humorous yet quite uncontrollable delusions of intellectual grandeur. Much work remains to be done to unravel the process by which the slippage of learning and erudition occurred from the popular image of the early modern Scotsman. But it seems likely that Scott's immense influence will once again prove to have been crucial.

167. This ubiquitous encomium used by Spotswood was significantly repeated in Nicolson, *Scottish Historical Library*, p. 99. It also, for example, provided the most natural eulogy on the Edinburgh civic authorities, for their 'encouraging all vertuous Actions and Learning', George Sinclair, *The Principles of Astronomy and Navigation* (Edinburgh, 1688), A2r, and in Shields's thunderous condemnation of those who controlled the schools and universities in order 'to poison the fountains of all learning & virtue', *Hind Let Loose*, p. 288.

168. James I of Scotland was to be legitimated retrospectively by historians who noted how he had been 'a great Encourager of Arts and Sciences', Anderson, *Collections*, p. xxvii, and one who 'advanced the Arts and Sciences … founding Schools and Seminaries of Learning at home', Stewart, *A Short Account*, p. 64. In short, as an anonymous Jacobean historian had it, James I 'was a gude, learned, vertuous, and just prince', *A Trewe Description of the Nobill Race of the Stewards* (Amsterdam, 1603), unpaginated.

169. That the Renaissance and Reformation were not only synchronous but intimately connected in Scotland's intellectual history was clear to early modern authors like Thomas Crauford, who observed in 1708 that 'God in his Mercy began to restore the Light of good Letters, together with the Light of the Gospel throughout Europe', *Notes and Observations*, p. 1.

170. Robert Baillie, *An Historical Vindication of the Government of the Church of Scotland* (London, 1646), A2r.

171. Ross, *Marrow of Historie*, A2r–A2v.

172. Furthermore, 'having Letters, he finds wherewith he can be made wiser … Therefore, we see, that science to a man of warre is a brave Mistresse, teaching him to doe all things as they did in old times', *Monro His Expedition*, II, 196.

173. *Hamlet*, II, ii, 327–8.

174. For his understanding of historical causality it is more than likely that Buchanan was indebted to the insistence of his French contemporaries upon the inclusion of causality in any meaningful historical account. Certainly, some of his own Scottish successors were familiar with Jean Bodin's *Six Books of the Republic* (1576), perhaps the most influential exposition of historical causality to emerge in the second half of the sixteenth century. Among Bodin's Scottish readers seem to have been Craig, *De Unione Regnorum*, p. 224; Godscroft, *History*, p. 418; and Rutherford, *Lex Rex*, p. 237.

175. A brooding awareness of external forces had been displayed, in a most influential way, by Guicciardini, who had observed 'all those calamities with which miserable mortals are usually afflicted', *History of Italy* (ed. and transl.), S. Alexander (New York, 1969), p. 3. A less pessimistic prognosis, but still retaining the passive mood with which the fate of mankind was often described in Scotland, was Boece's claim that prudence consisted in knowing 'weill al realmes and pepill sa thirlitt to mutabilite of fortoun', *Hystory*, fo. lxxxxv r(2).

176. Buchanan, *History*, p. 55.

177. *ibid.*, p. 94. Buchanan's deft negotiation between Fortune and Providence charts the necessary progress of a scholar who was by temperament and education a humanist, but by allegiance a loyal supporter of the Protestant and Jacobean parties to whom providentialism had acquired a precocious importance. Other late sixteenth-century historians, moreover, display the same equivocation between the Calvinist and the humanist vocabularies. The anonymous Gordon metrical history, for example, showed great terminological versatility: having just expatiated convincingly on 'the flood of God's admyred trueth … ', the poet almost immediately reverted to the humanist vision and embedded his narrative deep within the conflict between the Marquis of Huntly's 'noble heart' and his 'smoth slydeing fortune', in which 'the Godes' (significantly plural) lurk just off-stage, *Surgundo*, pp. 20–34. On the whole, however, and like Buchanan in the *History*, it was humanist Fortune which predominated at least until the second half of the seventeenth century.

178. Buchanan, *History*, Book XIII, p. 6. Conversely, and in an interpretation which was to remain in currency even during the Enlightenment, a loyal supporter of Mary Queen of Scots could explain her career precisely in terms of countervailing Fortune. She was a lady who, 'by the misffortunes of the time, and the rebellions of her wicked subjects, shall be involved in

a wordle of cares and tumults, till at length she should be splitt upon a rock, as the end of all her miseries', Herries, *Historical Memoirs*, p. 1. Likewise, her learned apologist Adam Blackwood in 1587 portrayed her wisdom and Stoic forbearance as so pitted against an unkind Fortune, as she 'so wiselie gowerned her selff befor, and so constantlie and patientlie suffered adversities', that she deserved even to receive the English crown, *History*, p. 101.

179.   To Guicciardini, for example, it was never enough simply to be virtuous. All one's best plans, wisdom, judgement and morality, would come to nought if 'one does not have similar good fortune on one's side', *History of Italy*, p. 57.

180.   Bellenden, 'Vertue and Vyce', p. 21.

181.   *ibid.*, p. 30.

182.   Gordon, *Famous History*, p. 1.

183.   *ibid.*, p. 3.

184.   *ibid.*, p. 10.

185.   *ibid.*, p. xii. The nineteenth-century editor of the anonymous MS chronicle of 1579 argues that its author had been a copyist of David Chambers ('Camerarius') and his French text known as *The History of Scotland, England, Germany, France, and the Papacy* (1557), itself in the relevant passages a gloss on Boece's history. Unsurprisingly, therefore, the author drops effortlessly into an appropriately humanist causal idiom, describing the Bruce as one who, 'be ressone of his ewill fortoune in the begining he wes left of all his freindis and subiectis', *Chronicle*, p. 64.

186.   Gordon, *Famous History*, p. 12.

187.   *ibid.*, p. 24.

188.   *ibid.*, p. 20.

189.   The characterisation of Fortune as a capricious but seductible woman was, of course, essential to Machiavelli's particularly permissive account of causality: 'I think it may be true', he considered, 'that Fortune governs half of our actions but that even so she leaves the other half more or less in our own power to control', *The Prince* (ed. and transl.), R. M. Adams (New York, 1970), p. 70. Fortune gave to men the Aristotelian 'material, on which they could impose whatever form they chose', *ibid.*, p. 17. Elsewhere, Machiavelli had considered that Fortune might indeed permit a man to shape his own destiny, for 'when it wants a man to take the lead in doing great things, it chooses a man of high spirits and great virtue who will seize the occasion it offers him', *Discourses* (ed. and transl.), B. Crick (Harmondsworth, 1970), p. 371. Buchanan likewise spoke of Fortune as 'an Handmaid', *History*, Book XIII, p. 6, again using femininity to suggest the latitude and pliability inherent in his vision of causality, as did the anonymous Jacobean metrical poet whose own affected difficulty in speaking was supposedly due to the fact that 'my fortoune's proude| To triumph over me, and to tirranisse,| Hir frounces constraines me for to temporisse', *Surgundo*, p. 2.

190.   Grahame, *Anatomie of Humors*, D3r.

191.   *ibid.*, A2v.

192.   Monipennie, *Scots Chronicles*, p. 121.

193.   Johnston, 'Historie', p. 370.

194.   *ibid.*, p. 404. The observation that 'the highest shall become the lowest' informed many humanist ruminations on the burning issue of mutability, and Scottish historical discourse inherited its vocabulary, as in Sir Robert Gordon's evocation of 'fortune's ficklenes, turning upsyd down whatsoever seemeth high in this world', *Genealogical History*, p. 178. As a humanist motif, it had been central to several writers, including Castiglione, who saw Fortune as 'burying in the depths those most worthy of being exalted', *Book of the Courtier* (ed. and transl.), C. S. Singleton (New York, 1959), p. 120.

195.   Johnston, 'Historie', p. 377.

196.   *ibid.*, p. 379.

197.   Godscroft, *History*, p. 215. Such calm acceptance of unkind Fortune could also itself assume a virtuous dimension, as in Mary Stuart, 'A princess of many virtues, but still crossed with the frowns of Fortune, which she bore with great courage and magnanimity to the last', George Crawfurd, *The History of the Shire of Renfrew* (ed.), W. Semple (Paisley, 1782), p. 59. This recapitulates her encomium in Spotswood, *History*, p. 357. See also Herries, *Historical Memoirs*, p. 1.

198.   Balfour, *Works*, I, 121. Similarly, to the self-effacing Gordon poet it was his own 'belaboured braine' with which he struggled in vain to beg 'a smylle from fortoune ... ', *Surgundo*, p. 2.

The notion that virtue overcame Fortune was equally familiar to the anonymous genealogist who in 1695 saw Patrick Lesley of Kincragie as 'a vertuous and frugall Gentleman', a man 'with a very small & broken fortune' who with 'industrie & virtue hath recovered it', *The Genealogie of the Surname of Lesley* (Aberdeen, University Library, MS 2201), p. 47. 'Fortune' and 'industrie' here, of course, begin to acquire their typically modern commercial nuances.

199. Maitland, *History*, p. 87.
200. Ross, *History*, a3r.
201. Lindsay, *History*, p. iv.
202. Cicero, the leading example in most Scottish minds, insisted that, despite misfortunes, 'the active life is of the highest merit', *De officiis*, I, 6, and thus avoided the necessitarian fatalism of some of his Stoic colleagues. Likewise, more recently, Sir Thomas More had advocated a realistic and pragmatic attitude towards those things which were beyond human foreknowledge or control: 'You wouldn't abandon ship in a storm just because you couldn't control the winds', he chided: *Utopia* (ed. and transl.), P. Turner (Harmondsworth, 1965), p. 63.
203. James VI, *Basilikon Doron*, p. 61.
204. *ibid.*, p. 61. James, at least in the eyes of his supporters, was himself intellectually and morally equipped to challenge Fortune. He was a man, claimed the Gordon poet, 'Whose holines, whose pius sanctitie,| Whose wertue and whose learning did agrie ... ', *Surgundo*, p. 45.
205. Monro, *Monro His Expedition*, II, 36. Again, Monro stressed that it was his 'delight' to 'try the Conclusions of Fortune against his enemies; forcing Fortune to make him her Favourite, and sometimes her Master', *ibid.*, II, 130. As a daring and battle-scarred veteran of the Continental wars, Monro was seemingly at home in this most Machiavellian of idioms, shot through, once again, with the tell-tale images of femininity and amorousness which so often characterised a permissive and opportunistic humanist causality.
206. Melville, *Memoires*, b2r.
207. *ibid.*, b2r.
208. Urquhart, *Tracts*, p. 113.
209. Drummond, *History*, p. 253.
210. *ibid.*, p. 188.
211. That Stoicism was a vivacious and accessible discourse, well able to flourish in seventeenth-century Scotland, was much owing to the intellectual influence it had enjoyed since the English Renaissance. See J. H. M. Salmon, 'Stoicism and Roman Example: Seneca and Tacitus in Jacobean England', *Journal of the History of Ideas*, 50 (1989), 199–225. A later Scottish example would be Robert Ferguson who was in 1673 clearly an avowed admirer of 'the Stoiks who of all the Philosophers were the most renowned Moralists', *Sober Inquiry*, p. 231. Mark Goldie paints a picture of Ferguson's radical circle in 'The Roots of True Whiggism, 1688–1694', *History of Political Thought*, 2 (1980), 192–236.
212. Ross, *History*, p. 647. An allusion to *Prov.* 30: 4, interesting not least because, with consequences in Scotland that we shall later see, divine determinism was here located specifically in the context of a biblical admission of intellectual weakness: 'And I have not learned wisdom. Neither have I the knowledge of the Holy One ... '.
213. *ibid.*, p. 465.
214. Ross, *Mystagogus Pedagogus*, p. 94. That Stoic retiredness was by the 1640s in Scotland an attractive proposition for an episcopalian but an indication of moral weakness in presbyterian eyes is arguably confirmed by Gordon of Rothiemay's earnest though unconvincing defence of Dr William Lesley, an Aberdonian academic deposed by the Covenanters. He was apparently 'a man of great reading, a painefull student', Gordon pleaded, 'who delyted in nothing else but to sitte in his studye, and spend dayes and nights at his booke, which kynd of lyfe is opposite to a practicall way of living'. Lesley's Stoic passivity made him hard to defend, and Gordon admitted as much when he expressed his own regret that Lesley had not left 'mor behynde him of his learned workes' and 'could scarce ever be gottne drawne for to speacke in publicke'. Gordon concluded by claiming that it was simply Lesley's moral humility, his 'naturall bashfullnesse', which had led him to his awkward and widely condemned solitude, *Scots Affairs*, III, 231.
215. *ibid.*, p. 94.
216. *ibid.*, p. 97.

217. See for example the bucolic retreat described in 'Lycidas', in *Milton: Poetical Works* (ed.), D. Bush (Oxford, 1979), pp. 142–7.

218. 'If by Fortune here is understood that blinde Idol of the Gentiles, then to asscribe the effects of Virtue to Fortune, is not so much malice as madness: for such a Fortune is nothing. But if, with wise men, wee mean by Fortune God's Providence, then to asscribe the effects of virtue to Fortune, is not malice but wisdom', Alexander Ross, *Som Animadversions and Observations upon Sir Walter Raleigh's Historie of the World* (London, 1648), p. 39. Explicitly adopting Sallust's frank admission that '*In omnia re dominatur Fortuna*', Ross confirmed the essentially Stoical character of his providential determinism.

219. In defending his clearly vulnerable proclivity for seclusion, Ross in 1652 used the classic argument of the Stoic recluse: 'I have been content hitherto, rather to converse in the *Stoicall* School of *Zeno*', he bashfully admitted, 'then in the *voluptuous Garden of Epicurus*', *History*, a3v. Simione Grahame had earlier made clear his own identical commitments: 'I hate this miserable sect of *Epicurians*', he railed, 'who onely loves to eate, sleepe, and drinke', *Anatomie of Humors*, F1r. Stoicism evidently was an obvious and attractive alternative.

220. The *Moral Essay* has recently been reprinted in facsimile in B. Vickers, (ed.), *Public and Private Life in the Seventeenth Century: The Mackenzie-Evelyn Debate* (New York, 1986), and located within the classical and Renaissance convention of academic argument exemplified by Cicero's *Paradoxa Stoicorum*.

221. Sir George Mackenzie of Rosehaugh, *A Moral Essay Preferring Solitude to Publick Employment* (London, 1685), p. 107. Originally published at Edinburgh in 1665.

222. *ibid.*, p. 36. An earlier Scottish observer, who had not, however, drawn the same solipsistic conclusion, was nevertheless only too aware of the especial dangers facing those in positions of leadership: 'Be examples we may learne', remarked John Colville, 'how that tyme in short space dois exalt men to digneteis and honors, and at another season dryvis thayme to extreme calamitie and miserie, and speciallie thais that huntis the courties of Prencis', 'Historie', p. 252. Time, in this instance, was synonymous with the harsh Stoic version of Fortune. Like many Jacobean propagandists, Colville was also caught up in the ideological apocalypticism of his milieu, hence perhaps his precocious historical providentialism: 'God, wha, be his eternall providence, dois governe bayth the hewin and the earth', he proclaimed, *ibid.*, p. 249.

223. Mackenzie of Rosehaugh, *Moral Essay*, p. 39.

224. *ibid.*, p. 39.

225. Mackenzie of Rosehaugh, *Moral History*, pp. 71–2.

226. Sir George Mackenzie of Rosehaugh, *A Moral Paradox: Maintaining, That it is Much Easier to be Virtuous than Vicious* (London, 1669), p. 80. Here, his Stoicism may have led him to use the term 'Fortune' rather than 'Providence', but the deterministic implication remains the same. As the philosopher is satisfied by good thoughts rather than material success or physical influence, he is the best equipped to achieve happiness in a fatalistic scheme.

227. Sir George Mackenzie of Rosehaugh, *Religio Stoici* (Edinburgh, 1665), p. 12.

228. As Thomas Sloane remarks, the '*vita contemplativa* veered inexorably towards stoicism, and the stoics were on the whole, too rational, too denying of body and flesh for most humanists'. But they '*did* place a premium on man's sufficiency, whereas the Augustinians constantly insisted on man's dependence upon God – a quality that would force most humanists, given the choice, to veer back towards the stoics again', *Donne, Milton*, p. 88. Scottish humanists thus had a complex relationship with Stoicism, mistrustful of its passivity and its disturbing proclivity for private meditation, yet drawn instinctively to its humane flavour and rational virtues in ultimate preference to dogmatic Christian accounts of determinism.

229. Erigena, who had argued that 'Predestination hath no Place', was considered by Mackenzie to have been the perpetrator of notions which were 'Extravagant and Whimsical', *Lives and Characters*, I, 49–58. Yet Calvin, too, on the other hand, offered a deterministic doctrine of '*Predestination, Election*, and *Reprobation*', as well as an argument for civil disobedience, which Mackenzie implied had justly been 'rejected by most of the *Protestant* Churches', *ibid.*, II, 459. Stoicism, as Mackenzie's approving references to Sallust confirm, would have provided a congenial solution to a classic conundrum, though one which inevitably drew fire from both Calvinists and humanists. In the case of his namesake Mackenzie of Rosehaugh, moreover, Stoicism may also have been the philosophy intuitively appealing to a scholar whose *Institutions of the Law of Scotland* (Edinburgh, 1684) stood firmly in the grand

tradition of natural jurisprudence, which itself drew heavily upon the central Stoic concepts of law, reason and nature.

230. Burnet, *Historie*, I, 81. Indeed, Burnet's view of a man's 'ballast' is redolent of Drummond's eulogy on the Earl of Traquair, which we have already discussed, *History*, p. 253.

231. Burnet, *Historie*, I, 409.

232. *ibid.*, II, 234.

233. Another example, from 1705, is James Anderson's vision of 'the various Turns of Fortune in a long and bloody War', *Historical Essay*, p. 251. In 1693, moreover, an anonymous episcopalian author had showered praise upon one who had 'by extraordinary Management, put your self beyond the greatest Reach and Malice of Fortune', [Crockat?], *Scotch Presbyterian Eloquence*, A2v, an invocation of virtuous capacity and countervailing malevolent destiny clearly rooted in a vestigial humanist causality.

234. Crauford, for example, listed the achievements of writers from Boece to Spotswood, but lamented that, in 1681, the divines, who had been so productive, 'are here so unhappily distracted by the divisions now on foot, that they have no heart to undertake or advance any considerable design in learning', *History*, B4r–a1v. More notoriously, Boswell records how, when journeying by sea from Ulinish to Talisker in the autumn of 1773, Dr Johnson had railed against the Scots, saying that 'they had been a very learned nation for a hundred years, from about 1550 to about 1650; but that they afforded the only instance of a people among whom the arts of civil life did not advance in proportion with learning', James Boswell, *The Journal of a Tour to the Hebrides* (ed.), P. Levi (Harmondsworth, 1984), p. 308. This perception even survived into the historiography into the present century, with the claim that 'Scots letters had a glorious period .... which began when James I returned from his English prison ... [and] did not cease till Drummond of Hawthorne-Glen died – the last Scots writing man before civil war and religious bitterness and cruel poverty made an end of letters and art', J. Watson, *The Scot of the Eighteenth Century* (London, 1907), p. 319.

235. John Knox, 'An Answer to the Cavillations of an Adversary Respecting the Doctrine of Predestination', *Works*, 5 vols (ed.), D. Laing (Edinburgh, 1856), V, 25.

236. *ibid.*, V, 26.

237. *ibid.*, V, 28.

238. *ibid.*, V, 32. It is interesting to speculate as to whether this Scottish discussion of the relative merits of free will and predestination after the Reformation merely echoed an earlier debate in Scotland. This is certainly a possibility suggested in A. Broadie, 'William Manderston and Patrick Hamilton', *Innes Review*, 37, (1986), 25–35.

239. Knox, 'Predestination', V, 32.

240. *ibid.*, V, 34. Intriguingly, and though I have suggested that Alexander Ross was something of a Stoic, he was no more keen than Knox or Drummond would have been to admit to it. He observed, indeed, that the Stoics had been incorrect in having 'fastned to Fate an inevitable necessitie, and give it the power over the minde and will of man: of which *Ovid* and *Juvenal*': *Marrow of Historie*, p. 9.

241. Montesquieu, *The Spirit of the Laws*, 2 vols (ed. and transl.), T. Nugent (Aberdeen, 1756), I, 1–2.

242. Knox, 'Predestination', V, 98–9.

243. Of the intimate relationship between predestination and a providential history, it has been observed that 'Knox's doctrine of absolute providence demanded that he maintain a philosophy of history in which the hand of God intervened in all events', Kyle, 'Divine Providence', p. 403. This was a relationship which the ecclesiastical histories of the seventeenth century also illustrated.

244. Petrie, *Compendious History*, p. 352.

245. Shields, *Hind Let Loose*, p. 330.

246. *ibid.*, p. 2.

247. Row, *History*, pp. 106–7. As his son reminds us, Row was 'a great observer of the passages of providence in his tyme', a major activity for the dogmatic Calvinist seeking to explain historical events, *ibid.*, p. 479.

248. Robert Burns, *Poetical Works* (ed.), J. L. Robertson, (London, 1963), pp. 86–9.

249. James Hogg, *Private Memoirs and Confessions of a Justified Sinner* (ed.), J. Casey (Oxford, 1981). Originally published in 1824.

250. In Calvinist America, indeed, the notion that 'secularization' and the 'de-divinization of the

universe' were underway before 1700, and intensified after that date, has been powerfully challenged in studies such as J. F. Berens, *Providence and Patriotism in Early America, 1640–1815* (Charlottesville, Va., 1978), an explicit rejoinder to Peter Gay and the 'pagan' model of the American Enlightenment. Berens argues convincingly that American identity and historical consciousness were powerfully influenced by providentialism in a seventeenth-century world increasingly dominated – as Scotland – by war and revolution.

251. See C. M. Shepherd, 'Newtonianism in Scottish Universities in the Seventeenth Century', in Campbell and Skinner (eds), *Origins and Nature of the Scottish Enlightenment*, pp. 65–85. Also Emerson, 'Natural Philosophy', which traces the important connections between the Calvinist search for 'innumerable proofs' of God's Will and the first dawn of scientific determinism in Scotland.

252. See J. C. D. Clark, *English Society, 1688–1832: Ideology, Social Structure, and Political Practice During the Ancien Regime* (Cambridge, 1985), esp. pp. 173–9.

253. Godscroft, *History*, p. 322.

254. Ross, *Mystagogus Pedagogus*, p. 125.

255. Mackenzie of Rosehaugh, *Religio Stoici*, p. 35.

256. Keith, *History*, p. 477.

257. It seems, for example, surprisingly ill-judged to claim that 'In historical writing it became increasingly unfashionable after the mid seventeenth century to explain events in terms of God's providence', K. Thomas, *Religion and the Decline of Magic*, 2nd issue (Harmondsworth, 1978), p. 127.

258. It is possible, however, that Abercromby, as the subtle proponent of a Jacobite rebellion, was entertaining 'revolution principles' for his own very different ends. But, at the same time, Providence still, of course, offered an attractive account of a hierarchical social structure to which Jacobite conservatives would also have been instinctively drawn. See J. Viner, *The Role of Providence in the Social Order* (Philadelphia, 1972), esp. pp. 95–113.

259. Abercromby, *Martial Atchievements*, I, 56. Another later seventeenth-century historian also observed how 'The Hand of Heaven ... cast the empire of the best part of the known World into the lap of the *Romans*', Sir James Turner, *Pallas Armata: Military Essayes of the Ancient Grecian, Roman, and Modern Art of War* (London, 1683), p. 33.

260. Abercromby, *Martial Atchievements*, I, 57.

261. *ibid.*, I, 339.

262. John Spurr argues that providentialism was useful to Restoration Anglicans both in the defence and in the strident criticism of the restored Caroline monarchy, as well as in a commentary on English public morality in general. See '"Virtue, Religion, and Government": the Anglican Uses of Providence', in T. Harris, P. Seaward and M. Goldie (eds), *The Politics of Religion in Restoration England* (Oxford, 1990), pp. 29–47.

263. For example, Henry VIII 'was a great Instrument in the Hands of Providence for many good Ends'. Burnet, *Historie*, III, 173. Of course, Henry, putative champion both of Protestant reformism and of honest Tudor government, seemed a providential character in either a Whig or a presbyterian analysis.

264. *ibid.*, II, b2r.

265. Paterson, *Enquiry*, p. 126.

266. Paterson, *Enquiry*, p. 126.

267. *ibid.*, p. 126.

268. *ibid.*, p. 22.

269. *ibid.*, p. 127.

270. M. G. Finlayson, 'Clarendon, Providence, and the Historical Revolution', *Albion*, 22 (1990), esp. 622. As Finlayson suggests, if one thing is more striking than the providentialism which suffuses Clarendon's definitive *History of the Rebellion* it is the breathtaking unpreparedness of some modern scholars to recognise it.

271. Wallace, *Description*, p. 40.

272. Rae, *History*, p. 249.

273. Robert Wodrow, *Analecta: or, Materials for a History of Remarkable Providences; Mostly Relating to Scotch Ministers and Christians*, 4 vols (Edinburgh, 1842), III, 474.

274. *ibid.*, II, 301–2. On the wider use of such arguments see J. Garrett, *The Triumphs of Providence: The Assassination Plot, 1696* (Cambridge, 1980).

275. Fleming, *Fulfilling of the Scripture*, a7v–a8r.

276. *ibid.*, p. 151. This scenario, derivative of *Matt.* 10:30, reflects a recurrent notion in Scottish Calvinist theology, that of the *physicus concersus*, which asserted that the essence of God energised and directed each and every action in Creation, including the most apparently trivial. For a discussion of this doctrine, see J. Walker, *The Theology and Theologians of Scotland*, 1560–1750 (Edinburgh, 1982), p. 55. Originally published in 1872, and, incidentally, another excellent example of the still-influential Victorian view that Enlightenment Moderatism represented an unhealthy and secularising condition in the presbyterian body politic.
277. Dalrymple, *Collections*, A2v.
278. Cromarty, *Historical Account*, p. 128.
279. Mackenzie of Rosehaugh, *Religio Stoici*, p. 30.

PART TWO

The Enlightenment in Scotland
1740–1800

CHAPTER THREE

Enlightened Identity and the Rhetoric of Intention

T HAT THERE WAS a considerable tradition of historical scholarship in Scotland from the Reformation to the early eighteenth century we have now established beyond reasonable dispute. We have identified the common assumptions which supported it and, most importantly perhaps, the cultural values by which its development was both conditioned and legitimated. As a result we find ourselves in a strong position to offer an account of Scottish Enlightenment discourse in a longer intellectual perspective. The main business of this chapter will be to examine in particular those points at which enlightened scholarship is commonly thought to have deviated from the prior tradition in Scotland. In effect, we shall be trying to rethink the relationship which Scottish Enlightenment scholarship bore to its immediate native predecessor. This will involve us in three related inquiries. The first will consider the claims of enlightened scholars and their later acolytes that they were truly the harbingers of an intellectual revolution. We will see that the case for acknowledging a methodological transformation of historical writing in Scotland is weakened both by a comparison with earlier Scottish scholarship and by the rigorous criticism to which it was in fact subjected by eighteenth-century scholars themselves. It will even be argued that some enlightened authors questioned the dubious credentials of this revolution. Not a few, I will suggest, retained a keen interest in earlier Scottish scholarship, seeking to defend its central assumptions and premises against the critical onslaught of the more vociferous modernists. Our next aim will then be to readjust the narrow thematic focus in which previous students have often tended to conceive the Scottish Enlightenment achievement. I shall argue here that the eighteenth century gave rise to a historical movement which was both much larger and in some ways less innovative than has usually been recognised. Important developments, associated with economic progress, political stability, and religious tolerance, certainly tended to distinguish enlightened scholarship from what had gone before. But I will suggest that historical writing in Scotland also continued to display a degree of polemical commitment and a concern for crucial traditional interests which, on the whole, limited the extent of innovation. Thirdly and finally, we shall examine how Scottish scholars now chose to articulate their own moral and social purpose as historians. It will emerge that, in spite of the condemnation of earlier exponents meted out by enlightened self-publicists, the Calvinist and humanist rhetoric of intention positively prospered in Scotland during the period of the Enlightenment. This continuity of self-conscious purpose, I shall argue, urges above all that we reassess the traditional image of eighteenth-century Scottish historical scholarship. Only then, of course, would we be in a position to appreciate the prodigious intellectual legacy of the Scottish past. Only then, too, could we begin to understand what actually happened to the historical discourse of Calvinism and humanism as it finally helped create Scotland's enlightened age.

I: ENLIGHTENED IDENTITY AND THE PLACE OF THE PAST

In the years after 1740 the Scottish tradition of historical writing experienced an expansion quite unparalleled in its long and turbulent history. Noticeably, the volume of scholarship and the much larger number of contributors began to attract wider recognition, in precisely the way in which most sixteenth- and seventeenth-century Scottish authors had failed to do. The least meticulous inspection of a typical library catalogue tells us just how right was the Edinburgh schoolmaster John Lawrie in 1783 to refer to 'this learned age, when men almost of all professions are seized with the cacoethes scribendi'.[1] Likewise, it seemed to Donald MacNicol, minister and polemical opponent of Dr Samuel Johnson, that the Scottish 'learned professions' had indeed transformed the intellectual landscape: in particular, he claimed in 1779, 'The province of history, is, in a manner, yielded up to them'.[2] As these lavish tributes suggest, however, there was a striking corollary of this tangible expansion of historical scholarship. This was the considerable increase in the traditional propensity of Scottish historians for reflecting upon and evaluating the state of their own discipline. What the historians' commentary was now helping to construct, it seems, was nothing less than an enlightened identity. This involved a dissociation from the intellectual past and an elevation of the present. It also relied strongly upon the widely held belief that Scottish historical scholarship was in the forefront of a truly revolutionary and 'enlightened age'.[3] In reassessing the assumption that an Enlightenment divided the scholarship of Hume and Robertson in some fundamental respect from that of their Scottish predecessors, therefore, we clearly need to begin by finding the way in which it was alleged that previous historical scholarship in Scotland had been both different and inferior. It should then be possible to consider the origin of these charges, to examine the devious ways in which they were frequently supported, and ultimately to consider whether any contradictory or conflicting views might also have been offered. Such an approach might allow us with confidence to evaluate the suggestion, both of enlightened scholars and their later admirers, that eighteenth-century scholarship actually carried through a conscious and sharp break with the ideas, interests and assumptions of the Scottish past.

Certain enlightened commentators, of course, were happy to concentrate attention merely upon the manifestly greater popularity of historical scholarship by the middle of the eighteenth century. The editor Walter Ruddiman, for example, remarked in 1754 that histories had only recently become popular in Scotland, 'the curiosity of inquiring into past events not having become, till of late years, so universal'.[4] The Enlightenment, in other words, was a heady brew comprising a quart of greater scholarly productivity and several pints of unrestrained public enthusiasm. Others, however, among them the idiosyncratic John Pinkerton, were prepared at times to launch the most blistering qualitative attacks upon earlier Scottish scholarship. Pinkerton in particular focused upon the actual area in which recent improvements were thought to have been made. Pinkerton declared himself 'Struck with the deplorable state of the ancient history of his country'.[5] Shame was in his view the only appropriate response to the previous historical canon. It had been, his *History of Scotland* luridly claimed, 'for five centuries, a field of the blackest forgery, falsification, and perversion of all authorities'.[6] Pinkerton was in truth probably less willing than most to swallow whole the suggestion that things had recently improved. But it is clear at least that he was concerned essentially with the question of methodology, a matter for discussion to which other contemporaries also often devoted themselves. William Maitland, for example, was the strident author of the *History and Antiquities of Scotland* (1757). Maitland, moreover, was no less convinced than Pinkerton that it was the methodological differences in particular which allowed one accurately to distinguish an earlier and inferior Scottish scholarship from the more polished efforts of an enlightened age. Earlier work, he suggested, had been richly deserving of 'the despicable and infamous epithets of fable and falshood, which has justly made us the mock of our neighbours'.[7] Alongside Adam Ferguson's aloof rejection of earlier scholarship as 'the mere conjectures or fictions of subsequent ages', then, there were others equally concerned to develop methodological argument against older work. This polemic sought to establish the credentials of an 'enlightened' modern scholarship by condemning decisively the errors and falsehoods of the past.[8] Lord Hailes's notoriously disparaging description of earlier work as 'trash', and William Guthrie's high-handedness towards work which he thought 'lame and often fabulous', are simply further examples of this approach.[9] Such claims effectively distanced modern scholars from the putative intellectual bankruptcy of their ancestors as they tried to raise the reputation of Scottish letters to unprecedented heights.

Two things, however, emerge from what we have so far heard from this deafening chorus of self-congratulation. First, the retrospective scholarly criticism which sustained Enlightenment confidence in its own unique achievements was focused very much upon the orthodox question of previous scholarly methodology. This, indeed, was something to which a host of earlier Scottish authors, as we know, had made no less hostile reference. Before even the professed scepticism of Thomas Innes for a 'history stuffed with fables', there was for example James Anderson's ostentatious contempt for scholarship which seemed 'overgrown with Legends and Miracles and Visions ... and larded

with many Romantick Fables', and George Buchanan's stock humanist rejection
of that 'mixture of vain Fables' which he found in the works of his major
rivals.[10] Secondly, we need to notice the nature of the inspiration for
'enlightened' modernity in historical scholarship. It was this, after all, which
promised an end to what the scholar-physician William Alexander patronisingly
termed 'the gloom of ignorance which had for ages enveloped the human
mind'.[11] This confidence in short seems to have derived, above all else, from a
methodological comparison with contemporary science and philosophy. But the
reliance of the Enlightenment upon such an over-worked and deeply vulnerable
allusion to science and philosophy equally renders its participants open, at very
best, to the charge of self-delusion. This is a state of affairs which obviously
demands closer inspection. In the first instance, the modern scholar would do
well to note the origins of the rhetoric of experimental science and methodological innovation. This was something to which many eighteenth-century
Scotsmen were patently addicted. But it had in fact been almost as much a
commonplace of early modern scholarly literature as the oratorical posturing
and moralistic utterances with which we are already so familiar.

In seeking to endow humane scholarship with the laurels won for natural
science by Bacon and Newton, for example, authors like Hume, and even Walter
Anderson, were simply following a convention to which numerous seventeenth-
century scholars had also freely subscribed.[12] Thomas Hobbes, for example, had
set out boldly to reconstruct what he termed 'civil science': the tract *De Cive*
explicitly acknowledged the intellectual debts the political scientist owed to the
inspiration of Euclidean geometry.[13] For Descartes, meanwhile, it had equally
been 'the demonstrations of the geometers' which had led the philosopher to
look afresh and with new self-assurance at the principles of human knowledge.[14]
Now Scottish historians saw in the techniques of experimental science a means
to revolutionising their own discipline. The advocate James Grant was one,
suggesting in *The Origin of the Gael* that historical truth was now 'to be
ascertained by facts and experiment alone'.[15] George Turnbull, too, saw truths
emerging 'from Facts ascertained by observation, and not from abstract,
imaginary Theories and Hypotheses'.[16] Yet their scholarship in both cases
continued to conform to the traditional narrative conventions. It blended
evidence from a variety of documentary and other sources, as well as a measure
of speculative inference. It managed to produce a subjective and highly
questionable commentary which still drew the fire of unconvinced contemporaries like Thomas Somerville.[17] The dubious shades of orthodox documentary
scholarship, it seems, very often merely skulked behind the more fashionable
façades of science and philosophy. Ostentatious empiricism and the uncritical
idealisation of mathematical and Newtonian science did little, in reality, to
improve the majority of Scottish scholarship.

Other aspects of the methodological critique, moreover, lose something of
their revolutionary credibility when subjected to comparison with earlier and
wider Scottish thought. The possibility that enlightened scholarship had

suddenly grasped the potential value of historical 'experience' because of a novel analogy with the scientifc 'experiment' is revealed as particularly remote. One finds, for example, the Edinburgh professor Alexander Tytler in 1782 pronouncing history a discipline which 'adds to our own an immense treasure of the experience of others'.[18] Here, however, one should be reminded directly of the similar figurative flourishes of earlier Scottish humanists. Experience, in particular, had been apostrophised in Scotland from an early date. From Alexander Monro, for example, had come the view that history 'might furnish us with very many sad Experiments'.[19] Even earlier, in 1681, and in the vehement Calvinism of the elder Robert Fleming, were to be found the most eloquent apostrophes directed to the virtues of historical experience. 'O what an empty thing should Religion be if it had not this word experience in its grammar', he wrote: experience was 'that secret and sure mark whereby the Christian knoweth the Scripture is of God, how thus the Lord hath oft sealed their instruction in a dark plunge'.[20] The 'enlightened' notion of experience, then, was both historical and conventional. In any case, it clearly provided David Hume with an audience and a reading public already fully alerted to the unique value of experience in polemical use. Hume, indeed, demonstrated his own entirely conventional understanding of historical 'experience' by observing in the manner of Alexander Ross how it 'extends our Experience to all past Ages, and to the most distant Nations', without which truly 'we should be for ever Children in Understanding'.[21] Historical experience was in this way a storehouse of examples revered by most earlier Scottish scholars. Historical evidence was at the same time more vigorously to be imported into a novel Scottish exploration of mental philosophy. But a philosophical method was not, as its enthusiasts are sometimes thought to have implied, being systematically and innovatively applied to history. Philosophy and science, as for Hobbes and Descartes, were simply re-emphasising to Scottish scholars the particular value of 'experience'. We are right to feel that we are in essence dealing with a sense of modernity which relied fundamentally upon an allusion to science and philosophy. But as such, it is one which can only be regarded with suspicion. Accordingly we might also now reconsider what the same enlightened commentators and self-publicists were actually doing when they advertised their commitment to the philosophical 'conjecture'. This was, after all, the particular device upon which their largely unquestioned reputation as methodological revolutionaries has in recent times most depended.

Much, of course, has been written about the Scottish Enlightenment conversion to the use of the 'conjecture' in historical scholarship.[22] It is unlikely that even the wily Dugald Stewart, whose retrospective and highly tendentious assessment of the enlightened intellect has all too often been accepted as definitive, intended to sow the seeds of quite such confusion when he claimed that the Scottish historians of primitive society had been 'under the necessity of supplying the place of fact by conjecture'.[23] Here, as much as anywhere else, there has been a tendency to ascribe meaning to a historical rhetoric on the basis of the utterances of the smallest constituency of Enlightenment authors. Unsurprisingly this has led to a misunderstanding of the role actually played by 'conjecture' in Scottish historical thought. Reference, I would argue, needs to be made again to the wider community of Scottish scholars addressing the question. This evidence in fact suggests that the 'conjecture' was regarded with a considerable degree of ambivalence during the eighteenth century. This reaction, of course, was natural enough in view of the apparent derivation of the 'conjecture', once more, from the dubious though fashionable analogy with philosophy and science. James Grant, for example, writing as late as 1814, considered that 'Conjecture, hypothesis, and speculative opinions, however plausible and ingenious', ought simply to be 'rejected as unwary guides, ever liable to delusion and error'.[24] Similarly, John Lanne Buchanan, in criticising Pinkerton for his primitivist researches, concluded that he was 'not singular in his conjecture... he only joins [previous scholars] in their mistake'.[25] The Advocates' librarian and bibulous Jacobite Walter Goodall observed the same fault in contemporary as well as in prior Scottish scholarship. He found himself lamenting with regard to Pictish matters that 'the conjectures of most authors, ancient and modern ... are vague and unsatisfactory'.[26] Many scholars active in eighteenth-century Scotland, then, clearly recognised that the 'conjecture' was the continuation of an earlier and equally questionable historical technique. But they also feared the use of what Gilbert Stuart termed 'their glosses and conjectures'.[27] These, we know, were increasingly being justified in an enlightened idiom by a specious comparison with the parallel achievements of philosophy and science, a trend with which some contemporaries profoundly disagreed. Robert Heron, for example, the celebrated debtor, miscellaneous writer, and sometime assistant to Hugh Blair, was to be found urging his Scottish colleagues in 1794 to admit their ignorance rather than feign a sophistical understanding of history based on rash speculation: 'let us rather confess this uncertainty' pleaded his *New General History*, 'than fondly embrace conjecture for historical truth'.[28] Even more concerned by the dangerous and self-deluding attractions of the philosophical allusion was John Pinkerton. As always he was only too willing to offer blunt advice to his contemporaries: 'If we trust conjecture, or philosophical nonsense', he revealingly warned, 'there is no end'.[29] Consequently, it would be foolish to think that the 'conjecture' received an uncritical acceptance in enlightened Scotland.[30] It would, moreover, be unwise to dismiss these comments as irrelevant to an assessment of the use of inference and speculative comparison by prominent authors like Hume and Ferguson. Their critics clearly insinuated that this unfounded but popular allusion to the philosophical method was responsible for the potential demise of a straightforwardly factual and unimpeachable moral history. In this way contemporaries pointed directly to the dubious character of Dugald Stewart's later claim that historical scholarship in Scotland had itself acquired a revolutionary new basis during the eighteenth century.

Even some of those Scotsmen prepared to entertain the seductive notion that history might indeed embrace the empirical techniques of science and philosophy were forced to admit the severe limitations of their enterprise. 'Fanciful conjectures and ingenious hypotheses', conceded George Wallace, 'ought always to yield to express testimony and to authentic facts'.[31] Slightly less reserved was William Borthwick, a diligent and progressive Midlothian scholar. His *Remarks on British Antiquities* (1776) took it 'for granted, that, in a question which cannot be proved by legal authority, probabilities and conjectures may be used'.[32] Yet Borthwick's admission only confirms the critics' wounding accusation. The 'conjecture' was itself a traditional device, and one rehabilitated only by a perilous borrowing from the language of contemporary philosophical and scientific method. Indeed, the defence of the 'conjecture', when it was undertaken by enlightened Scotsmen, was frequently conducted in these same limited terms. Borthwick was not alone in thinking that a calculation of probabilities was justified in the absence of extant evidence: Lord Kames and William Robertson, for example, were prominent among those who addressed themselves directly to the justification of the specifically 'probable conjecture'.[33] Such optimistic pronouncements from historians perhaps consciously echoed David Hume's recent *Treatise* (1740). This had contained persuasive arguments for 'PROBABILITY or reasoning from conjecture', a technique closely related to the epistemological process of conjunction by which discrete ideas were thought to be 'associated' or 'conjoined' and then assessed according to the probabilities suggested by custom and experience.[34] A direct philosophical analogy thus offered to legitimise those historical flights of speculative fancy which, on balance, seemed both reasonable and probable. This was surely the happy situation which led the fertile imagination of John Pinkerton to claim that the conventional ac-cumulation of historical evidence was itself a process in which 'a thousand little facts must be conjoined; a thousand falsehoods exploded'.[35] Yet in locating the defence of the 'conjecture' in its Scottish context one might equally recall arguments drawn from the earlier tradition. These speak eloquently of the advantages and disadvantages to be gained from the use of this most difficult of devices.

One example might be Robert Fleming, who had set out his intention in 1701 'to conjecture, with some just grounds of probability'.[36] A second could be Thomas Innes, whose *Critical Essay* proclaimed its author's willingness to employ the 'probable conjecture' in primitivist studies.[37] But the possible first Scottish intimations of this discussion go back much further. Perhaps amongst the earliest Scottish critics of the device was Adam Blackwood, Buchanan's opponent. Blackwood had thought the humanist's 'coniectures ar so colde, that I am amazed howe the inventor of them durste digresse from reason ... .'.[38] Later Mackenzie of Rosehaugh, too, had questioned men's capacity 'by conjecture to fall upon that medium by which providence intends to infer their ruin'.[39] In short, the 'conjecture', or the use of tenuous evidence, inference, and comparison, was no invention of the eighteenth century. Nor was it the creation of that small handful of its most eminent authors later so effectively canonised by Dugald Stewart. As with the claims for 'experience', philosophy itself was not actually entering history in the way that its acolytes disingenuously suggested. Analogy and imaginative reconstruction were in fact familiar if vexatious techniques in Scotland. This situation only ensured the avowedly refurbished 'conjecture' what appears to have been its decidedly mixed reception among enlightened Scotsmen.[40] The heightened use of methodological parallels with science and philosophy thus had brought unprecedented opportunities for the rhetorical justification of those important techniques which Dugald Stewart later elevated to the hallowed status of 'conjectural or theoretical history'.[41] 'Experiment' seemed indeed to reaffirm the empirical value of 'experience', and so by extension of 'conjecture'. But we have grounds again for a healthy scepticism in response to the mischievous suggestions of enlightened self-publicists. There is scant sign that they were in this respect the architects of a credible methodological revolution.

The idea that all previous historical work was to be rejected as 'fable and falshood' must therefore be understood as a part of the more general tendency among Scotsmen attracted by philosophy and science. They came to believe that their own inferences had actually been sanctioned afresh by the recent successes of probabilistic experimentation and Humean epistemology. The ambient sense of methodological innovation which this induced undoubtedly helped enlightened historical modernists to proclaim themselves the coming men. No less obviously it sustained the mood of missionary zeal in which some openly chastised their supposedly unreconstructed colleagues. To the impatient George Wallace, for example, it seemed as if David Hume was indeed 'the only Scotchman' who had so far 'ever attempted that philosophical method with any success'.[42] Consciousness of the experimental methodology as it was supposedly applied to historical studies, moreover, also allowed authors like the inconsistent Pinkerton to pronounce the eighteenth century 'as glorious for Scotish literature, as the preceding had been adverse'.[43] This assumption of methodological purity even led on to the conclusion, voiced by Adam Ferguson in the *History of Civil Society* (1767), that the modern historian's principal task was simply to rewrite the speculative and flawed earlier accounts 'with the accomplishments of a learned and a polished age'.[44] Attractive assertions of an infectious intellectual revolution contracted from other disciplines were thus able to become a central characteristic of 'enlightened' history. As James Grant freely admitted, Scottish minds now advertised themselves as having become enlightened specifically by means of 'science and philosophy'.[45] For precisely this reason we would ourselves do well to doubt the claim that enlightened historical writing had actually divorced itself from the prior tradition in Scotland.

The professed methodological dissociation of the Enlightenment from its Scottish precursors, meanwhile, was often accompanied by an open acknowledgement of the less propitious political and material circumstances in which previous Scottish historians had had to work. The immediate purpose of such comments was of course to elevate the present by condemning the turbulence and uncertainty of the past. But they also usefully illustrate the fact that the eighteenth-century historian's sense of his own modernity owed at least as much to recognition of a new political and social milieu as to any substantial revolution in historical method.[46] Toleration, commercial expansion, social change, and urbanisation, each of which was identified and commented upon by many influential observers, provided ready support for the widespread proclamation of an intellectual revolution in history. On such manifest developments the reputation of Scottish scholars, by their own account, was rapidly coming to depend. Hume's famous elevation of Bacon and modern science, for example, was set specifically against the conveniently contrasting background of 'scholastic learning and polemical divinity'.[47] Alexander Kincaid, meanwhile, openly disdained the 'illiberal rejudices, flowing from narrow and unenlightened minds', which he suggested had inhabited his poor country in former times.[48] These comments painted an alluring picture, one clearly as long on dislike for the religious tone of the past as it was short on intrinsic grounds for approving of modern scholarship. The developments to which they so frequently alluded were in truth explanations only for the greater social status, security, and audience, enjoyed by enlightened authors in what was unquestionably a more tranquil and prosperous age. The 'enlightened' author wished to stress how much he had distanced himself from the inferior scholarship of the past. Yet his chosen polemical stance again aligned him only with earlier Scottish scholars like James Anderson. Their criticism of prior scholarship, too, had very often been part of an aloof presbyterian condescension towards the 'Dark and Superstitious Ages' which had allegedly produced it.[49] Allusions to the social and political context, then, implied the essential modernity of enlightened scholarship and the inferiority of previous work. But like so many other unconvincing protestations of modernity, they cannot in themselves be taken as evidence of a substantive change in the techniques of Scottish historical discourse.

On the contrary, declarations of intellectual independence which relied so obviously upon references to toleration, stability, and wealth, should excite only the most suspicious of reactions. One finds, for example, William Guthrie arguing that the fabulousness of existing scholarship in Scotland was entirely attributable to the 'destruction of the Scottish monuments of learning and antiquity'.[50] But Guthrie also unwittingly implied that much of the alleged difference between past and present historical writing consisted only in the circumstantial changes which had rendered both modern scholars and their material sources secure. Equally, William Semple anticipated the intoxicated enthusiasm of more recent commentators. He joyously contrasted the 'refinement' of the 'present enlightened period' with the 'barbarous ages' which had preceded it.[51] Yet Semple was far from substantiating this sense of 'enlightenment' by a plausible display of new scholarly methodology. Indeed, he seems to have been content to observe with unconscionable smugness how 'Scotland has made more improvement in agriculture, mechanics, and literature, than in any three centuries before'.[52] Again a scholar turns out to have relied upon the evidence of economic and social progress to suggest the intellectual stature of his own scholarly age. More broadly, of course, there was alongside this a strong awareness of those more diffuse manners and social developments which the minister of Stichill, George Ridpath, thought had served to 'polish and adorn a more tranquil period'.[53] Such observations again lent vital colour to the wholly desirable illusion that a fundamental change had truly occurred in the motivation and character of Scottish scholarship. The emotive antithesis of turmoil and tranquillity was by this means linked productively to that of fabulousness and experimentalism. This merely enhanced the confident claims of those who wished to portray themselves as in the vanguard of a new kind of Scottish learning. Dugald Stewart, for example, that late and great disciple of 'conjectural' history, could scarcely have approved wholeheartedly of the scholarship which had been current during what he had elsewhere excoriated as 'the long night of Gothic barbarism'. Illuminated only by the single exception of George Buchanan, this was a phase, Stewart implausibly suggested, which had come to an end as late as the middle of the seventeenth century.[54] Of course, we have already seen what should always have been recognised. The literary sterility of late sixteenth- and seventeenth-century Scotland, the 'neglect of literature' which a myopic Pinkerton had contrived to find, had supposedly been the inevitable consequence of these less favourable worldly circumstances.[55] But it was itself an insidious though persuasive myth. It now appears that this might even have been a myth constructed by ambitious Enlightenment self-publicists like Guthrie, Semple, and Hume, embellished and perpetuated by subsequent scholars from Dugald Stewart to the modern historians. All of them, it seems, would have been flattered to derive their own disciplines from the apparently sanitised and respectable intellectual milieu of the eighteenth century. This its participants had triumphantly proclaimed a uniquely 'learned and polished age'.[56] As inhabitants of one of the prospective 'cultivated and enlightened nations' of the world, this was fundamentally a self-delusion in which eighteenth-century Scotsmen and their academic successors have strongly needed to believe.[57]

We cannot, it seems, simply take eighteenth-century triumphalism at face value. Indeed we would perhaps be well advised also to take a second look at Enlightenment perceptions of the literary past. It seems justified to ask in particular whether any more sympathetic analysis of previous Scottish historical scholarship was also to be found at the same time. In fact – and, given the diversity of eighteenth-century scholarship, surely not a surprise – it seems that George Buchanan's humanist battle-cry, his full-throated exhortation to the defence of national scholarship, was actually heeded by the less millenarian elements within the considerable learned community of enlightened Scotland.

The specific defence of earlier Scottish historians as eloquent and gifted public spokesmen was regularly attempted. Some authors found no shame at all in seeking to cover themselves, and by extension their own enlightened community, in the reflected glory of the inherited Calvinist and humanist tradition of history. In this respect the studied ambivalence of William Robertson, for example, was probably typical. Without the Union of the Crowns, Robertson argued, Scotland 'would still have been able to maintain some equality with other nations, in the pursuit of literary honour'.[58] This of course tied the enlightened Principal of the University of Edinburgh to the oratorical and public-oriented posture of post-Reformation historians like Crauford and Drummond, men disoriented and bewildered by the removal of their royal audience. Yet the *History of Scotland* (1759) also suggests that Robertson was still prepared to concede nevertheless the survival in Scotland of a rich potential for national literature. This was despite the damage reputedly done to Scottish historical oratory by the political changes of 1603. Indeed, a surprisingly generous perspective on prior scholarship saw Robertson go on to heap praise on a number of eloquent Scotsmen. These included Fletcher of Salton, one of those who had showed themselves 'still capable of generous sentiments, and, notwithstanding some peculiar idioms, ... able to express themselves with energy, and with elegance'.[59]

Nor was Robertson unique in his ambiguous approach to the intellectual past. The first *Edinburgh Review* (to which Robertson was actually an important contributor) likewise claimed in 1755 that a lack of a 'standard of language' had been instrumental in retarding the proper growth of Scotland's literary culture. But its authors nevertheless granted that the seventeenth century had seen a number of praiseworthy Scottish attempts at scholarly endeavour: 'Amid all the gloom of these times', they confessed, 'there were still some men who kept alive the remains of science, and preserved the flame of genius from being altogether extinguished'.[60] Maitland's continuator of course clung tenaciously to his author's notion that earlier Scottish scholarship had been incorrigibly fabulous. However, the anonymous patriot magnanimously still allowed that 'no nation can boast of more elegant historians than the Scottish'.[61] Continuing notions of Scottish literary eloquence, then, stemming ultimately from a sympathy with the oratorical pretensions of a Calvinist and humanist tradition, drove a number of eighteenth-century authors. These also included the antiquarian and naturalist Sir John Dalyell, who warned in 1798 that 'When a native of Scotland writes in English, he writes in fetters'.[62] The enlightened membership of the Select Society, of course, unavoidably echoed George Buchanan in their preferences. They longed for an edificatory Scottish literature couched in the common language of the greatest contemporary scholars. Less Anglophile intellects like Dalyell, however, still followed Hume of Godscroft in upholding the Scots tongue itself as the natural vehicle for Scottish national eloquence. They argued persuasively that 'National antiquities must be expressed in national language'.[63] Both groups in their different ways continued to seek for

Scotland the sort of international learned reputation which, on Calvinist and humanist premises, depended crucially upon a scholarly *eloquentia*. The expressiveness and style of Scottish scholarship still mattered as much as the substance. Even the most dismissive Enlightenment authors found themselves obliged at least to concede the eloquence and literary style of earlier Scottish scholars.

More broadly, the moralistic and edificatory qualities of earlier Scottish scholarship were recognised and applauded by their enlightened successors. Notwithstanding a predictable jibe at the methodological limitations of the great humanist, for example, John Lawrie was still determined to see Buchanan's admirable *History of Scotland* included in the modern school curriculum. To his mind, the unhealthy prevalence of foreign texts 'might very easily be obviated, by masters introducing into schools Buchanan's elegant history of Scotland, which, if not equal to Salust or Livy, is at least superior to any modern production of the kind, although in some particulars he is found somewhat fabulous, as most ancient histories are'.[64] William Duff, too, was happy to echo the advice of his own illustrious Scottish predecessors. The *History of Scotland* (1749) announced his continuing adherence to the Calvinist and humanist vision of a didactic history: it was still fundamentally, he insisted, 'a direct mean (as Bishop Burnet justly observes) to make men wiser and better'.[65] Accordingly, Duff led the way in representing for his readers, not the dissociation of the present historical milieu from the past, but in fact the deliberate continuation of the glorious traditions of Scottish historical scholarship. His own scholarship, he suggested, was admirable because, rather than in spite of, its comparability 'with all the others of our Scotch historians, viz. *Buchanan, Lesly, Drummond, Spotswood, Calderwood, Melvill, Lindsay of Pitscotty, Anderson, Campden, Keith, and Innes*'.[66] In similar vein the Earl of Buchan in 1780 proudly recalled the long line of Scottish historians and antiquarians to whom he anticipated his contemporaries succeeding through their generous support of the recently mooted Society of Antiquaries. Craig, Skene, Balfour, Scot, Drummond and Dalrymple were his favourites. These were merely to be matched in his own day, Buchan trusted, by the likes of Kames, Blair, Tytler, Goodall and Arnot.[67] Even John Pinkerton could be found agreeing on occasion with such cloying sentiments. He fancied that in the seventeenth century it had been, amongst others, Gordon of Straloch and Scot of Scotstarvet who had managed to alleviate the supposed literary gloom.[68]

It remains true, of course, that few of those so strenuously resuscitated by Duff and Buchan had ever managed to attract for themselves an international reputation. Consequently it was all too easy for averted enlightened eyes (as for more recent observers) to overlook the Scottish contribution to early modern historical learning. As Hugh Blair accurately observed in 1783, Britain as a whole had never been 'eminent for its historical productions', except (of course) for 'the celebrated Buchanan'.[69] But one explanation for the obscurity of the earlier tradition is obvious. Scottish historical scholarship very much reflected the peculiarly intense concentration of its authors upon a derivative Calvinist and humanist agenda. This, as we have extensively seen, was relevant to an audience who were at ease with a forceful vernacular, one striving energetically after an audible *eloquentia*. Meanwhile the theoretical load borne by the historical tradition, as well as the more colourful political and religious polemic which had also distinguished it, made it even more exclusive and introspective. Scotsmen as a result came to possess what seemed to its critics a savage and parochial historical discourse. It long remained sharply focused on the burning issues of audience, scholarly virtue and causality. It was at the same time still further clouded by what Buchanan notoriously diagnosed as the 'perfervid genius' of his countrymen. Foreigners or outsiders simply would not have been able to recognise the credentials of this discourse. Much less would they have been equipped or inclined to participate in such an impenetrable blend of social unease and factional venom. The alternating silence and criticism which earlier Scottish scholarship drew from the more cosmopolitan Enlightenment scholars may for these reasons be judged as understandable as it was rhetorically necessary. William Borthwick was surely even more correct than he intended when observing that, for all the Scottish public's recent interest in classical and oriental antiquities, 'certainly the Antiquities of their own country have at least an equal claim to their attention'.[70] In Scotland this had always, and inevitably, been the case.

From beneath a smothering triumphalism which has dominated so much of our own thinking about its relationship to earlier Scottish scholarship there have therefore emerged reasons for doubting some of the central claims made on behalf of an 'enlightened' historical revolution. There are tantalising signs that Enlightenment scholars themselves sometimes refused to participate in the wholesale destruction of their own intellectual heritage. The crescendo of self-congratulation which sustained the image of the methodological revolution owed much to a conventional allusion to the methods of science and philosophy. But the rhetoric of 'experience', and even the notorious claims made for the 'conjecture', were in fact long anticipated in Scotland. As a result they were subjected to the most penetrating criticism by historians who suspected that revolution to be both dubious and dangerous. Much more polemical weight, of course, was lent by easy reference to spectacular contextual developments. Economic and social change, religious tolerance, political stability, and the polite culture and literary expansion which they facilitated, were all effortlessly summoned up by modernist historians. These were arguably the reflexive response for eighteenth-century men in need of support for the perennial humanists' claim that they had disengaged themselves successfully and irremediably from the errors and commitments of the scholarly past. Yet a discussion of their predecessors conducted in a less affectatious tone allowed many commentators to voice a different, and, we may now suspect, more plausible conclusion. Enlightened scholarship, they agreed, was greatly indebted to a preceding tradition in Scotland. Its achievements, and especially those most

relevant to an 'enlightened' audience, were as a result to be identified and
exalted. The eloquent and learned character of earlier Scottish scholars in
particular received the most fulsome praise. Their moralistic and didactic
qualities, too, were not only recognised, but came to be advertised anew as the
standards to which an 'enlightened' scholarship should itself aspire. An
iconoclastic Enlightenment, whose special status at first sight relied on the
destruction of old reputations, was thus in some respects being forced at the
same time to acknowledge the continuing influence of its Scottish predecessors.
'We are reformed from popery', grumbled the resigned John Pinkerton,
echoing an equally perceptive Lord Hailes, 'but not from Hector Boethius':[71]
in a wider sense which surely escaped its unusual author, this statement aptly
describes the prodigious native intellectual inheritance within which eighteenth-
century scholarship in Scotland had necessarily to work. From the babble of
enlightened triumphalism, therefore, an intriguing conclusion surely begins to
emerge. The 'revolutionary' self-confidence characteristic of eighteenth-
century history in Scotland, it seems, may actually have been founded to a
significant extent upon a methodological illusion induced by its own extravagant
humanist pretensions. The question to pursue next is whether we could find
more persuasive evidence of intellectual revolution in the actual themes and
subjects to which Scottish historians were now enthusiastically addressing
themselves.

II: INNOVATION AND TRADITION

I have already more than once suggested that the historian of ideas should try
to avoid a constricting focus merely upon the more prominent figures of the
time. Instead, I have argued that we ought to embrace those whom Adam Smith
in 1776 called the 'unprosperous race of men'.[72] These were the men of letters
in Scotland who have had less recognition from posterity. But they certainly
contributed much to the cacophony of criticism and celebration which we have
just encountered. This broader community, as we have already begun to see,
provides a context in which to assess the extent and meaning of the triumphal
claims transmitted from within enlightened scholarship. Indeed, it promises to
allow Enlightenment studies as a whole to break out of their quasi-biographical
ghetto and to enter at last the exciting territory properly belonging to the
unconstrained history of ideas.[73] It will later permit us to grasp the intention and
purpose of historical discourse as it was understood by a full range of authors in
eighteenth-century Scotland. But at this point the most useful function of the
wider population of contributing authors is to allow us to examine further the
central question posed by the expansion of historical scholarship in Scotland
after 1740. In the light of what we now know of sixteenth- and seventeenth-
century Scottish discourse, and particularly because we have seen just how
misleading could be the scholars' self-serving estimation of their own historic
contribution, the problem is perhaps now best phrased like this: In what ways
did Enlightenment scholarship in Scotland actually represent a significant

change from that which had gone before? And to what extent were any innovations in theme or focus reflected across the broader community of eighteenth-century Scottish historians?

The specific themes developed by enlightened historians have attracted a large portion of the recent work devoted to understanding the Scottish Enlightenment. The possibility of considering the Scottish inquiry as an important source of modern social science, in particular, has led to a great deal of interest in the emergence of the theme of historical materialism in the eighteenth century.[74] The key players in this movement have been identified as Adam Smith and John Millar, with important further contributions by others like Adam Ferguson and Lord Kames. A significant part of their collective efforts certainly owed something in addition to the unashamed use of the 'conjectural' technique at which we have just looked: interpretations were speculated, particularly in the case of primitive societies, which drew confidently upon the lessons and principles deduced from more familiar cases. Modern interest in their work, however, has been most obviously represented in the works of Ronald Meek, whose formidable and often subtle historiographical influence we have already considered;[75] though it is important to remember that we could find versions of this 'materialist' interpretation before the work of Forbes and Meek, and at least as far back as the beginning of the present century.[76] Out of this encounter of subsequent academic scholarship with the central texts of enlightened Scotland emerged a broad consensus. Scottish discourse, it was claimed, had produced in the eighteenth century a theoretical model which linked the character and social institutions of an historical age with its typical form of economic organisation. In tracing the successive emergence of hunting, pastoral, agricultural, and commercial economies, the Scottish literati, it was believed, were in some sense outlining and explaining the evolution of society from its very earliest to its most advanced stages. Each of them, of course, was additionally characterised by distinctive institutions, ranging from legal systems and political organisations to aesthetic preferences and sexual manners. It thus seemed that a true 'science of society', an all-embracing theoretical scheme, was in the making.[77] Yet the bolder and more rigid materialism discerned by Meek, however, has now largely been rejected. Instead there has emerged an interpretation which stresses instead the different interests and emphases of the leading Scottish participants in this enterprise. Recent work has highlighted Smith's essentially jurisprudential concerns in formulating his social typology. Some have come to the understanding that his apparently definitive four-stage theory was itself a late and largely peripheral development.[78] Enlightened scholars, it now seems, may actually have employed their materialistic descriptions in a less coherent and less profound way than was formerly supposed. One of the conventional thematic characteristics of the small circle of great literati therefore looks significantly less epochal than it once seemed.

Our own ultimate concern of course remains with the evidence of intellectual continuity in Scotland manifested in the evolution of moral attitudes towards scholarship and learning. But it still seems necessary to examine this point as we ask what we can now say about the Scottish Enlightenment, in its widest embodiment, as an innovative phase in the development of historical scholarship. In the first instance it is significant that there is fresh doubt that there existed a unitary and revolutionary 'school' of enlightened scholars in eighteenth-century Scotland. This offers welcome encouragement to our own attempts to place the historical works of figures like Smith and Ferguson in their wider and longer Scottish context. Very obviously, this revisionism limits the extent to which one can ascribe entirely innovative interests to the Scottish Enlightenment as a whole. So the texts once associated with historical materialism are gradually proving capable of being relocated within broader contemporary scholarship in Scotland. They are increasingly understood in particular as standing potentially in closer relationship to the moral preoccupations of an earlier historical tradition. At the same time a possible function served in Scotland by the tentative discussion of property relations and modes of production has also begun to emerge. Andrew Skinner, for one, has insisted that the Scottish materialist classification of societies was essentially descriptive rather than explanatory. If property relations characterised but did not singularly cause the distinctive phases of social evolution, then this, too, effectively increases the number of enlightened Scotsmen who might in fact be said to have subscribed to such a system.[79] Simultaneously we now see that it may have been the dual imperatives of manners and jurisprudence which were leading the most famous Enlightenment historians into a study in what turned out to be embryonic political economy and sociology. This was of course a project broadly cognate with the influential example of their French contemporaries. But equally the same influences might have been pushing less eminent scholars in eighteenth-century Scotland into an equivalent interest in the changing status of property and so of morality. This would certainly make sense of the tendency of scholars like Robert Henry to describe the development of historical society *inter alia* in both moral and material terms.[80]

Nor would an emphasis on this broader history of manners only support the convictions of those who persist in seeing Scottish historical materialism basically as the answer to a specifically post-Union dilemma. Scotland's economic improvement and social change may indeed have seemed to threaten the classical notions of political society and citizenship to which its leading citizens still aspired. As Nicholas Phillipson and others have argued, this would still have forced its scholars to reformulate along commercial lines their moral prescriptions for its strength and stability.[81] But the identification of an incipient history of property merely as part of this wider inquiry into the origins and nature of social institutions and moralities also has other implications. In particular it encourages a view more consistent with what we have seen of the prior Scottish tradition as an edificatory and intensely moralistic discourse.[82] Francis Hutcheson, to many the philosophical founding father of Scotland's

Enlightenment, claimed with his Scottish predecessors that manners enjoyed a justified pre-eminence among the potential range of historical concerns: the 'superior Pleasure then of History', he believed, 'must arise, like that of Poetry, from the Manners'.[83] The study of manners and social norms on this account again grew naturally out of the conventional moralistic concerns of Scottish scholarship. Materialism, in its somewhat limited Enlightenment manifestation, was part of this attempt by eighteenth-century scholars to reconcile their nation's accelerating commercialisation and Anglicised manners with the axioms entrenched by commitment to a traditional social theory. The exaltation of scholarly virtue and the search for rational leadership were, as we shall see, becoming more rather than less frenetic in Scotland as the century progressed. The moral dimension to historical change, then, would have seemed especially fascinating to humanist scholars in eighteenth-century Scotland. Such minds were now busy contemplating the modification in an increasingly commercial society of the very nexus of social relations and moral values in terms of which their own vital scholarly function had long been defined.

There is a yet more significant result of this effective relocation of eighteenth-century Scottish materialism within a developing history of manners. This is that a much larger number of historians can be seen to have been in some way involved in the enterprise. Smith and Millar of course need no introduction. Adam Ferguson's classical taxonomy of 'hunting and fishing', 'pastoral', 'agricultural' and 'commercial' societies is also well known. But others turn out to have employed similar materialist descriptions when they sought, in Sir John Dalrymple's famous words, to establish a history of manners which explained 'how men arrived from the most rude to the most polished state of society'.[84] Alexander Kincaid, for example, the historian of Edinburgh, openly sought to paint 'a general picture of the manners of the time throughout all Scotland'.[85] His was a history which paid special attention to a 'barbarity' now conceived as a cultural rather than as a strictly economic phase. Equally William Semple's edition of Crawfurd's *History of the Shire of Renfrew* (1782) traced the history of agriculture and manufacturing around Paisley. This was done, Semple showed, with the intention of highlighting only one aspect of the historical developments through which he believed civilisation's broader manners had progressed. His interest in 'barbarism', for example, was clearly as a moral dimension of 'the melancholy Gothic'. His fascination for that which he called 'feudal' also had everything to do with the chivalry and brutal conduct which the term connoted, and little, if anything, with its vestigial association with an agrarian economy.[86] For Hugh Blair, meanwhile, the state of property was likewise of concern when it was an integral part of the history of manners, society and custom. His treatment of primitive society in the *Lectures*, for example, was typical of a Scottish materialist 'school' only in its considerable idiosyncracy. He curiously compressed the categories of 'hunting or pasturage' which for Ferguson were the names of distinct stages of development. But in the *Critical Dissertation* Blair also dwelled long and poignantly upon the 'tenderness and sublimity' which were his own chief interest in primitive Celtic society.[87] Moral circumstances or manners, then, seem to have been broadly what scholars like Hugh Blair were concerned to address. Property relations and material subsistence were important only in so far as they comprised part of more fascinating and pertinent moral and institutional changes. We may say that Scottish 'materialism' was therefore developed specifically for use in reconstructing a more satisfactory history of manners. Its inconsistencies and deficiencies as a self-contained system are as a result less historically problematic than was once thought. The perplexingly different terminologies employed by Smith, Millar, Robertson and Blair, for example, seem untroubling. The apparently contradictory claims of some contemporaries that in historical evolution we might actually reach 'an acme of refinement, which degenerates into the basest corruption', now also matter less.[88] After all, a relentlessly progressive and consistent system of materialist social science was in no way the result at which they were aiming. Material developments, though certainly rendered more significant by contemporary economic advances and by French thought, were at this stage still locked firmly into a developing moral history. This was concerned principally with manners and values and, consequently, as the melancholy Gilbert Stuart put it, centred upon specifically moral questions such as how 'Refinement and property were to open up the selfishness of mankind'.[89]

The history of property which characterised the historical scholarship of eighteenth-century Scotland may thus be understood only as a special case in a longer cultural continuum. It was enhanced by contemporary economic and intellectual trends, but was consistent still with the slowly-evolving Scottish exploration of morality and manners begun by Hector Boece. At a time of increasing social and economic change in Scotland, and with the position and cultural role of her scholars profoundly affected by this transformation, an explanation of such developments seemed ever more necessary for a satisfactory account of morality in history. Yet it is important not to lose sight of other aspects of enlightened historical scholarship which more directly and straightforwardly can be traced to what has been the main subject of our own study, the moral discourse developing in Scotland during the sixteenth and seventeenth centuries. On the one hand, the greater emphasis upon economic affairs undoubtedly influenced the character of the orthodox narrative history in the Enlightenment. Hume's *History*, for example, took great care to detail the emergence of new systems of property ownership, as well as of the moral and cultural changes associated with them.[90] But on the other hand, many of the political and religious squabbles which had scarred the earlier Calvinist and humanist tradition survived. Though somewhat tempered by the soothing balms of enlightened stability and tolerance, they continued to distinguish Scottish scholarship in the later eighteenth century. It would be too much to suggest that the anti-Catholic venom of John Lawrie's *The Completion of Prophecy* (1781) and Somerville's *History of Political Transactions* (1792), or even the controversy generated by the publication of anti-Whig narratives by James Macpherson and Sir John Dalrymple, were exactly typical of Scottish scholarship in an enlightened age. Yet they were only among the most colourful and extreme examples of partisanship to prosper in the eighteenth century.

The Scottish tradition of historical writing still remained, at bottom, a vehicle for factional bickering and the fiercest polemic. In civil scholarship, the eighteenth century saw the modification rather than the dissipation of the political disputes which had raged around the traditional bones of historical contention. Radical humanist politics, in particular, went into long-term decline. But even so, both Buchanan's reputation and a topical interest in his political philosophy survived into the new revolutionary age born out of the mature European Enlightenment. Robert Macfarlane's edition of the *Dialogue Concerning the Rights of the Crown of Scotland* (1799), for example, was particularly relevant in the context of recent events in France. In a curious way, moreover, John Home's historical drama *The History of the Sieges of Aquileia and Berwick* (1760) arguably looked back even further. It contained strong echoes of both the late medieval and Calvinist humanist historical traditions, now brought forth to aid Scotland's attempt to prove her martial virility in the continuing saga of the militia campaigns. Its direct equation of Scottish with classical history, and its concentration upon the fourteenth-century wars with England and the struggle of Scotsmen to throw off the shackles imposed by an imperialistic foreign enemy were all the more effective for being deeply evocative of the country's scholarly past. More typical, perhaps, was William Guthrie's *General History of Scotland* (1767–8). This, whilst still including an account of Boece's 'first forty-four kings', regarded both them and their political connotations as frankly 'imaginary'.[91] Increasingly, and in tune with wider political discourse in eighteenth-century Britain, it was the virtues of a mixed constitution rather than the brazen assertion of the right to revolt which now dominated the historical discussion. The study of constitutional and property law was of even greater interest now that Scotland's peculiarities had been thrown into sharper relief by the parliamentary union with England. Accordingly it was an area for which meticulous scholars like Gilbert Stuart, John Millar and Lord Hailes now showed special concern in a number of major works.[92] More generally, and perhaps inevitably, the focus of Scottish historians now tended towards 1688 and the rather different political questions which that most problematic of revolutions had raised. At the same time the public status of history itself was undergoing important changes. It was now, for example, that history was finally institutionalised as an academic discipline in its own right at the reformed universities of Edinburgh and Glasgow.[93] Yet it would be misleading in the extreme to suggest for these reasons that a clean intellectual break had occurred.

In fact, eighteenth-century scholars displayed an undiminished interest in the classic cruxes of the earlier tradition. The debate on Scotland's national origins, for example, precipitated by Fordun and controversially intensified by Boece

and Buchanan, continued. It was even carried to new heights of acrimony by
fervent Enlightenment scholars like John Pinkerton and John Lanne Buchanan,
men only too keen to idolise the Pict or the Celt. Some, of course, were moved
to write by the vexatious contemporary stimulus of the Ossianic poems. But all
were conspicuously equipped with the skills and concerns developed within the
early modern Scottish tradition of antiquarian primitivism and philological
speculation. These included men as different as John Williams, William Nimmo
and William Maitland, who attempted, once and for all, to provide the definitive
account of Scotland's earliest history.[94] Nor were eighteenth-century scholars
remiss in applying themselves to the renovation of other aspects of the
traditional Scottish narrative account. The stormy thirteenth and fourteenth
centuries, the English claim to sovereignty over Scotland and the uncertain
legitimacy of King Robert III all came under the intense and fruitful scrutiny
of scholars such as the Lords Hailes and Kames, who clambered eagerly on to
the increasingly profitable bandwagon of enlightened historical writing.[95] Mary
Stuart of course had been the subject of the most rancorous earlier controversy.
She now simply became the perplexing focal point of specialist eighteenth-
century examination. With the issue revolving centrally around the disputed
authorship of the so-called 'Casket Letters', this was again an area in which the
traditional humanist and linguistic preoccupations of Scottish scholars could
come to the fore. Walter Goodall, William Tytler, and latterly Thomas
Robertson, each produced voluminous studies devoted to her controversial
career. At the same time more versatile historians like Lord Hailes and William
Robertson continued in their panoptic narratives to find in the unfortunate
queen a natural subject for measured comment.[96] In sum, the Scottish
Enlightenment brought an intensified interest in historical manners and
property relations, as well as the demise of humanist politics in history. But it
also built solidly upon the documentary, philological, and antiquarian concerns
of the earlier Scottish political tradition. What it achieved was both an expansion
and the further development of Calvinist and humanist scholarship.

   Broadly similar observations, moreover, apply in relation to the eighteenth-
century fate of Scottish religious scholarship. Just as radical humanism faded
away, so religious history was now less obviously dominated by presbyterian
polemic and the traditional ecclesiological debate. More superficially, though
perhaps as significant, it is difficult to identify the enlightened successors of
Knox, Calderwood, Kirkton and Shields. After Wodrow and Innes in the 1720s,
and except for the singular contributions of Andrew Stevenson and John
Skinner, the conventional narrative religious history disappeared from view
until the Evangelical revival of the early nineteenth century. The Enlightenment, as conventional historiography maintains, was in Scotland truly an age
of ostentatious tolerance and greater even-handedness in religious scholarship.
It ushered in a more benign climate. In this the exceptional atheist, like David
Hume, could carry to destructive lengths the familiar humanists' task of
subjecting the phenomenon of organised religion to the same historical analysis

as all other human institutions.[97] But once again this is only the more well-known part of a much larger and more complex picture in Scotland. Very many eighteenth-century historians, including some of the best known, were not attempting to secularise history. On the contrary, they seem to have set out, like Knox and Shields, to justify church and faith in empirical terms, to entrench them by locating them in their properly historical perspective. To Gilbert Stuart, for example, portraying the 'actors in the Reformation' in their true historical context was a humanist exercise in adept revisionism rather than an act of vigorous demolition. The purpose inherited from the seventeenth-century controversialists remained to show the reformers 'asserting their natural independency, and vindicating the political rights of their nation'.[98] The Elgin minister Lachlan Shaw simply followed suit. He combined in the *History of the Province of Moray* (1775) both a conventional fascination for Celtic primitivism and philology, and a more innovative interest in historical property and manners, with a lengthy and violent assault upon the credentials of popery and superstition.[99] William Guthrie, too, recapitulated without embarrassment the orthodox presbyterian account of Buchanan and Petrie. The arrival of bishops in Scotland was still held by Guthrie to have plunged her catastrophically into 'that long darkness which for many ages overspread Europe'.[100] Alexander Kincaid, meanwhile, detailed the sheer ferocity of the Edinburgh reformers (nevertheless conceding his own grudging admiration), and William Robertson, as befitted a historian who was also Moderator of the General Assembly of the Kirk, delivered a cool and discriminating assessment of Knox and Melville, as well as a relatively favourable account of Covenant theology.[101]

Committed authors like the ministers Robert Wallace and John Witherspoon naturally used the learned and elegant historical essay specifically as an enlightened vehicle for the defence of biblical authority or in order to satirise an allegedly lukewarm Kirk hierarchy.[102] And apparently secular historians like Lord Kames, John Campbell and Maitland's continuator still in their narratives wrote enthusiastically of the Reformation, directing their refined historical scorn at the moral and intellectual consequences of popery in all its insidious manifestations.[103] The more intriguing purposes to which these continuing religious polemics now made their polished and enlightened contributions will be one of our central concerns in the next chapter, when we explore the deeper consequences of the Calvinist and humanist heritage for the nature of eighteenth-century attitudes towards scholarship and society. But at this stage, it is important that we note what was happening in the midst of relatively greater tolerance and the integration of religious affairs into the mainstream civil narrative history of Scotland. Enlightenment scholarship was continuing to display, in its preoccupation with exploring and justifying much of Scotland's clouded religious history, many fundamental links with an older Scottish scholarly tradition.

Given this broad overview of Enlightenment historical scholarship, a clear answer to the question as to whether the period was marked by thematic innovation remains rather elusive. At best, we might return the appropriately Scottish verdict of 'not proven'. On the one hand, we have the emergence after 1740 of a stronger interest in the history of property, and in economic affairs in general. This is undoubtedly a feature of Scottish scholarship which deserves the wide recognition which it has traditionally received. Familiar authors, most obviously Smith and Millar, moved some way in the direction of systematising their analysis. Many others, meanwhile, followed them in developing a typology in which the stages of social evolution were described most commonly by reference to economic characteristics. At the same time, much of the old political venom in Scottish scholarship, long sustained by and against a rich strain of radical humanist polemic, seems to have dissipated. Hanoverian stability and London government combined to render Scotland, at least by its own unimpressive standards, a peaceful and a harmonious country. Religious toleration and relative ecclesiastical equanimity also distinguished the period of the Enlightenment from all too much of the recent Scottish past. So it would be surprising had not historical scholarship likewise ceased to focus so intensely upon the strident hagiography and heavily loaded church history in which the Calvinist and humanist tradition in Scotland had been nurtured.

But beyond and even within the charmed circle of the most brilliant and famous of the Edinburgh literati, eighteenth-century Scottish scholarship also has another, less familiar, tale to tell. A fervent enthusiasm for the history of property was scarcely less evident among unspectacular authors like Guthrie, Semple, and Shaw. Yet here it was all the more obviously part of a fundamental concern with the historical evolution of social forms, of manners, and most crucially, of morality. This, indeed, merely confirms the most recent trend in the study of the work of Smith and Millar. This has been to emphasise the incoherence, the variability and the essentially moral and jurisprudential objectives, with which the analysis of property had been conceived. It also leaves open, as we shall see more extensively in the next chapter, the possibility of exploring the reasons for which a history of manners, and consequently of property, was of such interest to the confident and scholarly eighteenth-century recipients of Calvinist and humanist social theory. But at this stage the wider perspective on Enlightenment scholarship at least has reminded us how political history continued to be focused upon many of the same issues and controversies as before. The evidence of the Celtic and Pictish languages, the independence of Scotland and the uncertain virtues of Mary Stuart, all continued to exercise the most able scholarly minds. Equally, religious history was modified rather than rejected by the large majority of committed Enlightenment scholars. The historicisation of religion, though begun by Knox for rather different purposes, merely continued in the balmy years of moderation and politeness.[104] The Scottish Enlightenment thus in practice substantially accorded with the shifting image of itself revealed in the ambiguous rhetoric which we have already examined. Thematic innovation generated much noise. As a result it captured most of the subsequent attention. But in a less strident, more mundane way, tradition also continued to make its influence felt. It remained effective in determining the proper subjects for historical discussion. It also prescribed the stances and modes of argument which eighteenth-century authors would invariably adopt. What, then, of the fundamental purposes and social function of scholarship as they had been understood and so eloquently defended by the Scottish historians of the sixteenth and seventeenth centuries? To what extent did a further development of those underlying Calvinist and humanist attitudes towards intellectual activity and to the social leadership now take place? And how might this powerful cultural legacy have directed and informed the historical inquiry as it structured, indeed gave critical momentum to, the accelerating discourse of Scotland's Enlightenment? These are basic questions which can no longer be postponed.

III: THE PURPOSE OF ENLIGHTENED SCHOLARSHIP

There is, I have argued, less scope than was once thought for viewing the historians of the Scottish Enlightenment as working effectively against a prior tradition of historical scholarship in Scotland. Despite the condemnation of the methodology of the past generated in some quarters, there was a substantial degree of obvious continuity. There was, perhaps, even a harmonious counterpoint, albeit in a minor key, one recognising the survival of considerable elements of the Calvinist and humanist traditions of scholarship in Scotland. I have also suggested that, despite the emergence of a much wider interest in the history of property and of manners, conventional political and religious scholarship, often allied to the old technical humanist preoccupations of philology, antiquarianism and primitivism, remained very much to the fore. It would consequently be possible to feel that we have at least dispatched some of the more widely held and erroneous presuppositions with which people have so often approached 'enlightened' history in Scotland. Now, however, we need to go further and examine the eighteenth-century rhetoric of scholarly intention. This might enable us to see more clearly the intellectual project upon which Scottish historians of the Enlightenment actually understood themselves to be embarking. Eighteenth-century historians certainly still regarded their work as profoundly edificatory in character. They directed it specifically at the moral education of a social leadership in full accordance with their strongly Calvinist and humanist inheritance. This, I will further suggest, led them at the same time to retain a clear sense of the importance of instilling and cultivating virtue in a receptive audience. It also obliged them to express their belief in the continuing necessity of explaining causality as a major historical phenomenon. These issues, as we shall see, formed the essential core of the historians' own account of an 'enlightened' scholarship. As a result they must surely provide the best historical basis for understanding the function of history in eighteenth-century Scotland. With a firm grasp of their earnest intentions, wrung from the unequivocal words of the participants themselves, we could even hope to appreciate in the next chapter the interplay of these fundamental cultural assumptions as they motivated and directed scholarly discourse in eighteenth-century Scotland.

In the first instance, it seems clear that our authors proposed a deeply conventional purpose for history in an enlightened age. Scholars in Scotland considered that theirs remained an educative and a pre-eminently moralistic discipline. The avowedly dispassionate social science of the modern academy, or even the heavily loaded positivism of Comte, was conspicuously unable to emerge among practitioners whose primary task was still, above all else, the moral improvement of their impressionable Scottish audience. History, its exponents reiterated time and again, could learn and develop through the slow acquisition of new information. Consequently it was able to provide models and examples for the edification of those in society who were charged with important social and moral responsibilities.[105] John Bonar, minister at Cockpen and a Jeremiac Calvinist of the old school, was in this respect at least only typical of his times. Bonar argued vehemently in the unpublished *History of Tyre* (1758) that reading history 'for Amusement only … drudging through its Volumes from a mere shew of Vanity' was in fact 'to abuse History, not to use it'.[106] Information alone, mere intellectual gratification, was not the purpose of true historical scholarship. On the contrary, 'the proper end of such application', he fulminated, 'ought to be a constant improvement in public, & in private virtue'. Indeed, Bonar argued, 'the pursuit of that Knowledge, which has no tendency to make us better men, or more useful Members of Society, is but a specious idleness; and its acquisition only a more creditable ignorance'.[107] Of course, in articulating these claims for history Bonar was effortlessly regurgitating a much older Scottish line of rhetorical argument. This had originated, as we have already seen, in the perceived need to defend learning from possible accusations of impiety or indolence. It seems that a Calvinist and humanist rhetoric of historical intention was so deeply ingrained in Scottish minds by the eighteenth century that their recapitulation of its truisms and clichés could come to seem tiresome and even perfunctory. 'To expatiate on the pleasure and profit which are derived from History, when the world appears to be so sensible of its utility', observed one commentator, 'would be only to fill an exhausted theme with needless repetitions'.[108] Yet this was a duty which the enlightened historian still invariably performed. Indeed, with little sign of genuine remorse he inflicted his congenital urge for self-explanation upon a Scottish audience now equally weary of such familiar justification.

Enlightened historians in Scotland thus still unashamedly proclaimed, as in the case of John Adams of Aberdeen, that 'Without a competent knowledge of mankind, we shall be but ill qualified to act our part on the theatre of the world'.[109] Such a humanist conclusion of course followed easily from an equally established premise. This was voiced, for example, by the lawyer Andrew Stevenson, and provided yet another striking harmony with the 'experiential' concerns of contemporary moral philosophy: 'by a few hours reading the history of past times', he claimed, 'we may learn more than can be acquired by our experience for many years'.[110] Naturally, however, Stevenson was far from alone in holding this conventional view originally found, for example, in John Spotswood. The radical Glaswegian minister John Gillies was another who repeated that he would write history 'not for the amusement of an idle hour, but as an instructive lesson to posterity'.[111] Edification, rather than simply inquisitive exploration, remained in this view the only defensible focus for the author's attention. History was uniquely fitted for these tasks. It was 'the vehicle of a profusion of instructing, persuading, enlightening, elevating knowledge, more beneficial to human life', thought Robert Heron, 'then all the former productions of literary genius'.[112] In beginning his majestic *History of the Roman Republic* (1783), therefore, Adam Ferguson was coining a typically well-phrased aphorism. But it was one which in fact merely voiced the deeply ingrained humanist purpose of Scottish scholarship: 'To know it well', he proclaimed of history, 'is to know mankind'.[113] The last three words, of course, effectively summarised the general understanding of the Scottish historians of this period. Indeed, they deliberately echoed Alexander Pope in defining the project to which European intellectuals of the Enlightenment avidly subscribed. This was a project which certainly employed some clever philosophical metaphors and topical scientific analogies. But it did so fundamentally in order to defend what we can appreciate to be the established moralistic purpose of historical scholarship in Scotland.

The continued elevation of history to this supreme educational role in the moral study of human nature, moreover, still entailed the Scottish historian adopting a dual persona. He was to be at the same time both teacher and judge, a delicate balance whose striking was captured admirably by the evocative imagery of the Edinburgh professor, John Hill, in a paper presented to the Royal Society of Edinburgh in 1784: 'His sensibility to every moral sentiment', Hill advised, 'not only detects the least symptom of what is good or bad in human conduct, but is accompanied with an immediate apprehension of the one and abhorrence of the other'.[114] The partisan requirement for moral discrimination did not on this account vitiate the case for impartiality. Indeed, it remained the case, as Hill reiterated to his audience, that 'His mind, like a faithful mirror, reflects every thing precisely as it is seen'.[115] The humanist's obligation to seek accuracy in exposition and description, however, was no stronger than that to moral commitment and appropriate comment in the evaluation and judgement of historical conduct. This was of course a requirement with which Sir Robert Gordon and Gilbert Burnet in an earlier age, though perhaps not Malinowski, Marc Bloch or Talcott-Parsons in our own, would have been agreeably familiar.[116] In the same vein, when dealing with the sins of the past, it was claimed by William Robertson in the *History of Scotland* (1759) that 'History relates these extravagances of the human mind, without pretending to justify, or even to account for them'.[117] The creation of an accurate narration was here again regarded merely as the necessary prerequisite to the most informed and definitive judgement of men's actions and motivation. The proper explanation of human behaviour was inevitably to be couched in moralistic terms. Indeed, it was even sometimes argued that by its very recapitulation by scholars the immorality of the past would stand condemned. The St Bartholomew's Day massacre, for example, was deemed especially suitable for historical narration precisely because of its unspeakable horrors. For Walter Anderson, minister of Chirnside, in the *History of France* (1769), it seemed 'just and fit to have the authentic narrative of it translated to posterity; that mankind may ever remember with disgust, the horrid effects caused by fanatic zeal and bigotry in a nation'.[118] Similarly, William Smellie, publisher and founding editor of the *Encyclopaedia Britannica*, asserted in a determinedly republican idiom that 'The most important end of history is to promote liberty and virtue, to which impartial history will always be favourable'.[119] Impartiality and accuracy clearly led on inevitably in an enlightened setting to moral commitment rather than to social science. Nicely sensitive to the increasing taste for literary sentimentalism, then, Gilbert Stuart was only expressing with typical finesse a humanist juxtaposition of factual scrupulousness and strongly moralistic intention: 'Her weeping eye is the indication of an instructive sorrow', he gushed, 'and while her bursting heart, mourns over the crimes, the calamities, and the wretchedness of ages that are past, she records them with fidelity as a lesson to succeeding ages'.[120]

As in the rhetoric of the sixteenth and seventeenth centuries, these educative and moralistic urges retained a sharp focus even in an enlightened age. George Buchanan had himself insisted that 'the words and deeds of those, who hold the helme of publick affaires' needed to be 'written as it were in a publick monument, as *Horace* saith', and 'set before all men for imitation'.[121] Successive historians in Scotland had consequently sought to address those who might most benefit from such instruction. Enlightened scholarship again was no exception. It expressed on many occasions its Ciceronian desire to speak directly and effectively to an attentive social leadership. William Duff, for example, echoed *De officiis* in a way which befitted an accomplished eighteenth-century classical scholar. Duff sought nothing less by his scholarship than 'to prepare, form, and furnish the Minds of young Gentlemen of Figure and Distinction, to give them lively Ideas of high Life, to fix generous Principles of True Morals, of Government and Conduct in the different Spheres of publick Life, instructing by Examples of past Ages how to act in like Circumstances in the different Stations and Offices of Trust and Power'.[122] Others, like the more obscure John Belfour, claimed more generally in their work to be addressing those 'who are engaged in the active scenes of life'.[123] He was bent on encouraging a study 'most conducive both to their amusement at home, and to their advantage with society'. C. A. Gordon of Aberdeen, meanwhile, dedicated his own genealogical work to the Duke of Gordon, and hoped to provide in it an 'abundance of perfect Models, for your noble and rising Genius to copy all the Excellencies, which make the great Man'.[124] In short, history still sought out a readership of social leaders, of energetic and practically-minded men 'bent on useful knowledge'. These should have been men who, in Lord Kames' elegant phrase, hopefully felt 'the dawn of patriotism, and who in riper years enjoy its meridian warmth'.[125] The proper audience for enlightened history remained the public-oriented and active men of Scotland. These were the potentially 'great men', the men, above all, to whom social leadership, a position of unquestioned value, was the proper role.

Few could therefore have doubted Sir John Dalrymple's judgement that 'To mark the singular features of singular characters, is one of the chief provinces of history'.[126] Great men, his contemporaries insisted, continued to be the preferred Scottish audience, as well as the natural subject, of a profoundly moralistic history. The question of their uncertain identity in an enlightened age must consequently be a major focus of our own attention in the next chapter: economic change and accelerating social fluidity only turn out to have made the need for clear leadership in Scotland all the more pressing and its absence all the more frustrating. But it remained at the same time a matter of the utmost concern to Scottish historians that the means by which a leadership could effectively direct and underwrite the social and moral development of the community were still shrouded with uncertainty. Not only were causal affairs intrinsically difficult to fathom. Calvinist and humanist discourse also offered two sharply different accounts of causality. Both gave much latitude for individual interpretation and such scope for uncomfortable conclusions as effectively to guarantee a continuing debate in an enlightened age. The historians of the Enlightenment as a result acknowledged of necessity the obligation to explain the underlying dynamic of historical development. The scientific analogy, particularly with the physical sciences, served in this respect only to confirm historians in their ingrained belief that causality, the search in history for what Hutcheson called 'secret Causes', was indeed an essential focus of scholarly concern.[127] It was in any case necessary for a fundamentally moralistic tradition to seek a better understanding of the precise and effective way in which a Scottish leadership should be instructed to act. A plausible account of causality, whatever else it might be thought to offer, still needed to be a central objective of a history. This would remain the case so long as it sought to identify the role of a moral elite in the public sphere, and to encourage the pursuit of virtue in its most active and influential manifestations.

Alexander Tytler was professor of history at Edinburgh, and was adamant on the importance of this point. He saw clearly that 'the most important purposes of history, [are] the tracing of events to their causes, the detection of the springs of human actions, the display of the progress of society, and the rise and fall of states and empires'.[128] In expressing himself in this way, however, Tytler was simply confirming again the forcefulness and continued clarity of the inherited humanist rhetoric of history. The 'springs of human action' had in fact been among the most common motifs of causality among early modern Scottish authors like Sir James Melville, betraying the very considerable extent to which their rhetoric had come to dictate the language in which the purpose and meaning of history could be discussed by successors like Duff and Forbes.[129] Other historians, meanwhile, like the lawyer Andrew Stevenson, took an adjacent rhetorical track. Stevenson said that he endeavoured to extract from history the essential 'connection between causes and effects' in the human world.[130] This was an enterprise which again took on contemporary pertinence in the light of Scottish philosophical interests of the time, with Hume's jargon lending a modish gloss to the perennial concerns of the humanist historian. Some, like Kames, took to an even more fashionable mechanistic vocabulary. It was evident, Kames noted in the *Historical Law Tracts* (1758), that 'Events and subordinate incidents are, in each of these, linked together, and connected in a regular chain of causes and effects'.[131] Others, however, including the royal chaplain George Turnbull, still thought it the quintessential task of history 'to connect human affairs, and to take an united view of God's moral providence'.[132] Such scholars were still of course striving to retain a thoroughly Christian idiom throughout. But in their vigorous search for what another clergyman, George Ridpath, called 'circumstances, causes, and consequences', all the historians of enlightened Scotland nevertheless retained a clear Calvinist and humanist sense of their traditional obligations.[133] Causality was of interest for moral and public rather than for purely scientific or philosophical reasons. It was essential, as Alexander Gerard, professor of divinity at King's College, Aberdeen, had it, for 'the true historian' not to satisfy himself with a mere recital of the facts. Instead, the scholar 'places facts in connexion, he rises to the sources of actions, and he pursues them through their consequences'.[134] Only the truly moral historian was in Gerard's opinion 'plainly actuated by the relation of cause and effect'.[135]

So we are brought back, in conclusion, to the profoundly conventional and moralistic tone with which eighteenth-century historical writing in Scotland engaged in its somewhat high-flown and repetitive self-justification. James Dunbar most eloquently exemplifies this, in tacit agreement with his own distinguished Scottish predecessors. The duties of the modern historian were in the eyes of the professor at King's College, Aberdeen, still consistent with, and defined by reference to, the finest ancient moralists. For the literary man, Dunbar explained, 'to stop the career of Vice is the ultimate end of well-directed ambition. That was felt by the great writers of antiquity. They erected a temple to Virtue, and exhausted on the opposite character all the thunder of eloquence'.[136] Given such a self-conscious rhetorical orientation, it is hardly surprising that the need to discuss causality was, as we have seen, justified in essentially ethical terms. The task was, as that other persuasive Aberdonian George Turnbull put it, one of giving the audience 'proper parts of our own history in particular' and educating them specifically in 'the characters of the persons who were chiefly concerned in those transactions, the different parts they acted, and the different motives and views they were actuated by in all their behaviour'.[137] History throughout the Enlightenment, as in the time of George Buchanan, was directed towards the moral explanation of motivation and outcome. It remained as a result the belief of Scottish authors like the clergyman

Thomas Somerville that it would 'contribute not only to instruction, but to moral improvement'.[138] Indeed, apparent failure to meet this requirement still ensured a hostile reception in eighteenth-century Scotland, providing the most obvious target for critical invective. In attacking Hume's work, for example, the loquacious Robert Heron felt that its greatest weakness lay in the very fact that it seemed to diminish the moralistic potential of history. It threatened to obviate its natural function as a weapon in the unceasing conflict between virtue and vice: 'What moral principles can the ingenuous reader learn from the Historical pages of HUME', he railed, 'save a contempt, not of superstition only, but of all religious principles; a cold, sceptical indifference to all the virtue and vice which human conduct displays'.[139] But this was demonstrably not Hume's intention. And it was an accusation which even the 'Great Infidel' seems, like Godscroft before him, both to have anticipated and rejected. Speaking with the same rhetorical voice as Heron, and in discernibly the same register, Hume himself cast history in a humanist and moralistic mould. It was unique, he claimed, in helping man 'to cherish with the greater anxiety that science and civility which has so close a connection with virtue and humanity, and which, as it is a sovereign antidote against superstition, is also the most effective remedy against vice and disorders of any kind'.[140] The compulsion to present history in this deeply conventional way, indeed to regard departure from traditional intentions as the most reprehensible of scholarly sins, was evidently over-whelming to the Scottish historian in an enlightened age. The authors of the Enlightenment were, after all, still in so many respects using a language first found among Scotland's post-Renaissance scholars. With consummate skill it defined, directed and defended the tradition of scholarship that had been passed on to the Enlightenment. Its continuing acceptance and relevance actually limited for the moment the scope for questioning the *raison d'être* of their own scholarly activities. Robert Heron seems only to have exemplified this essential continuity in the conceptualisation of scholarship in Scotland, despite his acutely topical glance at the social tableau of enlightened Edinburgh: 'Every Coffee-house Critic can tell you', he observed, unconsciously melding the worlds of Scriblerius and Hector Boece, 'that *History* is the best *School of Morality*'.[141]

IV

I have argued that beneath the ostentatious rejection of the past there survived within the broader scholarly community of the eighteenth century clear indications of continuity with an older tradition of scholarship in Scotland. Some enlightened minds readily acknowledged their inheritance from what we earlier identified as Calvinist and humanist sources. But the grounds on which other authors actually distanced themselves from previous scholarship in Scotland also seem to have been less than convincing. Their claims of revolution invariably comprised only a rhetorical allusion to contemporary philosophy and science. This was conjured up to justify a continuation of the older practice of plausible speculation which had itself often been defended in strikingly similar terms. All too often, it seems, budding intellectual revolutionaries were forced back upon scurrilous remarks relating to political, religious and social change, by which the methodological deficiencies of prior scholarship, and the corresponding virtues of their own 'enlightened' alternative, were meant to be implied. Equally, the Enlightenment witnessed the emergence of a recognisable economic history, albeit as part of a still more important and less eye-catching inquiry into manners and morality. Yet political and religious issues continued to a very great extent to dictate the substance of enlightened scholarship and the matters to which its practitioners very largely addressed themselves. More fundamentally eighteenth-century authors still necessarily conceived history as being an educational genre and claimed to practise it for what were essentially didactic purposes. They viewed the identification and instruction of the Scottish élite as their pre-eminent scholarly task. At the same time the historians of the eighteenth century inherited and acknowledged the specific obligation to consider causality in a historical context, and so to trace the relationship between cause and effect in human affairs. In all of their statements on the nature and purpose of history, Scotland's enlightened historians thus expounded what we can now appreciate to have been an essentially Calvinist and humanist view of their work. As admirers of Voltaire, Diderot and Montesquieu, they easily imagined themselves the heirs of the classical moralists. But they also spoke with the assurance and deliberation characteristic of their own less eminent Scottish predecessors, to whom they frequently looked back with a mixture of despair and pride. These were, it is true, only the professed objectives of an evocative rhetoric, ones obviously derived from a much older tradition of Scottish scholarship and originally constructed in very different times. It is to the far-reaching intellectual consequences of this apparent continuity of scholarly purpose in the Scottish Enlightenment that we must now turn.

NOTES

1. John Lawrie, *The History of the Wars in Scotland* (Edinburgh, 1783), p. 1. The classical allusion is to Juvenal, *Satires*, vii, 52. A professed 'Itch for Scribbling' was responsible for Dougal Graham's crude metrical history in 1746, a continuation of the genre established by medieval Scotsmen like Blind Harry and continued in the seventeenth century by Alexander Tyler and Scott of Satchells. See his *Impartial History of the Rise, Progress, and Extinction of the Late Rebellion in Britain*, 5th edn (Glasgow, 1787), p. 5.

2. Samuel Johnson, *Journey to the Western Islands of Scotland* (Glasgow, 1817), p. 503. This had originally appeared in Donald MacNicol, *Remarks on Dr Samuel Johnson's Journey to the Hebrides* (1779).

3. Among the historians who spoke of an 'enlightened age' were the church historian John Skinner, *An Ecclesiastical History of Scotland* (London, 1788), pp. 22–3, and Gilbert Stuart, *History of the Reformation*, p. 206.

4. Sir John Scot, *The Staggering State of the Scots Statesmen*, (ed.), W. Ruddiman (Edinburgh, 1754), a2r.

5. John Pinkerton, *An Enquiry into the History of Scotland*, 2 vols (London, 1789), II, iv.

6. *ibid.*, II, 5.

7. Maitland, *History and Antiquities*, I, 52.

8. Ferguson, *Civil Society*, p. 115. Equally David Hume believed that the Enlightenment

marked the attempt to construct 'a new Scene of Thought' in historical writing, *Letters*, 2 vols (ed.), J. Y. T. Grieg (Oxford, 1932), p. 1, a development in which methodological improvements were thought to be of central importance.

9. Lord Hailes, *Annals of Scotland from the Accession of Malcolm III Surnamed Canmore to the Accession of Robert I* (Edinburgh, 1776), p. 262 n. William Guthrie, *A New Geographical, Historical, and Commercial Grammar and Present State of the Several Kingdoms of the World* (London, 1777), p. 148.

10. Innes, *Critical Essay*, I, 249. Also Anderson, *Historical Essay*, p. 15, and Buchanan, *History*, p. 1.

11. William Alexander, *The History of Women*, 2 vols (London, 1777), II, 64.

12. Hume regarded Newton as nothing less than 'the greatest and rarest genius that ever arose for the ornament and instruction of the species', *The History of England*, 3 vols (London, 1875), III, 780. To Walter Anderson, moreover, he was 'the incomparable geometrician and philosopher', *The Philosophy of Ancient Greece* (Edinburgh, 1791), p. 465.

13. Thomas Hobbes, *De Cive* (ed. and transl.), B. Gert (Atlantic Highlands, 1978), p. 92.

14. See the 'Discourse on the Method' in *Descartes: Philosophical Writings* (ed. and transl.), N. Kemp Smith, (London, 1952), p. 147.

15. James Grant, *Thoughts on the Origin and Descent of the Gael* (Edinburgh, 1814), p. 13.

16. George Turnbull, *A Treatise on Ancient Painting* (London, 1740), p. vii.

17. Somerville, for example, feared that the allusion to philosophical methods would tend to 'engender suspicions, and to nourish, especially in the young mind, a habit of scepticism', *The History of Political Transactions* (London, 1792), p. xx. Equally, the schizophrenic mind of John Pinkerton reacted with hostility to the 'reasoning ignorance ' which he attributed to rationalists from Aristotle to Voltaire, *History* , II, 51, and openly questioned the ability of the latter, 'and a few other ignorant theorists', to provide a systematic explanation of the human condition, *A Dissertation on the Origin and Progress of the Scythians or Goths* (London, 1787), p. 115.

18. Alexander Tytler, *Plan and Outline of a Course of Lectures on Universal History, Ancient and Modern* (Edinburgh, 1782), p. 2. For parallels see Spotswood, *History*, A5r, and Ross, *History*, a1r.

19. Monro, *Apology*, p. 17.

20. Fleming, *Fulfilling of the Scripture*, a7r–a7v. This also recalls the scholarly, almost Humean, enthusiasm for experimental/experiential methods found in the presbyterian polemicist William Rait in 1671, who had attempted to 'labour to know experimentally the power of the Christian Religion', *Vindication*, e1r. See also Lithgow's interesting choice of title, *A True and Experimentall Discourse*, recounting his experience as 'an Eye witness' to the siege of Breda.

21. David Hume, 'Of the Study of History', *Essays, Moral and Political*, 2 vols, 2nd edn (Edinburgh, 1742), I, 74. The humanist notion that an absence of historical 'experience' resulted in intellectual puerility had earlier been voiced by Ross, *History*, a1r. The antiquarian and publisher Thomas Ruddiman, too, more obviously spoke with the rhetorical voice of his Scottish antecedents when recommending monarchical government as 'confirmed by the Experience of all Ages', *An Answer to the Reverend Mr. George Logan's Late Treatise on Government* (Edinburgh, 1747), p. 392. Here, despite the contemporary philosophical resonances, was a statement of historical utility straight out of the presbyterian and humanist traditions of the past.

22. The best detailed statement of the conventional kind is H. Höpfl, 'From Savage to Scotsman: Conjectural History in the Scottish Enlightenment', *Journal of British Studies*, 17 (1978), 19–40. Bryson's *Man and Society* was perhaps correct to emphasise how much conjecturalism entailed the use of speculative reconstruction, whilst E. C. Mossner, 'Gladys Bryson, "Man and Society"', *Philological Quarterly*, 25 (1946), 136–42, wisely pointed to the significance of contemporary philosophy in suggesting the legitimation of the conjecture. Stuart Piggott gives a good account of its anthropological connotations, though fails, in an otherwise excellent interpretation, to highlight the earlier Scottish currency of this resonant defence of speculation and inference, *Ruins in A Landscape: Essays in Antiquarianism* (Edinburgh, 1976), pp. 151–5. Recently, Emerson, 'Conjectural History', with its emphasis upon the Calvinist and classical origins of reconstructive history, especially such works as Lucretius' *De Rerum Natura*, offers by far the most telling analysis of a more mundane reality.

23. Dugald Stewart (ed.), *Works of Adam Smith*, 6 vols., (Edinburgh, 1811–12), V, 452.

24. Grant, *Origin of the Gael*, p. 13.

25. John Lanne Buchanan, *A Defence of the Scots Highlanders in General and Some Learned Characters in Particular* (London, 1794), p. 119. A similar and slightly earlier condemnation of previous Scottish scholarship came from the Aberdonian moral philosopher James Beattie, who remarked that what 'passes for the history of those dark ages is in many particulars little better than conjecture', *Dissertations Moral and Critical* (London, 1783), p. 533. Nevertheless, Beattie himself decided that 'a conjecture may be formed of the distracted state of those feudal governments, in which the nobility had acquired great power, and high privileges', *ibid.*, p. 542.

26. Walter Goodall, *An Introduction to the History and Antiquities of Scotland* (London, 1769), p. 5.

27. Gilbert Stuart, *An Historical Dissertation Concerning the Antiquity of the English Constitution* (Edinburgh, 1768), p. vi.

28. Robert Heron, *A New General History of Scotland* (Perth, 1794), p. 7.

29. Pinkerton, *Dissertation*, p. 115.

30. Something of the suspicion surrounding speculative inference and comparison derived from the continuing claim, inherited likewise from earlier Scottish scholarship, that history required unquestionable accuracy and authenticity in order to fulfil its allotted role. The minister of Dalmeny, Thomas Robertson, for example, maintained that 'The standard of History is Truth', *The History of Mary Queen of Scots* (Edinburgh, 1793), p. 70. Stuart, too, sought to raise 'not ... a monument to my prejudices, but to build a Temple to Truth', *The History of Scotland from the Establishment of the Reformation Till the Death of Queen Mary*, 2 vols (London, 1782), I, A2v. Conjectures, it seems, the stuff of men dangerously trying to make history mimic the natural sciences, put this project in doubt.

31. George Wallace, *The Nature and Descent of Ancient Peerages* (Edinburgh, 1785), p. 39.

32. William Borthwick, *Remarks on British Antiquities* (Edinburgh, 1776), p. 67.

33. Kames considered that the delayed emergence of Scottish feudalism could be explained by a series of 'probable conjectures', *Essays on Several Subjects Concerning British Antiquities* (Edinburgh, 1747), p. 4. William Robertson, moreover, anticipated providing his readers with 'probable conjectures with regard to the plan of God's providence', *The History of Scotland*, 2 vols (London, 1759), I, 4. In a similar vein, relating the device to philosophy and probabilistic reasoning, see Andrew Stevenson on 'prudential conjectures', *The History of the Church and State of Scotland*, 3 vols (Edinburgh, 1753–7), I, b1v, and both James Dunbar, *Essays on the History of Mankind in Rude and Uncultivated Ages* (Dublin, 1782), p. 118, and Lord Kames again, *Historical Law Tracts*, 2 vols (Edinburgh, 1758), I, 385, on 'rational conjectures'.

34. David Hume, *A Treatise of Human Nature*, 3 vols (Edinburgh, 1739–40), I, 220. Hume's discussion of the 'association of ideas' occurs a little earlier, *ibid.*, I, 157–83.

35. Pinkerton, *History*, I, vi. From 'conjunction' to 'conjecture' was of course only a small logical and semantic step.

36. Fleming, *Epistolary Discourse*, p. 24.

37. Innes, *Critical Essay*, II, 536.

38. Blackwood, *History*, p. 85.

39. Mackenzie, *Moral Essay*, p. 39.

40. Even this sense of impending damnation seems to have been shared by those previous scholars who had employed the conjecture. Thomas Innes, for example, was not only prepared to employ what he recognised as the probabilistic 'conjecture', but was very much aware of the opprobrium which this speculative device had always tended to invite. Excusing himself, he said that 'though [he had] been sometimes obliged for want of vouchers, to make use of conjecture', he had always usually tried to cover himself by the use of notes and references, *Critical Essay*, I, xlix. Thus critics like Heron and Pinkerton themselves had their Scottish forebears, from whose assaults Innes was attempting to protect himself.

41. Stewart, 'Dissertation', I, 4.

42. George Wallace, *Thoughts on the Origin of Feudal Tenures* (Edinburgh, 1783), pp. 39–40.

43. Pinkerton, *History*, I, li.

44. Ferguson, *Civil Society*, p. 120. One who had already perceived and taken up the challenge of modernising the Scottish canon (and significantly its eloquence) was John Gordon of

Buthlaw, who sought to render in 'the fashion of a more felicitous age' the work of Fordun. The latter, Gordon claimed, had been 'overwhelmed in the refuse of the fourteenth century', 'ignorant of all elegancies', and as a result 'behoved to speak according to the manner of the times, that is, rudely', John Gordon, 'A Dissertation Concerning the Marriage of Robert Seneschal of Scotland with Elizabeth More', *Scotia Rediviva*, 1 (1826), p. 181. Originally published in Latin in 1759.

45. Grant, *Origin of the Gael*, p. 379.

46. As a recent scholar observes of the Enlightenment, 'None of its participants doubted that the literary renaissance was an integral part of the "Awakening of Scotland" in the economic and other social spheres', D. Kettler, *The Social and Political Thought of Adam Ferguson* (Columbus, Ohio, 1965), p. 16. Such realisation of contextual change can only have strengthened the scholars' conviction that their own work had acquired a new and firmer basis.

47. Hume, *History*, III, 114.

48. Alexander Kincaid, *History of Edinburgh* (Edinburgh, 1787), p. 91.

49. Anderson, *Historical Essay*, p. 85.

50. Guthrie, *New Grammar*, p. 148. The 'inhabitants of no country', William Borthwick agreed, 'have been more unfortunate in the preservation of their ancient writings', *Remarks*, p. 1.

51. Crawfurd, *History*, p. v. An example of the continuing tendency to make use of broad contextual brush-strokes in preparing the way for announcing an intellectual revolution might be the somewhat loaded description of pre-Enlightenment Edinburgh as stagnating in 'pious, squalid, post-medieval gloom ... a dark undeveloped land', Stocking, 'Lord Kames', p. 67.

52. Crawfurd, *History*, p. 9. A similar reliance upon economic and social observations to construct an identity for modernity was to be found, for example, in Sir Robert Gordon's references to 'the great increase of trade, and the superior wealth' acquired by Scotsmen since 1707, *In the Question Concerning the Peerage of Sutherland* ([ ], 1771), p. 80.

53. George Ridpath, *A Border History of Scotland and England* (London, 1776), p. iv. Identification with an 'enlightened age' had clearly percolated through even to the scholars of rural Roxburghshire, where Ridpath's journal was to record his delight and admiration when reading the works of friends like Hume, Robertson, and Smith, and his corresponding disdain for earlier authors like Abercromby. See *Diary of George Ridpath, Minister of Stitchel, 1755–1761* (ed.), J. B. Paul (Edinburgh, 1922).

54. Stewart, 'Dissertation', I, 44. Indeed, Stewart claimed that, after Buchanan, 'the name of Scotland, so early distinguished over Europe by the learning and the fervid genius of her sons, disappears for more than a century and a half from the history of letters', *ibid.*, I, 47–8. Although Stewart appears to have been unable to extend the same chronological scale to the more proximate case of Scottish scholarship, he was happy to trace Montesquieu's project, for example, back to Bodin in the sixteenth century, *ibid.*, I, 40, 154. Not only do we now know that the relative obscurity of Scottish scholarship (about which Stewart was at least correct) did not detract from its significance or vibrancy, but we can begin to appreciate from Stewart's perspective just how important must have been an instinctive dislike of 'Gothic gloom' in leading him to denigrate the methodology and so the historical achievements of earlier ages. Conversely, a lover of the Gothic, like the singular John Pinkerton, could be expected to attempt the deconstruction of the Enlightenment achievement, hence, perhaps, his barbed comment that his was an age in which 'ignorance is called philosophy', *History*, I, 200.

55. Pinkerton, *History*, I, xlvi.

56. Ferguson, *Civil Society*, p. 120.

57. William Barron, *History of the Colonization of the Free States of Antiquity* (London, 1777), p. 3.

58. Robertson, *History of Scotland*, II, 257.

59. *ibid.*, II, 260.

60. *Edinburgh Review*, 1 (1755), i–iii.

61. Maitland, *History and Antiquities*, I, i.

62. Sir John Dalyell, *Fragments of Scottish History* (Edinburgh, 1798), p. iv.

63. *ibid.*, p. iv.

64. Lawrie, *History*, p. 3.

65. William Duff, *A History of Scotland* (London, 1749), a1r.
66. *ibid.*, a1v.
67. Lord Buchan, *Discourse Promoting a Society for the Investigation of the History of Scotland* ([ ], 1780), pp. 17–23.
68. Pinkerton, *History*, I, xlvii.
69. Hugh Blair, *Lectures on Rhetoric and Belles Lettres*, 2 vols (London, 1783), II, 284.
70. Borthwick, *Remarks*, p. v–vi. As Robertson concurred, 'No period in the history of ones own country can be considered as altogether uninteresting', *History of the Reign of the Emperor Charles V*, 2 vols (Dublin, 1762), I, 5.
71. Pinkerton, *History*, I, xxii.
72. Adam Smith, *An Inquiry into the Nature and Causes of the Wealth of Nations*, 2 vols (London, 1776), I, 165. The perilous existence and fleeting influence of the intellectual was also significantly in Hume's mind. He observed that Hobbes' eclipse was 'a lively instance, how precarious are all reputations founded on reasoning and philosophy', *History*, III, 505. The social and moral position of Scottish intellectuals, commonly known as 'literati' from Burton's original coinage in *The Anatomy of Melancholy* (1621), was, of course, a matter of the most profound personal concern to scholars in an enlightened age. As we have seen, Robert Burton was himself steeped in the obsessions of Boece, Buchanan and the Stoics, as well as (possibly) Simione Grahame and Jacobean Scottish scholarship.
73. Despite the obvious interpretative advantages of a much wider range of authors, the study of the Continental Enlightenment remains, like in Scotland, handicapped by a disproportionate emphasis upon 'the interpretation of the works of four figures generally acknowledged to be the principals of the age ... ', S. Gearhart, *The Open Boundary of History and Fiction: A Critical Approach to the French Enlightenment* (Princeton, NJ, 1984), pp. 14–15. As with Scotland, this allows the achievements of the few both to be distorted by their supporters and marginalised by the doubters.
74. General intimations of the future consequences of Scottish materialism inform such contributions as Skinner, 'Economics and History', Lehmann, *John Millar*, and A. C. Chitnis, *The Scottish Enlightenment* (London, 1976), esp. pp. 91–123.
75. See especially Meek's *Ignoble Savage*, his 'Marxist Sociology', and Duncan Forbes, 'Scientific Whiggism: Adam Smith and John Millar', *Cambridge Journal*, (1954), 643–70.
76. Pascal 'Property and Society', written in 1938, was, as we mentioned earlier, a pioneering example, although such works as Small's *Adam Smith*, from 1907, also took Scottish materialism to be a vital source for later social and economic science.
77. See particularly the analysis of William Robertson's views, which lie at the heart of Meek's interpretation in 'Marxist Sociology', esp. pp. 37–8, and which had earlier sustained Pascal's arguments in 'Property and Society', esp. p. 177.
78. Typical of recent revisionism is Andrew Skinner's 'Scottish Contribution', a study which specifically re-examines Meek's claims and the suggestion that Adam Smith in particular was an 'economic determinist'. Others who have recently discussed this question include Haakonssen, *Science of a Legislator*, esp. pp. 178–89, and D. Winch, 'Adam Smith's enduring particular result', in Hont and Ignatieff (eds), *Wealth and Virtue*, esp. pp. 259–60.
79. Smith's uses of the materialist classification of historical societies, it seems, 'did not in themselves constitute an *explanation* of the process of transition between stages ... ', Skinner, 'Scottish Contribution', p. 93.
80. A fine example of the place of economic history within a universal study of culture and manners comes in Henry's profession that his work on Scotland had to offer 'a distinct view of the religion, laws, learning, arts, commerce, and manners of its inhabitants, in every age', *The History of Great Britain*, 6 vols (London, 1771–93), I, iii.
81. See Phillipson in 'Towards a Definition of the Scottish Enlightenment', in P. Fritz and D. Williams (eds), *City and Society in the Eighteenth Century* (Toronto, 1973), pp. 125–48. Also John Robertson in 'The Scottish Enlightenment at the Limits of the Civic Tradition', in Hont and Ignatieff (eds), *Wealth and Virtue*, pp. 137–78.
82. As Henry put it, 'The history of manners will probably be esteemed, by many readers, the most agreeable and entertaining part of history', *History*, I, 429.
83. Francis Hutcheson, *An Inquiry into the Original of Our Ideas of Beauty and Virtue*; *in Two Treatises* (London, 1725), p. 72. Hutcheson later went further, adding that 'HISTORY derives its chief Excellence from the representing the Manners and Characters', *ibid.*, p. 244.

84. Sir John Dalrymple, *An Essay Towards a General History of Feudal Property* (London, 1758), p. ix.

85. Kincaid, *History*, p. 15. 'Barbarity' was frequently invoked, as at *ibid.*, pp. 1, 16, 56, 62, though each time not (as in Smith) with any direct reference to a state of property relations, but rather in order to locate something within the history of manners.

86. Crawfurd, *History*, p. 9.

87. Blair, *Lectures*, I, 100, and *A Critical Dissertation on the Poems of Ossian* (London, 1763), p. 20.

88. Hugo Arnot, *The History of Edinburgh* (Edinburgh, 1779), p. 51.

89. Gilbert Stuart, *A View of Society in Europe in its Progress from Rudeness to Refinement* (Edinburgh, 1782), p. 69.

90. Direct evidence that Hume, too, analysed property relations and economic developments only as part of a moral and social inquiry might be his explanation that feudalism arose 'from the excess itself of that liberty', *History*, I, 115.

91. William Guthrie, *General History of Scotland*, 10 vols (London, 1767–8), I, D4r.

92. Amongst the greatest contributions were Gilbert Stuart, *Observations Concerning the Public Law and Constitutional History of Scotland* (Edinburgh, 1779), Kames's *Historical Law Tracts*, and John Millar's *An Historical View of the English Government* (London, 1781), as well as Lord Hailes' long-unpublished *Historical Account of the Senators of the College of Justice of Scotland, Since its Institution in* 1532 (Edinburgh, 1842).

93. See D. B. Horn, 'University of Edinburgh and the Teaching of History', *University of Edinburgh Journal*, 17 (1953–4), 161. Also, for the founding of the Edinburgh Chair of Universal History, see his *University of Edinburgh*, p. 41. On the Glasgow Chair of Ecclesiastical History, instituted in 1716, see Mackie, *University of Glasgow*, p. 193. Roger Emerson, moreover, explains how between 1717 and 1753 all five universities began to teach history as a separate discipline in its own right, 'Conjectural History', p. 75.

94. See John Williams, *An Account of Some Remarkable Ancient Ruins Lately Discovered in the Highlands and Northern Parts of Scotland* (Edinburgh, 1777). Nimmo made use of the 'Names of rivers, mountains, and cities', *General History of Stirlingshire* (Edinburgh, 1777), in much the same way, for example, as Scottish precursors like Henry Maule, *History*, p. 19; Major repeatedly, *History of Greater Britain*, e.g. pp. 3, 18, 38, 50, 52–3; or even John Cunningham's anonymous *Essay Upon the Inscription of Macduff's Crosse in Fyfe* (Edinburgh, 1678). Maitland, too, notably proclaiming 'language, a proof perhaps more certain than that of historical authority', *History and Antiquities*, I, i, obviously owed much to the sort of early modern British antiquarianism explored in S. Piggott, 'Antiquarian Thought in the Sixteenth and Seventeenth Centuries', in L. Fox (ed.), *English Historical Scholarship in the Sixteenth and Seventeenth Centuries* (London, 1956), pp. 93–114.

95. On the fourteenth century, see e.g. Lord Hailes, *Remarks Concerning the History of Scotland* (Edinburgh, 1773), esp. pp. 40–88. Likewise Kames's *Essays*, Hailes's *An Examination of Some Arguments for the High Antiquity of Regiam Majestatem*; and an Inquiry into the Authenticity of Leges Malcolmi* (Edinburgh, 1769). Also see Thomas Ruddiman's, *Dissertation Concerning the Competition for the Crown of Scotland* (Edinburgh, 1748).

96. See William Tytler, *An Historical and Critical Enquiry into the Evidence Against Mary Queen of Scots* (Edinburgh, 1769), who considered Mary to be guilty as charged, and the earlier Walter Goodall, *An Examination of the Letters of Mary Queen of Scots*, 2 vols (Edinburgh, 1754), who protested her innocence. Thomas Robertson's *History* likewise sought to rehabilitate Mary as, to a lesser degree, did Hailes's *Remarks* and William Robertson's *History of Scotland*.

97. Hume's *The Natural History of Religion* (London, 1757) was unquestionably the most forward-looking. But much more typical and numerous examples of the historicisation of religion were the efforts, for example, of Lord Hailes, including the *Historical Memorials Concerning the Provincial Councils of the Scottish Clergy* (Edinburgh, 1769), and the *Disquisition Concerning the Antiquities of the Christian Church* (Glasgow, 1783).

98. Stuart, *History of the Reformation*, p. iv. Stuart's familiarity with earlier Scottish scholarship is one of the clearest traits to emerge in his long overdue biography, W. Zachs, *Without Regard to Good Manners: A Biography of Gilbert Stuart, 1743–1782* (Edinburgh, 1992).

99. Lachlan Shaw, *The History of the Province of Moray* (Edinburgh, 1775), esp. pp. 233–381.

100. Guthrie, *New Grammar*, p. 144.

101. Kincaid, *History*, p. 20 et seq., and Robertson, *History of Scotland*, II, esp. 1–90, 164–5.
102. Robert Wallace, *Dissertation on the Numbers of Mankind in Antient and Modern Times* (Edinburgh, 1753); John Witherspoon, *The History of a Corporation of Servants Discovered a Few Years Ago in the Interior Parts of South America* (Edinburgh, 1765).
103. See particularly Maitland, *History and Antiquities*, II, 772 et seq., and John Campbell, *A Full and Particular Description of the Highlands of Scotland* (London, 1752), p. 15. Kames, moreover, spoke enthusiastically of 'the intimate connection that true religion has with morality', emphasising the benefits of presbyterianism and contrasting them with Catholic worship. Catholicism, he insisted, was 'crowded with ceremonies' and consequently, with obvious echoes of the Calvinist and humanist criticism of empty rhetoric, like 'the Italian opera, which is all sound, and no sentiment', *Sketches of the History of Man*, 2 vols (Edinburgh, 1774), II, 430, 479. Such admirers of presbyterianism and purveyors of the traditional historiography of course far outnumbered during the eighteenth century the unbelievers like David Hume.
104. A persuasive case for seeing Robertson in particular as a direct successor of Knox has been made by a recent scholar, whose concluding rhetorical question is 'Had this secularity not, in fact, been bequeathed to the Enlightenment by Knox himself and the historical command that he has had over the interpretation of the Scottish reformation?', M. Fearnley-Sander, 'Philosophical History and the Scottish Reformation: William Robertson and the Knoxian Tradition', *Historical Journal*, 33 (1990), 338.
105. As a recent student remarks, the historians of the eighteenth century in general, and Scottish practitioners in particular, inherited a 'long tradition of classical justifications for historical writing and did little to modify them', M. Phillips, 'Macaulay, Scott, and the Literary Challenge to Historiography', *Journal of the History of Ideas*, 50 (1989), 119–20. It was only after Scott, Romanticism, and the explosion of the new theories of poetics, that the nineteenth-century finally buried the rhetoric and practice of this tradition.
106. John Bonar, *The History of Tyre* (New College Library, Edinburgh, MSS Box 27, X156, 1/5), pp. 16-17. I am grateful to Richard Sher for bringing this manuscript to my attention.
107. *ibid.*, p. 17. Here Bonar reaches out for an unacknowledged quotation from Bolingbroke, itself a purple passage taken from Tillotson, which reads 'The true and proper object of this application, is a constant improvement in private and in public virtue. An application to any study, that tends neither directly nor indirectly to make us better men and better citizens, is at best but a specious and ingenious sort of idleness ... and the knowledge we acquire by it is a creditable kind of ignorance, nothing more', *Letters*, I, 14–15.
108. John Belfour, *A New History of Scotland* (London, 1770), p. iii.
109. John Adams, *Curious Thoughts on the History of Man* (Dublin, 1790), A2r. For an earlier usage, see Maule, *History*, p. vii, on the 'theatre of man's life'.
110. Stevenson, *History*, I, b1r. Spotswood had also once spoken of the advantage of history that 'in a few hours reading, a man may gather moe Instructions out of the same ... [than many men] can possibly learn by their owne experience', *History*, a5r. Mis-spelling original.
111. John Gillies, 'A Discourse on the History, Manners, and Character of the Greeks', in his (ed.), *The Orations of Lysias and Isocrates* (London, 1778), A1r.
112. Heron, *New General History*, p. xvi. That history was in fact the very finest means to the improvement of morality was a possibility implicit in one of the debates of the Newtonian Society, an Edinburgh undergraduate forum: 'Whether has civil history or moral treatises the greatest tendency to improve our morals', they asked. Debated on 27 July 1762 and found in 'Roll of Miscellaneous Questions to be debated in the Newtonian Society', *Newtonian Society Minute Book*, 1760–64, (Edinburgh, University Library, MSS Gen. 1423). Perhaps this crucial question, and certainly its most likely answer, was suggested by Francis Hutcheson who, with apparent disregard for his own profession as a moral philosopher, argued that because of their lively and engagingly naturalistic use of example, 'the *Epic Poem* or *Tragedy*, give a vastly greater Pleasure than the Writings of a *Philosopher*, tho both aim at recommending *Virtue*', *Inquiry*, p. 241.
113. Adam Ferguson, *The History of the Roman Republic*, 3 vols (London, 1783), I, 3.
114. John Hill, 'An Essay upon the Principles of Historical Composition', *Transactions of the Royal Society of Edinburgh*, 1 (1784), 79. Robert Heron, too, saw a judicial role for the historian, envisaging him becoming 'the impartial and inflexible judge of mankind', *New General History* , p. xii.

115. Hill, 'Essay', p. 86.
116. Marc Bloch, for example, one of the most notable of modern theorists, tells us that 'There are two ways of being impartial: that of the scholar and the judge'. Naturally, they have 'a common root in their honest submission to the truth'. But when the scholar has 'observed and explained, his task is finished. It yet remains for the judge to pass sentence', *The Historian's Craft* (ed. and transl.), P. Putnam, (Manchester, 1984), pp. 138–9. Hill, Heron, and even Hume, denied this characteristically modern distinction with all the power at their disposal. Hume, indeed, thought that 'The Writers of History, as well as the Readers, are sufficiently interested in the Characters and Events, to have a lively Sentiment of Blame or Praise; and, at the same Time, have no particular Interest or Concern to pervert their Judgment', 'Of the Study of History', I, 77. Disinterest, but not uninterest, was the disposition of the narrator; this aided rather than forestalled the ultimate judgement.
117. Robertson, *History of Scotland*, I, 311.
118. Walter Anderson, *The History of France*, 2 vols (London, 1769), II, 337.
119. William Smellie, *Literary and Characteristical Lives of John Gregory, Lord Kames, David Hume, and Adam Smith* (Edinburgh, 1800), p. 64.
120. Stuart, *History of Scotland*, I, 202. That accuracy necessarily led to a fit moral conclusion also seems to have been Francis Hutcheson's influential opinion: 'The representing the Actions themselves, if the Representation be *judicious, natural, and lively*, will make us admire the *Good*, and detest the *Vitious*, the *Inhuman*, the *Treacherous*, and *Cruel*, by means of our *moral Sense*, without any Reflections of the *Poet* to guide our *Sentiments*', *Inquiry*, p. 241.
121. Buchanan, *De Jure Regni*, p. 62.
122. Duff, *History*, A3r.
123. Belfour, *New History*, p. iv.
124. C. A. Gordon, *A Concise History of the Ancient and Illustrious House of Gordon* (Aberdeen, 1890), p. xi. Originally published in 1754.
125. Kames, *Sketches*, I, v.
126. Sir John Dalrymple, *Memoirs of Great Britain and Ireland*, 2 vols (Edinburgh, 1771), I, 46.
127. Hutcheson, *Inquiry*, p. 72.
128. Tytler, *Plan and Outline*, p. 5. Hume, too, shared the Calvinist and humanist view of the scholar's task: when an 'Event is supposed to proceed from certain and stable Causes, he may then display his Ingenuity, in assigning these Causes', 'Of the Rise and Progress of the Arts and Sciences', *Essays*, II, 53.
129. Duff, for example, sought the 'reasons, springs, and grounds of transactions', *History*, a1r, whilst Hume considered 'the true springs and causes of every event', *Natural History*, p. 16. The 'secret springs' of the world form the subject of an explicitly Newtonian rumination on determinism, in Duncan Forbes, 'Reflexions on the Sources of Incredulity with Regard to Religion', in *Works* (Edinburgh, 1752), p. 162. But the Jacobean courtier Melville was also to be heard urging us to 'discover those hidden Springs of Affairs, which give motion to all the vast Machines ... ', *Memoires*, a2r.
130. Stevenson, *History*, b1r.
131. Kames, *Historical Law Tracts*, I, v. Later, Kames expressed a similar hope that 'reason' would be 'exercised in discovering causes and tracing effects through a long chain of dependencies', *ibid.*, I, xii. This sort of mechanistic vocabulary might tempt the modern student to regard it as evidence of a materialist philosophy. But another Scottish writer anticipated this temptation, and explained that the use of terms like 'wonderful mechanism' was purely figurative. 'I only use the term metaphorically to those effects ... produced in consequence of such fixed laws as are independent of the will. It hath therefore no reference to the doctrine of the materialist, a system which, in my opinion, is not only untenable, but absurd': George Campbell, *The Philosophy of Rhetoric*, 2 vols (London, 1776), I, 288 n.
132. George Turnbull, *Observations upon Liberal Education* (London, 1742), p. 393. Similarly, Robert Wallace understood the function of 'the moderns' to be to study better 'those hidden connexions which may be traced in the ways of providence', *Various Prospects of Mankind, Nature, and Providence*, (London, 1761) p. 22.
133. Ridpath, *Border History*, p. vii.
134. Alexander Gerard, *An Essay on Genius* (London, 1774), p. 221. That causality was a moral rather than a scientific question was also emphasised by Gerard's Aberdonian friend and contemporary William Duff. Having enjoined the historian to record 'reasons, springs, and

grounds of transactions', Duff further encouraged him 'to make such observations ... as from them to draw proper morals and observations', *History*, air.

135. Gerard, *Genius*, p. 221.
136. Dunbar, *Essays*, Preface.
137. Turnbull, *Observations*, p. 171.
138. Somerville, *Political Transactions*, p. xxii.
139. Heron, *New General History*, p. xxxix.
140. Hume, *History*, I, 700. Significantly, the terms 'antidote' and 'remedy' suggest a history which searches out the cause of a moral malaise, and seeks to minister to it. Such a pathological vision of vice and immorality often characterised Scottish historical thought, as we saw in authors like Boece and Alexander Ross. Hume had elsewhere merely affirmed his moral commitments as a scholar, remarking that 'Historians have been, almost without Exception, the true Friends of Virtue', 'Of the Study of History', I, 75. Having drawn upon a republican resource which we have seen had long been familiar in Scotland, Hume went on to insist that even '*Machiavel* himself discovers a true Sentiment of Virtue in his History of Florence', *ibid.*, I, 75–6.
141. Heron, *New General History*, p. xxxviii.

CHAPTER FOUR

Historians and Orators

The Rise and Fall of Scholarly Virtue

ILLIAM SEMPLE OBSERVED in 1782 that 'The historian is universally acknowledged to hold a distinguished rank, in the circle of literature'.[1] Most of his Scottish contemporaries, as we have seen, shared this keen sense of their own social function as educators and moralists. Their rhetoric of scholarly intention certainly expressed this view with great vehemence and alacrity. To regard Enlightenment history as anything less than a self-consciously edificatory discourse would as a result seem needlessly perverse. But beyond the eloquent theorisation of their own activities, the practice of the eighteenth-century historians, I shall argue, substantially bears out this view. It is clear, in particular, that the Scottish historians still acted as though they were public orators and preachers. Indeed, this feeling was now to be of crucial significance in orienting the work that they produced. In the first instance, we shall see that it still meant a keen focus upon the great orators of the past. More widely, it also entailed the sometimes rather speculative attribution of eloquence and rhetorical prowess to a motley assortment of historical dignitaries. The intention of both of these strategies would still seem to have been to demonstrate the ultimate descent of the modern historical author from an ancient line of orators and preachers, as well as to provide an analysis of the uses to which such a status should be put.[2] Having identified in this way the historical function of the moral rhetorician and illustrated the crucial role of oratory in society, we shall find that the Scottish writer remained unwilling to have his historical text merely proceed to mull over a stultifying record of 'what King reigned in such an Age, and what Battles were fought, which common History teacheth, and teacheth little more'.[3] Enlightened historians instead went significantly further than their Scottish forebears. They no longer presented oratory simply as a vital characteristic of the legitimate social leader, probably the limit of their predecessors' ambitions. Eighteenth-century historians, it turns out, now increasingly associated it directly with the possession of learning, claiming in the process that it thereby legitimated the leadership of Scottish historians and intellectuals themselves. With this far more portentous conclusion having been reached, enlightened historical discourse in Scotland became an arena for the definition and propagation of rational virtue. This gave force to the crucial suggestion that history had the power to mould a society in its own image. Nor was even this the end of the enlightened scholar's task. The conventional remit of the Scottish historian had obliged him also to offer an account of causality. This was an area in which the resources of the Calvinist and humanist tradition were now to be stretched to their limits. What emerged was an intensified conflict between scholarly virtue and determinism. Trapped by the language and perceptions of their predecessors, Scottish scholars, I shall argue, were ultimately denied, in their hour of earthly glory, the very justification for their social leadership which Calvinist and humanists had always craved. With these momentous and far-reaching ends in view, however, like the enlightened Scottish historians before us, it is necessary to begin simply with their intensely Ciceronian enthusiasm for the art of oratory in its historical context.

1: IN DEFENCE OF ENLIGHTENED ORATORY

When James Dunbar observed that the ancient writers had been the great worshippers of virtue, and had 'exhausted on the opposite character all the thunder of eloquence',[4] he was speaking symbolically on behalf of the broader Scottish historical community: 'Animated with the views, not with the genius of the ancients', he claimed, 'I occupy the same ground'.[5] The approving tone and the identification of eloquence as the pre-eminent tool of the influential public moralist are entirely consistent with the thinking of his contemporaries. But they are consistent also with the detailed working-out of the complex historical attitude towards rhetoric which we explored in the earlier Scottish tradition. Scotsmen, as we have already seen, had developed a sophisticated understanding of the importance, and the potential dangers, of a reliance upon the sheer verbal felicity of the orator. This concern in fact affected the scholarship of an enlightened age no less than it had the efforts of Buchanan or James VI. There are, indeed, palpable signs that a Calvinist and humanist ambivalence towards rhetoric continued to inform the Enlightenment mind, perhaps still haunted by the spectres of Jesuit casuistry and the tortuous argumentation of the Schoolmen.[6] However, the value of linguistic skill in framing and propagating true and useful moral knowledge was also over-whelmingly recognised by the Scottish historians. *Eloquentia* had yet to acquire in Scotland quite those unwelcome connotations of sophistry and superficiality which had slowly been emerging in England and elsewhere.[7] Indeed, it could be argued that a heightened awareness of the vital role of accurate and articulate communication in moral affairs actually underlay eighteenth-century expressions of anxiety as to the integrity and manipulability of rhetoric.

It is certainly possible, for example, to find persuasive evidence of a distaste for modern trends in the practice of public speaking, a development which is entirely consistent with what we have seen was a much older Scottish commitment to the traditional moralistic and exhortatory purposes of oratory. Hugh Blair, of course, is a fine case in point, commenting with obvious alarm in his *Lectures on Rhetoric and Belles Lettres* (1783) upon 'those public and promiscuous Societies, in which multitudes are brought together who are often of low stations and occupations, who are joined by no common bond of union, except an absurd rage for Public Speaking'.[8] The use of oratorical methods for purposes fundamentally unconnected with the proper business of public discourse was to conventional minds little more than a misuse. Oratory remained for Blair, as for his Scottish predecessors, indissolubly linked to notions of moral edification. These required that the orator be a man of high personal integrity and a pre-eminent example in his public-spiritedness to those he was attempting to persuade. He had to be, in short, a 'good man', with 'ardent sentiments of honour, virtue, magnanimity, and publick spirit'.[9] After all, as Blair insisted, 'the most renowned Orators, such as Cicero and Demosthenes, were no less distinguished for some of the high virtues, as Public Spirit and zeal for their country, than for Eloquence'.[10] To the professor of rhetoric and belles lettres at Edinburgh, it was a matter for public concern that in contemporary Scotland there were men who declaimed with 'no other object in view, but to make a show of their supposed talents', and institutions which were accordingly 'not merely of an useless, but of an hurtful nature'.[11] Such a sense of the dangers of a misdirected and empty rhetoric, moreover, can only have been heightened by the understanding of David Hume that, even in the most important public discourse, all too often, ' 'tis not reason, which carries the prize, but eloquence'.[12]

Having refused to concede the vital ground of public oratory to those bent on mere ostentatious display or academic squabbling, men like Blair and Adam Ferguson could at least hope to use their positions in the pulpit and the lecture-halls to exercise the true public purpose of the medium. Indeed, these two were distinguished professors at Edinburgh and amongst the very greatest preachers and lecturers in what was still an age of great public speakers.[13] But in the wider intellectual community of the Scottish Enlightenment, the desire to hold the public ear led authors to take to writing with renewed vigour and determination. Most of them, moreover, would immediately have shared Lord Kames's view that a historian 'who hath a genius for narration, seldom fails to engage our belief'.[14] Humane scholarship remained in enlightened Scotland a vehicle not so much for academic analysis as for the most persuasive and polished didactic eloquence. Fortunately for them, and perhaps also for a reading public who were thus spared a barrage of unadulterated moral instruction, the Scottish historical tradition in particular continued to provide a congenial and ductile medium in which this rhetorical function could be acted out. Blair wistfully commented that 'We have Historians, we have Poets of the greatest name; but of Orators, or Public Speakers, how little have we to boast?'[15] But this was very much a rhetorical question. We know from their self-conscious posture how completely early modern Scottish historians felt they had managed to usurp the orator's laurel.

Donald MacNicol's view, for example, was that Scottish intellectuals and the gentlemen of the 'learned professions' were not simply notable for their 'knowledge and talents': they could also articulate and disseminate their wisdom, for 'in the pulpit, and at the bar, they have no superiors'.[16] It was to the same men that he considered history 'in a manner, yielded up'.[17] Small wonder, then, that the Scottish historians of the Enlightenment now reinforced their own credentials as orators by illustrating the power of oral and literary exhortation to change the course of history. Fletcher of Salton, for example, was portrayed by Sir John Dalrymple as having influenced men by conjuring up nothing less than 'all the fire of ancient eloquence'.[18] It was Fletcher's 'glowing eloquence', in particular, which was thought by George Wallace in his *Ancient Peerages* to have alerted his countrymen to 'the real situation of the community'.[19] On the other hand, though to much the same purpose, Dalrymple argued that Viscount Dundee himself had been awakened to his duty 'by the perusal of antient poets, historians, and orators', and had been inflamed 'still more, by listening to the antient songs of the highland bards'.[20] In more general terms, however, it was to be George Campbell's influential *Philosophy of Rhetoric* (1776) which best epitomised the view that oratory served to inspire men in their public duty. Having offered a theoretical 'analysis of persuasion', he swiftly illustrated his claims with an exemplary reply directed to a hypothetical, but clearly convincing, orator: 'Your eloquence hath fired my ambition, and makes me burn with public zeal ... ', he effused, 'there is nothing which at present I would not attempt for the sake of fame, and the interest of my country ... I am instantly at your command'.[21] This seems to have been a succinct account of what the enlightened scholar still hoped he could achieve when he adopted the pose of the greatest historical and classical orators.

   A forceful strain of oratorical skill, however, was also claimed by eighteenth-century scholars to be characteristic of the greatest historical civilisations. With undisguised deference to the classical commentators, who had associated public speaking with political liberty and the obligations of responsible citizenship, eloquence remained for the enlightened Scotsman, as David Daiches reminds us, the mark of a public-spirited man.[22] From an appreciation of these two positions, and a burgeoning Scottish affiliation to the ideas associated with the late Earl of Shaftesbury, followed Blair's inevitably misty-eyed apostrophisation of Athens: 'Eloquence there sprung, native and vigorous', he wrote, 'from amidst the contentions of faction and freedom, of public business, and of active life'.[23] At the same time, an anonymous Aberdonian chronicler, clearly besotted with the 'tyranical power' enjoyed by Pericles over the Athenians, was in little doubt as to its source: 'it was his Eloquence and integrity that maintained him against Cimon, Thucydides and all his opponents for forty years'.[24] Similarly, the Glaswegian professor William Wight was clear that 'eloquence, its power and effect' were central to an understanding of the achievements of Greek society, when he drew up the curriculum to be followed by his impressionable university students.[25] It was also increasingly fashionable to address similar comments to societies much closer to home. Of England it was said by William Guthrie that 'no nation in the world can produce so many examples of true eloquence'.[26] Lord Kames likewise commented that 'Eloquence triumphs in a popular assembly ... [it] flourished in the republics of Athens and of Rome; and makes some figure at present in the British house of Commons'.[27] Such comments though, for all their contemporary utility to a Hanoverian Whig propagandist, only built successfully upon the profound Scottish concern for political eloquence exhibited throughout the earlier tradition.

Alongside this unflagging determination to lay bare the secular and political use of rhetoric, so evocative of republican humanist thought in Scotland, the Enlightenment historians continued to assert the necessity of a preaching, moralistic, inspirational, and spiritual oratory, which had traditionally been vested in an active and diligent ministry. Hovering mediately between the shades of Cicero and Knox, like their Scottish predecessors, the enlightened historians would not meekly relinquish the oratorical functions of the Calvinist clergy. After all, some scholars were themselves ministers. Many others, as James Cameron tells us, were dutiful adherents of the Scottish Kirk. All in any case believed, as humanists, that their rhetoric had a powerful spiritual and moralistic potential which could not lightly be cast aside.[28] Whilst the civil discord and intolerance occasioned by the Reformation were almost always condemned by historians like the Edinburgh publisher Alexander Kincaid, bent on supporting the modern 'restoration of public tranquility',[29] there was sometimes also a deeply felt and instinctive sympathy for the modern fruits of the reformer's efforts: a religion that was 'rational and simple',[30] 'mild and gentle'.[31] Most pertinently, however, the role of public oratory in the Reformation was expounded with great attention and not a little admiration. Knox, for example, according to Gilbert Stuart, had 'pointed all the thunder of his eloquence against idolatry'.[32] For William Duff, who succeeded Turnbull as professor of moral philosophy and logic at Aberdeen, 'his declamations against luxury, vice, and pride, had every character of that natural antipathy which cannot be counterfeited or dissembled'.[33] For his part, Melville was regarded by Stuart as having been 'fond of disputation, hot, violent, and pertinacious'.[34] The preachers were said in Hugo Arnot's popular *History of Edinburgh* (1779) to have fulminated too hotly against 'sensual enjoyments'. But it was admitted that their duty was nevertheless to recommend 'their followers to keep their appetites and passions in due subjection'.[35] The responsible use of spiritual oratory was therefore an important focus of Enlightenment concern, just as it had exercised the Calvinist and humanist scholars of the past.

Unsurprisingly, the religious misapplications of rhetoric, and especially its role in fanning the flames of bigotry and encouraging impetuous violence, were now very firmly dealt with: but significantly, it was again the perversion rather than the potential of moralistic oratory which offended the purveyors of enlightened toleration. The reckless 'industry and rhetoric of the preachers', for example, in blowing the people into a 'combustion', seemed to the urbane Gilbert Stuart the very height of irresponsibility.[36] Arnot, too, thought that rhetoric was corrupted by those who had been merely 'practising on the passions of the vulgar'.[37] For William Robertson, moreover, himself a leading preacher of the day, it was diminished by those who had 'excited their hearers to the most desperate and lawless actions'.[38] Even to a lesser light like the merchant and scholar John Gibson, the Glaswegian Reformation seemed an object lesson in the proper employment of oratory: 'extemporary effusions of zeal', he regretfully observed, 'were substituted in place of theological lectures'.[39] Subsequently the use or abuse of oratorical responsibility by the spiritual leaders of Scottish society was a matter of acute concern to the Enlightenment historians. It was plain, for example, that the presbyterian clergy had generally played a crucial role in weakening support for the Jacobite rebellion in 1745: the ministers, according to John Campbell, preaching 'with the Sword of the Gospel, gained a greater conquest over those hot-headed Gentry' than Cope and the Hanoverian army.[40] But there were also some preachers, William Maitland insisted in the *History of Edinburgh* (1753), who had left 'their Flocks...destitute of Pastors, when there was never more Occasion for Protestant Ministers to exert themselves'.[41] Evidently, the performance or abdication of the duty of moral oratory was still thought to have a considerable impact on the public condition of Scotland, even up to the present time.

The art of oratory, we may conclude, enjoyed a seminal, if subsequently overlooked, position in the historical work of the Scottish Enlightenment. As Thomas Somerville enthusiastically reflected in 1792, history abounded 'with examples of eloquence, courage, integrity, and patriotism', four matters to which any self-respecting humanist historian in Scotland still had immediately to attend.[42] Loaded with the rich connotations of republican political thought and a Calvinist commitment to a preaching ministry, both of which also looked back to a more recent Scottish tradition of thought, the condition of rhetoric and public speaking, in particular, afforded the enlightened historian an opportunity to gauge the moral and political state of society. Eschewing Blair's purist attitudes, a less doctrinaire historian, like Hugo Arnot, might actually rather approve of the recent rash of 'societies instituted by young men for the improvement of public speaking', seeing the bodies frequented by impressionable foreign visitors like Benjamin Constant as veritable 'schools of education'.[43] Even though a sublime oratory was normally regarded as the peculiar preserve of the most auspicious ages in human history, as when the Greek poets had been to Walter Anderson 'the first public orators',[44] it would always prove a valuable indicator of the state of social development. Alexander Kincaid, for example, could speak of the 'times of barbarity and ignorance, when people were less versant in quibbling and chicanery', a comment again not without its barbed allusion to the modern abuse of rhetorical skill.[45] But the opposite conclusion remained available for a confirmed admirer of primitive society like Adam Ferguson: 'Savage society', he thought, amongst other more predictable accolades, might equally be characterised by 'eloquence'.[46]

Having identified this continuing and wide-ranging preoccupation with the role of eloquence and the rhetorician, it clearly behoves the modern student to ask why the historians of the Scottish Enlightenment might have wished still to associate themselves in this way with an oratorical tradition. This question arises not least in view of the steady dissociation of oratory and learning which had been taking place in many other countries over the same period.[47] We have already seen that the historians consistently claimed that their work was directed at the education of Scotland's social leaders. I have also suggested that a glaring deficiency in this particular line of rhetoric, at least prior to the Enlightenment, had always been any consensual definition of the specific social group to whom the historians saw themselves as appealing. It is this very evident concern for the historical status of rhetoric which in fact provides the resolution to our problem. The Scottish Enlightenment historians were indeed, I shall argue, engaged in offering a lucid description of the men to whom the Scottish social leadership ought to fall, even if no previous social class or professional group was alone deemed suitable. The persuasive skills of course remained essential weapons in the armoury both of the public-spirited citizen and the conscientious preacher. The art of rhetoric, we have seen, already equipped a man for leadership in the Enlightenment, as it had done in the Scottish past. But, as the practical accomplishments of the enlightened and learned gentleman, not least in a society increasingly celebrated for its prominent and influential advocates, ministers, and professors, these skills now placed the eloquent man of letters in a position of great and unprecedented opportunity. In a way in which only the social developments in Scotland since 1680 could plausibly sustain, and with the political changes of the early eighteenth century merely compounding the older feeling that neither the aristocracy nor the monarchy would ever again fulfil the responsibilities of a virtuous and sympathetic audience, Scottish scholars themselves at last stepped into the theoretical breach, and pronounced themselves the moral and social leaders of their community.[48] The details of this remarkable development, as Calvinist and humanist social theory now took on an increasingly ideological function in supporting the actual dominance of an enlightened and learned elite, obviously require our immediate consideration.

II: The Scholar as Orator and Statesman

In demonstrating the continuing and crucial connection in Scottish Enlightenment history between eloquence and learning, which allowed the enlightened man of letters to stake his particular claim to the social leadership, a number of the acknowledged concerns of the historians might move into a strikingly sharper focus. The pursuit of virtue, the obsession with audience, and the fascination with language, would each repay consideration in the light of the ever-closer liaison which was emerging between oratory and scholarship. Our own approach, however, will be simply to explore the manner in which enlightened historians now reinforced the deeply Ciceronian conceptual linkage at the heart of this development. Scotsmen had long drawn upon Calvinist and humanist notions of the invariable historical importance of a vociferous but sensitive rhetoric in shaping the course of events. But now more and more historians asserted a view of the role of learned men who were characterised by their eloquence. They were thus able to portray their own intellectual contemporaries as the rightful leaders of Scotland's culture, political life, and moral improvement.[49] By sharpening the traditional Scottish focus upon the eminent orator, in particular, and reducing still further the small moral distance which lay between eloquence and wisdom, enlightened scholars, I shall argue, succeeded in emphasising to an unprecedented degree the claims of the intellectual to be regarded as the candidate best qualified for the leadership of society. In such an ambitious project, of course, James Grant's prescient comment that a study of the language might form the basis for a 'history of ideas'[50] would assume considerable contemporary significance: it was perhaps a hint of a history, first adumbrated in Smith's *History of Astronomy*, which would regard ideas as the business of the learned man, and language as the crucial medium by which his special influence in society could be traced. But, for the eighteenth-century Enlightenment, the Scottish historians seem largely to have restricted themselves to identifying and magnifying the modern and historical examples of eloquence and, more broadly, of learned leadership. This is the strategy which we shall primarily consider.

Those who could legitimately be characterised as both the practitioners of oratory and scions of learning were inevitably accorded special treatment. Most obviously, there was an explicit recognition by enlightened authors, as well as by the occasional eighteenth-century cynic, that the functions of the eloquent and ancient bard and the modern historian were in fact broadly analogous. The bards, after all, as Lord Kames pointed out, 'were the only historians before writing was introduced'.[51] It was, meanwhile, through the 'bards and Sannachies' that William Maitland's continuator thought that the 'historical poems' had been preserved.[52] The 'shannachies, or story-tellers' were successors to 'the ancient bards', who were for Guthrie clearly 'the historians, or rather the genealogists as well as the poets, of the nation and the family'.[53] By extension, moreover, other disseminators of an oral tradition, such as the Scandinavian 'scalds', could be treated similarly. They were seen by enthusiasts like John Pinkerton as 'not only the poets, but the historians and genealogists of the time'.[54] These men, of course, had in Blair's view long since acquired the pre-eminent status of the 'chief members of the state'.[55] Their eloquence and verbal ingenuity were the principal sources of their social influence, enabling them to take a commanding moralistic and edificatory position: in short, Kames argued, their oratory empowered them to elevate 'some into heroes', and to promote 'virtue in every hearer'.[56] In the light of this widespread perception, the fervour for bardic culture seemingly aroused by the recovery of the Ossianic cycle should surely provoke less surprise in the modern reader. It remains true that Macpherson was deviously adept at constructing for enlightened Scotsmen the sort of ancient literary tradition which they wished to discover. Yet he was by no means responsible for their antecedent desire to reinstate the Caledonian bards in the 'republic of letters'.[57] On the contrary, it seems that Macpherson was merely the most successful exploiter of an interest in the learned ancient orators. This the Scottish historical tradition had itself been instrumental in bringing to the fore, and the social conditions underlying the Enlightenment had simply made it more relevant than ever before.[58]

The Scottish bards, however, were to be only the most local and venerable of the eloquent and learned men rehabilitated by eighteenth-century historians as they sought to establish their own claims as a social leadership. Public speaking, it was clear, had always been an essential device for the transmission of learning and the conduct of public business, and this function attracted judicious comment from historians. Lachlan Shaw's *History of the Province of Moray* (1775), for example, observed that among the Druids, 'their literati' had been composed of several groups, 'who were their Divines, Philosophers, Poets, Orators, Physicians, and Judges in all causes'.[59] Just as the Aberdonian primitivist William Duff considered that the 'ingenious and learned Men' of medieval St Andrews had instituted 'publick lectures in the different Sciences, without any Reward, with a generous Intention of promoting Literature and polite knowledge',[60] so the modern debating society sought in Arnot's eyes to improve 'science in general, without having peculiar reference to any of its branches'.[61] These examples seemed just so much more evidence that linguistic eloquence was the conduit through which true and useful public knowledge must flow. A learned eloquence was also interposed at crucial junctures in national affairs. Sometimes here it was to be found adopting once again the nuance of a worryingly manipulable medium, as historians sought to define and limit its proper uses. Lord Hailes, for example, in pointing out that it was conventional among historians to ascribe the Scottish defeat at Falkirk to quarrelling, alleged in his *Annals of Scotland* (1776) that 'they make Bruce and Wallace talk across the river like two young declaimers from the pulpits in a school of rhetoric'.[62] Eloquence in men of letters even seemed vital to the maintenance of patriotic spirit. Hence, Hugh Blair focused attention on the unpleasant fate reserved for the Welsh bards by the all-conquering *Malleus Scottorum*: as the vocal guardians of an elemental and deeply historical national identity, they had been ruthlessly and quite deliberately exterminated.[63] Some authors of course preferred a haughty aloofness, at least from the oral historians of the past: Hume, for example, poured whiggish scorn upon non-literate history, intoning deeply that 'the history of past events is immediately lost or disfigured when entrusted to memory and oral tradition'.[64] But the historians of the Scottish Enlightenment nevertheless expounded a remarkably coherent view of the historical place of the learned orator. Even if they doubted the accuracy of an oral traditionary history, they recognised its eloquent and learned exponents as their functional ancestors. Having embraced the learned and influential orators of the past, it was then possible – indeed essential – for enlightened historians to paint a highly tendentious picture of the eminent role

of the various learned men across the broad canvas of history. This they could
do safe in the knowledge that a Scottish audience would appreciate the increased
significance attached to learning.

Like the men who were particularly gifted as orators, therefore, the 'learned'
in general were deemed by the self-interested eighteenth-century scholar to be
at their very best when actively engaged in public affairs. This can be no surprise
for, as John Pocock has suggested, it is possible to characterise the Enlightenment itself as a phase during which 'secular clerisies' emerged,
enthusiastically engaged in moral edification, in exhortation, and in patriotic
designs.[65] In 1753, for example, William Maitland surveyed the recent European
past, and noted the 'Many Advantages having accrued to the Publick from the
Studies and Labours of Learned and ingenious Men'.[66] They had excited 'a
generous Emulation among the *literati*' who had sought to unfold 'the most
occult Secrets of Nature, for the Benefit of Mankind'.[67] In the best traditions of
historical reinforcement, the Scottish historians accumulated favourable evidence from the past for their central proposition. The ideal social leader was to
be the public-spirited, eloquent, active and learned citizen. John Millar
certainly used this argument when the *Historical View of the English Government*
(1787) attributed the long 'influence and authority' of the clergy to their
'learning'.[68] Naturally, the study of history was also one of the finest means by
which a man could attain this desirable status. 'The study of Antiquities will
always be reckoned worthy of the notice of men of honour and industry', urged
the enthusiastic William Borthwick of Crookston, eager to endorse the claims of
Rochefoucauld.[69] It was transparently clear to this scholar, moreover, reflecting
the Calvinist and humanist vision of the active and industrious social leader, that
'Men devoted to habits of dissipation or of idleness, will not wish to promote
inquiries of this nature'.[70] Learning, no less than eloquence, it seems, fitted a
man for active leadership. It can be no surprise if, as Thomas Pennant's
correspondent reported, a whole train of English scientists and men of letters of
the past were now being idolised as heroes in enlightened Scottish circles.[71]

Andrew Henderson's *Dissertation on the Royal Line* (1771) actually provides
one of the finest examples of a historical analysis which emphasised the dual
importance of learning and eloquence, as well as a specific sense of history, as the
credentials of the Scottish leader. Taking as his text Tacitus' account of a
Caledonian chieftain confronting the Roman invaders, it seemed to Henderson
that the Roman author had 'marked down the emphatic Speech, of which no
Orator of ancient Greece or Rome needed be ashamed'. Here, in short, was a
Scotsman who possessed all the verbal felicity of a Demosthenes or Cicero, who
therefore epitomised the classical and humanist ideal of eloquent public
leadership in the very hour of national crisis. More significantly, however, the
chieftain's speech seemed remarkable to Henderson for being 'filled with proofs
of his acquaintance with the Annals of former times'. In other words, his
leadership was strengthened and legitimated in Enlightenment eyes by his
knowledge of history. Moreover, his speech was a model of classical eloquence,

couched in 'terms of politeness' and breathing 'a spirit of affection and tenderness to his country, full of all the sentiments of a Hero and of a man ... '.[72] Thus, his speech succeeded in inspiring admiration and acquiring authority because it accurately conveyed the presence of a learning which implied public spirit and patriotism in the speaker, the vital personal attributes of the legitimate Calvinist and humanist leader: with oratory and learning thereby fused in an ancient Scottish example of heroism, eloquent Scottish men of letters, no doubt like the Roxburghshire scholar and London bookseller Andrew Henderson himself, could themselves hope to achieve a high public status by virtue of their own undoubted scholarly accomplishments.

Nor, in this way, was the unusual intellectual versatility characteristic of the historian in particular discounted in numbering him amongst the eloquent and learned men most fit for public responsibility and respect: Tacitus, after all, had for the enthusiastic Blair managed to be 'The Philosopher, the Poet, and the Historian', all at the same time, and he remained one of the chief models for Scottish historians from Buchanan to Pinkerton.[73] Even to the presbyterian minister John Bonar, everyone seemed under a unique 'obligation to those who have transmitted to us the examples of former times': future ages would 'hold them in grateful remembrance when the manners of many Kings & Heroes shall be buried in everlasting oblivion'.[74] More generally, an eloquent learning itself could embrace the full breadth of philosophy and science in the pursuit of true and (which seemed to follow) useful public knowledge. Like the Highland Caledonian Society, men of learning were now enjoined by John Buchanan to 'contribute liberally to encourage their countrymen to make progress in the several kinds of improvement and refinement of manners'.[75] Like the later Roman emperors, too, who had 'sought the Interest of the World', Scottish gentlemen were encouraged by George Turnbull in his *Treatise* to 'raise again the perishing Arts, and decay'd Virtue of Mankind'.[76] This might take the form of writing history, or perhaps only of serving as one of those 'several learned men' for whose co-operation the author would feel obliged to doff his cap.[77] In dedicating his *Border History* (1776) to the Percies, therefore, the Roxburghshire clergyman and friend of Hume and Robertson was not indulging in empty flattery of the patrons of 'learning, commerce, and every elegant and useful art'.[78] Nor was the dissolute Robert Heron descending to meaningless formality in addressing his *New General History* (1794) to Sir John Sinclair, the statistician, who continued 'to promote the true interests of his country, and still more those of genuine philosophy'.[79] Both were in fact forcefully asserting a view of the ideal leaders of society. Enlightened Scottish scholars busily sought to reconstruct as the moral apex of society an audience of men who, like themselves, not only possessed learning and cultivation, but also encouraged its public dissemination.

The way was therefore open, and the obligation clearly recognised by the Enlightenment historian, to embellish the lives of historical luminaries with the various accomplishments of the rounded man of letters. This was a preoccupation which was also to dictate the Scottish historian's idiosyncratic preferences among the great men of the past, a tendency well illustrated in David Hume's *History of England*. In Hume's eyes, King Alfred, for example, had been both a great scholar and a champion of learning. Alfred had 'deemed it nowise derogatory from his other great characters of sovereign, legislator, warrior, and politician, thus to lead the way to his people in the pursuits of literature'.[80] Similarly, he portrayed Henry I (significantly Hume, like John Major before him, preferred the alternative name of 'Beauclerc') as a man whose wisdom and learning alone had preserved him from most of the 'pedantry and superstition which were then so prevalent among men of letters'.[81] When addressing the interpretation of Stuart parliamentary history, moreover, Hume chose to illustrate the character of Charles I's opponents by sharp intellectual contrast with preceding generations of political leaders. They had been mere 'barbarians, summoned from their fields and forests, uninstructed by study, conversation, or travel; ignorant of their own laws or history, and unacquainted with the situation of all foreign nations'.[82] A cynical retort might be that Hume's objection to the medieval knights of the shire rested on the simplistic realisation that they were not the polite, well-heeled gentlemen-lawyers of enlightened Edinburgh. But the caricatures remain important for what they imply about Hume's abiding interest in the intellectual tone of the past. At times, most obviously in his vivid cameos of the literary and scientific spirit of an age, Hume seems to have been engaged in sketching a history of learning not entirely dissimilar to the project later envisaged by James Grant or Robert Henry.[83] In this light, moreover, the well-documented Enlightenment interest in the historical development of language appears not to have been the exercise in academic sociological analysis which some modern commentators have suggested.[84] Instead it looks more and more like a deeply personal exploration by scholars of the linguistic context within which an intellectual community might live out their social function as the manufacturers and disseminators of learned ideas. In short, the characteristic enlightened 'history of manners' may simply have been pursued in order to reveal the causes and moral implications of cultural and intellectual development. This is a question which, as I have already argued, can only have seemed more relevant than ever to a confident community of aspiring Scottish intellectual and cultural leaders in an age of bewildering social, economic and political change.

Hume, however, was only the most successful Scottish historian of the day. The identification of an intellectual leadership throughout the different ages of history, it seems, was equally the business of the wider community of historians in eighteenth-century Scotland. A man who had a much higher opinion of the medieval mind than Hume, for example, but whose analysis similarly betrayed a determination to isolate the intellectual qualities of past generations, was William Guthrie. To Guthrie, the Scottish feudal elite 'were men who had seen the world, were conversant in the courts of Europe, masters of polite literature, and amiable to all the duties of civil and social life'.[85] This is hardly an advertisement for scholarly accuracy. Yet this picture nevertheless successfully achieved the author's intention of relating influential historical groups to the cosmopolitan and learned men of letters, and thus of associating the eloquent modern scholar with the undisputed social leadership in ages with even the least auspicious manners. From an only slightly less distorted perspective, the Aberdonian scholar William Duff claimed in the *History of Scotland* that James I of Scotland had been exemplary for his 'learning'. Indeed, he had sought 'to make his People a civiliz'd and polite Nation':[86] probably dubious history again, but also a bold attempt to locate an intellectual kingship in Scotland during one of the brief interludes in what the conventional Calvinist and humanist critique had held to be the prevailing turmoil and barbarism of the time. The same author, moreover, recognised in Bishop William Turnbull, the founder of Glasgow University, a man of admirable qualities, with 'a just Notion for polishing and reforming the Genius and Manners of the Nation'.[87] Duff's facility for transposing the educational altruism and polite affectations of the learned modern intellectual on to often spectacularly inappropriate historical figures appears, however, to have been widespread among enlightened Scottish authors. This further emphasises the extent to which the enlightened historian was exploring the different moral and social contexts of the past, committed principally to stressing the ubiquitous moral influence and universal suitability of the learned and virtuous leader. Only a preparedness unashamedly to misrepresent the intellectual strength and continuity of the Scottish past in this way could surely have led the Edinburgh lawyer Andrew Stevenson to the bizarre and incongruous conclusion that 'Never did this country abound more with learned men then in the *eighth* century'.[88] This determination to exalt the ability of learned men to dominate an age and win particular acclaim arguably even gave direction to Millar's virtual canonisation of Charles James Fox. The Whig genius was claimed to be a man with a mind 'superior to prejudice; equally capable of speculation, and of active exertion; no less conversant in elegant literature, than accustomed to animate the great scenes of national business ... '.[89] Neither the constraints of accuracy nor of tact, therefore, nor even the palpably inappropriate contexts in which scholarly orators were now being conveniently identified, seem to have been capable of hindering enlightened Scottish historians from worshipping at the altar of a supremely eloquent public learning.

This speculative streak, in which authors sought to associate a largely suppositious scholarship with the acknowledged legitimacy of previous public figures, ran even through some of the accounts of revolutionary change constructed by eighteenth-century historians. Adam Ferguson, for example, fancied that the founders of Rome herself could perhaps have been, at the same time, 'philosophers, statesmen, and able tutors';[90] which is to say, men imbued with learning, dedicated to its public employment and equipped to dispense it to succeeding generations. To Thomas Blackwell it seemed that the Augustan age had produced 'the greatest Revolutions of Fortune in the shortest Time', as well as having 'the greatest Men in these capacities in which the best and worthiest of Mankind chiefly strive to excell. LETTERS, ARTS, and ARMS'.[91] In Walter Anderson's view, meanwhile, the early success of the Reformation in France had been attributable to the leadership of the 'men of letters'.[92] Their adoption of heretical knowledge had set them in ultimately ill-fated opposition to the ignorant masses who had formed 'the fortress of the catholic church'.[93] Important material evidence could even be found to testify to the profound significance of the learned in times of great change. Those crucial vouchers of Scottish history, the charters around which so much scholarly controversy had always raged, were, for example, in Andrew Henderson's eyes, just 'so many tokens of there being learned men in the Kingdom'.[94] It was Henderson's most forthright contention, that there had been a distinguished druidical 'seminary of learning' in Scotland, and that 'from them were several learned men draughted', who had had a disproportionate impact on the history of their own times.[95] Yet perhaps the final words in illustration of the historical significance of learned men in the collective mind of scholars in eighteenth-century Scotland should be those of the Rankenian Society philosopher and royal chaplain George Turnbull, in the classic *Treatise on Ancient Painting* (1740). They encapsulate the central role conceived for learning and polite letters among the qualifications of the ideal leader and citizen. They also further indicate the apparently pressing need of the enlightened scholar, in changing times, to demonstrate that arts and learning were perforce the most valuable virtues – whatever the prevailing state of manners. Scipio, he claimed, was notable precisely for being 'so brave a Warrior, so great a Conqueror, so good a Citizen, and so polite a Scholar; so generous a Patron and Encourager of the fine Arts in peace, and the great Bulwark of his Country in war'.[96] These accolades, it seems, allowed the historians of the Enlightenment to present the most influential classical leaders in all circumstances as men both of learning and eloquence. And thus, we may conclude, they effectively prepared Turnbull's sympathetic contemporaries to accept the bid of enlightened Scottish intellectuals themselves for the vacant leadership of a dynamic modern 'republic of letters'.[97]

III: THE TRIUMPH OF INTELLECTUAL VIRTUE

Enough has now been said to suggest that the historians of the Scottish Enlightenment were employing their self-consciously oratorical role in order to elevate the man who possessed both eloquence and learning to a position of social leadership. This certainly allowed the eighteenth-century historian to continue to bask in the glorious afterglow of an ancient line of learned statesmen, much elaborated in previous Scottish humanist thought. But it also opens up further inquiries for the modern student. In particular, we need now to consider what use was made both of humanist public morality and the virtues of Calvinism in enlightened Scottish discourse as it sought to present the ideal social leader, above all else, as imbued with learning and reason. In short, we need to explore the means by which traditional moral legitimacy was conferred upon the increasingly dominant Scottish intellectual in an enlightened age. There appears to have been no new theoretical obstacle to learning playing the part of a humanist virtue in the social world of the Scottish Enlightenment. In the necessary compression of scholarly accomplishment and public character, enlightened scholars would have been much aided by the prominent position still occupied by the concept of public spirit in their thought. So long as learning itself oriented a man towards activities of public benefit, there would be an opportunity to consider it, again with deference to Shaftesbury's teachings, as bearing some special relation to the virtue of magnanimity.[98] But a parallel route to virtue also still suggested itself. This offered a rather different view to that generously inclined public learning which hearkened very obviously back to Cicero. In this more strongly Calvinist view, learning involved the exercise of the rational faculty, and was thus an unfailing indication of a man's moral submission to his reason. It would then be possible to associate it with a personal virtue of the first importance, one tracing its ancestry back through Scottish thinkers like Drummond and Ross, and ultimately back to Plato by way of the patristic Church. By either route the enlightened historian was able, no less than his Scottish predecessors, to invest both his own intellectual qualities and the scholarly inclinations of his colleagues with the precious legitimacy offered by 'virtue'.

In the first instance, it is clear that no traditional humanist virtue was held in higher esteem in eighteenth-century Scotland than what was still widely called 'public spirit'. The dutiful citizen, even if he was not a particularly learned individual, was exhorted to be like Sir Alexander Livingstone, courtier and counsellor to James II. In the words of William Nimmo, the historian of Stirlingshire, Livingstone had been 'one of those few statesmen who prefer the public good to their own private interest, and who never sacrifice the common weal to their owne private passions'.[99] This orientation, at least as an ideal, could be presented even as the *sine qua non* of the properly human character. 'Public spirit' for John Logan, clergyman, historian and orientalist, was amongst the several elevated 'names that have never been pronounced in the regions of Asia'. These were therefore places where 'the word mankind is without a meaning'.[100] When considered as the inclination of the learned man, however, public spirit elicited the particular approval of Scottish historians. The application of information and knowledge to the conduct of public business was a high priority among the obligations of the responsible citizen: as John Campbell put it, 'it is the Duty of every Person to contribute what he can for the Service of his Country', and to offer to those charged with important duties 'the necessary Information on every Subject he is acquainted with'.[101] Thomas Somerville, moreover, claimed in the *History of Political Transactions* (1792) that learning, especially when accomplished through historical inquiries, would itself 'afford repeated opportunities of inculcating principles of genuine patriotism upon those, who wish to understand and to pursue the true interests of their country'.[102] Similarly, in 1760, the 20-year-old William Smellie was in no doubt that it was biographies and other exemplary forms of history which were 'best calculated for inspiring [young minds] with a catholic love to the human race', a noble and idealistic expression of public spirit extended to its widest Stoical boundaries.[103] In much the same vein, moreover, Cicero, the paragon of men of letters, was in Turnbull's influential view characterised by a 'Fortitude and publick Spirit ... and a generous Love of Mankind and publick Good'. This was conceived of as being 'the very Essence of Virtue'.[104] It was therefore not wholly inappropriate for the judge Duncan Forbes of Culloden, a man notably ambivalent towards some aspects of the Enlightenment, to allege, with an intended ironical twist, that philosophy and learning had contrived in modern Scotland to portray themselves as elevating the 'social and public virtues'.[105]

   This continuing association of virtue with public spirit was of course not peculiar to Scotland. Deploying a pungently Florentine sense of his terms, Montesquieu had advised his readers that he was writing of a 'political virtue' which was 'directed to the public good'; he was concerned 'very little' with what was called 'private moral virtue', and 'not at all' with 'that virtue which relates to revealed truths'.[106] But the historians of the Scottish Enlightenment still seem, like so many of their native predecessors, to have been particularly concerned to develop this focus upon the public virtues into an elaborate defence of a resoundingly humanist learning. History, as John Bonar eloquently stated, was definitively the work of magnanimous patriots. 'Such Men have indeed been liberal Benefactors to their species', he observed, no doubt with at least one eye on his previous and contemporary colleagues in Scotland. With 'a noble Generosity', he boasted, 'they have consecrated a treasure, as a kind, of common stock for the moral use, & improvement of the community, not only in their own, but in all Succeeding ages'.[107] There was simply no room for doubt, as George Turnbull's influential *Treatise* also reiterated in unequivocal fashion, that humane learning, in the broadest sense, was intimately related to the pre-eminent virtue of public spirit. Hence, for example, the chaplain to the future King George III confidently observed of the Greek arts, that 'It is remarkable that they degenerated among them in proportion as Virtue and publick Spirit declined'.[108] The relationship between learning and public virtue was so crucial to enlightened thought that it needed constant reinforcement and explication. As Turnbull himself showed, it was still felt necessary to pre-empt the accusation that art and learning served only to 'soften and effeminate Men', or that, as a recurrent charge had it, they had been 'one principal Cause of the Ruin of the Roman State'.[109] Literature, history and art, for George Turnbull as for previous writers like Buchanan, James VI, Hume of Godscroft, and Montaigne, were not at all to be dismissed simply as the servants of sensuous corruption. Instead, and as Turnbull claimed in the strongest tone, the appreciation of art and the study of its history placed in 'young Minds the Love of true Knowledge, and the Love of Society, Mankind, and Virtue'.[110] Acutely aware of the vulnerability of art to aspersions of indolence and luxury, indeed, he felt compelled to proclaim that, on the contrary, they properly served only to 'promote and encourage Virtue'.[111] The artist, representative in his qualities and direction of the intellectual community of his day, was expected by Turnbull to employ his 'strong and lively Sense of Virtue' in guiding 'his Pencil to display the Beauties and Excellencies of Virtue, and the Turpitude of Vice'.[112] Only if the author of the edificatory composition was thus endowed with virtue and public spirit, as James VI had once insisted, would his creation serve its unquestionably proper purpose, the fostering of public virtue: after all, 'the immediate Effect of good moral or historical Pictures upon the Mind', Turnbull concluded, 'is either directly virtuous, or at least exceedingly strengthening and assistant to Virtue'.[113]

This powerful image of intellectual creativity, assuming the proportions of a virtue because of its practical and public orientation, was eloquently expressed in Turnbull's *Treatise*. It seems to have been widely grasped in the Scottish Enlightenment and to have been retained as a classic defence of learning from older Scottish scholarship. Restated and elaborated in his own *Observations Upon Liberal Education* (1742), Turnbull's arguments, drawn from the common stock of Calvinism and humanism, reinforced the intimate connection between 'wisdom and virtue', emphasising how minds might 'be very early formed to the sincere love of virtue' and the inseparable matter of acquiring 'the more useful arts and sciences'.[114] Similarly, in justifying the study of classical mythology, for example, that other outstanding Aberdonian classical scholar Thomas Blackwell pointed proudly to its 'End of promoting Learning and Virtue'.[115] His was a conception of learning in which 'the publick Good, Love of their Country' and 'Social Virtue', were always the motivation of the scholar and the intended response in the reader.[116] Adam Ferguson, likewise, in a significant recapitulation of his views on the peculiar importance of oratory, considered that 'in whatever manner men are formed for great efforts of elocution or conduct' in public life, 'it appeared the most glaring of all other deceptions, to look for the accomplishments of a human character in the mere attainments of speculation'.[117] The 'attainments of speculation', the abstract reflections of the private and detached scholar, were, as we saw in George Buchanan's meditation, precisely the equivalent in the learned lexicon of that art which pandered to the libidinous proclivities and that rhetoric which simply fanned the flames of faction and dissension: each attainment was morally vitiated when it neglected what the enlightened Ferguson now called 'the qualities of fortitude and public affection, which are so necessary to render our knowledge an article of happiness or use'.[118] Only when art, rhetoric, or more broadly, learning were committed to the public purposes of edification and instruction could they hope in his view to achieve the status of 'accomplishments of the human character', and their practise acquire the radiant colour of a virtue.[119] For this reason, the Scottish historian, like Ferguson, still earnestly sought to appear as a moralist and an educator, as one whose public spirit, and consequently whose virtue, was beyond question. Authorial intentions, as expressed to the community at large, had necessarily to be couched in public terms. Like the Midlothian scholar William Borthwick, therefore, in his *Remarks on British Antiquities* (1776), he would practise virtue and seek approval in Scotland principally through learned productions which were themselves defended explicitly as 'endeavours to serve my Countrymen'.[120]

I have already suggested, however, that a truly virtuous learning could still be accomplished in enlightened Scotland by means other than this single-minded humanist devotion to the public interest. Or rather, the familiar contours of Calvinist and humanist thought in Scotland also led the enlightened historian to address the question of personal virtue, and the ways in which it ought to relate to a rational learning. This overwhelmingly still prompted the conventional Scottish assertion that learning might assist the moral and spiritual improvement both of its exponents and its recipients. In Quintilian's influential view, this had amounted to the understanding that 'Virtue, though she gets her beginning from nature, yet receives her finishing touches from learning',[121] an understanding of individual moral improvement which Scotsmen since at least the time of Boece and Major had shared. It was therefore far from being simply a different or distinct route by which learning could be expressed as a virtue. In practice, the presentation of learning as an aid to spiritual strengthening and improved moral conduct remained, as we saw in the earlier period, substantially fused with the argument for a public-oriented learning which we have just recapitulated. The association of learning with the virtues of rational conduct and informed self-restraint offered a compelling explanation of the very reasons for which learning was itself held to be of profound public consequence. In both the public and the personal contexts, after all, vice and the passions continued to overshadow the thoughts of the historians. Both accordingly delimited the formulations of virtue which they could construct. It was still essential, of course, to restrict the opportunities for regarding a strictly rational virtue as an argument for a reclusive and private scholarly existence. Ross and Mackenzie had showed in the mid-seventeenth century that *otium* remained an available philosophical option. Yet in the brilliant incandescence of Scotland's energetic Enlightenment, this dangerous drift towards a gloomy and lethargic virtue was more undesirable than ever. Enlightened historians bound tightly the assertion of rational virtue to the classical defence of public orientation. This gave rise to a strenuous reinforcement of *negotium* rendered still more effective by a modern analysis of reason which again stressed the importance of a social and intellectual context in its operations. For the self-consciously learned followers of Cicero and Knox it was consequently possible to emphasise the potential of reason and of useful knowledge for containing the rampant passions and the brutal appetites of men. They could do so without ever seeming to discount the fundamentally public context within which they existed. As the professor of moral philosophy at Edinburgh, James Balfour, was able comprehensively to affirm, 'VIRTUE has ever been represented as the empire of the mind over the passions and affections'.[122]

Because of this redoubled concern for rational learning, many major texts of the Scottish Enlightenment might in one sense be considered as extended Calvinist essays on the unruly passions of man.[123] At any rate, it seems quite clear that the historians of the eighteenth century sought no less than their Scottish predecessors to identify and stigmatise the fatal consequences of luxury and ignorance. They attempted at the same time to portray learning and the applications of reason as the soundest bulwark against their corrosive influence. But they also had a penetrating eye for evidence of the mechanisms by which moral decay and corruption still crept up on the unwary and the uninstructed. This perception at times approached even the paranoid apocalypticism of the Reformation Calvinist, and certainly mirrored the feverish concerns of Alexander Ross. Gilbert Stuart, for example, diagnosed in the decline of chivalry 'a voluptuousness, and a luxury which, in the circle of human affairs, are usually to distinguish and to hasten the decline and fall of nations'.[124] John Gibson, too, noted with considerable poignancy in the *History of Glasgow* (1776) how, with the advancement of commerce, rhetoric had failed to halt the onset of vice: 'In vain did the clergy, these watchful pastors, declaim against this change of manners…. luxury advanced with hasty strides every day'.[125] Speaking from a more strongly Calvinist position, Robert Wallace, the eminent Edinburgh minister, commented on the same recent development and offered a distinctly puritanical remedy. Explicitly linking the analysis of unrestrained individual passion with a broader concern for the public welfare, he advised that 'it is not the prevalence of luxury, but of simplicity of taste among private citizens, which makes the public flourish'.[126] A similar appreciation of the consequences of individual moral laxity for the public condition, moreover, led Lord Kames to warn that it was at its most vulnerable when confronted by 'the epidemic distempers of luxury and selfishness'.[127] At the same time the Midlothian minister John Bonar only echoed Hector Boece's concern for the 'polity of manners': 'Vice as certainly enervates the body politic', he cautioned the enlightened citizens of Hanoverian Scotland, 'as Intemperance weakens & impairs the body Natural'.[128] In such a febrile Calvinist and republican atmosphere of all-enveloping corruption and vice, there was of course still ample scope for the enlightened historian to locate reason and learning in the vanguard of the virtuous counter-attack.

James Balfour's dictum that 'VIRTUE has ever been considered as a rational and enlightened principle',[129] though only a partial truth, underpins an exemplary illustration of the way in which an Enlightenment elevation of reason depended crucially for its moral efficacy upon the formative influence of education and learning. As Balfour himself explained, the rational principle, the 'REASON' which was 'the distinguishing characteristic of man'[130] could not be regarded as a comprehensive, innate capacity for deducing knowledge and reality merely by its own internal operations. Instead, in terms which would have been immediately familiar to others within the eighteenth-century school of Scottish experimental philosophy, as well as to educational theorists like George Turnbull, Balfour thought that the rational faculties were only 'the seeds and first principles of wisdom, and virtue'.[131] Reason may have been the tool which distinguished man from brute, which allowed, as Hume said, 'the discovery of truth or falshood'.[132] But it required the acquisition of experience and learning in order to make any advance in the direction of intellectual or moral improvement. This qualification looked back immediately to Scotland's native tradition of Calvinist anti-rationalism and served to highlight the public and social context within which private virtue had necessarily to be developed.[133] If permitted to 'lie altogether uncultivated', the rational potential would in Balfour's view 'contribute very little to raise him to that degree of happiness, perfection and dignity, of which Nature has certainly made him capable'.[134] As Adam Ferguson therefore generalised, with a strikingly similar organic metaphor, it seemed that 'The seeds of every form are lodged in human nature; they spring up and ripen with the season'.[135] Reason was indeed the principal example of those capacities with which man was originally equipped. From a position of elemental rational endowment, however, it was necessary for the improving individual to cultivate his faculties by social and intellectual experience. Progress did not bestow either reason or sentiment: but it allowed the reason to grow and to refine, and, as Ferguson at least earnestly hoped, 'to obviate the casual abuses of passion'.[136]

Given this general philosophical consensus on the nature and limitations of unassisted reason, a consensus which merely increased the importance of the relationship between public and private virtue, most historians of the Scottish Enlightenment could still stand enthusiastically for the proposition that learning (historical learning remaining unsurprisingly prominent) was of special moral importance. In its exponents, it was evidence of a refined power of reason and thus a connotation of superior virtue; to its audience and votaries, it offered unequalled opportunities to hone and improve their own rational faculties to their full moral potential. Thus, the learned man might practise erudition and scholarship for the purpose of cultivating his own rational powers. But he would claim with George Turnbull also to possess a wider public function, to 'inure Youth to reason, or compute from Experience only; that is, from Facts ascertained by Observation'.[137] Nor, in this approach, were the other Calvinist nuances of a rational virtue at all outmoded. It remained entirely possible for men like the dour Duncan Forbes to integrate into the analysis some claims for a 'rational discerning soul', which might indeed 'perceive the beauty, the order, the harmony of nature'.[138] Man had still been bequeathed a rational faculty as a consequence of his nature. But empiricism confirmed the Calvinist instinct, as Forbes said, that 'we have no capacity to conceive any idea of any thing that does not affect our senses ... besides those that affect our senses, of which, and of their powers or actions, we can know nothing':[139] this, then, was the faculty which some scholars still saw themselves as honing. Moreover, and notwithstanding

Hume's smothered attacks, the Argument to Design itself survived as a feasible Calvinist position in a debate in which a capacity for 'discerning' reason remained for many thinkers the focal point of mental philosophy.[140]

But the position of reason in the vision of Scottish Enlightenment history was, as we have already seen, not based upon its centrality to a rationalist philosophy.[141] Rather it was founded in a sense of the special ability of reason to challenge the passions. This was a fundamentally moralistic perception which touched to the core the prior Calvinist and classical notions of a rational virtue, and which Addison had more recently erected into the seminal dictum that 'Reason should govern Passion'.[142] Reason, suitably refined by learning, was thus indeed a virtue. It was one which counter-factually implied the riot of the desires and the derangement of orderly priorities. And, in intriguing ways to which Richard Sher has now drawn our attention, it therefore served the moralistic objectives of the severe Calvinist as much as the pragmatic humanist.[143] Hence it was only when unsound knowledge, irrationality, and indolent intellects, had filled the Scottish Kirk, that a luridly-described medieval corruption had taken hold. William Semple, for example, considered that 'Laziness, with a train of abuses, and then ignorance entered in .... The clergy acquired vast riches on that account, but in a course of years they resigned themselves to pride and luxury by all the basest methods ... '.[144] Ecclesiological polemic aside, Semple's line of attack was in fact widely characteristic of a traditional Scottish approach to rational virtue, drawing heavily upon both Calvinist and humanist resources. As Adam Ferguson claimed, also speaking unguardedly in the voice of the authentic Calvinist Jeremiah, 'The natural antidote of vice is restraint and correction'.[145] Such public disciplines were best imposed, as the earlier Scottish humanists would instantly have agreed, by the operations of individual reason.

For Enlightenment historians in Scotland, the successors of a distinguished line of Calvinist preachers, it remained the case that vice was the inevitable child of ignorance. The passions, it seemed, would always tend to overawe an inherently frail reason. With this perception, it was natural for Robert Heron, as "late" as 1794, to regard 'superstition' as an intellectual condition of false knowledge and irrational belief. It was simply the state of not being 'at this time eminently learned', from which the clergy had unavoidably descended into a corruption which was 'selfish, luxurious, proud, and hypocritical'.[146] For the St Andrews professor Robert Watson, too, it seemed that Phillip II of Spain was only the exception who proved the rule, disappointing what 'might be expected, that, in a virtuous prince, the sentiments of honour and humanity would, on some occasions, triumph over the dictates of superstition'.[147] In other words, virtuosity implied a degree of learning which ought to have been (but sadly was not) the very antithesis of Catholic superstition. Similarly, an anonymous reviewer of Keith's *An Historical Catalogue of the Scottish Bishops* (1755) noted with obvious approval that the author had denominated the 'credulity and superstition' which had 'prevailed among the people' as an invariable cause which 'did not fail of producing every where the same effects'.[148] Thus the continuing and vaguely hysterical denunciation of past ecclesiastical abuses in enlightened Scotland was especially significant when it focused disapprovingly upon the denial of learning and the espousal of irrational belief. Catholicism, in short, was perceived to be an intellectual as much as a spiritual malaise.[149] Here, then, a Calvinist rejection of superstition only underscored and gave additional substance to an Enlightenment faith in the moral necessity of pursuing a rational learning.

There remained, however, a secular harmony which analysed civil history in order to enhance the claims of learning to be a principal aid to moral self-control. Almost mouthing the words of his fellow Aberdonian Alexander Ross, we find George Turnbull, for example, extolling the Athenian emphasis upon 'the beauty, the dignity of self-domination, and rule over the passions'.[150] Naturally, he sighed, the key to personal continence lay in 'excelling others in wisdom and virtue, and in meriting thereby the esteem of all good men'.[151] Likewise, in a significant development of his own classic assertion of James I's public-spirited learning, Duff's *History of Scotland* went on to discuss the personal moral consequences for his courtiers of the king's failure successfully to introduce intellectual pursuits. His picture was concise, but no doubt richly suggestive to a Scottish audience familiar with the complementarity of private and public morality. It seemed to Duff that 'instead of Temperance, Study, and the Encouragement of Learning, Trade, and Manufactures', there were introduced merely 'Balls, Masquerades, Concerts, Feastings, ... '.[152] Interpreted by means of a damning analysis which in Scotland looked as far back as the civic humanism of Hector Boece, James seemed simply to have stimulated those activities which gratified the sensuous appetites, accelerating the moral corruption both of his courtiers and the country, and failing to restrain it through the medicinal cultivation of a virtuous learning and rational self-control.[153] To the anonymous author of *The General History of the World* (1763), meanwhile, it remained abundantly clear that a Calvinist and humanist moral analysis of civil government still obtained. States existed, by divine will, only to ensure 'the keeping of strict discipline, the encouragement of labour and industry, of liberal arts, and all social virtues'. These were themselves instrumental in 'the suppression of such vices as weaken government, and introduce a corruption of morals'.[154] Lord Kames, too, suggested that to 'prevent or to retard such fatal corruption', it was best to cultivate the 'fine arts', for 'riches so employ'd, instead of encouraging vice, will excite both public and private virtue'.[155] Significantly, therefore, Kames not only claimed that the actual patronage of art encouraged virtue because it was public-oriented. He was in fact equally concerned with the private consequences of the resulting aesthetic cultivation. This, as Turnbull had already forcefully argued, both instructed directly in the ways of virtue, and encouraged the rational faculties, refining them and allowing them to strengthen and control the mind.

Reason, then, properly cultivated by learning, was a discriminating guide for individual morality, and the faculty to which the humanist orator, the Calvinist preacher, and consequently the enlightened historian, saw themselves as appealing.[156] Along with the assertion of public spirit, which we examined earlier, it provided the enlightened man of letters, no less than Scottish scholars of the past, with a potent argument for the moral and social importance of learning and, by recent extension, for the rightful pre-eminence and 'greatness' of the learned. Learning, as we have seen, continued to hold an appeal compatible with the Calvinist mind in search of an acceptable antidote to personal immorality. It was consistent also with a humanist determination to exalt the public over the exclusively private activity. Each route had always offered a means to attaining a recognisable virtue. But it now permitted the Scottish man of letters, always a prominent figure in historical discussions, to take advantage of the more propitious social circumstances of an enlightened age, and acquire precisely the additional dimension of moral legitimacy which his successful bid for the social leadership would require. George Turnbull's account in 1742 of the men encountered by the young Cicero in the Mediterranean cities can, then, be read as a striking and essentially allegorical evocation of the position of social leadership then eagerly being acquired in Scotland by her men of learning: they were simply 'the great and eminent', he insisted, 'not so much for their birth and wealth, as for their virtue, knowledge, and learning; men honoured and reverenced in their several cities, as the principal patriots, orators, and philosophers of their age'.[157] Virtue was suggested by his own association with moral learning and reason, and confirmed by his ostentatiously public orientation. The Scottish historian, on what we have seen so far, could at last look forward to moral legitimacy as the pre-eminently eloquent voice of Scotland's future.

IV: Causes, Consequences and the Problem of Rational Leadership

They had used history to present the intellectual elité as the men morally best equipped to lead Scottish society. It was thus incumbent upon eighteenth-century historians to offer an explanation of historical causality in which rational intention played a central role. Conventional discussions of the causality underlying historical change in the Scottish Enlightenment nevertheless have rightly focused on the dominance of a so-called 'theory of unintended consequences'. Broadly speaking, it seems fair to generalise that this doctrine held that large-scale historical change, and especially in the development of social structures and institutions, occurred *not* as the intended result of planned activity or legislative action but as the unintended outcome of multifarious individual initiatives. This account, however, has unfortunately been analysed more for its later importance in political economy and liberal philosophy than for its contemporary significance in the historical evolution of Scottish thought. Yet if the reconstruction of the Scottish social leadership seems to have been attempted by a wide community of scholars, men employing materials derived very largely from a rich and still-potent seam of Calvinism and humanism in Scotland, then the modern student is surely obliged at least to question the wisdom of this openly anachronistic approach. Our analysis of previous Scottish discussions of historical causality has already, for example, cast considerable doubt on the notion that providentialism had entered into a terminal decline by the early years of the eighteenth century. The Stoic concept of Fortune and especially the Calvinist vision of Providence actually continued to enjoy similar longevity. Both still provided in particular a fertile resource for eighteenth-century historians in need of deterministic explanations for events in the human sphere. This legacy of unintention, it seems, now tipped the precarious balance which in Scotland had long been maintained between reason and determinism, and did so finally and decisively in favour of the latter. The enlightened discussion of causality was therefore to prove perhaps the most problematic as well as the most prodigious aspect of the eighteenth-century Scottish inquiry. It was also one which can be understood only in the wider context of the Calvinist and humanist discourse of the Scottish past.

In the first instance, there is much evidence that historical scholars in enlightened Scotland still reached out to a recognisably providentialist framework in explaining both the general course of history and a remarkably diverse sequence of particular events. William Robertson, for example, one of the most eminent and enlightened historians of the day, assured his audience that 'the supreme Being conducteth all his operations by general laws'.[158] This was of course a conventional association of the general Providence with a Stoic faith in the mechanisms of Nature. The philosopher James Balfour, moreover, agreed with him. Balfour was to be found arguing that a general Providence was in fact necessary to make sense of our experience. A world 'fluctuating at random, without an intelligent ruler, without a common and beneficent parent', would be awful, he claimed, for 'life itself (as the Emperor Antoninus justly observed, without God, and Providence, is not worth the possessing'.[159] To yet another, the Aberdonian classicist Thomas Blackwell, it was equally evident that we should develop a Stoic acquiescence to the workings of a bountiful and benevolent universe. We ought not 'to foolishly wish for Things contrary to the Order of Nature and all-wise Destination of Providence', since that 'grand Instructress' had designated the course of events.[160] So comprehensive and infallible was the 'original Plan of Providence' envisaged by Lord Kames, meanwhile, writing in the *Essays Concerning British Antiquities* (1747), that it was simply an impiety to think it in any way 'insufficient to answer his Purposes'.[161] Nor ought such expressions of determinism to surprise the modern scholar familiar, as we should now have become, with the prevailing contours of Scottish thought during most of the century before 1740. No statement of a general Providence should be regarded as exceptional in the context of the dominant Newtonian natural philosophy of late seventeenth- and eighteenth-century Scotland. This triumphantly took as its foundation what Colin MacLaurin, professor of mathematics at Edinburgh, in 1748 called the 'great mysterious Being, who made and governs the whole system'.[162] So long as the *Principia Mathematica* ruled in the universities, God still seemed overwhelmingly the most likely ruler of a mechanical universe, of what Forbes of Culloden now confidently and with deliberate finality pronounced 'a perfect machine'.[163]

However, it seemed plain to Scottish thinkers, in keeping with MacLaurin's immensely influential account, that it was not God's 'intention, that the present state of things should continue forever without alteration'.[164] Such a conclusion explains the habitual recourse of historians to the interposition of divine direction, in the form of what the Calvinist would still have recognised as 'special Providences'. Those interventions were local intrusions of God's will serving to direct events more conspicuously towards an unseen divine objective. They remained an integral part of historical explanation in the eighteenth-century Scotland. As a typically panglossian George Turnbull remarked, it continued accordingly to be a proper objective of education to impart 'just ideas of providence, and the administration of the world, by pointing out the wise and good final causes every where pursued in it'.[165] To the special influence of Providence could be attributed in this way an assortment of those momentous but isolated occurrences which seemed unheralded in the human sphere. The fortuitous discovery of the mariner's compass, for example, 'when Providence decreed men were to pass the limits within which they had been so long confined',[166] or the transfer of 'the sovereignty of the world' to the Romans, as Providence had 'decreed',[167] were both explained in this way, by historians as eminent and otherwise as self-confidently modernist as William Robertson and William Maitland. The Calvinist doctrine of instruments, moreover, continued to provide an explicit means for presenting individuals as the sometimes unwitting local agents of an unfathomable divine Providence. Robertson, for example, saw Knox, in his *History of Scotland* (1759), as 'the instrument of Providence for advancing the Reformation'.[168] This was a direct recapitulation of descriptions of Knox we saw offered by earlier Calvinist scholars like John Row. In a similar manner, William Semple, the editor and continuator of Crawfurd's *History of the Shire of Renfrew* (1782), observed that 'the wise God put it in the hearts of some to breath after a reformation'.[169] Again Semple was merely elaborating, in an enlightened idiom, upon the received presbyterian interpretation of crucial historical events. So it should not seem unusual to find that, in Robertson's eighteenth-century eyes, the disciples had been 'only instruments in the divine hand, for the execution of wise purposes, concealed from themselves'.[170]

Providence, thus conceived, also retained its traditional controlling interest in moral matters and in the punitive treatment of vice. Nor can even this be regarded as surprising in view of the feverish concern for public morality which we have seen remained endemic in Scottish historical scholarship. Adam Smith, for example, readily invoked 'the providential care of its Author'.[171] This promised to explain how the human moral faculty, fortuitously though rather curiously, had come to consider outcomes as well as intentions in the evaluation of conduct. God, it seemed to Smith, was providentially concerned to have the moral calculus underline the importance of worthy actions as well as of good intentions. Many an 'event of providence' had similarly tended to occur in human affairs, according to the censorious Tory minister Thomas Somerville, to 'reprobate the imprudence, as well as the immorality of that maxim, That it is lawful to do evil, when good may be obtained by it'.[172] Moreover, in the direct punishment of immoral conduct, Providence could still take a most conspicuous part. In the turmoil of the French wars of religion, for example, the Border minister Walter Anderson thought that it had been as if 'providence had intended a long and signal punishment of her insults on the principles of humanity and the civil privileges of mankind'.[173] Similarly, for the distinguished advocate and miscellaneous scholar Sir John Dalrymple, the Civil War was also to be regarded as a case of Providence intruding so as to 'render dissension, as well as union, beneficial to mankind.'[174] In acknowledging the use of Providence in such contingent historical explanations, as well as emphasising how proper and defensible was the practice, moreover, William Robertson seems to have taken Luther's successes as the paradigm case: they were, quite simply, the *History of Charles V* (1762) claimed, 'operations which historians the least prone to credulity and superstition, must ascribe to that Divine Providence which can, with infinite ease, bring about events that to human sagacity appear impossible'.[175] As if to confirm his confidence in the thorough acceptability of this numbing vision of destiny even to a great Enlightenment historian, Robertson went on to maintain that the Reformation itself had been merely 'the natural effect of many powerful causes prepared by peculiar providence, and happily conspiring to that end'.[176] And we must remember that Robertson was only the most distinguished of a large number of enlightened authors. Very many others continued to rely in the same way upon both a general providential scheme and a series of individual divine interpositions. The inadequacy of human foresight and comprehension, it seems, was not only an established fact with which many Scotsmen were happy to work. It was part of a divinely ordained and benevolent scheme: the Lord indeed sent 'ane to heaven and ten to hell', as Burns' awestruck Holy Willie claimed, and did so 'no for ony guid or ill they've done … '.[177] This acceptance of human weakness and of the essential irrationality of outcomes ensured a historical causality still broadly cognate with the Calvinist metaphysics of their more purblind and tenacious Scottish predecessors.

Enlightened Scottish historians could therefore not have been simply in retreat from providentialism, as the conventional account of their position implies. Authors like the Perthshire clergyman John Bonar, feverishly gathering together the manuscript *History of Tyre* (1758) as an antidote to the moral ills of the Hanoverian polity, were typical rather than marginal. They demonstrably shared a vocabulary and conceptual framework with men as indisputably 'enlightened' as Robertson and Ferguson. Bonar's equation of history and prophecy may itself have looked back to Fleming and even to Napier: 'The

Prophecy limits this State of Subjection & Servitude to 70 years', he proclaimed, and 'History shows us that it was just of this Duration'.[178] But his providential faith that 'all Events depend upon God', and that 'the Conduct of his providences towards Men will always bear a relation to their character & behaviour', was scarcely out of tune even with the words of his most distinguished and optimistic contemporaries.[179] On the contrary, I have argued, they were themselves manifestly still writing a conventional form of history. This, in spite of what we have seen to be some hyperbolic claims to be a rigorously secular and scientific discipline, continued in fact to find both a need and a use for the traditionally inscrutable moral operations of Providence. The pervasive influence of Providence at crucial explanatory junctures in the historical account, then, as well as in the general metaphysical statements of Scottish historians at all levels, positively clamours for attention from modern students. This is so not least because, as our earlier analysis showed, it makes eminent sense of the otherwise confusing developments which occurred in Scottish thought during the tumultuous century before the Enlightenment. It would therefore be foolish indeed to suppose that Thomas Robertson's almost Miltonic claim in 1793, to be presenting historical pictures in order to magnify 'the ways of Providence to man',[180] was either exceptional or anachronistic in an enlightened age. So forceful were some of the continuing assertions of providential causality, even in the closing years of the century, and in men otherwise as skilful and elegant as Smith and Robertson, that one would instead be well advised to look again at the conceptualisation of historical change in the Scottish Enlightenment. The 'first task of historians of ideas and culture', John Dwyer rightly reminds us, 'is to place their subjects within appropriate and particular discursive domains'.[181] In doing so an examination of the continuing use of Stoic Fortune in eighteenth-century discourse provides precisely that vital additional perspective.

That Fortune retained a significant place in Enlightenment thought was, it turns out, not just the malicious allegation of a few of its more critical contemporaries like Duncan Forbes of Culloden. It was a fact that was admitted, and even trumpeted, by some of the most distinguished historians of the day. James Dunbar, for example, stated in untypically laconic fashion that 'Fortune governs events'.[182] This expressed a familiar Stoic view of unfathomable change, one which was especially common amongst those historians, like Adam Smith, who elsewhere professed an adherence to providential determinism. In reinforcing his own insistence on the beneficial circumstance of man's judgement of moral actions, indeed, Smith himself claimed that 'Fortune, which governs the world, has some influence where we should be least willing to allow her any, and directs in some measure the sentiments of mankind, with regard to the character and conduct both of themselves and others'.[183] In the Scottish Enlightenment, as in the later seventeenth century, Fortune was now more often conceived as an unyielding and uncontrollable director of outcomes. Rather than the somewhat lax, even vulnerable Renaissance body, it was increasingly seen as a fiercely Stoic entity which served to thwart the most noble of intentions and rendered the rational calculation of moral outcomes often hopelessly wide of the mark: as Thomas Robertson put it in 1793, when defending Mary Queen of Scots from her worst critics, it seemed 'just to observe, that fortune, as well as injustice and malice, was against her'.[184] Yet the resulting suggestion of fatalism – once so vigorously attacked by John Knox – remained a slurr on any self-respecting enlightened man of letters. It was a stigma which Kames certainly sought to shrug off when he was formally accused of embracing necessitarian theology in the *Essays on the Principles of Morality and Natural Religion* (1751). It was also one from which Walter Anderson furiously tried to defend his Stoic heroes. They were men, he claimed, who had lacked those fatalistic implications 'subversive of any free agency in man'.[185] In other words, enlightened scholars, and especially those who employed it, attempted to suppress what they identified as the anti-rationalist implications of Stoic Fortune. These posed a clear threat to the ability of men involved in the affairs of the world both to decide and to act effectively. A Stoic scepticism of rational foresight did, however, grow organically out of their proclivity for a deterministic vision of Fortune which itself had a great deal in common with traditional Calvinist metaphysics. As David Hume and James Beattie in their different ways both chose to illustrate, Stoicism offered a compelling account of virtue in an uncontrollable and unpredictable world.[186] Acceptance of this offer had only been encouraged by its broad consistency with a strongly anti-rationalist Calvinist determinism, which was itself prospering anew in the same disturbing and deeply uncertain environment.

The aspect of Stoicism which seems especially to have earned the admiration of such historians, moreover, as of some of their Scottish predecessors, was the ability it gave to accept misfortune in the public arena with apparent equanimity. Or rather, Stoicism seemed the philosophy perhaps best able to offer causal determinism in the external world without actually allowing men to overlook the obligations of virtuous conduct – a fatalistic tendency encouraging precisely that private seclusion whose taint they seem most to have feared. Smith's *Theory of Moral Sentiments* (1759), for example, claimed that it was unquestionably 'the philosophy which affords the noblest lessons to magnanimity'. Smith even suggested that Stoicism was the consummate public-oriented philosophy, the 'best school of heroes and patriots'.[187] It allowed men to overcome disappointment in their worldly affairs and to retain a necessary faith in the benevolent design and the 'wisdom which directs all the events of human life'.[188] In particular, by emphasising the moral imperative of virtuous conduct, Stoicism at least sought to avoid what Walter Anderson, again following his Scottish predecessors, identified as the most pernicious effect of determinism: a solipsistic urge for private meditations, a dulling and enervating fatalism, a 'belief in an invidious disposition in the fates, and the doom of the gods against a constant and undisturbed prosperity to mortals'.[189] The ideal Enlightenment Stoic, then, would accept his almost inevitable disappointment in the world with calm resignation. He would strive manfully (though with little success) to shape the future in his own rational and virtuous image, rather than simply retreat with Alexander Ross into a safe and secluded *otium*. Outcomes in the public sphere, however, were to be awaited with no great certainty. This remained regrettably true whatever the simultaneous injunctions to activity and virtue. Indeed Stoicism, to its critics, offered a role for reason only in a cultivated moral seclusion, and provided no account of an effective rational causality in the public arena. As Beattie's *The Minstrel* so shamelessly expressed it, only 'the shade of Academus' grove', the pursuit of science and scholarship where 'cares molest not, discords melt away', gave any hope of worldly peace of mind. Stoicism therefore gazed sadly at the public domain. But ultimately it turned away in dejection, pining in solitude only for 'virtue lost, and ruin'd man'.[190] The exaltation of virtuous aims and rational outcomes in the public domain certainly continued. Yet precisely because in this way it offered no hope of foreseeable results, and as William Drummond had once feared, Stoicism itself was not an account of causality likely ultimately to inspire many men to purposeful historical action. A retreat from effective rational intention, it seems, was sheepishly though unmistakably gathering pace. The so-called doctrine of 'unintended consequences', with its enhanced reliance upon the utter causal inadequacy of human wisdom in the public domain, can appear in this context only as an even more dangerous development. For it was one which clearly intensified rather than resolved the fatalistic difficulties long identified by Scottish authors in both of these problematical older traditions.

The extent to which Scottish thought by 1770 had nevertheless come to rely upon unintentional outcomes in historical explanation has certainly not been over-emphasised by the existing historiography. The disjunction between intention and outcome, as is usually recognised, did indeed offer to reconcile the pursuit of private profit with the public welfare. But more broadly, it also represented in Scotland the final and widespread success of a doctrine of unintention. This in effect brought to secular maturity the deeply familiar separation of human decision and consequent effect which had been implicit in orthodox Calvinist and Stoic discussions of causality offered by previous Scottish scholars otherwise as diverse as Hume of Godscroft and Mackenzie of Rosehaugh.[191] Lord Kames, a familiar spokesman for obdurate Calvinist thinking in an enlightened age, actually considered a theory of unintentional outcomes central to a traditional Calvinist providentialism. He also provides an unwitting illustration, therefore, of just how little distance in fact separated modern unintention and orthodox theistic fatalism: 'it appears agreeable to the plan of Providence', Kames observed in the *Sketches on the History of Man*, 'that we should have but an obscure glimpse of futurity'.[192] Moreover, he later added, 'a knowledge of future events, as far as it tends to influence our conduct, is inconsistent with a state of trial, such as Providence has allotted to man in this life'.[193] In precisely the same unperturbed secular idiom, meanwhile, Adam Smith, another who had espoused both a providentialist and a Stoic causality, notoriously considered the unseen operations of an 'invisible hand', the very embodiment of unintended consequences, as not at all 'the worse for the society'. Again, that intention and an expectation of public benefits were 'no part of it' seemed to Smith admirably suited to a causal mechanism regulating aggregate economic activity.[194] To the enlightened providentialist or Stoic, then, the unintentionality responsible for large-scale historical phenomena was structural rather than incidental to the model. It was this feature, indeed, which was held to be responsible for ensuring that outcomes would remain obscure and that the force of 'passion and interest', rather than vain discerning reason, would be the most likely origin of historical change. As the pious Forbes of Culloden dutifully recognised of God's Creation: the 'brutal appetites, and enjoyments, are nicely proportioned to their ends'.[195] Unintention was thus an essential part of an awe-inspiring but benevolent design, by which those blind and irrational instincts were unwittingly applied to profound historical purposes.

With unintention so blessed by Stoicism and consistent also with Calvin's familiar divine determinism, the rule of the inchoate passions over frail reason in eighteenth-century Scotland was probably assured. Indeed, in a sometimes panglossian universe, their triumph could often be thought productive of the most beneficial ends. From a suitably optimistic theological starting-point, Hugo Arnot, for example, now openly admired 'the wisdom of Providence, which so disposes of human actions, as to make the passions and interests of men, leading them to indifferent, and sometimes criminal pursuits, productive of the most happy events'.[196] Similarly, when seen from the human perspective, Dunbar, the Aberdonian philosopher already encountered as an acolyte of Stoic Fortune, considered historical events were indeed 'more justly reputed the slow result of situations than of regular design'.[197] In a startling attack on classical patriotism, moreover, the celebrated '*amor patriae*' of the ancients, the Glaswegian minister John Gillies argued that the Greek city states had likewise triumphed because of unintentional rather than deliberate individual action. They had in fact acted without rational purpose, he claimed, and 'with no other object in view in all their civil contests, but private interest and ambition'.[198] Not uninfluenced by this stinging assault on reason, one could argue, was even Scott himself, contrasting in his great heroine Flora MacIvor the natural vigour and spontaneity of her 'reality of feeling' with the acquired dissemblance, the mere 'gloss of politeness', instilled by too rigorous an education.[199] Reason and the House of Hanover may have triumphed, but the author's preferences are still abundantly clear. Defeated by a remorselessly rational world, Flora yet retains the passion and the essentially heroic humanity to which Scott still found himself irresistibly drawn. Unintentional consequences and the blind passions, therefore, and according to an entirely orthodox Calvinist position, could combine to reduce the strictly rational virtues to impotent and even fatalistic subordination.[200] This remarkable convergence of intellectual currents in enlightened anti-rationalism of course makes it all the more regrettable that classical political economy, in the hands of recent commentators like Hutchison and Hirschman, has not been permitted to reveal its specifically Scottish pre-history.[201]

Calvinist-inspired arguments for the considerable causal power both of unintentionality and the irrational passions, however, were not only applicable under strictly historical circumstances. Unintention and its immeasurable influence could not so safely be bounded by mere narrative or fictional time. Indeed, Smith himself provided a clear reminder of their relevance to Scotsmen in explaining the most recent and topical of social developments. The modern economic division of labour, he famously claimed in the *Wealth of Nations*, was simply the 'necessary, though very slow and gradual consequence of a certain propensity ... which has in view no such extensive utility' as the generation of wealth.[202] In a similar vein, William Robertson explained the recent extermination of the American Indians as an unintentional outcome of other actions. It was emphatically 'Not the result of any system or policy'.[203] Much more expansively, meanwhile, the distinguished 'common sense' thinker and professor of moral philosophy at Glasgow, Thomas Reid, in no sense a practising historian, also made striking use of unintended consequences in his *Essays on the Active Powers of Man* (1788). 'We have seen how, by instinct and habit', he wrote, 'man, without any expence of thought, without deliberation or will, is led to many actions, necessary for his preservation and well-being, which, without those principles, all his skill and wisdom would not have been able to accomplish'.[204] Even more redolent of his Scottish theological background, to which he was most notably to have recourse in his spirited philosophical tussles with David Hume, Reid regarded this system – which had apparently constructed his own world – as testifying indisputably that 'the wise Author of our being hath implanted in human nature many inferior principles of action'. These, 'with little or no aid of reason or virtue, preserve the species, and produce the various exertions, the various changes and revolutions which we observe upon the theatre of life'.[205] Calvinist anti-rationalism, it seems, had once again induced in the eighteenth-century scholar the conclusion that reason and virtue were unreliable guides. The divine determinism of unintended consequences, with the 'Author of our being' providentially harnessing the instinctive passions, was instead, as Thomas Blackwell had lately preached, the invariable motor of change.[206] The unintentional, an essential element in Calvinist thought, was thus not only central to the classic eighteenth-century Scottish account of historical causality. It also implied the causal priority of the ignorant passions, and gave at the same time a worrying twist to the perennial problem of fatalism. This was profoundly threatening to the active and rational social theory inherited from Boece, Buchanan and Drummond. In this the capacity of learned and virtuous minds both to understand and to direct historic developments had of course always been central.[207]

The character of the enlightened exploration of historical causality, then, was wholly consistent with the deeply problematical evolution of the Scottish intellectual tradition. At the same time it was also vigorously subversive of some of the central claims which we have seen still clearly supported the Enlightenment scholarly enterprise. In particular, unintentional consequences, like Stoic or providential fatalism, had the potential to undermine those vital pretensions to a rational social leadership which were sustained elsewhere in eighteenth-century Scottish thought by an intensified emphasis upon the pre-eminent oratorical, moral and intellectual qualifications of the scholarly community. Discomfort might be the least that we should expect from historians committed in this way to vitiating what had by now become their own ideological defence; and discomfort, or something very like it, is surely betrayed by their fragmentary attempts specifically in causal explanation to protect their suddenly less-than-persuasive arguments for the power of learning and virtue. David Hume, no less, actually conceded in the *History of England* that, alongside the 'mixture of accident' which attended upon momentous long-term develop-ments, there still remained 'a small ingredient of wisdom and foresight'.[208] Thomas Reid, too, Hume's great philosophical opponent, offered 'little or no aid' from 'reason and virtue' to the onward march of events. But he nevertheless left open the intriguing possibility that these capacities, qualities 'of the latest growth', might yet have some 'little' influence over developments.[209] Such vestigial claims for the efficacy of the Calvinist and humanist virtues were buried amid powerful evocations of causal unintention. They could of course be neither as frequent nor as expansive as the much more forceful statements found elsewhere in the same enlightened texts. Both Hume and Reid notably failed to go further, or to offer a defensible role for human reason specifically whilst expounding a causal explanation of historical events. A similar unwillingness to relinquish hold on the learned virtues, even in causal explanation, probably affected Adam Ferguson, often regarded as the consummate opponent of rationalist pretensions and mythological legislators. Ferguson was to offer them a residual role in the most portentous of historical developments. Rome's founders, his *History of the Roman Republic* (1783) unconvincingly announced, may indeed have been learned men who 'with a perfect foresight of the consequences, suggested the maxims which gave so happy a turn to the minds of men in this infant republic'.[210] Like Hume, then, Ferguson apparently considered that human 'foresight', which we have already seen to be the very antithesis of unintention and so of Enlightenment causality, might still play an important if sporadic part in the direction of events. Even in his expositions of unintentional causality, it seems, the rational man of learning could neither quite manage nor afford to silence the last defiant echoes of the older humanist account.

Evidence of the profound theoretical difficulties beginning to be provoked by causal determinism in the last decades of the eighteenth century thus surfaces upon closer analysis of Enlightenment historical thought. Even John Pinkerton, that chimerical intellect largely beyond the pale of enlightened respectability, seems in this respect to have been as one with his more orthodox contemporaries. Pinkerton observed in 1787 that human affairs 'by no means proceed according to reason, speculation, or philosophy'. But he also tantalisingly claimed, though again without further elaboration at this point, that the 'various contingencies' of existence might still somehow 'be learned from ancient authors'.[211] Occasional prevarication, then, strongly suggests that the enlightened Scottish historian was increasingly being torn in two. Engaged in pronouncing the doom of reason and learning as effective causal influences, he can have been only too aware of the considerable damage likely to be inflicted by such rigorous unintentionality upon the long-standing claims of Scotland's learned élite. These were still being faithfully enunciated by almost every other element of his text. Anti-rationalism, we have seen, grew powerfully out of a rich heritage of Calvinist historical thinking in Scotland. The parallel discursive influences of modern natural philosophy or of Hanoverian political discourse did nothing but further strengthen the providential or Stoic causality, and so the insistence upon mechanistic unintention, of most enlightened Scottish historians. This did not at first, it seems, prevent the eighteenth-century successors of Boece and Buchanan from speaking with their customary purpose and confidence to a uniquely receptive audience. After all, their astonishing success as intellectuals in actually winning-over the Scotland of their day gave them little initial cause for self-doubt. But their Calvinist inheritance had nevertheless finally and fatefully to be reckoned with. The eventual consequences of such a disturbing development for the coherence, even the very plausibility, of enlightened discourse, are matters to which we must therefore of necessity return in our conclusion.

V

The construction of an enlightened history in Scotland, then, saw both the practical triumph and the increasing disablement of a heroic enterprise originally begun by Calvinists and humanists in the sixteenth century. An enlightened history with one hand still offered to bestow upon the Scottish scholar all the lavish honours due to the virtuous, eloquent and learned orator. But with the other it threatened to snatch away the laurels of the rational leader, denying him any special causal influence over the political, economic and social affairs of a modern Scottish community. The oratorical posturing of the Scottish historian, of course, seems largely to have inhered until the end of the eighteenth century, giving him the public ear to which all of his many subsequent claims were directed. More broadly, the equation of oratory and learning allowed the enlightened Scottish scholar himself finally to justify a position of social leadership, underwritten by complementary and deep-seated Calvinist and humanist presuppositions. Virtue, moreover, that characteristic obsession of all earlier Scottish historians, continued to be freely available to those who practised fastidiously the irreplaceable arts of moral scholarship. To a great extent, therefore, the assertion of rational virtue served ideologically to underpin the undoubted transformation of the Scottish scholar in the eighteenth century from a nervous recipient of patronage to the pre-eminent leader of his community. Yet even as those increasingly justifiable claims were being advanced by means of what had by now become a supremely eloquent and influential historical tradition, profoundly dissonant chords were also reaching their own disturbing crescendo. Calvinism and humanism had at first brought the Scottish historian, confident and well-equipped, into an enlightened age. Additionally, they had offered him materials for constructing a persuasive ideological defence of his social pre-eminence. But, in the final analysis, they also contained within themselves at least the potential seeds of his downfall. Reason and rational intention, those humanist qualities to which Scotsmen had long responded with the most extreme ambivalence, were by the end of the century under increasing attack from within the intellectual community itself. The eighteenth-century Scottish triumph of rational virtue, as a direct result, would turn out to be a vulnerable and a fragile thing.

NOTES

1. Crawfurd, *History*, p. v.
2. That this was the purpose in mind was occasionally indicated by an explicit comment. Thus, we find the almost dynastic account of the intellectual succession: 'after the revival of letters we began with *Eruditi*, next we had Poets, then Orators, then Metaphysicians, then Geometricians', before the modern advent of 'history'. Pinkerton, *History*, I, vi-vii.
3. This criticism of traditional history was taken from Guarini, the translator of Tasso, but it epitomised the Scottish attitude towards the morally uninstructive in history. See [Thomas Blackwell], *Letters Concerning Mythology* (London 1748), p. 113. The text is an anonymous collection of alleged correspondence, purportedly published by the friends of a deceased author. In fact, Blackwell was responsible and he survived until 1758.
4. Dunbar, *Essays*, Preface.
5. *ibid.*, Preface.
6. One, for example, considered that the slackening of interest in oratory might in part be the result of the 'superior good Sense of the Moderns, who reject, with Disdain, all those rhetorical Tricks, which may be imploy'd to seduce the Judges...', David Hume, 'Of Eloquence', *Essays*, II, 19. This suspicion of oratorical sophistry, and the frantic anxiety that an author might actually 'disguise the weritie' of his argument by mere 'painted eloquence', looked back in Scotland at least to Adam Blackwood, who had made this telling point in his assault in 1579 upon Buchanan's humanist oratory, *History*, p. 21.
7. See Grassi, *Rhetoric as Philosophy*, whose thesis is that the early modern period saw the gradual uncoupling of philosophy and oratory, and the evolution of a modern suspicion towards the agile and over-dextrous use of language. It is, however, better to see this momentous shift towards post-humanism occurring only in late eighteenth-century Scotland, as explained in Reid, *Party-Coloured Mind*, p. 12.
8. Blair, *Lectures*, II, 240.
9. *ibid.*, I, 13–14.
10. *ibid.*, II, 231.
11. *ibid.*, II, 240. John Macpherson, minister at Sleat on the Isle of Skye, wrote similarly in condemnation of 'That philosophy which tends neither to strengthen the mind, or improve the happy feelings of the heart', *Critical Dissertations on the Origin, Antiquities, Language, Government, Manners, and Religion of the Ancient Caledonians, Their Posterity the Picts, and the British and Irish Scots* (London, 1768), p. 150.
12. Hume, *Treatise*, I, 2.
13. Thomas Somerville, then minister at Jedburgh, looked back fondly to this period and reflected in glowing terms on the eloquence merely of Scotland's presbyterian clergy: the orators of the Kirk alone included a constellation of stars, including Blair, Dick, Walker, Wallace, Wishart, Drysdale, Robertson and Erskine, *Life*, pp. 57–62.
14. Lord Kames, *Elements of Criticism*, 2 vols (Edinburgh, 1769), I, 100.

15. Blair, *Lectures*, II, 39.
16. Johnson, *Journey*, p. 503.
17. *ibid.*, p. 503.
18. Dalrymple, *Memoirs*, I, 6. Robert Henry, the Edinburgh minister and antiquarian, likewise noted with approval that the Druids had opportunities 'to display their eloquence, and to discover its great power and efficacy – as, when they were teaching their pupils in their schools – when they discoursed in public to the people on religious and moral subjects – when they pleaded causes in a court of justice – and when they harangued in the greatest councils of the nation ... ', *History*, I, 279. Scotland's professors, ministers and lawyers already enjoyed the first three prerogatives: the Enlightenment bid fair at last to offer them the fourth.
19. Wallace, *Ancient Peerages*, p. 18.
20. Dalrymple, *Memoirs*, I, 46.
21. Campbell, *Philosophy of Rhetoric*, I, 200–2.
22. For example, David Hume equated liberty with eloquence, observing that 'Of all the polite and learned Nations, *Britain* alone possesses a popular Government, or admits into the Legislature such numerous Assemblies as can be suppos'd to lye under the Dominion of Eloquence', 'Of Eloquence', II, 11–12. On this political dimension see D. Daiches, 'Style Périodique and Style Coupé: Hugh Blair and the Scottish Rhetoric of American Independence', in Sher and Smitten (eds), *Scotland and America*, pp. 209–26.
23. Blair, *Lectures*, II, 13. See also Robert Henry's view of the social prominence and political value accorded to eloquence in Greece and Rome, a fact of clear relevance to the eloquent and upwardly-mobile scholar in Hanoverian Scotland: 'While these illustrious nations enjoyed their liberties, their greatest Orators were esteemed the greatest men, had the chiefest sway in all their public councils, and were advanced to the highest honours in their respective states', *History*, I, 296. For an influential source, see Shaftesbury's comment on the Greeks, that 'With their Liberty they lost not only their Force of Eloquence, but even their Stile and Language it-self', in his 'Advice to an Author', *Characteristicks of Men, Manners, Opinions, Times*, 2nd edn, 3 vols ([ ], 1714), I, 219.
24. [ ], *Historical Notes to 1748* (Aberdeen, University Library, MS 614), fo. x(v).
25. William Wight, *Heads of a Course of Lectures on the Study of History* (Glasgow, 1767), p. 5. See also his *Heads of Lectures on the Study of Civil History* (Glasgow, 1772).
26. Guthrie, *New Grammar*, p. 205.
27. Kames, *Sketches*, I, 140. Hume, however, considered that the modern age had not produced orators to equal the ancients: though lists of other worthy men of letters and poets might indeed be drawn up, yet 'what Orators are ever mentioned?', 'Of Eloquence', II, 12.
28. 'That the Enlightenment flourished in Scotland at the hands of so many of its church leaders is probably in large measure due to its intellectual humanist heritage', Cameron, 'Humanism and Religious Life', p. 175.
29. Kincaid, *History*, p. 27. Kincaid's qualified enthusiasm for the reformed religion owed much to the general belief that it approached 'to the democratic form of civil government', as voiced by Alexander Wight, *A Treatise on the Laws Concerning the Election of the Different Representatives of Scotland to the Parliament of Great Britain* (Edinburgh, 1773), p. 43, a view which also again marked the continuing utility of presbyterian humanist polemic in an enlightened age.
30. Adams, *Curious Thoughts*, p. 295. The words belong to Kames.
31. Guthrie, *New Grammar*, p. 147.
32. Stuart, *History of the Reformation*, p. 114.
33. Duff, *History*, p. 272.
34. Stuart, *History of Scotland*, II, 164.
35. Arnot, *History*, p. 167.
36. Stuart, *History of the Reformation*, p. 119.
37. Arnot, *History*, p. 118.
38. Robertson, *History of Scotland*, II, 90.
39. John Gibson, *History of Glasgow* (Glasgow, 1777), p. 81.
40. Campbell, *Full and Particular Description*, p. 41.
41. William Maitland, *The History of Edinburgh* (Edinburgh, 1753), p. 129. The case of the ministers and their belated employment of eloquence in the service of political stability and

enlightened values also concerned Andrew Henderson, anonymous historian of the Jacobite rebellion, who noted how once 'the Ministers of the Gospel returned, the silent Sabbaths cease, and Sermon begins in the Churches' as 'With Flows of Eloquence, and Streams of Persuasion, they recommended loyalty to their King, a Regard for their Country, Liberty, and Laws', *The History of the Rebellion, 1745 and 1746* (Edinburgh, 1747), p. 108. Once again, of course, Scottish oratory was seen as the successful fusion of narrow presbyterian and republican-humanist public interests.

42. Somerville, *Political Transactions*, p. 382.
43. Arnot, *History*, p. 428. Such organisations were invaluable: there was 'no better environment for a man with scholarly aspirations nor indeed a better training for a future public speaker', D. Wood, 'Constant in Edinburgh: Eloquence and History', *French Studies*, 40 (1986), 151–66.
44. Anderson, *Ancient Greece*, p. 6.
45. Kincaid, *History*, p. 56.
46. Ferguson, *Civil Society*, p. 143.
47. See e.g. R. S. Pomeroy, 'Locke, Alembert, and the anti-rhetoric of the "Enlightenment"', *Studies on Voltaire and the Eighteenth Century*, 154 (1976), 1657–75.
48. One of the most significant transformations turning mid-eighteenth-century Scotland into a society ripe for intellectual leadership was the development of the urban provincial culture examined in R. L. Emerson, 'The Enlightenment and Social Structure', in Fritz and Williams (eds), *City and Society*, pp. 99–124. More particularly, the years at the close of the seventeenth century had seen the emergence of Scotland's legal, scientific, and clerical professionals to social eminence, a development on which the social credibility of an 'enlightened' intelligentsia was subsequently to rest. See Hugh Ouston in Craig, *Scottish Literature*, II, 11–31. The Union with England in 1707, and the transfer of political power to London, as Nicholas Phillipson suggests, would further have strengthened their claims to be considered the natural heirs of the aristocrats and statesmen, 'Culture and Society'. The removal of other claimants from the scene, moreover, would only have exacerbated the difficulty of locating the scholar's audience, ultimately allowing the Calvinist and humanist elevation of rational learning to run its course and buttress their own growing sense of having assumed the social leadership.
49. The extent to which enlightened scholars in particular regarded themselves as orators has, of course, been seriously underplayed in modern considerations, though a timely corrective is John Dwyer's observation that 'the eighteenth-century Scots did not view themselves as sociologists. They regarded themselves as civic moralists and rhetoricians', *Virtuous Discourse*, p. 3. Also Kenneth Simpson has recently observed how the legal education to which so many enlightened authors were subjected tended to make 'presentation, style, and rhetoric' an important priority in their writing, *The Protean Scot: The Crisis of Identity in Eighteenth-Century Scottish Literature* (Aberdeen, 1988), esp. pp. 11–12. That the Ciceronian junction of the oratorical and prudential arts still greatly influenced even the most forward-looking Enlightenment theoreticians seems clear from George Campbell's continuing conviction that 'there is no art whatever hath so close a connexion with all the faculties and powers of the mind, as eloquence, or the art of speaking', *Philosophy of Rhetoric*, I, p. 13.
50. Grant, *Origin of the Gael*, p. 29.
51. Kames, *Sketches*, I, 121.
52. Maitland, *History and Antiquities*, I, ii. The Jacobite scholar Drummond of Balhaldy offered a different and intensely provocative assessment of the literati's identification with the bards. Clearly censuring the pompous erudition and insipid politeness of Whig, Hanoverian, presbyterian Edinburgh and its emerging intellectuals, Drummond made a spiteful comparison between the 'Highland Bard', who truly had 'no ostentation of learning, no allusions to antient fable or mythology, no far-fetched similes, nor dazeling metaphors … ', and the modern polite poet, with his 'affected ornaments', devoid of 'that glow of imagination and noble flame of fancy' which marked out the genuine ancient orator, *Memoirs*, p. 155. See also the anonymous admirer of the bards in the *History of the Earls and Dukes of Argyll to 1776* (Edinburgh, National Library of Scotland, Adv. MS 34.5.22), esp. pp. 1–2.
53. Guthrie, *New Grammar*, p. 124.
54. Pinkerton, *History*, I, 273.
55. Blair, *Lectures*, I, 12.

56. Kames, *Sketches*, I, 306. Likewise, John Macpherson of Sleat observed how 'They exerted the whole force of their genius in perpetuating the memory of departed heroes, in exciting the nobles to walk in the same paths of activity and glory ... to cultivate the generous and manly virtues ... ', *Critical Dissertations*, p. 220.

57. Macpherson observed that the 'character of the ancient Britons [was] formed on the poems of the Bards'. More particularly, 'the Bards inculcated the purest morals on their countrymen, and comprehended in their songs all those virtues which render a man truly great, and deservedly renowned', *Introduction to the History of Great Britain and Ireland* (London, 1771), p. 201. Earlier Scottish examples of admiration for the 'Bards & shenachies' arise in the early 1720s in Campbell, 'Genealogical Account', p. 190, and of course in the 1730s in John Drummond's evident fascination for the 'Highland Bard' who 'sung or recited his verses after the manner of the antients, and who inherited no small portion of their spirite and simplicity', *Memoirs*, p. 155.

58. Macpherson's enthusiastic reception can only further have been facilitated in an age of dominant preachers, lawyers and professors by his emphasis upon the importance of the oratorical function of the learned. This element in his work shines through in his earliest offerings, as, for example, in the bardic refrains and mournful dirges of Vinvela and Ossian in 'Fragments of Ancient Poetry, Collected in the Highlands of Scotland', in R. and J. Dodsley (eds), *Fugitive Pieces on Various Subjects, By Several Authors*, 2 vols (London, 1761), II, pp. 117–62, originally published in 1760. Even earlier, and later suppressed by Macpherson himself (probably because it was the openly fictitious piece in which he had first hit upon his winning formula), see *The Highlander: A Poem in Six Cantos* (Edinburgh, 1758), where perorations and stirring elegies abound.

59. Shaw, *History*, p. 227.

60. Duff, *History*, p. 43. Even more intriguingly, the same north-eastern bastion of religious conservatism, Aberdeen, was also to produce that great proto-Romantic allegorical poem of the age, James Beattie's *The Minstrel, in Two Books: with Some Other Poems* (London, 1779), a work which looked back to explain how 'THE MINSTREL fared in days of yore', in days when Scotland had been, in evocative Calvinist and humanist terms, 'Inflexible in faith; invincible in arms', *ibid.*, pp. 2–6.

61. Arnot, *History*, p. 430.

62. Hailes, *Annals*, p. 263.

63. Blair, *Lectures*, I, 15 n. For an equally scathing attack on Edward I for his destruction of Scotland's literary muniments, see Andrew Henderson, *A Dissertation on the Royal Line and First Settlers of Scotland* (London, 1771), p. 28.

64. Hume, *History*, I, 1. Later Henry Mackenzie's overdue investigation into the authenticity of Ossian used the same argument, that 'the preservation of such long and connected poems, by oral tradition alone, during a course of fourteen centuries, is so much out of the ordinary course of human affairs, that it requires the strongest reasons to make us believe it', *Report of the Committee of the Highland Society of Scotland, Appointed to Inquire into the Nature and Authenticity of the Poems of Ossian* (Edinburgh, 1805), p. 6. But this was not an Enlightenment invention. In 1692 Alexander Monro had observed that it was not possible to preserve the memory of events 'unless they are *timeously* committed to writing. Unwritten tradition goes but a short way', *Apology*, p. 54. Perhaps again, therefore, this rigorously sceptical aspect of Enlightenment Whig history had early affinities with Scottish Protestantism and humanism, and their scrupulous insistence upon the solid textual analysis of written testimony.

65. J. Pocock, 'Post-Puritan England and the Problem of the Enlightenment', in P. Zagorin (ed.), *Culture and Politics from Puritanism to the Enlightenment* (Berkeley, Calif., 1980), pp. 91–111.

66. Maitland, *History of Edinburgh*, p. 355.

67. *ibid.*, p. 355.

68. Millar, *Historical View*, p. 455.

69. William Borthwick, *An Inquiry into the Origins and Limitations of the Feudal Dignities in Scotland* (Edinburgh, 1775), p. vii.

70. *ibid.*, p. vii.

71. As the anonymous contributor relates, with distinct echoes of Gray's recent *Elegy Written in a Country Churchyard* (1751), 'Your Divines, your Philosophers, your Historians, your Poets, have found their way to our sequestered vales, and are perused with pleasure even by

our lowly swains; and the names of Tillotson, of Atterbury, of Clerk, of Secker, of Newton, of Locke, of Bacon, of Lyttelton, of Dryden, of Pope, of Gay, and of Gray, are not unknown in our distant land', Thomas Pennant, *A Tour in Scotland*, 1769 (Chester, 1771), p. 247.

72. Henderson, *Dissertation*, pp. 42–3.

73. Blair, *Lectures*, II, 279. The utility of history in complementing other learned and practical accomplishments of course gave its exponent a very special claim to social eminence in an enlightened community. This was admirably captured by Scott in his *alter ego* Pleydell, who acutely observes that 'A lawyer without history or literature is a mechanic, a mere working mason; if he possesses some knowledge of these, he may call himself an architect', in 'Guy Mannering', III, 205.

74. Bonar, *History of Tyre*, pp. 15–16. To George Campbell, moreover, a knowledge of history seemed 'to adorn the character of a pastor, and render him respectable ... procuring him in general a more favourable reception with mankind', In particular, it reinforced his eloquence with learning, giving 'double weight to everything he says', and ensuring that 'even princes refrain from talking, and the nobles lay their hand upon their mouth', *Lectures on Ecclesiastical History*, 2 vols (London, 1800), I, 8.

75. Buchanan, *Defence of the Scots Highlanders*, A3r.

76. Turnbull, *Treatise*, p. 100.

77. Crawfurd, *History*, p. vi.

78. Ridpath, *Border History*, p. v.

79. Heron, *New General History*, Dedication.

80. Hume, *History*, I, 54. Indeed, he argued, echoing once again his Scottish predecessors, Alfred's achievement was to recognise that 'good morals and knowledge are almost inseparable', *ibid.*, I, 53. The equation of virtue and learning was thus still central to the historical analysis of an enlightened age. Equally, Robert Henry saw Alfred as the paradigm scholar-leader, 'an eloquent orator, an acute philosopher, an excellent historian, mathematician, musician, and architect, and the prince of the Saxon poets', *History*, II, 349 – in fact, everything for which the enlightened intellectual seemed or wished to stand. By 'speaking on all occasions in praise of learning, – and by making it the great road to preferment, both in church and state', *ibid.*, II, 356, Alfred seemed to have striven to create nothing less than the model oratorical and intellectual leadership.

81. Hume, *History*, I, 191. See Major, *History of Greater Britain*, p. 143.

82. *ibid.*, III, 61 n. See Abercromby, *Martial Atchievements*, I, b1r.

83. Grant, *Origin of the Gael*, p. 29, refers to a 'history of ideas', whilst Henry's *History*, I, 248, itself attempts to reconstruct 'the history of learning'. The possibility of such an inquiry, as well as an urgent reassertion of its moral utility, is prefigured in David Hume, 'Arts and Sciences', II, 53–100.

84. See L. Formigari, 'Language and Society in the Late Eighteenth Century', *Journal of the History of Ideas*, 35 (1974), 275–92, and C. J. Berry, 'Adam Smith's *Considerations* on Language', *Journal of the History of Ideas*, 35 (1974), 130–8.

85. Guthrie, *New Grammar*, p. 139.

86. Duff, *History*, p. 61. James I was a favourite object of Enlightenment praise, and, as we saw earlier, a recipient of lavish compliments from many sixteenth- and seventeenth-century authors, for much the same reasons. George Wallace, for example, excused James's failure permanently to attach the Scottish aristocracy to 'the elegancies of cultivated life' on the typically unlikely grounds of their unaccountable predilection for 'proud and gloomy castles', *Ancient Peerages*, p. 242.

87. Duff, *History*, p. 85.

88. Stevenson, *History*, I, 24. But Stevenson was by no means the first to see learned Scotsmen in the least propitious of times. Before even George Mackenzie's *Lives and Characters*, a monument to the devious Augustan imagination, there had been the Jacobean scholar Sir Thomas Craig, fancying, with scarcely more plausibility, that the seventh century had been a golden age of Scottish letters, exemplified by their alleged foundation of the universities of Paris and Pavia, *De Unione Regnorum*, pp. 379–80. And as a particularly unashamed example of this genre, no one should forget Dempster's *Historia Ecclesiastica Gentis Scotorum* (1627). Even these had their antecedents, however, as when John Major had claimed (with greater accuracy) that during the time of Charlemagne Scotland had sent to France men 'better furnished with learning than in all other parts of the [world]', *History of Greater Britain*, p.

102, or when in 1594 a Scottish Jesuit had listed 'men eminent for the fame of their learning' in medieval Scotland, Thomson, 'Antiquity', p. 129.

89. Millar, *Historical View*, p. vi. The 'man of letters' was widely presumed also to possess many other advantages by virtue of his learning, as the controversial James Macpherson explained: access to foreign archives, in particular, was 'a favour seldom if ever refused' to the cosmopolitan and virtuous scholar, *Original Papers Containing the Secret History of Great Britain*, 2 vols (Dublin, 1775), I, 6.

90. Ferguson, *Roman Republic*, I, 10. In emphasising the scholarly credentials of Roman leaders, Ferguson merely followed the lead given by the Augustan reviewer George Mackenzie, who had observed, with Quintilian, that Caesar '*Spoke, Wrote, and Fought by the same Spirit*', a fact whose pertinence was hammered home by Mackenzie's insistence that in Scottish history, too, 'our Greatest Scholars were our Greatest Statesmen', *Lives and Characters*, A1r–A1v. With minds like Hailes and Kames on the bench, and with David Hume having performed diplomatic services in Paris, it would only have appeared to Ferguson that such confidence had in no small way been justified.

91. Thomas Blackwell, *Memoirs of the Court of Augustus*, 2 vols (Edinburgh, 1753–5), p. 3.

92. Anderson, *History of France*, I, 195.

93. *ibid.*, I, 196.

94. Henderson, *Dissertation*, p. 16.

95. *ibid.*, p. 15.

96. Turnbull, *Treatise*, p. 36. Acquiring the same credentials had been urged upon his sixteenth-century fellow Scotsmen by John Major, who strongly approved of 'the example of the Romans, whose most illustrious generals were men well skilled in polite learning', *History of Greater Britain*, p. 48.

97. This entails a much greater significance, indeed an ideological role, for the many references to this idealised community. Hume, for example, wrote to Blair using the term 'commonwealth of letters', quoted in Mackenzie, *Report*, p. 8. Other Scottish examples include Sir John Dalrymple in 1758, *Feudal Property*, p. x.; William Tytler in 1769, *Historical and Critical Enquiry*, p. i; John Pinkerton in 1789, *History*, II, 12; and John Buchanan in 1794, *Defence of the Scots Highlanders*, p. 180, each using the phrase 'republic of letters'. But variants occurred more widely, as in 1777 when William Guthrie referred to 'the republic of learning and the arts', *New Grammar*, p. 204.

98. 'There is no real Love of Virtue, without the Knowledg of *Publick Good*', Lord Shaftesbury, 'An Essay on the Freedom of Wit and Humour', *Characteristicks*, I, 106–7. On the evidence of the prior Scottish tradition, this explains why Shaftesbury became so popular in Scotland, rather than making him the originator of their concern for public virtue. Thus Francis Hutcheson, the greatest populariser of the views of 'the late Earl of SHAFTESBURY' was speaking an only too familiar language when he reminded his audience that Mandeville had been wrong to deny an instinctive inclination to the service of the public: 'may not another *Instinct* toward the *Publick*, or the *Good* of others', he asked, 'be as proper a Principle of *Virtue* as the *Instinct* towards *private Happiness*?', *Inquiry*, p. 176.

99. Nimmo, *History*, p. 345. For possible plagiarism see Alexander Ross's description of Cato, as one of a few who 'preferred the publick good to their owne private interests', *History*, p. 21.

100. John Logan, *A Dissertation on the Manners and Spirit of Asia* (London, 1787), pp. 12–13. The Stoic notion of public spirit as the essence of all genuine humanity was very much abroad in enlightened Scotland, and it was in some ways reflected in the astonishing success of Addisonian polite letters. The sentiment that 'every Action of any Importance, is to have a Prospect of Publick Good ... without this a Man as I before have hinted, is hopping instead of walking, he is not in his entire and proper Motion', was universally applauded, as in [Joseph Addison], *The Spectator*, 16 vols (London, 1724), I, 6, 45. This seminal essay had originally appeared in March 1710–11.

101. Campbell, *Full and Particular Description*, p. 1.

102. Somerville, *Political Transactions*, p. xxii. Equally, learning and the public virtues were inseparable even in the fevered ruminations in 1746 of Robert Edgar, the Dumfriesshire burgess and historian. Recounting a failed earlier project to 'build an Colledge with some Professors of Philosophy &c', a scheme originally fostered by a Provost of Dumfries 'who wished for the public good', Edgar trusted and hoped that these plans might still make it an

eminent centre of learning: 'a new generation of Inhabitants of a more public spirit will probably arise in Divine Providence', he piously suggested, *An Introduction to the History of Dumfries*, (ed.), R. C. Reid (Dumfries, 1915), pp. 39–41.

103. William Smellie, 'A Dissertation on the Means of Supporting and Promoting Public Spirit', appended to his posthumous *Lives*, p. 364.

104. Turnbull, *Treatise*, p. 103.

105. Forbes, 'Reflexions', p. 112.

106. Montesquieu, *Spirit of the Laws*, I, 25 n.

107. Bonar, *History of Tyre*, p. 16.

108. Turnbull, *Treatise*, p. 92. On Turnbull's considerable philosophical influence, especially on Thomas Reid, as well as the curious though significant failure of Dugald Stewart to identify him as a leading player in the Enlightenment, see D. F. Norton, 'George Turnbull and the Furniture of the Mind', *Journal of the History of Ideas*, 36 (1985), 701–16. His educational importance, in which respect he has likewise been considerably underestimated, is examined in M. A. Stewart, 'George Turnbull and Educational Reform', in Carter and Pittock (eds), *Aberdeen and the Enlightenment*, pp. 95–103.

109. Turnbull, *Treatise*, p. xxiii.

110. *ibid.*, p. v.

111. *ibid.*, p. xxiii. This critical perspective, jarring uncomfortably with many of the diversifying intellectual tendencies of the wider Enlightenment, has plausibly been seen as one of the peculiar reasons leading Scottish scholars to feel such an affinity with the idiosyncratic Rousseau, who, in the *First Discourse*, had had the temerity to question the artifice and veneer of polite French civilisation, and especially its insipid and sophistical learning. See R. A. Leigh, 'Rousseau and the Scottish Enlightenment', *Contributions to Political Economy*, 5 (1986), 1–21.

112. Turnbull, *Treatise*, p. 84.

113. Turnbull, *Treatise*, p. 183. Turnbull is representative of a forceful educational philosophy underpinning Scottish historical writing in the Enlightenment. This has received inadequate attention, and the misconceptions blighting it are typified in H. Hutchison, 'An Eighteenth-Century Insight into Religious and Moral Education', *British Journal of Educational Studies*, 24, (1976), 233–41, which makes painful reading for anyone wishing to disavow a teleological account of later ideas. Taking the *Treatise of Education* (Edinburgh, 1743) by James Barclay as his text, Hutchison claims that his author's frequent criticism of rote learning and dry information identifies him as a precursor of modern Marxist theorists. Of course, and as the copious evidence of early modern Scotsmen makes clear, Barclay was in fact merely part of a Calvinist and humanist intellectual culture in which the moralists' mistrust of irrelevant learning was endemic. His arguments, viewed in this context, and alongside men like Turnbull, are neither exceptional nor precocious, though the more significant because of this.

114. Turnbull, *Observations*, p. 2.

115. [Blackwell], *Letters*, p. iv.

116. *ibid.*, p. 223.

117. Ferguson, *Civil Society*, pp. 274–5.

118. *ibid.*, p. 275.

119. *ibid.*, p. 275.

120. Borthwick, *Remarks*, p. viii.

121. Quintilian, *De institutione oratoria*, xii. As a classical theorist both of education and rhetoric, Quintilian had been an obvious point of reference for scholars throughout the early modern period. Jonson, Milton and Dryden were among his more distinguished English disciples.

122. James Balfour, *A Delineation of the Nature and Obligation of Morality* (Edinburgh, 1763), p. 50.

123. Men in the eighteenth century, as Edward Young, the Augustan churchman, makes clear, still thought it entirely possible to 'consider a Treatise on the Passions, as a History of Themselves', *A Vindication of Providence*, 2nd edn (Berkeley, Calif., 1984), A4v. Bolingbroke, the disenchanted Tory exile, noted, and not without misgivings, that 'history, true or false, speaks to our passions always', *Letters on the Study and Use of History*, 2 vols (London, 1752), I, 13. It is also perhaps significant that Hugh Blair, the arbiter of enlightened Edinburgh's literary tastes, advertised Macpherson's supposititious Gaelic translations as 'The history of human imagination and passion', *Critical Dissertations*, p. 1. And Hume, too,

thought that in history itself we learn that 'love is not the only Passion, that governs the Male-World, but is often overcome by Avarice, Ambition, Vanity, and a thousand other Passions', 'Of the Study of History', I, 69–70.

124. Stuart, *View of Society*, p. 142.

125. Gibson, *History*, p. 115.

126. Wallace, *Dissertation*, p. 160. For Wallace's career see H. R. Sefton, 'Rev. Robert Wallace: An Early Moderate', *Records of the Scottish Church History Society*, 16 (1966), 1–22.

127. Kames, *Sketches*, I, 449.

128. Bonar, *History of Tyre*, p. 4.

129. Balfour, *Delineation*, p. 205.

130. *ibid.*, p. 23.

131. *ibid.*, p. 13. Scotsmen almost universally believed, as the Edinburgh historian and public archivist David Macpherson saw it, that 'men of liberal education' would acquire a 'candour and ingenuity' above the common stock, *Geographical Illustrations of Scottish History* (London, 1796), b1r.

132. Hume, *Treatise*, III, 6.

133. See, for example, James Durham's almost Lockeian conviction in the 1650s, that, with respect to the moral use of reason, 'seing men are not born skilful in any common occupation, till it be taught them: it is no marvel therefore that they be undextrous as to the main things', *Commentarie*, p. 173. Innate knowledge and proficiencies were clearly thought unlikely.

134. Balfour, *Delineation*, pp. 13–14.

135. Ferguson, *Civil Society*, p. 188.

136. *ibid.*, p. 146.

137. Turnbull, *Treatise*, p. vii.

138. Duncan Forbes, 'A Letter to a Bishop Concerning Some Important Discoveries in Philosophy and Theology', in *Works*, p. 25. An earlier Calvinist exponent of this minimal or 'critical' rationalism had been William Rait of Dundee, who in 1671 had supposed 'the Readers of Scripture rational men, & that reason in its own line may be helpful to them for understanding scripture', *Vindication*, p. 69.

139. Forbes, 'Letter to a Bishop', pp. 15–16. A seminal account of the human rational faculties among men of Forbes's time was that of Francis Hutcheson, whose moral and aesthetic philosophy attributed to 'the AUTHOR of Nature' men's limited power of reason: 'Men have *Reason* given them, to judge, and compare the Tendencys of Actions', *Inquiry*, p. 186.

140. For a persuasive assertion of Hume's Calvinist credentials as an anti-rationalist, see S. Sutherland, ' The Presbyterian Inheritance of Hume and Reid', in Campbell and Skinner (eds), *Origins and Nature of the Scottish Enlightenment*, pp. 131–49. For even earlier Scottish scepticism of the 'folly' of thinking 'that any human scrutinie can finde out mysteries that are so unsearchable', however, see Mackenzie of Rosehaugh, *Religio Stoici*, p. 28.

141. For Hume most obviously, there was little flirtation 'with the rationalism of Voltaire. Hume did not believe that man behaved in terms of reason alone. He was dominated by his passions, he was affected by the customs of society', J. R. Hale, *The Evolution of British Historiography* (London, 1967), p. 25. Again, Schneider correctly observes that the 'Scots are keenly aware of the limitations of reason ... plainly connected with their strong sense of its non-rational foundations', *Scottish Moralists*, p. xx. See also J. V. Price, 'Concepts of Enlightenment in Eighteenth-Century Scottish Literature', *Texas Studies in Literature and Language*, 9 (1967), 371–9. Even the great architect of Scottish attitudes had, after all, claimed 'that nature and reason are not only unable to lead us to true knowledge of God, but ... they have bene maistresses of all errors and idolatrie', Knox, 'Predestination', V, 396–7.

142. *The Spectator*, I, 6, 45. This strictly moralistic notion of reason has usefully been distinguished by Hayek from what he calls the 'constructivist rationalism' of Descartes, 'Kinds of Rationalism', in his *Studies in Philosophy, Politics, and Economics* (Chicago, 1967), pp. 82–95. The moral or 'critical' rationalism of the Scottish tradition usually denied the innate constructive powers of this other tradition, and thus justifies in this sense the label of 'anti-rationalism' which I have employed throughout.

143. George Turnbull, once again, makes this absolutely clear: 'He alone is truly virtuous', he advised, following the Greek axiom coined by Strephon, 'who sincerely abhors moral evil as such, and places his supreme satisfaction in acting conformably to his reason and moral conscience', *Observations*, p. 68. Sher explains the recrudescence of Calvinist moralism in

revolutionary America in 'Witherspoon's *Dominion of Providence* and the Scottish Jeremiad Tradition', in his and Smitten (eds), *Scotland and America*, pp. 46–64.

144. Crawfurd, *History*, p. 301.

145. Ferguson, *Roman Republic*, II, 323.

146. Heron, *New General History*, pp. 431–2. Andrew Henderson too poured cultivated presbyterian scorn upon the rebellious MacDonalds and other truculent Catholic clans: 'Their Religion recommends an Abhorrence of the Ecclesiastical Constitution; no Arts and Sciences prevailing among them, their Exercise is the Sword, and Education the Accounts of their Sea-Fights', *History*, pp. 14–15.

147. Robert Watson, *The History of the Reign of Phillip the Second, King of Spain*, 2 vols (Dublin, 1777), II, 409.

148. *Edinburgh Review*, 2 (1755), pt. III, 18. This reviewer is customarily identified as William Robertson, and his subject was Robert Keith's episcopalian *An Historical Catalogue of the Scottish Bishops Down to the Year* 1688 (Edinburgh, 1755), which in denying the significance of the Culdees and in locating Scotland's early religious history firmly within the orbit of Roman orthodoxy, managed to challenge the traditional sacred cows of presbyterian scholarship. Hume, too, was no friend of a Catholic Church which had, he claimed, and to the detriment of the arts and sciences, 'engrost all the learning of the times', 'Arts and Sciences', II, 70.

149. For example, John Gibson characterised the citizens of medieval Glasgow as probably 'the same as they are found to be in many Roman catholic countries at this day; their connections with the priests would render them credulous and superstitious, consequently they would be exceedingly ignorant', *History*, p. 74.

150. Turnbull, *Observations*, p. 32.

151. *ibid.*, p. 32.

152. Duff, *History*, p. 54.

153. Duff's distrust of 'Feastings', in particular, was an especially stark reminder of the moral lexicon employed by earlier Scottish authors in the tradition of Hector Boece, so much so that one wonders whether Dr Johnson's malicious comments on the meagreness of the Scots' cereal diet might have been regarded as a matter for moral pride rather than shame even in the middle of the eighteenth century. In Robert Monro, for example, we find an unfeigned outrage at gastronomic excess, which Duff's analysis merely echoes: after the victories of the 1630s, there had been such a moral decline 'that we could not sleepe without a good bed, our stomackes could not digest a Gammon of Bacon or cold Beefe without mustard, so farre were we out of use', *Monro His Expedition*, p. 47. The unsavoury aroma of gustatory vice had also offended the sensitive Jacobean nostrils of Sir Thomas Craig, who rejoiced that Scotsmen did not readily surrender themselves to 'temptations of the table', *De Unione Regnorum*, p. 382, and later Sir Robert Sibbald was to condemn the ancient Britons for yielding to the pleasures of 'costly Feasts and fine Intertainments', *Historical Inquiries*, p. 2. For further enlightened alarmists, see William Maitland's continuator, *History and Antiquities*, II, 610, with his calls for sumptuary legislation, and Ferguson, *Roman Republic*, I, 273, with his similar suggestions for limiting 'the ostentation of wealth'.

154. [ ], *The General History of the World, From the Creation, Till the Dispersion, and the Establishment of Kingdoms* (Edinburgh, 1763), p. 153.

155. Kames, *Elements*, I, p. vii.

156. Pertinently located in a discussion as to the nature and purpose of oratory, Hugh Blair defined reason, the target of rhetorical address, as 'that power of the mind which in speculative matters discovers truth, and in practical matters judges of the fitness of means to an end', *Lectures*, I, 16.

157. Turnbull, *Observations*, p. 315. This is, of course, a classic exposition of the Calvinist and humanist vision of the ideal moral community, replete with its leadership of oratorical scholars, men of both private and public virtue who had specifically refuted the defensive claims of heredity and money to make themselves the patriotic elite. It is also, needless to say, highly significant that Turnbull later underscored the reliance of this vision of Enlightenment social reality upon earlier Scottish ideas with a gloss on Juvenal's familiar and ubiquitous maxim, 'that virtue alone is true honour and solid durable happiness', *ibid.*, p. 398.

158. William Robertson, *The Situation of the World at the Time of Christ's Appearance*, 3rd edn (Edinburgh, 1759), p. 6.

159. Balfour, *Delineation*, pp. 24–5. Unclosed brackets original.
160. [Blackwell], *Letters*, p. 79.
161. Kames, *Essays*, p. 204.
162. Colin MacLaurin, *An Account of Sir Isaac Newton's Philosophical Discoveries* (London, 1748), p. 22. If Maclaurin represents the triumph of Newtonian mechanics in natural philosophy, it is useful to remember that this was part of a broader trend to see scientific knowledge in a distinctly theological light. In discussing the intellectual influence of this system among men who shared 'a common commitment to a religious version of the natural world', John Christie has recently drawn attention, for example, to Plummer's chemical theory and the Boerhaaveian mechanistic anatomy being taught in Scotland at the same time: 'For all of these men, nature was itself an artefact, to be understood ultimately in terms of the causes and purposes which the Deity had used, and installed in the design of Creation', Craig, *Scottish Literature*, II, esp. 295.
163. Forbes, 'Letter to a Bishop', p. 120. Outside Scotland, moreover, the Cartesian model continued to inspire similarly mechanistic and deterministic theories, perhaps most controversially in La Mettrie's *L' Homme Machine* (1747), an account which was feared partly because of its fatalistic implications for reason and virtue. Yet significantly, Newtonian science and philosophy were regarded with studied ambivalence by the carping voice of post-Enlightenment pessimism, who lamented in 1829 that his was 'not an Heroical, Devotional, Philosophical, or Moral Age, but, above all others, the Mechanical Age'. Its pernicious materialist philosophy, lately compounded by the harsh and cold Benthamite calculus of Utilitarianism, seemed to sound the death knell of human ingenuity and moral inspiration: 'Men are grown mechanical in head and heart', he sighed, ' ... They have lost faith in individual endeavour, and in natural force, of any kind', Thomas Carlyle, 'Signs of the Times', *Edinburgh Review*, 49 (1829), 441–4.
164. MacLaurin, *Account*, p. 387.
165. Turnbull, *Observations*, p. v. Equally, that other Aberdonian scholar James Beattie considered that the progress of learning and the emergence of creative genius was itself plain proof that 'a wise and good Providence governs the world', *Dissertations*, p. 162. Beattie's position, of course, was defined by the need to offer a polemical defence of religious and everyday belief in response to the assaults of Hume and the Edinburgh sceptics. See N. T. Phillipson, 'James Beattie and the Defence of Common Sense', in B. Fabian (ed.), *Festschrift für Rainer Gruenter* (Heidelberg, 1978), pp. 145–54.
166. William Robertson, *The History of America*, 2 vols (London, 1777), I, 38. On the same subject in 1697, Andrew Fletcher had observed how 'Such odd Consequences, and of such a different Nature, accompany extraordinary Inventions of any kind', *Discourse*, p. 8. Unforeseeable and unrelated consequences seem to have been essential also to Fletcher's characteristically dour interpretation of history.
167. Maitland, *History and Antiquities*, I, 38. For similar earlier examples see both Abercromby, *Martial Atchievements*, I, 56, and Turner, *Pallas Armata*, p. 33.
168. Robertson, *History of Scotland*, II, 35.
169. Crawfurd, *History*, p. 301.
170. Robertson, *Situation of the World*, p. 13. This vision, moreover, had scarcely changed since the time when Gilbert Burnet had employed the same phrases, *Historie*, III, 173, or even from James Kirkton's presbyterian encomium on Knox, *Secret History*, p. 7.
171. Adam Smith, *The Theory of Moral Sentiments*, 4th edn (London, 1774), p. 187.
172. Somerville, *Political Transactions*, p. 24.
173. Anderson, *History of France*, II, 413–14.
174. Dalrymple, *Memoirs*, I, 18.
175. Robertson, *Charles V*, I, 367.
176. *ibid.*, I, 399.
177. Burns, *Poetical Works*, pp. 68–9.
178. Bonar, *History of Tyre*, Prediction III.
179. *ibid.*, p. 1.
180. Robertson, *History*, p. 186. The Puritan echo also resounded elsewhere in an enlightened age, as in Robert Wallace's hopes that his scholarship might 'vindicate eternal providences, and justify God to man', *Various Prospects of Mankind, Nature, and Providence* (London, 1761), p. 331.

181. J. Dwyer, 'The Imperative of Sociability: Moral Culture in the Late Scottish Enlightenment', *British Journal of Eighteenth-Century Studies*, 13, (1990), 169.

182. Dunbar, *Essays*, p. 114. The philosophical Dunbar was particularly aware of the anti-rationalism of unintention implicit in the Stoic account of Fortune: 'Even the actual promoters of the most important interests of mankind', he went on, 'have seldom anticipated, in idea, the progressive consequences of their own plans', *Essays*, p. 114.

183. Smith, *Moral Sentiments*, p. 185. Again, the feminine characterisation perhaps recalled something of the Machiavellian idiom of earlier Scottish humanists, *pace* Buchanan. Another adept exponent of this style was the Jacobite and Russian commander Alexander Gordon of Auchintoul, in whose own fluctuating and exceedingly perilous career were to be found many of those reverses and unexpected occurrences for which the Florentine and Roman accounts had been classically suited. Gordon wrote of Peter the Great, for example, that despite his occasional poor judgement, 'even in this, his good fortune (which had been his faithful companion all along) did not abandon him', *The History of Peter the Great, Emperor of Russia*, 2 vols (Aberdeen, 1755), II, 31. Gordon, of course, was an anachronism, a throwback to the sub-Renaissance world of Drummond and Urquhart: Smith's feminine nuances, however, did not prevent him from outlining a much more rigid and mechanical causality, more in sympathy with his own times.

184. Robertson, *History*, p. 183. The Stoics, and especially Epictetus, Marcus Antoninus, and Juvenal, were recognised by no less a moralist than Thomas Reid as proponents of 'the Providence of the Deity', therefore establishing to the satisfaction of an enlightened Scottish philosopher that the 'Oracles of Right Reason correspond exactly with the Oracles of Divine Wisdom in the Christian Religion'. See J. C. Stewart-Robertson, 'Cicero among the Shadows: Scottish Prelections of Virtue and Duty', *Rivista Critica di Storia della Filosofia*, 38 (1983), pp. 26–7.

185. Anderson, *Ancient Greece* p. 532. He went on to condemn 'the modern *Necessitarians*', who seemed 'to need a fatalistic brand of fortune' which was quite unacceptable. An equally illuminating rejection of the charge of Stoic indolence was more subtly attempted by William Robertson, who detected those 'distinguished doctrines' in India, doctrines, he insisted, which were 'formed only for men of the most vigorous spirit', *An Historical Disquisition Concerning the Knowledge Which the Ancients Had of India* (Dublin, 1791), p. 287.

186. Not unlike Mackenzie or Ross before him, Hume suggested that by the mere 'Pursuit of Pleasure, you more and more expose yourself to Fortune and Accidents, and rivet your Affections on external Objects, which Chance may, in a Moment, ravish from you'. Instead, one should seek wisdom and virtue: 'The Temple of Wisdom is seated on a Rock, above the Rage of the fighting Elements, and inaccessible to all the Malice of Man', 'The Stoic', II, 122–3. Again echoing Ross, Hume's philosophical opponent James Beattie displayed with less detachment the advantages accruing to the Stoic, praising 'Nature's true sons, the friends of man and truth!' in a world where 'All feel th'assault of fortune's fickle gale', *The Minstrel*, pp. 22, 33.

187. Smith, *Moral Sentiments*, p. 105.

188. Smith, *ibid.*, p. 103.

189. Walter Anderson, *The History of Croesus, King of Lydia* (Edinburgh, 1755), p. 55.

190. Beattie, *The Minstrel*, pp. 42–59.

191. An example from the middle of the seventeenth century would be the observation of Mackenzie of Rosehaugh in 1665 that events occur because of 'such unexpected beginnings, that none can see in (or apprehend the least danger by) them', *Moral Essay*, p. 39. Even earlier, and closely linked to his discussion of 'God's Providence', Hume of Godscroft had explained in the 1620s how history displayed 'men's actions, which arrive often to unexpected events, and sometimes to such ends as are quite contrary to the Actors intentions', *History*, Preface. More recently, Henry Maule had in 1706 approved of the 'palpable and Egyptian darkness' which God had ordained to prevent sinful and ignorant men from being able 'to perceive the vials of his wrath which are ready to be poured upon them', *History*, p. 40.

192. Kames, *Sketches*, II, 359. Such mordant emphasis upon a providential unintention translated very smoothly in a colleague like Ferguson into an apparently secularised adumbration of 'unintended consequences'. For example, 'Every step and every movement of the multitude', Ferguson observed, ' ... are made with equal blindness to the future', *Civil Society*, p. 187.

Yet even here, reference to the redolently Calvinist sub-text was hard to avoid, as Ferguson went on to focus on Cromwell, the archetypal English Calvinist leader, who had famously concluded that 'a man never mounts higher than when he knows not whither he is going'. Calvinist-inspired unintentionality, it appears, surfaced even in one of the most polished and eloquent statements of 'secular' determinism.

193. Kames, *Sketches*, II, 393. Kames had also observed that 'The system of Providence differs widely from our wishes; and shall ignorant man venture to arraign Providence? Are we qualified to judge of the whole, when but so small a part is visible?', *ibid.*, I, 381.

194. Smith, *Wealth of Nations*, II, 35. Smith, of course, was introducing to the world an individual who 'neither intends to promote the publick interest, nor knows how much he is promoting it' when 'he intends only his own gain'. It was the 'invisible hand' which served 'to promote an end which was no part of his intention'. The influential studies of Duncan Forbes, 'Scientific Whiggism', and R. K. Merton, 'The Unanticipated Consequences of Purposive Social Action', *American Sociological Review*, I, (1936), esp. 894–5, both greatly overestimate the revolutionary character of this model of unintention classically expounded by Smith.

195. Forbes, 'Thoughts on Religion', p. 6.

196. Arnot, *History*, p. 16. The 'general Passions and Interests' also seemed to David Hume the causes of the 'domestic and the gradual Revolutions of a State', which were thus almost impossible rationally to explain, 'Arts and Sciences', II, 55.

197. Dunbar, *Essays*, p. 37. As Lois Whitney remarks, it seemed clear that there was no longer 'the possibility of the old duality of passion and reason and the supposition that virtue arises only from the victory of reason over passion', *Primitivism and the Idea of Progress in English Popular Literature of the Eighteenth Century* (Baltimore, Md., 1934), p. 40.

198. Gillies, 'Discourse', p. lxxii.

199. Sir Walter Scott, *Waverley; Or, 'Tis Sixty Years Since* (ed.), C. Lamont (Oxford, 1986), p. 101.

200. In Alasdair MacIntyre's enigmatic account as to 'why the Enlightenment project had to fail', it is precisely because, after Calvin, 'reason is powerless to correct our passions', that the attainment of the classical Aristotelian virtues is finally put in doubt. Moreover, he says, 'it is not unimportant that Hume's views are those of one who was brought up a Calvinist', *After Virtue: A Study in Moral Theory* (London, 1981), pp. 49–51.

201. See e.g. T. Hutchison, *Before Adam Smith: The Emergence of Political Economy, 1662–1776* (Oxford, 1988), which, despite an encouraging title, offers little on the historical tradition out of which men like Smith and Steuart emerged, and nothing at all on the Scottish Calvinist heritage of anti-rationalism. Equally, Hirschman, *Passions and Interests*, though an invaluable study in its detailed analysis, provides a historical perspective in which Calvin is mentioned only twice, and no consideration whatsoever of a Scottish tradition of passionate discourse. It is almost inevitable that we are blankly informed that 'similar ideas' to Montesquieu simply 'crop up' in eighteenth-century Scotland, *ibid.*, p. 81.

202. Smith, *Wealth of Nations*, I, 16.

203. Robertson, *History of America*, II, 348.

204. Thomas Reid, *Essays on the Active Powers of Man* (Glasgow, 1788), p. 141.

205. *ibid.*, p. 141. A contemporary non-historical author who likewise displayed a considerable indebtedness to unintended consequences was James Burnett, Lord Monboddo. His account of the work of bees, patently based on Mandeville's notorious *Fable of the Bees* (1721), would nevertheless have appealed precisely because of its Calvinist and anti-rationalist resonances. The bee, he wrote, 'acts by Intelligence, though she has it not herself, but by an Intelligence much superior to the human, no less Intelligence than the Divine', *Antient Metaphysics: or, the Science of Universals*, 6 vols (Edinburgh, 1779–99), II, 299–300.

206. That the 'Intentions of Providence' were themselves responsible for 'these dismal Shocks, that seem to make Mankind the alternate Sport of the Elements and their own Passions', had earlier been the opinion voiced in the influential [Blackwell], *Letters*, p. 219.

207. This interpretation of Scottish historical thought perhaps provides a perspective in which MacIntyre's intriguing view that the Enlightenment 'inherited incoherent fragments of a once coherent scheme of thought and action' becomes more understandable, *After Virtue*, p. 53. In rejecting the classical and scholastic renditions of causality, the Enlightenment ensured the fatal opposition of a virtuous and dynamic morality and an obdurate and determinist reality.

208. Hume, *History*, I, 704.
209. Reid, *Essays*, p. 141. This may also have been the uncomfortable conclusion of William Robertson who, rather apologetically, ascribed to occasional figures like Rizzio an ability to shape and dominate otherwise insuperable historical forces. See the interesting discussion of this quirk in P. Moore, 'The Nature of Theoretical History and its Application in the Works of William Robertson' (unpublished Ph.D. dissertation, University of Edinburgh, 1975), esp. pp. 285–98.
210. Ferguson, *Roman Republic*, I, 10–11. This apparently contradicts Ferguson's own more famous analysis of 'foresight', which had in 1767 given rise to the maxim that we erroneously 'ascribe to a previous design, what came to be known only by experience, what no human wisdom could foresee ... ', *Civil Society*, p. 188. It was this logical doom, perhaps, from which Ferguson later perceived the need to rescue the Roman founders.
211. Pinkerton, *Dissertation*, p. 115. Perhaps Hume had something similar in mind when observing in 1742 that, despite the problems in exploring the 'general Passions and Interests' behind social change, yet still nothing could be 'a more proper Subject of Reasoning and Observation', 'Arts and Sciences', II, 55.

CHAPTER FIVE

'Signs of the Times'

The End of the Enlightenment?

THE SCOTTISH ENLIGHTENMENT died with a whimper, it is usually supposed, some time between 1800 and 1830. In 1831 Sir Walter Scott, its last and greatest creative spirit, was dead. Its most brilliant prodigy of the next generation, Thomas Carlyle, was to depart from Edinburgh in 1834, tempted by the more rarified intellectual atmosphere of London and Cheyne Walk. Even earlier, in 1828 and 1816 respectively, Dugald Stewart and Adam Ferguson had followed Smith, Robertson and Blair to the grave. During the same period a revival in the educational life of Cambridge and Oxford was allowing them slowly to replace the ossifying universities of Edinburgh and Glasgow as the premier seats of learning in an expanding British empire. Thereafter in England, too, it was to be Bentham, Dickens, Macaulay, Arnold and Mill – all of course influenced by Scottish thought but essentially English and metropolitan in their preoccupations – who would dominate a new Victorian age. Even in Scotland itself, discussion of its intellectual triumphs sank irretrievably into the past tense, as wistful biographies of the great and late literati began to appear. Elderly men like Lord Cockburn and Robert Chambers now increasingly recalled in their memoirs the anecdotes and achievements of a bygone golden age.[1] Carlyle, the great critic of the times, even reflected in 1829 with deliberate finality on the 'wisdom, the heroic worth of our forefathers, which we have lost'.[2] The local intelligentsia, meanwhile, from both the Tory and the radical wings, also assailed with fatal effect the once-unchallenged ascendancy of a Whig politics of culture.[3] The signs were sometimes confusing but the 'Athens of the North', it gradually became obvious, no longer enjoyed the clear cultural hegemony. The Enlightenment in Scotland was over.

Our long journey through a major strand of Scottish thought since the sixteenth century therefore appears to have a disappointingly tame ending. The extraordinary success of eighteenth-century Scottish culture had truly been that of an age when, as a cock-sure Alexander Carlyle had seen it in 1760, 'the genius of the Scotch never shone with greater lustre than now'.[4] But this exuberance was to end only seventy years later in what seemed at the time to be Scotland's almost total eclipse. Indeed, there had then followed what must likewise seem to us a depressingly familiar story. Scotland was apparently reduced by the middle of the nineteenth century to the sort of yellowing provincialism associated with the virtual absence of cultural innovation. Of her contemporary intellectual life and activity, little or nothing good was to be heard. There occurred at the same time the generation of a basically fictitious national identity. By the 1850s this had produced what Tom Nairn has scathingly termed 'the great tartan monster', which has ever since loomed over the frozen and unchanging landscape of '*kitsch* Scotland'.[5] Thus the country of Hume and Smith during the Victorian era concocted for a credulous world a bogus and distinctly mildewed Scottish nationhood, a misleading though apparently desirable artefact closely linked in spirit with the captivating but strikingly unintellectual romanticism of Scott's deeply atmospheric novels. Where, however, one might reasonably ask, had the brash vigour and unrestrained confidence of the Enlightenment gone? Why, in any case, had an extraordinary culture of endeavour and intellectual attainment faded away so rapidly and apparently so completely? Of course these are weighty questions, ones which could in themselves very easily justify another substantial study. But it seems an inescapable obligation, having travelled this far, to offer in valediction at least some form of retrospective upon the eighteenth-century Scottish achievement. In doing this, it becomes clear that our exploration of historical discourse actually casts a most intriguing light upon the essential character of the Enlightenment in Scotland. It also offers an illuminating insight into some of the many possible reasons for its seeming demise.

Clearly a good deal of the conventional line of thinking on these matters has already been ruled out of court by the account of Scotland's fluctuating intellectual history which has been sketched in this study. The Enlightenment, it has been suggested, was founded at the intellectual level upon an assertion of the immense social utility of learning. This was a claim, however, which drew on arguments themselves firmly embedded in rich local traditions of Calvinist and humanist scholarship. These, indeed, had had a profound influence over the evolution of Scottish historical thought since at least the sixteenth century. In particular an intimate relation had slowly been established between the specifically intellectual qualities of eloquence, wisdom and rationality on the one hand, and the corresponding moral values deemed to be necessary for social leadership on the other. This had ensured that eighteenth-century scholars would be able to strike a resonant chord when they claimed their rightfully pre-eminent place in Scottish society. They had long, by their own reckoning, possessed the necessary rhetorical skills for leadership. They now confidently took up the commanding position vacated by the orators, politicians and rabble-rousing preachers of the past. Eighteenth-century intellectuals were able, it seems, through their role as pedagogues, to act out the binding obligations of the generous public benefactor. At the same time, an ostentatious attachment to rationality rendered possible within the recesses of their finely tuned minds at least a potential for the eventual mastery of the wilder and more destructive passions. In short, Scotland's scholars could believe that they now had an unequalled claim to the conspicuous possession of moral virtue, that quality which more than any other was still thought to qualify a man for leadership. The elaborate but mutually reinforcing arguments of Calvinist and humanist discourse had thus by the eighteenth century conspired to make possible a truly momentous conclusion. This, it appears, was positively ideological in its implications, and clearly distinguished this country from other supposedly more 'enlightened' societies. As David Spadafora has acutely observed, 'only in Scotland, where the elite cherished and encouraged ideas and intellectual activity, did the Enlightenment come to be an integral part of the establishment'.[6] In Scotland the man of letters himself could hope to enjoy not only supremacy but absolute legitimacy as the effective leader of his community.

That Scotland's eighteenth-century intellectual vigour thus rested confidently on deep foundations in established cultural discourse is not, of course, the end of the matter. Indeed, it only makes it more difficult than ever to accept the basic tenor of conventional wisdom: the Enlightenment, on this reading at least, simply could not have been a marginal activity carried on by a few brilliant but isolated intellectual malcontents. The philosophical genius of David Hume, the narrative abilities of Robertson and the explanatory flair of Smith and Ferguson, may understandably have captured the subsequent limelight. Helped by some shrill triumphalism and not a little also by the subtle discrimination bequeathed to posterity by Dugald Stewart's judiciously modernist mind, a handful of historical demi-gods naturally came to hold centre-stage. But their sustaining belief in the social and moral value of learning, and their motivating determination to transform Scottish society on that basis, manifestly embraced a very much wider constituency of active and ambitious eighteenth-century authors. These included dedicated public moralists such as the Aberdonians George Turnbull, William Duff, and Gilbert Stuart, eloquent historians committed unswervingly to the proper use of oratorical influence. Amongst the energetic ministers and theologians who participated in the determined elevation of the man of letters in Scottish society were George Ridpath, Lachlan Shaw, Robert Henry and Hugh Blair. Lawyers like Andrew Stevenson and Lord Hailes, meanwhile, emphasised to their audience in Scotland the potential historical impact of reason and learning. At the same time obscure scholars – the forgotten William Borthwick of Crookston and the scarcely better-remembered Alexander Gerard are good examples – believed themselves to be contributing in their own more ponderous way to the same edifying national enterprise. Historical discourse, it seems, was the natural medium for a veritable host of able and like-minded intellectuals. They saw themselves by the eighteenth century not merely as adding to the accumulated canon of national scholarship. They felt themselves now to be collectively the architects and guardians of a newly virtuous and learned society in Scotland, one which would be defined and shaped by its moral scholarship. For such men, becoming 'enlightened' palpably meant much more than simply the construction and dissemination of formal historical knowledge. Learning more than ever implied the acquisition of the moral and social credentials deemed to be necessary for full and responsible membership of a civilised modern community. As scholars holding the public ear, therefore, the literati of the Scottish Enlightenment seemed to themselves both competent and numerous enough at last to set about rebuilding this kind of society in precisely their own deeply learned image.

This emerging picture of course does violence to the received image of the Enlightenment in Scotland as both limited and largely ephemeral. But it also does little, at first sight, to explain the strange and sudden death of that country's culture in the following century, remarked upon by perplexed observers from Lord Henry Cockburn to Marinell Ash.[7] On the contrary, it was surely one of the more convincing features of the traditional view of the Scottish En- lightenment – and certainly a main reason for its abiding appeal – that it appeared at least to contain within itself a plausible explanation for the seeming collapse of Scotland's relatively short-lived intellectual and cultural supremacy. Indeed, convention offered a disarmingly simple use of logic to great explanatory effect. Scotland, it was insisted by Buckle, had before the eighteenth century possessed no intellectual sophistication. Violence, dissension and a suffocating theology had stifled her native talent. She had consequently had little or no creative energy to call her own. Foreign, and predominantly English, influences were responsible, in the eyes of most later scholars, for inspiring the eighteenth- century endeavours of a small number of extremely unusual men. Such Enlightenment as Scotland ever came to possess, therefore, had the shallowest of roots. Serious historical scholarship was a delicate foreign flower in what remained essentially an inhospitable soil. The bracing winds of Evangelical reaction and political controversy at first caused it to wither. The rather more congenial climate offered elsewhere, both by industrial England and a beckoning empire on which the sun increasingly never set, then conspired to finish it off. Promising or unusually able Scotsmen – from Carlyle to Andrew Carnegie and beyond – thereafter took the high road to London and a widening world. The Enlightenment in Scotland, it seemed safe to say, was after all an aberrant phase which had disappeared almost as expeditiously as it had allegedly arrived. Its fragility, of course, not only made accounting for its emergence much less problematical for the historian, but also rendered the explanation of its rapid dissipation rather more straightforward. With once more a stunted and underdeveloped cultural life, deprived of intellect and shorn of wit, normality in Scotland had apparently been restored.

This persuasive though unedifying picture, however, conflicts sharply with the main thrust of our study thus far. We would be right as a result to question our own explanation of Scotland's intellectual development were it at the last to appear incapable of encompassing also the apparent waning of the Scottish Enlightenment with which this story closes. The first point to be made in outlining a possible response to this concluding challenge would actually be to draw the most direct parallel between interpretations of the origins and explanations of the end of this singular phase in Scottish history. We have seen extensively throughout our journey just how misleading has been the hoary myth that the Enlightenment condensed, as it were, out of nothing. It was in fact generated and sustained to a large extent, it seems, from within the resources provided by Scotland's peculiar social and intellectual heritage. What I would now like to suggest is that the view that by the 1830s Scotland had simply sunk back again into her customary intellectual moribundity may well need to be treated with at least equal suspicion. There was of course beyond dispute a savage mockery now being meted out by fashionable opinion to the stock caricature of the boorish 'Scotch feelosopher'. Undoubtedly there was also a relative quietness, even perhaps a tinge of melancholy reflectiveness, to be found in post-Enlightenment discussions of the status and significance of Scottish learning: Cockburn and Chambers are again the obvious representatives in Scotland of the *fin de siècle* mood. But these mellow tones need not necessarily be taken to testify to the effective suffocation of intellectual vigour in Scotland. It is at least possible that what had long been demanded and anticipated, a natural cause for intense analysis and vociferous self-congratulation when it finally arrived, had in the end come to seem only mundane and common. What is more, it may for the same reasons very quickly have become ripe for underestimation and demolition. Possibly acceptance rather than rejection of Scottish ideas and influence underlay the unrelieved tedium which seems by the 1830s to have characterised men's increasingly jaded contributions to this now-familiar discussion.

There is, without question, reason enough to doubt the real extent of the putative decline in the influence of Scottish pedagogy during the nineteenth century. Scottish educational theory and practice still made their characteristic influence felt, not least, as Anand Chitnis has shown, in the English schools and academies.[8] The same is true of the emerging colleges and universities of North America. There not only Reid and Stewart but also Blair, Campbell, Witherspoon, and later James McCosh, long retained a vice-like grip on the substance and delivery of academic provision.[9] One should certainly take account also of those leading British politicians of the nineteenth century who continued to benefit from the distinctive educational style of the Scottish universities: Brougham, Palmerston and Russell, for example, and later Balfour and Haldane, all spent their formative years at the University of Edinburgh, whilst Melbourne and later Campbell-Bannerman were future premiers among the glittering alumni of nineteenth-century Glasgow. To these, one should probably add professors as influential in their different fields as Robert Knox and Thomas Saintsbury, as well as distinguished scientists, economists and philosophers like John Playfair, James Ferrier and Sir William Hamilton. Each of these magnetic teachers carried on with considerable aplomb after 1800 an established tradition of brilliant exposition and effective pedagogy associated since at least the seventeenth century with Scotland's solid presbyterian schooling and its eloquent university faculties. At the same time it would even be possible to make a credible plea for Thomas Carlyle actually to be seen as the natural heir and successor of Scotland's early modern scholars. His profound scepticism of reason yet his open hostility towards the Utilitarian philosophers who seemed to threaten the heroic and the instinctive may, as I have already suggested, have owed a great deal to the venerable Calvinist sense of the ultimate primacy in human motivation of the irrational passions. His claim in *On Heroes, Hero-Worship and the Heroic in History* (1841), meanwhile, that historical significance was the prerogative of 'Great Men', and specifically of the 'Man of Letters', was likewise in both terminology and spirit to be an obvious point of contact with the moral discourse of earlier humanists in Scotland such as Scott of Satchells and Alexander Monro. Of influential and historically-minded teachers and of concerned public moralists, then, nineteenth-century Scotland could clearly still produce more than its fair share.

Nor should we allow ourselves to overestimate the fall from literary grace of Scotland's creative men of letters. Scott may have died in 1831, an overworked and debt-ridden man. But his prodigious influence on the nineteenth-century mind, and not only in the technical development of historical literature and antiquarianism stimulated by his *Tales of a Grandfather* (1828), if anything only grew stronger as time progressed. The emerging modern novel, for example, derived incalculable benefits from the raging fashion for imaginative fiction largely whipped up by Scott's formidable virtuosity and the stunning international success of the *Waverley Novels*.[10] Romantic poetics and aesthetic theory, moreover, would be difficult to imagine in their classic form without the impact of his wide-ranging activities in poetry and prose. Elsewhere the hold exerted in the early nineteenth century by Macpherson's *Ossian* – Napoleon's favourite reading – and the lasting popularity throughout Europe as a whole of Burns's inspirational poetry, would have to be weighed. Hogg's *Justified Sinner*, and later the historical adventures of Stevenson in particular, were to lend disproportionate weight to Scotland's substantial literary reputation. Nor, if we are looking for evidence of the continuation of older Scottish currents of thought beyond the early years of the new century, should we discount the familiar providentialism eventually articulated in John Galt's masterpiece of narrative fiction, *The Annals of the Parish* (1821).[11] The *Edinburgh Review* and *Blackwood's Magazine*, too, were always to the outside world much more than merely the mouthpieces of virulent Whig and Tory ideologues. The former, as Biancamaria Fontana's recent work has rightly suggested, was amongst the most respected literary and political journals of the early nineteenth century.[12] The flood-tide of northern influence, then, did not quickly ebb away. Alongside such prospering enlightened institutions as the *Encyclopaedia Britannica* and *Chambers' Encyclopaedia*, these periodicals continued to give to raised Scottish voices, like those of Francis Jeffrey and John Gibson Lockhart, the kind of moral authority and judgemental *gravitas* to which their sixteenth-century forebears like Boece and Lindsay had only been able to aspire. The past, as defined and articulated in both popular literature and serious journalism in the nineteenth century, would clearly have looked far different without these continuing Scottish contributions.

At the same time, the significance of Scottish science, medicine and philanthropy was scarcely to diminish. Indeed, by the nineteenth century those formidable agents for change had been effectively adopted, even in many cases institutionalised, in British public life. Arguably the Scottish commitment to 'improvement', for example, had acquired an even greater influence as it shaped the hospitals, schools and wider civic and cultural life of early Victorian Britain. It now justified innumerable philanthropic foundations and probably also encouraged progressive social reform in response to the 'Condition of England' debate. Even the studious obsessions of the countless philosophical and scientific societies which illuminated the otherwise grimy industrial townscape – such as the Manchester Mechanics' Institute and the Sheffield Lit. and Phil. –, would perhaps bear further examination for Scottish influence. All of these developments have in any case plausibly been attributed by Anand Chitnis to the pervasive ethos of the 'clubbable', civic-minded and, above all, inveterately curious Scottish literati.[13] John Robertson has shown us, meanwhile, how the basic conceptual architecture supporting the dominant ideological structures of the middle decades of the century – free trade and constitutional liberalism – can also both be traced back to Scotland and the early years of modern political economy: 'Manchester School' opposition, and later the tenets of Gladstonian governmental practice, were moulded ultimately, it seems, in the supple hands of Adam Smith himself.[14] Even those works after the fashion of William Lehmann and Ronald Meek, which I earlier suggested had given an unfortunate impression of the essential function of the Enlightenment in Scotland, do nevertheless have considerable value in this respect.[15] These and other studies illustrate very graphically the extent to which the crowded agendas of nineteenth-century European political and social discourse, as well as of academic fashion – of economics, of nascent sociology, of phrenology and philosophy of mind –, were profoundly affected by the continuing if sometimes misconstrued influence of Scottish teachings as popularised by men like Sir William Hamilton and Dugald Stewart.[16] Literature, ideas, and intellectual programmes, then, remained Scotland's most durable and most valuable exports in the nineteenth century. The exaggerated swagger and actual social dominance of the intellectuals which had characterised its own Enlightenment may have gone forever. But Scotland for some appreciable time remained in the wider world inevitably a cultural and intellectual force to be reckoned with.

Yet all of this, one feels, can still only be a part of this perplexing story, a partial response to the continuing challenge of defining and explaining the limits of the Scottish Enlightenment. It would certainly be unwise to think that after 1800 Scotland's intellectual life merely continued to function as before. After all, within Scotland itself recognition of what from a more recent perspective looks like 'the relatively sudden disintegration of a great national culture', was to be even more inescapable.[17] No Humes or Robertsons now published scholarship which would enchant the wider reading public: the fusty record societies and documentary editions which flourished through the industry of Victorian scholars were still a far cry from the speculative flights and all-encompassing interests of their recent Scottish predecessors. As a result, no visitor to nineteenth-century Edinburgh would have found 'fifty men of genius and learning' to take by the hand.[18] In the recent pithy description offered by Michael Fry, Scotland's problematical history and identity were thereafter 'locked for safekeeping in the kailyard'.[19] There are even strong grounds for believing that the 'failure of intellectual nerve', diagnosed so astutely by George Davie was indeed a sickness affecting those Victorian Scotsmen charged with upholding the integrity of the northern university curriculum.[20] And a crippling loss of national self-confidence now certainly afflicted a consciously post-enlightened generation of commentators, including the critical Carlyle, the reflective Stewart, and the deeply nostalgic Henry Cockburn. The most promising response, I would argue, to these more obdurate interpretative problems, would actually be to look in the direction of the acute ideological difficulties now emphasised by our own account of enlightened historical discourse. The Enlightenment had been made possible by an unprecedented confidence in the status and historical importance of rational learning. How vulnerable must have been that tenuous achievement, therefore, to the corrosive effects of a thoroughgoing doctrine of 'unintended consequences', one which struck a powerful chord within much older traditions of Scottish historical thought? A serious 'failure of intellectual nerve' among disillusioned Scottish scholars and teachers would perhaps in these circumstances have been an entirely plausible outcome. We have seen signs that a rigorous questioning and doubting of the ability of rational men effectively to change the course of history was developing in Scotland by the end of the eighteenth century. This would have been fraught with obvious dangers for the purveyors of such a self-consciously rational and reformist Enlightenment. Indeed, only that triumph of an unbridled anti-rationalism within the human sciences could perhaps have brought about the rapid dissipation of precisely that bullishness and sense of collective purpose which had characterised and motivated the Scottish Enlightenment in its most brilliant and productive phase.

To the world at large, then, Scottish cultural influence did not quickly fade – the evidence for its survival abroad is clear enough. But in Scotland itself the Enlightenment had been tangible as an episode within and an eloquent discussion of that country's hitherto peculiar social development. The signs of decay were therefore all the more remarkable. Scottish society was already by 1800 reeling under the simultaneous impact of several other debilitating changes. The Scottish middle classes, it seems, were at last being hurriedly sucked into the Anglicised metropolis by the brute force of political and social circumstance. Renewed nationalism and emergent Anglophobia were among the unsettling developments to be seen at this time.[21] Equally, sharpened political divisions and social disharmony were being countered only by the suffocating impositions of a reactionary London government: radical political programmes, shadowy liaisons with the French Jacobins, even an abortive insurrection in Edinburgh itself, were the stuff of a new and suddenly dangerous age.[22] To cap it all, even greater economic change was irreversibly altering the agenda of topical public discourse. Industrialisation reached new heights during the 1790s. Urban squalor and the pernicious 'division of labour' soon came to haunt a fresh generation of commentators like Francis Horner and Thomas Carlyle. In these fluid circumstances it would be no surprise at all if the local factors which had long made Scottish society so unusual and problematic for interested thinkers were suddenly reduced in significance. With this swiftly changing and uncertain context, then, the victory of blind 'unintended consequences' would itself have been entirely consistent. It would also have been able to have an even more startling and rapid effect upon beleaguered reason and virtue. The famous misgivings of Edmund Burke probably show us as much. These were to many influential thinkers now bewildering times of revolution and political upheaval. They were therefore also unpropitious times for the advocacy of any kind of deliberate social reform or for the rational restructuring of society. To a deeply conservative society such as Georgian Britain, indeed, the events in France can only have seemed an unspoken argument in favour of caution and pro-crastination, and certainly against the 'new conquering empire of light and reason'.[23] The essential vanity of this ambitious empire had always, of course, attracted in Scotland the thinly veiled mockery of convinced sceptics from Knox through Mackenzie to Hume. But now it seemed an even more terrifying proposition, one which was positively destructive of a hitherto peaceful and prosperous social order. It is hardly surprising, then, that there emerge suggestive signs of an explicit distrust of the claims of reason in human affairs beginning to spread contagiously in Scotland by the turn of the nineteenth century. The Whig lawyer Francis Jeffrey, for example, used the *Edinburgh Review* in 1804 to denounce with unfettered sarcasm the pretentious rationalism and reductionism which had so recently underlain the 'Science of Man': 'We cannot decompose our perceptions in a crucible', he chided, 'nor divide our sensations in a prism'.[24] The dynamic morality and impulsive feeling behind human actions could no longer, it seems, safely be the subjects of rational prediction or scientific explanation.[25] Nor was it any longer an uncontentious truism that intention and calculated design were simply the natural, orderly engines of a benevolent social progress.[26] Virtue and learning, too, were in quick time reduced to the same uncertain historical value.

As revealing in this context was the fear of cold science in moral affairs voiced a little later by Thomas Carlyle. Carlyle openly lamented in the *Edinburgh Review* in 1829 the apparently consummate failure of heroic morality and human creativity, once so promisingly advocated in Scotland by humanist scholars like Buchanan and Monro. This failure had been brought about, in Carlyle's eyes, not by the fleeting triumph of reason itself but by the accompanying mechanistic and scientific determinism of the wider Enlightenment, the very trend which we have seen implicated in the final dominance of unintention. After 'a rickety infancy, which never reached the vigour of manhood', he complained, the pursuit of moral and intellectual spirit had fallen 'suddenly into decay, languished, and finally died out, with its last amiable cultivator, Professor Stewart'.[27] Stewart himself, of course, has been something of an *éminence grise* in this study. But his status as probably the first and greatest post-Enlightenment teacher in Scotland must make him again a crucial figure at this late stage. Modern scholarship has surely been correct to think of Stewart that 'his expectations of the philosopher are more confident and ambitious' even than those of his more immediate enlightened predecessors.[28] Stewart was, however, clearly compensating in his urgent pleading for what had become increasingly uncertain in contemporary thought. In a celebrated contribution to the *Encyclopaedia Britannica* in 1815, he was genuinely to regret, merely anticipating Carlyle, what he too seems to have recognised and resented as the almost complete triumph of blind unintention. He roundly chastised d'Alembert, for example, who in a famous preface to the *Encyclopédie* had seemingly undermined the 'civilised and inquisitive individual' for whom Stewart still conceived a central historical role.[29] Elsewhere Stewart also huffily despatched Thomas Hobbes, in significant agreement with the English theologian Ralph Cudworth: to both the Cambridge Platonist and the Edinburgh moral philosopher it was clearly Hobbes' notorious materialist 'scheme of *necessity*' which was again the root of the problem. This had seemed, as Knox and Drummond had earlier said of the Stoics, 'to be equally inconsistent with the moral agency of man, and with the moral attributes of God'.[30] These measured attacks on unintention, however, like those of Carlyle from a different standpoint, simply came too late. In Stewart they were part of an unconvincing nostalgia for enlightened discourse, a discourse which at least had retained a self-interested commitment to the rational individual even whilst systematically destroying his classic historical function. Now the anti-rationalism notoriously peddled by Hobbes and lately enthroned by d'Alembert and La Mettrie seemed to its nervous opponents to have become absolutely rampant. Stewart clearly feared for the very survival of humanism and one sanitised form of Enlightenment civilisation. Carlyle pined for an older, more vigorous notion of spontaneity and moral leadership. But to both men the creative powers of reason and classical heroism seemed suddenly under mortal threat from a determinism recklessly unleashed on a largely unsuspecting world by the Enlightenment itself. As Carlyle sadly concluded, it now seemed that 'Practically considered, our creed is Fatalism ... . free in hand and foot, we are shackled in heart and soul'.[31] With Edmund Burke enthusiastically applauding this development and the diverse critics of the 'Science of Man' looking on with undisguised glee, a commitment to an effective intellectual leadership of society was thus being rendered completely untenable. Rational virtue, it was being concluded, was either untrustworthy or even impotent. It certainly looked incapable, least of all, of delivering the orderly moral regeneration of a dynamic industrial society beset by seemingly continual war and chronic political uncertainty. Scotland's once-confident 'Age of Reason', perhaps, could do little else in these circumstances but fall apart catastrophically from within.

What had occurred in eighteenth-century Scotland must therefore in retrospect seem a unique window of opportunity. For a time, a combination of civil harmony, religious toleration and increased wealth had offered Scottish scholarship a chance to flourish. This it had done with a vengeance. A long and sophisticated tradition of moral science and humane learning had in the hands of Hume, Smith and Robertson entered into a brief but intensely glorious golden age. More than this, the absence of social and political direction in Scotland had allowed its ambitious and increasingly successful scholars to achieve unparalleled eminence in society. Nor, at least from the scholars' point of view, could this exactly be said to have been accidental. Scottish scholarship since at least the sixteenth century – with Buchanan, Monro and Urquhart among the more strenuous – had been deliberately engaged in the forceful social advancement of rational virtue. Little wonder, then, that familiar arguments for the efficacy of learning were now wielded with the unfettered enthusiasm and brazen triumphalism which in such men as Alexander Carlyle and Gilbert Stuart so marked out the period of the Enlightenment in Scotland. The Scottish triumph of rational virtue was, after all, grounded in an exaggeration and substantiation of the more tentative expectations and long-thwarted ambitions of the stormy sixteenth century. It is salutary to note, however, that this longer and less discontinuous perspective on that transitory eighteenth-century achievement had nevertheless been offered by a perceptive but sadly untypical Victorian scholar. Only 'then, and not till then', wrote James Alfred Froude, when the nourishment of the Calvinist Reformation had been properly digested in Scotland, 'came the David Humes with their essays on miracles, and the Adam Smiths with their political economies, and steam engines, and railroads, and philosophical institutions, and all the other blessed or unblessed fruits of liberty'.[32] Had we listened to the cautious Froude rather than to the progressive and controversial Henry Buckle, of course, our view of the Scottish Enlightenment might have been far different. But the lesson for our own understanding remains available if we wish to take it. Scotland's enlightened discourse bore a very close relationship to its unique social and intellectual history. Its Enlightenment as a result was a long and painful time in coming. When it arrived, it was accompanied by open hyperbole, understandable celebration, perhaps even by a measure of relief. But these were almost inevitably short-lived. Scottish conditions, and again particularly Scotland's intellectual character, ensured that the sudden shattering of its rationalist pretensions would be as fatal as it was complete. The window of opportunity had closed. For the modern student this *denouement* suggests again what might once have seemed an unlikely conclusion. The Enlightenment, far from being a startling or deviant phenomenon in a Scottish context, actually offers an insight of unexpected clarity into the essential social and intellectual character of this most complex and misunderstood of early modern communities.

NOTES

1. Cockburn, *Memorials*; Robert Chambers, *Traditions of Edinburgh*, 2 vols (Edinburgh, 1825).
2. Carlyle, 'Signs of the Times', p. 458.
3. Pocock, *Virtue, Commerce, and History*, p. 310.
4. Alexander Carlyle, *The Question Relating to a Scots Militia Considered* (Edinburgh, 1760), p. 27.
5. Nairn, *Break-Up*, p. 116.
6. David Spadafora, *The Idea of Progress in Eighteenth-Century Britain* (New Haven, Conn., 1990), p. 261.
7. Ash, *Scottish History*, p. 11.
8. Chitnis, *Early Victorian English Society*, esp. pp. 41–4.
9. See e.g. Hoeveler, *McCosh* and Sloan, *Scottish Enlightenment*.
10. For evidence of his influence in the most unlikely places, see A. Katona, 'The Impact of Sir Walter Scott in Hungary', in A. Bell (ed.), *Scott Bicentenary Essays* (Edinburgh, 1973), pp. 271–83.
11. See J. MacQueen, 'John Galt and the Analysis of Social History', in Bell (ed.), *Scott*, esp. 334–6.
12. B. Fontana, *Rethinking the Politics of Commercial Society: The Edinburgh Review, 1802–1832* (Cambridge, 1985).
13. Especially in Chitnis, *Early Victorian Society*, pp. 146–73.
14. J. Robertson, 'The Legacy of Adam Smith; Government and Economic Development in the *Wealth of Nations*', in R. Bellamy (ed.), *Victorian Liberalism: Nineteenth-Century Political Thought and Practice* (London, 1990), pp. 15–41.
15. See e.g. Meek, 'Scottish Contribution' and Lehmann, *Adam Ferguson*.
16. See e.g. N. Waszek, *The Scottish Enlightenment and Hegel's Account of 'Civil Society'* (Dordrecht, 1988). For a less appreciative assessment by a modern psychologist see D. N. Robinson, 'The Scottish Enlightenment and its Mixed Bequest', *Journal for the History of the Behavioural Sciences*, 22 (1986), 171–7.
17. Nairn, *Break-Up*, p. 116.
18. Smellie, *Lives*, p. 161.
19. M. Fry, 'The Whig Interpretation of Scottish History', in I. Donnachie and C. Whately (eds), *The Manufacture of Scottish History* (Edinburgh, 1992), p. 83.
20. Davie, *Democratic Intellect*, p. 337.
21. Phillipson, 'Nationalism and Ideology', pp. 167–88.
22. The definitive study of Scotland's 'political awakening' at this time remains H. W. Meikle, *Scotland and the French Revolution* (Glasgow, 1912). But see H. Fraser, *Conflict and Class: Scottish Workers, 1700–1838* (Edinburgh, 1988), which suggests that continual friction and periodic disorder had in fact long been an underlying feature of Scottish social life.
23. Edmund Burke, *Reflections on the Revolution in France* (ed.), C. C. O'Brien (Harmondsworth, 1969), p. 171.
24. Francis Jeffrey, 'Stewart's Life of Dr Reid', *Edinburgh Review*, 3 (1804), 275. More widely on the pessimism undermining the confident values of Scotland's intellectuals, see Fontana, *Commercial Society*, pp. 170–80.
25. To John Pocock this emerging critique of Condorcet and Bentham, of 'administrative ideology' and of 'cold mechanical philosophy', spelled the end of an enlightened 'commercial humanism' in the 1790s. See 'Virtue, Rights, and Manners: A Model for Historians of Political Thought', *Political Theory*, 9 (1981), 68.
26. Again Jeffrey makes an instructive example, following Burke in claiming now that society 'is not like a piece of mechanism which may be safely taken to pieces, and put together by the hands of an ordinary artist', 'Mémoires de Bailly', *Edinburgh Review*, 6 (1805), 142.
27. Carlyle, 'Signs of the Times', p. 445.
28. Collini, Winch and Burrow, *Noble Science*, p. 42. It is therefore likely that any acolytes of the Scottish tradition in the next generation, such as James Mill and Thomas Macaulay, who wished to rebuild a role for the influential intellectual in society, would need first to disavow 'unintended consequences' altogether, *ibid.*, pp. 124–5.
29. Stewart, 'Dissertation', I, 3. It was likewise to be Carlyle's estimation that 'The French were the first to desert Metaphysics'.

30. *ibid.*, I, 67. See Phillipson, 'Scottish Enlightenment', pp. 38–40, for an account of Stewart's motivation in upholding the role of the 'virtuous expert' in society.

31. Carlyle, 'Signs of the Times', p. 457.

32. J. A. Froude, 'The Influence of the Reformation on the Scottish Character', in his *Short Studies on Great Subjects*, 2 vols (London, 1867), I, 171.

Bibliography

Economy prevents this bibliography from referencing more than the works fully cited in the text. However, for a guide to the collosal secondary literature relevant to Scotland's cultural and intellectual heritage, which underpins less specifically much that has been argued herein, the reader is referred to D. W. Allan, 'Virtue, Learning, and the Enlightened Historian. Calvinist Humanism and the Rise of Scottish Scholarship, 1550–1800' (unpublished Ph.D. dissertation, University of Cambridge, 1990). Additional primary sources can be identified from H. G. Aldis, *List of Books Printed in Scotland Before* 1700 (Edinburgh, 1904) and G. Averley (ed.), *Eighteenth-Century British Books: A Subject Catalogue* (Folkestone, 1979). Some valuable materials are also listed in D. and W. B. Stevenson, *Scottish Texts and Calendars. An Analytical Guide to Serial Publications* (Edinburgh, 1987).

Unpublished Sources

Edinburgh, National Library of Scotland
Adv. MSS 33.3.16–18   *General Historical Manuscripts*
Adv. MS 33.4.18   Richard Hay, *Life of Sir William Wallace*
Adv. MS 34.1.8   Richard Hay, *Ane Account of the Most Renowned Churches etc.*
Adv. MS 34.5.22   *History of the Earls and Dukes of Argyll*
Wodr. Qu. LII   Robert Wodrow, various
Wodr. Qu. XCVII   William Jameson, *The History of the Wisdom, Valour, and Liberty of the Ancient Albion-Scotish Nation*

Edinburgh, New College Library
X156, 1/5, Box 27   John Bonar, *The History of Tyre*

Edinburgh, University Library
MS Gen. 1423   *Newtonian Society Minute Book*, 1760–1764
MS Dc.1.64   [William Dunlop?], *Genealogies of the Nobility of Scotland*
MS Dc.4.12   *Chronicle of Scotland*

Aberdeen, University Library
MS 192   *Chronicle of the Kings of Scottis from Fergus Ferchard till* 1346
MS 614   *Historical Notes to* 1748
MS 615   *Historical Notes of Scotland to* 1757
MS 2201   *The Genealogie of the Surname of Lesley*

Glasgow, University Library
MS Gen. 372   James Graham, *An Account of the Expedition of William Earl of Glencairn etc.*
MS Gen. 1471   *Defence of the Independence of the Antient Kingdom and Church of Scotland*
MS Murray 304   Patrick Boyle, *Notes of History*

St Andrews, University Library
MS DA805.M2   *Memoirs Concerning the Affairs of Scotland*
MS D18.Y7C35   Gavin Young, *A Mappe of Mutationes etc.*

Printed Sources (*to* 1830)

The inevitably limited name-pool available to the scholarly community of a small country sometimes makes identification of a particular Scottish author or text difficult. To indicate the presence of separate individuals or works commonly known by the same names at different times, Roman numerals have been inserted in the Bibliography. These distinguish the unique men and works, in chronological order by date of birth and/or publication.

Abercromby, Patrick, *The History of the Campagnes of* 1548 *and* 1549 ([ ], 1707).
Abercromby, Patrick, *The Martial Atchievements of the Scots Nation*, 2 vols (Edinburgh, 1711–15).
Adams, John, *Curious Thoughts on the History of Man* (Dublin, 1790).
[Addison, Joseph], *The Spectator*, 16 vols (London, 1724).
Alexander, William, *The History of Women*, 2 vols (London, 1777).
Anderson, James, *Collections Relating to the History of Mary Queen of Scotland*, 3 vols (Edinburgh, 1727).
Anderson, James, *An Historical Essay Shewing that the Crown and Kingdom of Scotland is Imperial and Independent* (Edinburgh, 1705).
Anderson, Walter, *The History of Croesus, King of Lydia* (Edinburgh, 1755).
Anderson, Walter, *The History of France*, 2 vols (London, 1769).
Anderson, Walter, *The Philosophy of Ancient Greece* (Edinburgh, 1791).
Arnot, Hugo, *The History of Edinburgh* (Edinburgh, 1779).
Baillie, Robert, *An Historical Vindication of the Government of the Church of Scotland* (London, 1646).
Baird, William, *Genealogical Collections Concerning the Sir-Name of Baird* (ed.), W. N. Fraser (London, 1870).
Balfour, Sir James, *Historical Works*, 4 vols (Edinburgh, 1825).
Balfour, James, *A Delineation of the Nature and Obligation of Morality* (Edinburgh, 1763).
Barclay, James, *A Treatise of Education* (Edinburgh, 1743).
Barron, William, *History of the Colonization of the Free States of Antiquity* (London, 1777).
Beattie, James, *Dissertations Moral and Critical* (London, 1783).
Beattie, James, *The Minstrel, in Two Books: with Some Other Poems* (London, 1779).
Belfour, John, *A New History of Scotland* (London, 1770).
Bellenden, John, 'Vertue and Vyce', in R. and A. Foulis (eds), *Two Antient Scots Allegorical Poems* (Glasgow, 1750), pp. 17–38.
Blackwell, Thomas, *An Enquiry into the Life and Writings of Homer* (London, 1735).
[Blackwell, Thomas], *Letters Concerning Mythology* (London, 1748).
Blackwell, Thomas, *Memoirs of the Court of Augustus*, 2 vols (Edinburgh, 1753–5).
[Blackwood, Adam], *History of Mary Queen of Scots; A Fragment* (ed.), A. Macdonald, (Edinburgh, 1834).
Blair, Hugh, *A Critical Dissertation on the Poems of Ossian* (London, 1763).
Blair, Hugh, *Lectures on Rhetoric and Belles Lettres*, 2 vols (London, 1783).
Boece, Hector, *Hystory and Croniklis of Scotland* (ed. and transl.), J. Bellenden ([Edinburgh, 1542?]).
Bolingbroke, Viscount, *Letters on the Study and Use of History*, 2 vols (London, 1752).

Borthwick, William, *An Inquiry into the Origins and Limitations of the Feudal Dignities in Scotland* (Edinburgh, 1775).
Borthwick, William, *Remarks on British Antiquities* (Edinburgh, 1776).
Boswell, James, *The Journal of a Tour to the Hebrides* (ed.), P. Levi (Harmondsworth, 1984).
[Britton, John], *Modern Athens! Displayed in a Series of Views* (London, 1829).
Buchan, Lord, *Discourse Promoting a Society for the Investigation of the History of Scotland* ([ ], 1780).
Buchanan, George, *De Jure Regni Apud Scotos Dialogos* (ed. and transl.), Philalethes ([ ], 1680).
Buchanan, George, *Dialogue Concerning the Rights of the Crown of Scotland*, (ed. and transl.), R. Macfarlane (London, 1799).
Buchanan, George, *The History of Scotland* (ed. and transl.), J. Fraser (London, 1690).
Buchanan, John Lanne, *A Defence of the Scots Highlanders in General and Some Learned Characters in Particular* (London, 1794).
Burke, Edmund, *Reflections on the Revolution in France* (ed.), C. C. O'Brien (Harmondsworth, 1969).
Burnet, Gilbert, *The Historie of the Reformation of the Church of England*, 3 vols (London, 1681–1715).
Burnet, Gilbert, *The History of the Rights of Princes in the Disposing of Ecclesiastical Benefices* (London, 1682).
Burnet, Gilbert, *The Memoires of the Lives and Actions of James and William Dukes of Hamilton and Castleherald* (London, 1677).
Burnet, Gilbert, *Reflections on Mr Varillas' History* (Amsterdam, 1686).
Burnet, Gilbert, *A Vindication of the Authority, Constitution, and Laws of the Church and State of Scotland* (Glasgow, 1673).
Burns, Robert, *Poetical Works* (ed.), J. L. Robertson (London, 1963).
Burton, Robert, *The Anatomy of Melancholy* (ed.), H. Jackson (London, 1932).
Butler, Samuel, *Hudibras: The First Part* (London, 1663).
Byron, Lord, *English Bards and Scotch Reviewers*, 3rd edn (London, 1810).
Calderwood, David, *The True History of the Church of Scotland* ([ ], 1678).
Calvin, *Institutes of the Christian Religion*, (ed. and transl.), F. L. Battles, revised edn (London, 1986).
Campbell, Alexander, 'The Genealogical and Historicall Account of the Family of Craiginsh' (ed.), H. Campbell, *Miscellany of the Scottish History Society* (Edinburgh, 1926), IV, 117–299.
Campbell, George, *Lectures on Ecclesiastical History*, 2 vols (London, 1800).
Campbell, George, *The Philosophy of Rhetoric*, 2 vols (London, 1776).
Campbell, John, *A Full and Particular Description of the Highlands of Scotland* (London, 1752).
Carlyle, Alexander, *The Question Relating to a Scots Militia Considered* (Edinburgh, 1760).
Carlyle, Thomas, 'Signs of the Times', *Edinburgh Review*, 49 (1829), 439–59.
Castiglione, *The Book of the Courtier* (ed. and transl.), C. S. Singleton (New York, 1959).
Chambers, Robert, *Traditions of Edinburgh*, 2 vols (Edinburgh, 1825).
Chronicle of the Kings of Scotland, From Fergus the First to James the Sixth (ed.), J. W. Mackenzie (Edinburgh, 1830).
Cockburn, Henry, *Memorials of His Time* (ed.), W. F. Gray (Edinburgh, 1946).
[Colville, John], *The Historie and Life of King James the Sext* (ed.), T. Thomson (Edinburgh, 1825).

Craig, Sir Thomas, *De Unione Regnorum Britanniae Tractatus* (ed. and transl.), C. Sanford Terry (Edinburgh, 1909).

Crauford, James, *The History of the House of Este* (London, 1681).

Crauford, Thomas, *History of the University of Edinburgh from 1580 to 1646* (Edinburgh, 1808).

Crauford, Thomas, *Notes and Observations on Mr George Buchanan's History of Scotland* (Edinburgh, 1708).

Crawford, George, *The Peerage of Scotland* (Edinburgh, 1716).

Crawford, Matthew, *Proposals for Printing a General History of the Church of Scotland* ([ ], 1720?).

Crawfurd, George, *The History of the Shire of Renfrew* (ed.), W. Semple (Paisley, 1782).

[Crockat, Gilbert?], *Scotch Presbyterian Eloquence Display'd: Or, The Folly of their Teaching Discover'd* (Rotterdam, 1738).

Cromarty, Earl of, *An Historical Account of the Conspiracies of the Earls of Gowry and Robert Logan of Restalrig Against King James* (Edinburgh, 1713).

Cromarty, Earl of, *A Vindication of Robert III King of Scotland* (Edinburgh, 1695).

[Cunningham, John], *Essay Upon the Inscription of Macduff's Crosse in Fyfe* (Edinburgh, 1678).

Dalrymple, Sir James, *Collections Concerning the Scottish History* (Edinburgh, 1705).

Dalrymple, Sir John, *An Essay Towards a General History of Feudal Property* (London, 1758).

Dalrymple, Sir John, *Memoirs of Great Britain and Ireland*, 2 vols (Edinburgh, 1771).

Dalyell, Sir John, *Fragments of Scottish History* (Edinburgh, 1798).

Denina, Carlo, *An Essay on the Revolutions of Literature* (ed. and transl.), J. Murdoch (London, 1771).

Descartes, *Descartes: Philosophical Writings* (ed. and transl.), N. Kemp Smith (London, 1952).

[Drummond, John], *Memoirs of Sir Ewen Cameron of Locheil* (ed.), J. MacKnight (Edinburgh, 1842).

Drummond, William, *The History of Scotland* (London, 1655).

Drummond, William, *The Poetical Works of William Drummond of Hawthornden* (ed.), L. E. Kastner, 2 vols (London, 1913).

Dryden, John, *Plutarch's Lives*, 5 vols (London, 1688).

Duff, William, *Essay on Genius* (London, 1767).

Duff, William, *A History of Scotland* (London, 1749).

Dunbar, James, *Essays on the History of Mankind in Rude and Uncultivated Ages* (Dublin, 1782).

Dunbar, William, *Poems* (ed.), W. M. Mackenzie (Edinburgh, 1932).

Duncan, William, *The History of the Kings of Scotland* (Glasgow, 1722).

Durham, James, *A Commentarie Upon the Book of the Revelation* (Glasgow, 1680).

Edgar, Robert, *An Introduction to the History of Dumfries* (ed.), R. C. Reid (Dumfries, 1915).

The Edinburgh Review (I) (1755–6).

The Edinburgh Review (II) (1802–1929).

Erasmus, *The Colloquies of Erasmus* (ed. and transl.), C. R. Thompson (Chicago, 1965).

Erasmus, *The Education of the Christian Prince* (ed. and transl.), L. K. Born (New York, 1936).

Ferguson, Adam, *An Essay on the History of Civil Society* (Edinburgh, 1767).

Ferguson, Adam, *The History of the Roman Republic*, 3 vols (London, 1783).

Ferguson, Robert, *A Sober Inquiry into the Nature, Measure, and Principle of Moral Virtue* (London, 1673).

Fleming, Robert (I), *The Fulfilling of the Scripture* ([ ], 1681).

Fleming, Robert (II), *An Epistolary Discourse Concerning the Rise and Fall of the Papacy* (Edinburgh, 1790).

Fleming, Robert (II), *The History of Hereditary-Right* (London, 1711).

Fletcher, Andrew, *A Discourse Concerning Militia's and Standing Armies* (London, 1697).

Forbes, Duncan of Culloden, *Works* (Edinburgh, 1752).

Forrester, Thomas, *The Hierarchical Bishops Claim to a Divine Right* (Edinburgh, 1699).

Fowler, William, 'The Prince of Machiavelli', in *Works* (ed.), H. W. Meikle, 3 vols (Edinburgh, 1914–1936), II, 69–164.

The General History of the World, From the Creation, Till the Dispersion, and the Establishment of Kingdoms (Edinburgh, 1763).

Gerard, Alexander, *An Essay on Genius* (London, 1774).

Gibson, John, *The History of Glasgow* (Glasgow, 1777).

Gillies, John, *The Orations of Lysias and Isocrates* (London, 1778).

Goodall, Walter, *An Examination of the Letters of Mary Queen of Scots*, 2 vols (Edinburgh, 1754).

Goodall, Walter, *An Introduction to the History and Antiquities of Scotland* (London, 1769).

Gordon, Alexander, *The Lives of Pope Alexander VI and Caesar Borgia* (London, 1729).

Gordon, Alexander of Auchintoul, *The History of Peter the Great, Emperor of Russia*, 2 vols (Aberdeen, 1755).

Gordon, C. A., *A Concise History of the Ancient and Illustrious House of Gordon* (Aberdeen, 1890).

Gordon, James, *History of Scots Affairs from MDCXXXVII to MDCXLI* (ed.), J. Robertson and G. Grub, 3 vols (Aberdeen, 1841).

Gordon, John (I), *The Union of Great Britaine* (London, 1604).

Gordon, John (II), 'A Dissertation Concerning the Marriage of Robert Seneschal of Scotland with Elizabeth More', *Scotia Rediviva*, 1 (1826) 161–224.

Gordon, Patrick, *The Famous History of Robert the Bruce* (Edinburgh, 1718).

Gordon, Sir Robert, *In the Question Concerning the Peerage of Sutherland* ([ ], 1771).

Gordon, Sir Robert of Gordonstoun, *A Genealogical History of the Earldom of Sutherland* (Edinburgh, 1813).

Gordon, William, *The History of the Ancient, Noble, and Illustrious Family of Gordon*, 2 vols (Edinburgh, 1726–7).

Graham, Dougal, *Impartial History of the Rise, Progress, and Extinction of the Late Rebellion in Britain*, 5th edn (Glasgow, 1787).

Grahame, Simione, *The Anatomie of Humors and the Passionate Sparke of a Relenting Minde* (ed.), R. Jameson (Edinburgh, 1830).

Grant, James, *Thoughts on the Origin and Descent of the Gael* (Edinburgh, 1814).

Guicciardini, *The History of Italy* (ed. and transl.), S. Alexander (New York, 1969).

Guthrie, William, *General History of Scotland*, 10 vols (London, 1767–8).

Guthrie, William, *A New Geographical, Historical, and Commercial Grammar and Present State of the Several Kingdoms of the World* (London, 1777).

Hailes, Lord, *Annals of Scotland from the Accession of Malcolm III Surnamed Canmore to the Accession of Robert I* (Edinburgh, 1776).

Hailes, Lord, *Disquisition Concerning the Antiquities of the Christian Church* (Glasgow, 1783).

Hailes, Lord, *An Examination of Some Arguments for the High Antiquity of Regiam Majestatem; and an Inquiry into the Authenticity of Leges Malcolmi* (Edinburgh, 1769).

Hailes, Lord, *Historical Account of the Senators of the College of Justice of Scotland, since its Institution in* 1532 (Edinburgh, 1842).

Hailes, Lord, *Historical Memorials Concerning the Provincial Councils of the Scottish Clergy* (Edinburgh, 1769).

Hailes, Lord, *Remarks Concerning the History of Scotland* (Edinburgh, 1773).

Hay, Richard, *An Essay on the Origine of the Royal Family of the Stewarts* (Edinburgh, 1722).

Hay, Richard, *Genealogie of the Hayes of Tweeddale* (Edinburgh, 1835).

Hay, Richard, *A Vindication of Elizabeth More* (Edinburgh, 1723).

Henderson, Andrew, *Considerations On the Question Whether a Militia Ought to Extend to Scotland* (London, 1760).

Henderson, Andrew, *A Dissertation on the Royal Line and First Settlers of Scotland* (London, 1771).

[Henderson, Andrew], *The History of the Rebellion, 1745 and 1746* (Edinburgh, 1747).

Henry, Robert, *The History of Great Britain*, 6 vols (London, 1771–93).

Hepburn, Robert, *A Discourse Concerning the Character of a Man of Genius* (Edinburgh, 1715).

Heron, Robert, *A New General History of Scotland* (Perth, 1794).

Herries, Lord, *Historical Memoirs of the Reign of Mary Queen of Scots and a Portion of the Reign of King James the Sixth* (ed.), R. Pitcairn (Edinburgh, 1836).

Hill, John, 'An Essay upon the Principles of Historical Composition', *Transactions of the Royal Society of Edinburgh*, 1 (1784), ii, 76–98.

The History of the Seven Wise Masters of Rome (London, 1684).

Hobbes, Thomas, *De Cive* (ed. and transl.), B. Gert (Atlantic Highlands, 1978).

Hogg, James, *The Mountain Bard* (Edinburgh, 1807).

Hogg, James, *Private Memoirs and Confessions of a Justified Sinner* (ed.), J. Casey (Oxford, 1981).

Home, John, *The History of the Rebellion in the Year* 1745 (London, 1802).

Home, John, *The History of the Sieges of Aquileia and Berwick* (London, 1760).

Hume, David, *Essays, Moral and Political*, 2 vols 2nd edn (Edinburgh, 1742).

Hume, David, *The History of England*, 3 vols (London, 1875).

Hume, David, *Letters* (ed.), G. Birkbeck-Hill (Oxford, 1888).

Hume, David, *Letters*, 2 vols (ed.), J. Y. T.Grieg (Oxford, 1932).

Hume, David, *The Natural History of Religion* (London, 1757).

Hume, David, *A Treatise of Human Nature*, 3 vols (Edinburgh, 1739–40).

Hume, David of Godscroft, *The History of the Houses of Douglas and Angus* (Edinburgh, 1644).

Hutcheson, Francis, *An Inquiry into the Original of Our Ideas of Beauty and Virtue; in Two Treatises* (London, 1725).

Innes, Thomas, *The Civil and Ecclesiastical History of Scotland, AD80–818* (Aberdeen, 1853).

Innes, Thomas, *A Critical Essay On the Ancient Inhabitants of Scotland*, 2 vols (London, 1729).

James VI, *Basilikon Doron* (London, 1603).

Jeffrey, Francis, 'Mémoires de Bailly', *Edinburgh Review*, 6 (1805), 137–61.

Jeffrey, Francis, 'Stewart's Life of Dr Reid', *Edinburgh Review*, 3 (1804), 269–87.

Johnson, Samuel, *Journey to the Western Islands of Scotland* (Glasgow, 1817).

Johnston, Robert, 'The Historie of Scotland During the Minority of King James', *Scotia Rediviva*, 1 (1826), 361–470.

Kames, Lord, *Elements of Criticism*, 2 vols (Edinburgh, 1769).

Kames, Lord, *Essays on Several Subjects Concerning British Antiquities* (Edinburgh, 1747).

Kames, Lord, *Historical Law Tracts*, 2 vols (Edinburgh, 1758).

Kames, Lord, *Sketches of the History of Man*, 2 vols (Edinburgh, 1774).

Keith, Robert, *An Historical Catalogue of the Scottish Bishops Down to the Year 1688* (Edinburgh, 1755).

Keith, Robert, *History of the Affairs of Church and State in Scotland* (Edinburgh, 1734).

Kennedy, David, *The Late History of Europe* (Edinburgh, 1698).

Kincaid, Alexander, *History of Edinburgh* (Edinburgh, 1787).

Kirkton, James, *The Secret and True History of the Church of Scotland from the Restoration to the year 1678* (Edinburgh, 1817).

Knox, John, *A Faythfull Admonition* ([Zurich], 1554).

Knox, John, *The Historie of the Reformation of the Church of Scotland* (London, 1644).

Knox, John, *Works*, 5 vols (ed.), D. Laing (Edinburgh, 1856).

Lawrie, John, *The Completion of Prophecy: the Clearest Evidence of the Truth of Christianity* (Edinburgh, 1781).

Lawrie, John, *The History of the Wars in Scotland* (Edinburgh, 1783).

Lesley, John, *The History of Scotland* (Edinburgh, 1830).

Lesley, John, *A Treatise Touching the Right of Marie, Queene of Scotland, to the Croune of England* ([ ], 1571).

Leslie, Henry, *A Treatise of the Authority of the Church* (Dublin, 1637).

Lindsay, Sir David, *Works* (Edinburgh, 1709).

Lindsay, Robert, *The History of Scotland from 1436 to 1565* (ed.), R. Freebairn (Edinburgh, 1728).

Lithgow, William, *A True and Experimentall Discourse Upon the Beginning, Proceeding, and Victorious Event of this Last Siege of Breda* (London, 1637).

Lockhart, John Gibson, *Peter's Letters to His Kinsfolk* (ed.), W. Ruddick (Edinburgh, 1977).

Logan, John, *A Dissertation on the Manners and Spirit of Asia* (London, 1787).

Macgregory, John, *The Geography and History of Tournay* (Edinburgh, 1709).

Machiavelli, *Discourses* (ed. and transl.), B. Crick (Harmondsworth, 1970).

Machiavelli, *The Prince* (ed. and transl.), R. M. Adams (New York, 1970).

Mackenzie, Sir George of Rosehaugh, *Institutions of the Law of Scotland* (Edinburgh, 1684).

Mackenzie, Sir George of Rosehaugh, *A Moral Essay Preferring Solitude to Publick Employment* (London, 1685).

Mackenzie, Sir George of Rosehaugh, *Moral Gallantry* (London, 1669).

Mackenzie, Sir George of Rosehaugh, *The Moral History of Frugality and its Opposite Vices* (London, 1691).

Mackenzie, Sir George of Rosehaugh, *A Moral Paradox: Maintaining, That it is Much Easier to be Virtuous than Vicious* (London, 1669).

Mackenzie, Sir George of Rosehaugh, *Observations Upon the Laws and Customs of Nations* (Edinburgh, 1680).

Mackenzie, Sir George of Rosehaugh, *Religio Stoici* (Edinburgh, 1665).

Mackenzie, George, *Lives and Characters of the Most Eminent Writers of the Scots Nation*, 3 vols (Edinburgh, 1708–22).

Mackenzie, Henry, *Report of the Committee of the Highland Society of Scotland, Appointed to Inquire into the Nature and Authenticity of the Poems of Ossian* (Edinburgh, 1805).

MacLaurin, Colin, *An Account of Sir Isaac Newton's Philosophical Discoveries* (London, 1748).

Macpherson, David, *Geographical Illustrations of Scottish History* (London, 1796).

Macpherson, James, 'Fragments of Ancient Poetry, Collected in the Highlands of Scotland', in R. and J. Dodsley (eds), *Fugitive Pieces on Various Subjects, By Several Authors*, 2 vols (London, 1761), II, 117–62.

Macpherson, James, *The Highlander: A Poem in Six Cantos* (Edinburgh, 1758).

Macpherson, James, *Introduction to the History of Great Britain and Ireland* (London, 1771).

Macpherson, James, *Original Papers Containing the Secret History of Great Britain*, 2 vols (Dublin, 1775).

Macpherson, John, *Critical Dissertations on the Origin, Antiquities, Language, Government, Manners, and Religion of the Ancient Caledonians, Their Posterity the Picts, and the British and Irish Scots* (London, 1768).

MacUre, John, *A View of the City of Glasgow* (Glasgow, 1830).

Maitland, Sir Richard, *The History of the House of Seytoun* (ed.), J. Fullarton (Glasgow, 1829).

Maitland, William, *The History and Antiquities of Scotland*, 2 vols (London, 1757).

Maitland, William, *The History of Edinburgh* (Edinburgh, 1753).

Major, John, *A History of Greater Britain, as well England as Scotland* (ed. and transl.), A. Constable (Edinburgh, 1892).

Maule, Henry, *The History of the Picts* (Glasgow, 1818).

Melville, Sir James, *Memoires* (ed.), G. Scott (London, 1683).

Melville, James, *A Short Relation of the State of the Kirk of Scotland* ([Edinburgh], 1638).

Millar, John, *An Historical View of the English Government* (London, 1781).

Milton, John, *Milton: Poetical Works* (ed.), D. Bush (Oxford, 1979).

Milton, John, *Prose Works*, 1641–50, 3 vols (Menston, England, 1967).

Monboddo, Lord, *Antient Metaphysics: or, The Science of Universals*, 6 vols (Edinburgh, 1779–99).

Monipennie, John, *The Abridgement or Summarie of the Scots Chronicles* (Glasgow, 1820).

Monro, Alexander, *An Apology for the Clergy of Scotland* (London, 1692).

Monro, Robert, *Monro His Expedition With the Worthy Scots Regiment etc.* (London, 1637).

Montaigne, *Essais* (ed. and transl.), J. Florio (New York, 1907).

Montesquieu, *The Spirit of the Laws* (ed. and transl.), T. Nugent, 2 vols (Aberdeen, 1756).

More, Sir Thomas, *Utopia* (ed. and transl.), P. Turner (Harmondsworth, 1965).

Moysie, David, *Memoirs of the Affairs of Scotland* (Edinburgh, 1755).

Mudie, Robert, *The Modern Athens* (London, 1825).

Napier, John, *A Plaine Discovery of the Whole Revelation of St John* (Edinburgh, 1593).

Nicolson, William, *The Scottish Historical Library* (London, 1702).

Nimmo, William, *The General History of Stirlingshire* (Edinburgh, 1777).

Paterson, William, *An Enquiry into the State of the Union of Great Britain* (London, 1717).

Pennant, Thomas, *A Tour in Scotland*, 1769 (Chester, 1771).

Petrie, Alexander, *A Compendious History of the Catholick Church*, 2 vols (The Hague, 1662).

Pinkerton, John, *A Dissertation on the Origin and Progress of the Scythians or Goths* (London, 1787).

Pinkerton, John, *An Enquiry into the History of Scotland*, 2 vols (London, 1789).

Rae, Peter, *The History of the Late Rebellion Rais'd Against His Majesty King George, by the Friends of the Popish Pretender* (Dumfries, 1718).

Rait, William, *A Vindication of the Reformed Religion, From the Reflections of a Romanist* (Aberdeen, 1671).

Ramsay, Allan, *The Ever Green, Being a Collection of Scots Poems Wrote by the Ingenious before 1600*, 2 vols (Edinburgh, 1724).

Ramsay, John of Ochtertyre, *Scotland and Scotsmen in the Eighteenth Century* (ed.), A. Allardyce, 2 vols (Edinburgh, 1888).

Reid, Thomas, *Essays on the Active Powers of Man* (Glasgow, 1788).

Ridpath, George, *An Historical Account of the Antient Rights and Power of the Parliament of Scotland* (Edinburgh, 1703).

Ridpath, George of Stitchell, *A Border History of Scotland and England* (London, 1776).

Ridpath, George of Stitchell, *Diary of George Ridpath, Minister of Stitchel, 1755–1761*, (ed.), J. B. Paul (Edinburgh, 1922).

Rinuccini, Alamanno, 'De Libertate' (ed. and transl.), R. N. Watkins in *Humanism and Liberty: Writings on Freedom in Fifteenth-Century Florence* (Columbia, SC, 1978), pp. 193–223.

Robertson, Thomas, *The History of Mary Queen of Scots* (Edinburgh, 1793).

Robertson, William, *An Historical Disquisition Concerning the Knowledge Which the Ancients Had of India* (Dublin, 1791).

Robertson, William, *The History of America*, 2 vols (London, 1777).

Robertson, William, *The History of Scotland*, 2 vols (London, 1759).

Robertson, William, *History of the Reign of the Emperor Charles V*, 2 vols (Dublin, 1762).

Robertson, William, *The Situation of the World at the Time of Christ's Appearance*, 3rd edn (Edinburgh, 1759).

Ross, Alexander, *The History of the World – The Second Part in Six Books* (London, 1652).

Ross, Alexander, *The Marrow of Historie* (London, 1650).

Ross, Alexander, *Mystagogus Pedagogus, or The Muses Interpreter*, 2nd edn (London, 1648).

Ross, Alexander, *Som Animadversions and Observations upon Sir Walter Raleigh's Historie of the World* (London, 1648).

Row, John, *The History of the Kirk of Scotland* (Edinburgh, 1842).

Ruddiman, Thomas, *An Answer to the Reverend Mr. George Logan's Late Treatise on Government* (Edinburgh, 1747).

Ruddiman, Thomas, *Dissertation Concerning the Competition for the Crown of Scotland* (Edinburgh, 1748).

Rule, Gilbert, *A Vindication of the Church of Scotland* (Edinburgh, 1691).

Rutherford, Samuel, *Lex Rex: The Law and the Prince* (London, 1644).

Scott, David, *The History of Scotland* (London, 1727).

Scot, Sir John of Scotstarvet, *The Staggering State of the Scots Statesmen* (ed.), W. Ruddiman (Edinburgh, 1754).

Scott, Sir Walter, *Tales of My Landlord*, 3rd ser. (Edinburgh, 1819).

Scott, Sir Walter, *The Waverley Novels*, 12 vols (Edinburgh, 1819).

Scott, Sir Walter, *Waverley; or, 'Tis Sixty Years Since* (ed.), C. Lamont (Oxford, 1986).

Scott, Walter, *A True Historie of Several Honourable Families of the Name of Scot*, 2 pts (Edinburgh, 1776).

The Sevin Seages (ed. and transl.), J. Rolland (Edinburgh, 1578).

Shaftesbury, Lord, *Characteristicks of Men, Manners, Opinions, Times,* 2nd edn 3 vols
([ ], 1714).

Shaw, Lachlan, *The History of the Province of Moray* (Edinburgh, 1775).

Shields, Alexander, *Hind Let Loose: or, an Historical Representation of the Testimonies
of the Church of Scotland* ([Amsterdam], 1687).

A Short History of the Late Rebellion, And of the Conduct of Divine Providence
(Edinburgh, [1716])

Sibbald, Sir Robert, *Historical Inquiries Concerning the Roman Monuments and
Antiquities of Scotland* (Edinburgh, 1707).

Sinclair, George, *The Principles of Astronomy and Navigation* (Edinburgh, 1688).

Sinclair, George, *Satan's Invisible World Discovered* (Edinburgh, 1685).

Skinner, John, *An Ecclesiastical History of Scotland* (London, 1788).

Smellie, William, *Literary and Characteristical Lives of John Gregory, Lord Kames,
David Hume, and Adam Smith* (Edinburgh, 1800).

Smith, Adam, *An Inquiry into the Nature and Causes of the Wealth of Nations,* 2 vols
(London, 1776).

Smith Adam, *The Theory of Moral Sentiments,* 4th edn (London, 1774).

Smith Adam, *Works of Adam Smith* (ed.), D. Stewart, 6 vols (Edinburgh, 1811–12).

Smollett, Tobias, *The Expedition of Humphry Clinker* (ed.), L. M. Knapp (London,
1966).

Somerville, Thomas, *The History of Political Transactions* (London, 1792).

Somerville, Thomas, *My Own Life and Times* (Edinburgh, 1861).

Spotswood, John, *History of the Church of Scotland* (London, 1655).

Stair, Viscount, *Institutions of the Law of Scotland* (Edinburgh, 1681).

Stevenson, Andrew, *The History of the Church and State of Scotland,* 3 vols
(Edinburgh, 1753–7).

Stewart, Dugald, 'Dissertation Exhibiting a General View of the Progress of
Metaphysical, Ethical, and Political Philosophy, Since the Revival of Letters in
Europe', *Supplement to the 4th, 5th, and 6th Editions of the Encyclopaedia
Britannica* (Edinburgh, 1815–24), I, 1–166, and V, 1–257.

Stewart, Duncan, *A Short Historical and Genealogical Account of the Royal Family of
Scotland* (Edinburgh, 1739).

Stuart, Gilbert, *An Historical Dissertation Concerning the Antiquity of the English
Constitution* (Edinburgh, 1768).

Stuart, Gilbert, *The History of Scotland from the Establishment of the Reformation Till
the Death of Queen Mary,* 2 vols (London, 1782).

Stuart, Gilbert, *The History of the Establishment of the Reformation of Religion in
Scotland* (London, 1780).

Stuart, Gilbert, *Observations Concerning the Public Law and Constitutional History of
Scotland* (Edinburgh, 1779).

Stuart, Gilbert, *A View of Society in Europe in its Progress from Rudeness to
Refinement* (Edinburgh, 1782).

Surgundo (ed.), C. K. Sharpe (Edinburgh, 1837).

Symson, David, *A Genealogical and Historical Account of the Illustrious Name of
Stuart* (Edinburgh, 1712).

Thomson, George, 'The Antiquity of the Christian Religion Among the Scots' (ed.
and transl.), H. D. G. Law, *Miscellany of the Scottish History Society* (Edinburgh,
1904), II, 117–32.

A Trewe Description of the Nobill Race of the Stewards (Amsterdam, 1603).

Turnbull, George, *Observations upon Liberal Education* (London, 1742).

Turnbull, George, *A Treatise on Ancient Painting* (London, 1740).

Virtue, Learning and the Scottish Enlightenment

Turner, Sir James, *Pallas Armata: Military Essayes on the Ancient Grecian, Roman, and Modern Art of War* (London, 1683).

Tyler, Alexander, *Memoires of the Life and Actions of Johne King of Poland* (Edinburgh, 1685).

Tytler, Alexander, *Plan and Outline of a Course of Lectures on Universal History, Ancient and Modern* (Edinburgh, 1782).

Tytler, William, *An Historical and Critical Enquiry into the Evidence Against Mary Queen of Scots* (Edinburgh, 1769).

Urquhart, Sir Thomas, *Tracts* (ed.), G. Paton (Edinburgh, 1774).

Valla, Lorenzo, *De Rebus a Ferdinando Aragonaie Rege Gestis Libri Tres* (Rome, 1520).

Wallace, George, *The Nature and Descent of Ancient Peerages* (Edinburgh, 1785).

Wallace, George, *Thoughts on the Origin of Feudal Tenures* (Edinburgh, 1783).

Wallace, James (I), *A Description of the Isles of Orkney* (Edinburgh, 1693).

Wallace, James (II), *The History of Scotland* (Dublin, 1724).

Wallace, Robert, *Dissertation on the Numbers of Mankind in Antient and Modern Times* (Edinburgh, 1753).

[Wallace, Robert], *Various Prospects of Mankind, Nature, and Providence* (London, 1761).

Watson, James, *A Choice Collection of Comic and Serious Scots Poems Both Ancient and Modern*, 3 vols (Edinburgh, 1706–11).

Watson, James, *The History of the Art of Printing* (Edinburgh, 1713).

Watson, Robert, *The History of the Reign of Phillip the Second, King of Spain*, 2 vols (Dublin, 1777).

[Wedderburn, Robert], *The Complaynt of Scotland* (ed.), J. Leyden (Edinburgh, 1801).

Wight, Alexander, *A Treatise on the Laws Concerning the Election of the Different Representatives of Scotland to the Parliament of Great Britain* (Edinburgh, 1773).

Wight, William, *Heads of a Course of Lectures on the Study of History* (Glasgow, 1767).

Wight, William, *Heads of Lectures on the Study of Civil History* (Glasgow, 1772).

Williams, John, *An Account of Some Remarkable Ancient Ruins Lately Discovered in the Highlands and Northern Parts of Scotland* (Edinburgh, 1777).

Wishart, George, *The History of the King's Majesties Affaires in Scotland* ([ ], 1649).

Witherspoon, John, *The History of a Corporation of Servants Discovered A Few Years Ago in the Interior Parts of South America* (Edinburgh, 1765).

Wodrow, Robert, *Analecta; Or, Materials for a History of Remarkable Providences; Mostly Relating to Scotch Ministers and Christians*, 4 vols (Edinburgh, 1842).

Wodrow, Robert, *The History of the Sufferings of the Church of Scotland*, 4 vols (Glasgow, 1828).

Wright, William, *The Comical History of the Marriage Betwixt Fergusia and Heptarchus* (Edinburgh, 1717).

Young, Edward, *A Vindication of Providence*, 2nd edn (Berkeley, Calif., 1984).

Printed Secondary Literature (from 1830)

Anderson, J., *Sir Walter Scott and History* (Edinburgh, 1981).

Armstrong, B., *Calvinism and the Amyraut Heresy: Protestant Scholasticism and Humanism in Seventeenth-Century France* (Madison, Wisc., 1969).

Ash, M., *The Strange Death of Scottish History* (Edinburgh, 1980).

Bagehot, W., *Collected Works* (ed.), N. St John-Stevas 6 vols (London, 1965).

Baron, H., 'Calvinist Republicanism and its Historical Roots', *Church History*, 8 (1939), 30–42.

Baron, H., *In Search of Florentine Civic Humanism*, 2 vols (Princeton, NJ, 1988).

Barrow, G. W. S., 'The Idea of Freedom in Late Medieval Scotland', *Innes Review*, 30 (1979), 16–34.

Bauer, L. and Matis, H., 'From Moral Philosophy to Political Economy: The Genesis of Social Science', *History of European Ideas*, 9 (1988), 123–43.

Beales, D., 'Christians and *philosophes*: The Case of the Austrian Enlightenment', in his and G. Best (eds), *History, Society, and the Churches. Essays in Honour of Owen Chadwick* (Cambridge, 1985), pp. 169–94.

Becker, C., *The Heavenly City of the Eighteenth-Century Philosophers* (New Haven, Conn., 1932).

Bell, A. (ed.), *Scott Bicentenary Essays* (Edinburgh, 1973).

Bell, M. C., *Calvin and Scottish Theology* (Edinburgh, 1985).

Berens, J. F., *Providence and Patriotism in Early America*, 1640–1815 (Charlottesville, Va., 1978).

Berry, C. J., 'Adam Smith's *Considerations* on Language', *Journal of the History of Ideas*, 35 (1974), 130–8.

Berry, C. J., 'The Nature of Wealth and the Origins of Virtue', *History of European Ideas*, 7 (1986), 85–99.

Bevan, J., 'Seventeenth-Century Students and their Books', in G. Donaldson (ed.), *Four Centuries: Edinburgh University Life*, 1583–1983 (Edinburgh, 1984), pp. 16–27.

Black, J. B., *The Art of History: A Study of Four Great Historians of the Eighteenth Century* (London, 1926).

Blanning, T. C. W., 'The Enlightenment in Catholic Germany', in R. Porter and M. Teich (eds), *The Enlightenment in National Context* (Cambridge, 1981), pp. 118–26.

Bloch, M., *The Historian's Craft*, (ed. and transl.), P. Putnam (Manchester, 1984).

Bolgar, R. R., *The Classical Inheritance and its Beneficiaries* (Cambridge, 1973).

Bransford, V. V. 'The Patriotic Historians of Scotland', *Macmillans Magazine*, 76 (1897), 268–78.

Broadie, A., 'Continuity of Scottish Philosophy', *Cencrastus*, 25 (1987), 6–7.

Broadie, A., *The Tradition of Scottish Philosophy* (Edinburgh, 1990).

Broadie, A., 'William Manderston and Patrick Hamilton on Freewill and Grace', *Innes Review*, 37 (1986), 25–35.

Brown, I. G., *The Clerks of Penicuik: Portraits of Taste and Talent* (Edinburgh, 1987).

Brown, I. G., 'Critick in Antiquity: Sir John Clerk of Penicuik', *Antiquity*, 51 (1977), 201–10.

Brown, J. M., 'Taming the Magnates?', in G. Menzies (ed.), *The Scottish Nation* (London, 1972), pp. 46–59.

Brown, K. M., *Bloodfeud in Scotland*, 1573–1625: *Violence, Justice, and Politics in an Early Modern Society* (Edinburgh, 1986).

Bryson, G., *Man and Society: The Scottish Enquiry of the Eighteenth Century* (Princeton, NJ, 1945).

Buckle, H. T., *On Scotland and the Scotch Intellect* (ed.), H. J. Hanham (Chicago, 1970).

Burns, J. H., 'The Conciliarist Tradition in Scotland', *Scottish Historical Review*, 42 (1963), 89–104.

Cameron, J. K., 'The Church of Scotland in the Age of Reason', *Studies on Voltaire and the Eighteenth Century*, 58 (1967), 1939–51.

Cameron, J. K., 'Humanism and Religious Life', in J. MacQueen (ed.), *Humanism in Renaissance Scotland* (Edinburgh, 1990), pp. 161–77.

Cameron, J. K., 'Theological Controversy: A Factor in the Origins of the Scottish

Enlightenment', in R. H. Campbell and A. S. Skinner, (eds.), *The Origins and Nature of the Scottish Enlightenment* (Edinburgh, 1982), pp. 116–30.

Camic, C., *Experience and Enlightenment: Socialization for Cultural Change in Eighteenth-Century Scotland* (Edinburgh, 1983).

Camic, C., 'Experience and Ideas: Education for Universalism in Eighteenth-Century Scotland', *Comparative Studies in Society and History*, 25 (1983), 52–82.

Campbell, J., 'John Anderson, Minister of Dumbarton, and of the Ramshorn Kirk, Glasgow, 1698–1721', *Records of the Scottish Church History Society*, 9 (1947), 155–65.

Campbell, R. H. and Skinner, A. S. (eds), *The Origins and Nature of the Scottish Enlightenment* (Edinburgh, 1982).

Campbell, W. M., *The Triumph of Presbyterianism* (Edinburgh, 1958).

Cant, R. G., 'Origins of the Enlightenment in Scotland: The Universities', in R. H. Campbell and A. S. Skinner (eds), *The Origins and Nature Of the Scottish Enlightenment* (Edinburgh, 1982), pp. 42–64.

Cant, R. G., 'The Scottish Universities and Scottish Society in the Eighteenth Century', *Studies on Voltaire and the Eighteenth Century*, 58 (1967), 1953–66.

Carnie, R. H., 'Scottish Presbyterian Eloquence and *Old Mortality*', *Scottish Literary Journal*, 3 (1976), 51–61.

Carter, J. J. and Pittock, J. H. (eds), *Aberdeen and the Enlightenment* (Aberdeen, 1987).

Cassirer, E., *The Philosophy of the Enlightenment* (Princeton, NJ, 1951).

Charters, L., *Catalogues of Scotish Writers* (ed.), J. Maidment, (Edinburgh, 1833).

Cherno, M., 'John Knox as an Innovator in Historiographic Narration', *Clio*, 8 (1979), 389–403.

Chitnis, A. C., 'The 18th Century Intellectual Enquiry', *Cencrastus*, 25 (1987), 9–11.

Chitnis, A. C., 'The Eighteenth-Century Scottish Intellectual Inquiry: Context and Continuity versus Civic Humanism', in J. J. Carter and J. H. Pittock (eds), *Aberdeen and the Enlightenment* (Aberdeen, 1987), pp. 79–92.

Chitnis, A. C., *The Scottish Enlightenment* (London, 1976).

Chitnis, A. C., *The Scottish Enlightenment and Early Victorian English Society* (London, 1986).

Christensen, J., *Practicing Enlightenment. Hume and the Formation of a Literary Career* (Madison, Wisc., 1987).

Christie, G., 'James Durham as Courtier and Preacher', *Records of the Scottish Church History Society*, 4 (1932), 66–80.

Christie, G., 'Scriptural Exposition in Scotland in the Seventeenth Century', *Records of the Scottish Church History Society*, 1 (1926), 97–111.

Christie, J. R. R., 'The Origins and Development of the Scottish Scientific Community, 1680–1760', *History of Science*, 7 (1974), 122–41.

Clark, I. D. L., 'From Protest to Reaction: the Moderate Regime in the Church of Scotland, 1752–1805', in N. T. Phillipson and R. Mitchison (eds), *Scotland in the Age of Improvement* (Edinburgh, 1970), pp. 200–24.

Clark, J. C. D., *English Society, 1688–1832: Ideology, Social Structure, and Political Practice during the* Ancien Régime (Cambridge, 1985).

Clark, J. C. D., *Revolution and Rebellion. State and Society in England in the Seventeenth and Eighteenth Centuries* (Cambridge, 1986).

Clive, J., 'The Social Background of the Scottish Renaissance', in N. T. Phillipson and R. Mitchison (eds), *Scotland in the Age of Improvement* (Edinburgh, 1970), pp. 225–44.

Clive, J. and Bailyn, B., 'England's Cultural Provinces: Scotland and America', *William and Mary Quarterly*, 11 (1954), 200–13.

Collini, S., Winch, D. and Burrow, J., *That Noble Science of Politics: A Study in Nineteenth-Century Intellectual History* (Cambridge, 1983).

Conrad, S. A., *Citizenship and Common Sense: The Problem of Authority in the Social Background and Social Philosophy of the Wise Club of Aberdeen* (New York, 1987).

Couper, W. J., 'Robert Wodrow', *Records of the Scottish Church History Society*, 3 (1929), 112–34.

Cowan, E. J., 'Myth and Identity in Early Medieval Scotland', *Scottish Historical Review*, 63 (1984), 111–35.

Craig, C. (gen. ed.), *History of Scottish Literature*, 4 vols (Aberdeen, 1987).

Craik, Sir H., *A Century of Scottish History: From the Days Before the '45 to Those Within Living Memory* (Edinburgh, 1911).

Daiches, D., *The Paradox of Scottish Culture: The Eighteenth-Century Experience* (London, 1964).

Daiches, D., 'Style Périodique and Style Coupé: Hugh Blair and the Scottish Rhetoric of American Independence', in R. Sher and J. R. Smitten (eds), *Scotland and America in the Age of the Enlightenment* (Edinburgh, 1990), pp. 209–26.

Daiches, D., Jones, P. and Jones, J. (eds), *A Hotbed of Genius. The Scottish Enlightenment, 1730–1790* (Edinburgh, 1986).

Davie, G. E., *The Democratic Intellect: Scotland and Her Universities in the Nineteenth Century* (Edinburgh, 1961).

Davie, G. E., *The Scottish Enlightenment* (London, 1981).

Devine, T. M., 'The Scottish Merchant Community, 1680–1740', in R. H. Campbell and A. S. Skinner (eds), *The Origins and Nature of the Scottish Enlightenment* (Edinburgh, 1982), pp. 26–41.

Donagan, B., 'Providence, Chance, and Explanation: Some Paradoxical Aspects of Puritan Views of Causation', *Journal of Religious History*, 11 (1981), 385–403.

Donaldson, G., 'The Polity of the Scottish Church, 1560–1600', *Records of the Scottish Church History Society*, 11 (1955), 212–26.

Donaldson, G., 'Stair's Scotland: The Intellectual Heritage', *Juridical Review* (1981), 128–45.

Drummond, A. L. and Bulloch, J., *The Scottish Church, 1688–1843: The Age of the Moderates* (Edinburgh, 1973).

Duke, J. A., *History of the Church of Scotland to the Reformation* (Edinburgh, 1937).

Dunlop, E. and Kamm, A. (eds), *A Book of Old Edinburgh* (Edinburgh, 1983).

Dunn, J., 'The Identity of the History of Ideas', *Philosophy*, 43 (1968), 85–104.

Durkan, J., 'The Beginnings of Humanism in Scotland', *Innes Review*, 4 (1953), 5–24.

Durkan, J., 'The Cultural Background in Sixteenth-Century Scotland', in D. MacRoberts (ed.), *Essays on the Scottish Reformation* (Glasgow, 1962), pp. 274–331.

Durkan, J., 'Giovanni Ferrerio and Religious Humanism in Sixteenth-Century Scotland', *Studies in Church History*, 17 (1981), 181–94.

Dwyer, J., 'The Imperative of Sociability: Moral Culture in the Late Scottish Enlightenment', *British Journal of Eighteenth Century Studies*, 13 (1990), 169–84.

Dwyer, J., *Virtuous Discourse: Sensibility and Community in Late Eighteenth-Century Scotland* (Edinburgh, 1987).

Dwyer, J. and Murdoch, A. (eds), *New Perspectives on the Politics and Culture of Early Modern Scotland* (Edinburgh, 1982).

Edwards, O. D. and Richardson, G. (eds), *Edinburgh* (Edinburgh, 1983).

Emerson, R. L., 'Conjectural History and the Scottish Philosophers', *Canadian Historical Association Historical Papers* (1984), 63–90.

Emerson, R. L., 'The Edinburgh Society for the Importation of Foreign Seeds and Plants, 1764–1773', *Eighteenth Century Life*, 7 (1982), 73–95.

Emerson, R. L., 'The Enlightenment and Social Structure', in P. Fritz and D. Williams (eds), *City and Society in the Eighteenth Century* (Toronto, 1973), pp. 99–124.

Emerson R. L., 'Natural Philosophy and the Problem of the Scottish Enlightenment', *Studies on Voltaire and the Eighteenth Century*, 242 (1986), 243–92.

Emerson, R. L., 'Peter Gay and the Heavenly City', *Journal of the History of Ideas*, 28 (1967), 383–402.

Emerson, R. L., 'The Philosophical Society of Edinburgh, 1737–1747', *British Journal for the History of Science*, 12 (1979), 154–91.

Emerson, R. L., 'The Philosophical Society of Edinburgh, 1748–1768', *British Journal for the History of Science*, 14 (1981), 133–76.

Emerson, R. L., 'The Philosophical Society of Edinburgh, 1768–1783', *British Journal for the History of Science*, 18 (1985), 255–303.

Emerson, R. L., *Professors, Patronage and Politics: The Aberdeen Universities in the Eighteenth Century* (Aberdeen, 1992).

Emerson, R. L., 'Science and the Origins and Concerns of the Scottish Enlightenment', *History of Science*, 26 (1988), 333–66.

Emerson, R. L., 'The Scottish Enlightenment and the End of the Philosophical Society of Edinburgh', *British Journal for the History of Science*, 21 (1988), 33–66.

Emerson, R. L., 'Scottish Universities in the Eighteenth Century, 1690–1800', *Studies on Voltaire and the Eighteenth Century*, 167 (1977), 453–74.

Emerson, R. L., 'Sir Robert Sibbald, Kt., the Royal Society of Scotland, and the Origins of the Scottish Enlightenment', *Annals of Science*, 45 (1988), 41–72.

Emerson, R. L., 'The Social Composition of Enlightened Scotland: the "Select Society of Edinburgh", 1754–1764', *Studies on Voltaire and the Eighteenth Century*, 114 (1973), 291–330.

Fearnley-Sander, M., 'Philosophical History and the Scottish Reformation: William Robertson and the Knoxian Tradition', *Historical Journal*, 33 (1990), 323–38.

Fermia, J. V., 'An Historicist Critique of "Revisionist" Methods for Studying the History of Ideas', in J. Tully, (ed.), *Meaning and Context. Quentin Skinner and His Critics* (Oxford, 1988), pp. 156–75.

Figgis, J. N., *Studies of Political Thought: From Gerson to Grotius, 1414–1625* (Cambridge, 1907).

Finlayson, M. G., 'Clarendon, Providence, and the Historial Revolution', *Albion*, 22 (1990), 607–32.

Flew, A., *David Hume: Philosopher of Moral Science* (Oxford, 1986).

Flew, A., 'From ... The Virtue of Selfishness to the Invisible Hand', *Focus*, 1 (1980), 21–30.

Fontana, B., *Rethinking the Politics of Commercial Society. The Edinburgh Review, 1802–1832* (Cambridge, 1985).

Forbes, D., 'Scientific Whiggism: Adam Smith and John Millar', *Cambridge Journal*, 7 (1954), 643–70.

Formigari, L., 'Language and Society in the Late Eighteenth Century', *Journal of the History of Ideas*, 35 (1974), 275–92.

Franklin, J. H., *Jean Bodin and the Sixteenth-Century Revolution in the Methodology of Law and History* (Columbia, NY, 1963).

Fraser, H., *Conflict and Class: Scottish Workers, 1700–1838* (Edinburgh, 1988).

Froude, J. A., 'The Influence of the Reformation on the Scottish Character', in his *Short Studies on Great Subjects*, 2 vols (London, 1867), I, 146–77.

Fry, M., 'The Whig Interpretation of Scottish History', in I. Donnachie and C. Whateley (eds), *The Manufacture of Scottish History* (Edinburgh, 1992), pp. 72–89.

Galloway, B., *The Union of England and Scotland, 1603–1608* (Edinburgh, 1986).

Garrett, J., *The Triumphs of Providence: The Assassination Plot*, 1696 (Cambridge, 1980).

Gatter, F. L., 'On the Literary Value of Some Scottish Presbyterian Writings in the Context of the Scottish Enlightenment', in D. Strauss and H. Drescher (eds), *Scottish Language and Literature, Medieval and Renaissance* (Frankfurt, 1986), pp. 175–92.

Gay, P., *The Enlightenment*, 2 vols (New York, 1966–9).

Gearhart, S., *The Open Boundary of History and Fiction. A Critical Approach to the French Enlightenment* (Princeton, NJ, 1984).

Gibson, J. S., 'How did the Enlightenment seem to the Edinburgh Enlightened?', *British Journal of Eighteenth Century Studies*, 1 (1978), 46–50.

Goldie, M., 'Obligations, Utopias, and their Historical Context', *Historical Journal*, 26 (1983), 727–46.

Goldie, M., 'The Roots of True Whiggism, 1688–1694', *History of Political Thought*, 2 (1980), 195–236.

Graham, H. G., *Scottish Men of Letters in the Eighteenth Century* (London, 1901).

Grant, A. H., 'Earls and earldoms in late medieval Scotland, c. 1310–1460', in J. Bossy and P. Jupp (eds), *Essays Presented to Michael Roberts* (Belfast, 1976), pp. 24–40.

Grassi, E., *Rhetoric as Philosophy: The Humanist Tradition* (London, 1980).

Gray, H. H., 'Renaissance Humanism: The Pursuit of Eloquence', *Journal of the History of Ideas*, 24 (1963), 497–514.

Gray, J. R., 'The Political Theory of John Knox', *Church History*, 8 (1939), 132–47.

Griffiths, O. M., *Religion and Learning: A Study in English Presbyterian Thought* (Cambridge, 1935).

Haakonssen, K., *The Science of a Legislator: The Natural Jurisprudence of David Hume and Adam Smith* (Cambridge, 1981).

Hale, J. R., *The Evolution of British Historiography* (London, 1967).

Hamowy, R., *The Scottish Enlightenment and the Theory of Spontaneous Order* (Carbondale, Ill., 1987).

Hay, D., 'Scotland and the Italian Renaissance', I. B. Cowan and D. Shaw (eds), *The Renaissance and Reformation in Scotland* (Edinburgh, 1983), pp. 114–24.

Hayek, F. A., 'Kinds of Rationalism', in his *Studies in Philosophy, Politics, and Economics* (Chicago, 1967), pp. 82–95.

Hayek, F. A., 'The Use of Knowledge in Society', in his *Individualism and the Economic Order* (London, 1949), pp. 77–91.

Healey, R. M., 'The Preaching Ministry in Scotland's *First Book of Discipline*', *Church History*, lviii (1989), 339–53.

Henderson, G. D., *The Burning Bush: Studies in Scottish Church History* (Edinburgh, 1957).

Henderson, G. D., 'John Knox and the Bible', *Records of the Scottish Church History Society*, 9 (1947), 97–110.

Henderson, G. D., *Presbyterianism* (Aberdeen, 1954).

Henderson, G. D., *Religious Life in Seventeenth-Century Scotland* (Cambridge, 1937).

Hirschmann, A. O., *The Passions and the Interests. Political Arguments for Capitalism Before its Triumph* (Princeton, NJ, 1977).

Hoeveler, J. D., *James McCosh and the Scottish Intellectual Tradition* (Princeton, NJ, 1981).

Hollinger, D. A., 'Historians and the Discourse of Intellectuals', in J. Higham and P. K. Conkin (eds), *New Directions in American Intellectual History* (Baltimore, Md., 1979), pp. 42–63.

Hont, I. and Ignatieff, M. (eds), *Wealth and Virtue: The Shaping of Political Economy in the Scottish Enlightenment* (Cambridge, 1983).

Höpfl, H., 'From Savage to Scotsman: Conjectural History in the Scottish Enlightenment', *Journal of British Studies*, 17 (1978), 19–40.

Horn, D. B., *A Short History of the University of Edinburgh, 1556–1889* (Edinburgh, 1967).

Horn, D. B., 'Some Scottish Writers of History in the Eighteenth Century', *Scottish Historical Review*, 40 (1961), 1–18.

Horn, D. B., 'University of Edinburgh and the Teaching of History', *University of Edinburgh Journal*, 17 (1953–4), 161–72.

Howe, D. W., 'Why the Scottish Enlightenment was Useful to the Framers of the American Constitution', *Comparative Studies in Society and History*, 31 (1989), 572–87.

Hutchison, H., 'An Eighteenth-Century Insight into Religious and Moral Education', *British Journal of Educational Studies*, 24 (1976), 233–41.

Hutchison, T., *Before Adam Smith: The Emergence of Political Economy, 1662–1776* (Oxford, 1988).

Jack, R. D. S., *The Italian Influence on Scottish Literature* (Edinburgh, 1972).

Johnston, G. P., 'The First Edition of Hume of Godscroft's History', *Papers of the Edinburgh Bibliographical Society*, 4 (1901), 149–71.

Jones, P., 'The Polite Academy and the Presbyterians, 1729–1770', in J. Dwyer and A. Murdoch (eds), *New Perspectives on the Politics and Culture of Early Modern Scotland* (Edinburgh, 1982), pp. 156–78.

Jones, P., 'The Scottish Professoriate and the Polite Academy, 1720–1746', in I. Hont and M. Ignatieff (eds), *Wealth and Virtue: The Shaping of Political Economy in the Scottish Enlightenment* (Cambridge, 1983), pp. 89–117.

Jones, R. V., 'Physical Science in the Eighteenth Century', *British Journal of Eighteenth Century Studies*, 2 (1978), 73–88.

Joyce, M., *Edinburgh: The Golden Age, 1769–1832* (London, 1951).

Katona, A., 'The Impact of Sir Walter Scott in Hungary', in A. Bell (ed.), *Scott Bicentenary Essays* (Edinburgh, 1973), pp. 271–83.

Kelley, D. R., *Foundations of Modern Historical Scholarship: Language, Law, and History in the French Renaissance* (Columbia, NY, 1970).

Kennedy, W. J., *Rhetorical Norms in Renaissance Literature* (New Haven, Conn., 1978).

Kettler, D., *The Social and Political Thought of Adam Ferguson* (Columbus, Ohio, 1965).

Kinghorn, A. M., *The Chorus of History 1485–1558: Literary-Historical Relations in Renaissance Britain* (London, 1971).

Kratzmann, G., *Anglo-Scottish Literary Relations, 1430–1550* (Cambridge, 1980).

Kuehn, M., *Scottish Common Sense in Germany, 1768–1800: A Contribution to the History of Critical Philosophy* (Kingston, Ont., 1987).

Kyle, R., 'John Knox's Concept of Divine Providence', *Albion*, 18 (1986), 395–410.

Kyle, R., 'John Knox's Concept of History: A Focus on the Providential and Apocalyptic Aspects of His Religious Faith', *Fides et Historia*, 18 (1986), 5–19.

Lachman, D. C., *The Marrow Controversy* (Edinburgh, 1988).

Landsman, N. C., 'Witherspoon and the Problem of Provincial Identity in Scottish Evangelical Culture', in R. Sher and J. R. Smitten (eds), *Scotland and America in the Age of the Enlightenment* (Edinburgh, 1990), pp. 29–45.

Laurie, H., *Scottish Philosophy in its National Development* (Glasgow, 1902).

Law, A., *Education in Edinburgh in the Eighteenth Century* (London, 1965).

Leff, G., *History and Social Theory* (London, 1969).

Lehmann, W. C., *Adam Ferguson and the Beginnings of Modern Sociology* (New York, 1930).

Lehmann, W. C., *John Millar of Glasgow, 1735–1801: His Life and Thought and His Contributions to Sociological Analysis* (Cambridge, 1960).

Leigh, R. A., 'Rousseau and the Scottish Enlightenment', *Contributions to Political Economy*, 5 (1986), 1–21.

Levine, J., *Humanism and History: Origins of Modern English Historiography* (Ithaca, NY, 1987).

Lewis, C. S., *English Literature in the Sixteenth Century* (Oxford, 1954).

Lough, J., 'Reflections on Enlightenment and Lumières', *British Journal of Eighteenth Century Studies*, 8 (1985), 1–15.

Lyall, R. J., 'Politics and Poetry in Fifteenth and Sixteenth-Century Scotland', *Scottish Literary Journal*, 3 (1976), 5–29.

Lynch, M., 'Calvinism in Scotland, 1559–1638', in M. Prestwich (ed.), *International Calvinism, 1541–1715* (Oxford, 1985), pp. 225–55.

Lynch, M., *Scotland: A New History* (London, 1991).

MacCallum, N., *A Small Country: Scotland 1700–1830* (Edinburgh, 1983).

McCosh, J., *The Scottish Philosophy: Biographical, Expository, Critical, From Hutcheson to Hamilton* (London, 1875).

MacElroy, D. D., *Scotland's Age of Improvement* (Washington, DC, 1969).

MacIntyre, A., *After Virtue. A Study in Moral Theory* (London, 1981).

Mackenzie, A. M., *Scotland in Modern Times, 1720–1939* (London, 1941).

Mackie, J. B., *The University of Glasgow, 1451–1951* (Glasgow, 1954).

MacLeod, J., *Scottish Theology* (Edinburgh, 1943).

MacNeill, J. T., *The History and Character of Calvinism* (New York, 1954).

Macpherson, H., 'Alexander Shields, 1660–1700', *Records of the Scottish Church History Society*, 3 (1929), 55–68.

Macpherson, H., *A Century of Intellectual Development* (Edinburgh, 1907).

Macpherson, H., *The Intellectual Development of Scotland* (London, 1911).

Macpherson, H., 'Political Ideals of the Covenanters, 1660–1688', *Records of the Scottish Church History Society*, 1 (1926), 224–32.

MacQueen, J., 'Aspects of Humanism in Sixteenth and Seventeenth Century Literature', in his (ed.), *Humanism in Renaissance Scotland* (Edinburgh, 1990), pp. 10–31.

MacQueen, J., *The Enlightenment and Scottish Literature: Progress and Poetry* (Edinburgh, 1982).

MacQueen, J., *The Enlightenment and Scottish Literature: The Rise of the Historical Novel* (Edinburgh, 1989).

MacQueen, J., 'John Galt and the Analysis of Social History', in A. Bell (ed.), *Scott Bicentenary Essays* (Edinburgh, 1973), pp. 332–42.

MacQueen, J., 'Some Aspects of the Early Renaissance in Scotland', *Forum for Modern Language Studies*, 3 (1967), 201–22.

Macrae, D. G., 'Adam Ferguson, 1723–1816', in T. Raison (ed.), *The Founding Fathers of Social Science* (Harmondsworth, 1963), pp. 17–26.

Markus, T. A., *Order in Space and Society: Architectural Form and its Context in the Scottish Enlightenment* (Edinburgh, 1982).

Marshall, G., *Presbyteries and Profits: Calvinism and the Development of Capitalism in Scotland, 1560–1707* (Oxford, 1980).

Marwick, A., *The Nature of History* (London, 1981).

Mason, R. A., '*Kingship, Nobility, and Anglo-Scottish Union: John Mair's History of Greater Britain (1521)*', *Innes Review*, 41 (1990), 183–222.

Mason, R. A. (ed.), *Scotland and England: 1286–1815* (Edinburgh, 1987).

Mathieson, W. L., *The Awakening of Scotland. A History from* 1747 *to* 1797 (Glasgow, 1910).

Matthews, W., 'The Egyptians in Scotland: Political History of a Myth', *Viator*, 1 (1970), 289–306.

Maxwell, T., 'The Scotch Presbyterian Eloquence: A Post-Revolution Pamphlet', *Records of the Scottish Church History Society*, 8 (1944), 225–53.

May, H. F., 'The Decline of Providence?', *Studies on Voltaire and the Eighteenth Century*, 154 (1976), 1401–16.

Meek, R. L., 'The Scottish Contribution to Marxist Sociology', in J. Saville (ed.), *Democracy and the Labour Movement* (London, 1954), pp. 84–102.

Meek, R. L., 'Smith, Turgot, and the "Four Stages" Theory', in his *Smith, Marx, and After: Ten Essays in the Development of Economic Thought* (London, 1977), pp. 18–32.

Meek, R. L., *Social Science and the Ignoble Savage* (Cambridge, 1976).

Meikle, H. W., *Scotland and the French Revolution* (Glasgow, 1912).

Meikle, H. W., *Some Aspects of Later Seventeenth-Century Scotland* (Glasgow, 1947).

Merriman, M., 'James Henrisoun and "Great Britain": British Union and the Scottish Commonweal', in R. A. Mason (ed.), *Scotland and England: 1286–1815* (Edinburgh, 1987), pp. 85–112.

Merton, R. K., 'The Unanticipated Consequences of Purposive Social Action', *American Sociological Review*, 1 (1936), 894–904.

Minogue, K., 'Method in Intellectual History: Quentin Skinner's *Foundations' Philosophy*, 56 (1981), 533–52.

Mitchison, R., 'Patriotism and National Identity in Eighteenth-Century Scotland', in T. W. Moody (ed.), *Nationality and the Pursuit of National Independence* (London, 1978), pp. 73–95.

Mitchison, R. (ed.), *Why Scottish History Matters* (Edinburgh, 1991).

Morrell, J. B., 'The University of Edinburgh in the Late Eighteenth Century: Its Scientific Eminence and Academic Structure', *Isis*, 62 (1971), 158–71.

Mossner, E. C., 'Gladys Bryson, "Man and Society"', *Philological Quarterly*, 25 (1946), 136–42.

Nairn, T., *The Break-Up of Britain. Crisis and Neo-Nationalism*, 2nd edn (London, 1981).

Norton, D. F., 'George Turnbull and the Furniture of the Mind', *Journal of the History of Ideas*, 36 (1985), 701–16.

Oakley, F., 'On the Road from Constance to 1688: The Political Thought of John Major and George Buchanan', *Journal of British Studies*, 2 (1962), 1–31.

O'Malley, J. W., 'Content and Rhetorical Forms in Sixteenth-Century Treatises on Preaching', in J. J. Murphy, (ed.), *Renaissance Eloquence: Studies in the Theory and Practice of Renaissance Rhetoric* (Berkeley, Calif., 1983), pp. 238–52.

Pascal, R., 'Property and Society: The Scottish Historical School of the Eighteenth Century', *Modern Quarterly*, 2 (1938), 167–79.

Patrick, J., *Scotland: The Age of Achievement* (London, 1972).

Phillips, M., 'Macaulay, Scott, and the Literary Challenge to Historiography', *Journal of the History of Ideas*, 50 (1989), 117–33.

Phillipson, N. T., 'Adam Smith as Civic Moralist', in I. Hont and M. Ignatieff (eds), *Wealth and Virtue: The Shaping of Political Economy in the Scottish Enlightenment* (Cambridge, 1983), pp. 179–202.

Phillipson, N. T., 'Culture and Society in the Eighteenth-Century Provinces', in L. Stone, (ed.), *The University in Society*, 2 vols (Princeton, NJ, 1975), I, pp. 407–48.

Phillipson, N. T., *Hume* (London, 1989).

Phillipson, N. T., 'Hume as Moralist: A Social Historian's Perspective', in S. Brown (ed.), *Philosophers of the Enlightenment* (Hassocks, Sussex, 1979), pp. 140–61.

Phillipson, N. T., 'James Beattie and the Defence of Common Sense', in B. Fabian (ed.), *Festschrift für Rainer Gruenter* (Heidelberg, 1978), pp. 145–54.

Phillipson, N. T., 'Lawyers, Landowners, and the Civic Leadership of Post-Union Scotland', *Juridical Review* (1976), 97–120.

Phillipson, N. T., 'Nationalism and Ideology', in J. Wolfe (ed.), *Government and Nationalism in Scotland* (Edinburgh, 1969), pp. 167–88.

Phillipson, N. T., 'Politics, Politeness, and the Anglicisation of Early Eighteenth-Century Scottish Culture', in R. A. Mason (ed.), *Scotland and England: 1286–1815* (Edinburgh, 1987), pp. 226–46.

Phillipson, N. T., 'The Scottish Enlightenment', in R. Porter and M. Teich (eds), *The Enlightenment in National Context* (Cambridge, 1981), pp. 19–40.

Phillipson, N. T., 'Towards a Definition of the Scottish Enlightenment', in P. Fritz and D. Williams (eds), *City and Society in the Eighteenth Century* (Toronto, 1973), pp. 125–48.

Phillipson, N. T., 'Virtue, Commerce, and the Science of Man', *Studies on Voltaire and the Eighteenth Century*, 190 (1980), 750–2.

Phillipson, N. T. and Mitchison, R. (eds), *Scotland in the Age of Improvement* (Edinburgh, 1970).

Piggott, S., 'Antiquarian Thought in the Sixteenth and Seventeenth Centuries', in L. Fox (ed.), *English Historical Scholarship in the Sixteenth and Seventeenth Centuries* (London, 1956), pp. 93–114.

Piggott, S., *Ruins in A Landscape: Essays in Antiquarianism* (Edinburgh, 1976).

Pocock, J. G. A., *The Ancient Constitution and the Feudal Law* (Cambridge, 1957).

Pocock, J. G. A., *The Machiavellian Moment: Florentine Political Thought and the Atlantic Republican Tradition* (Princeton, NJ, 1975).

Pocock, J. G. A., 'Post-Puritan England and the Problem of the Enlightenment', in P. Zagorin (ed.), *Culture and Politics from Puritanism to the Enlightenment* (Berkeley, Calif., 1980), pp. 91–111.

Pocock, J. G. A., 'Texts as Events: Reflections on the History of Political Thought', in K. Sharpe and S. N. Zwicker (eds), *Politics of Discourse: The Literature and History of Seventeenth-Century England* (Berkeley, Calif., 1987), pp. 21–34.

Pocock, J. G. A., *Virtue, Commerce, and History: Essays on Political Thought, Chiefly in the Eighteenth Century* (Cambridge, 1985).

Pocock, J. G. A., 'Virtue, Rights, and Manners: A Model for Historians of Political Thought', *Political Theory*, 9 (1981), 353–68.

Pollard, S., *The Idea of Progress: History and Society* (Harmondsworth, 1968).

Pomeroy, R. S., 'Locke, Alembert, and the anti-rhetoric of the "Enlightenment"', *Studies on Voltaire and the Eighteenth Century*, 154 (1976), 1657–75.

Porter, R. and Teich, M. (eds), *The Enlightenment in National Context* (Cambridge, 1981).

Prestwich, M., *International Calvinism*, 1541–1715 (Oxford, 1985).

Price, J. V., 'Concepts of Enlightenment in Eighteenth-Century Scottish Literature', *Texas Studies in Literature and Language*, 9 (1967), 371–9.

[Pringle-Pattison, A. S.], *Scottish Philosophy: A Comparison of the Scottish and German Answers to Hume*, 2nd edn (Edinburgh, 1890).

Purves, J., 'First Knowledge of Machiavelli in Scotland', *La Rinascita*, 1 (1938), 139–42.

Rae, T. I., 'The Scottish Antiquarian Tradition', *Abertay Historical Society Publications*, 16 (1972), 12–25.

Rawson, E., *The Spartan Tradition in European Thought* (Oxford, 1969).

Reid, D., *The Party-Coloured Mind: Prose Relating to the Conflict of Church and State in Seventeenth-Century Scotland* (Edinburgh, 1982).

Rendall, J., *The Origins of the Scottish Enlightenment* (London, 1978).

Rendall, J., 'Scottish Orientalism: from Robertson to James Mill', *Historical Journal*, 25 (1982), 43–69.

Robertson, J., 'Andrew Fletcher's Vision of Union', in R. A. Mason (ed.), *Scotland and England: 1286–1815* (Edinburgh, 1987), pp. 203–25.

Robertson, J., 'The Legacy of Adam Smith: Government and Economic Development in the *Wealth of Nations*', in R. Bellamy (ed.), *Victorian Liberalism: Nineteenth-Century Political Thought and Practice* (London, 1990), pp. 15–41.

Robertson, J., *The Scottish Enlightenment and the Militia Issue* (London, 1985).

Robertson, J., 'The Scottish Enlightenment at the Limits of the Civic Tradition', in I. Hont and M. Ignatieff (eds), *Wealth and Virtue: The Shaping of Political Economy in the Scottish Enlightenment* (Cambridge, 1983), pp. 137–78.

Robinson, D. N., 'The Scottish Enlightenment and its Mixed Bequest', *Journal for the History of the Behavioural Sciences*, 22 (1986), 171–7.

Rothwell, H. (ed.), *English Historical Documents*, 1189–1326 (London, 1959).

Salmon, J. H. M., 'Stoicism and Roman Example: Seneca and Tacitus in Jacobean England', *Journal of the History of Ideas*, 50 (1989), 199–225.

Schneider, L., *The Scottish Moralists on Human Nature and Society* (Chicago, 1967).

Schwend, J., 'Nationalism in Scottish Medieval and Renaissance Literature', *Scottish Studies–Mainz*, viii (1986), 29–42.

Sefton, H. F., 'Rev. Robert Wallace: An Early Moderate', *Records of the Scottish Church History Society*, 16 (1966), 1–22.

Seigel, J. E., *Rhetoric and Philosophy in Renaissance Humanism* (Princeton, NJ, 1968).

Sekora, J., *Luxury: The Concept in Western Thought, Eden to Smollett* (Baltimore, Md., 1977).

Shapin, S., 'The Audience for Science in Eighteenth-Century Edinburgh', *History of Science*, 12 (1974), 95–121.

Shepherd, C. M., 'Newtonianism in Scottish Universities in the Seventeenth Century', in R. H. Campbell and A. S. Skinner (eds), *The Origins and Nature of the Scottish Enlightenment* (Edinburgh, 1982), pp. 65–85.

Sher, R., *Church and University in the Scottish Enlightenment* (Princeton, NJ, 1985).

Sher, R. and Murdoch, A., 'Literary and Learned Culture', in T. M. Devine and R. Mitchison (eds), *People and Society in Scotland*, 3 vols (Edinburgh, 1988), I, 127–42.

Sher, R. and Smitten, J. R., *Scotland and America in the Age of the Enlightenment* (Edinburgh, 1990).

Simpson, J. M., 'Scottish Enlightenment Studies: Three Routes Through a Busy Place', *Scottish Journal of Political Economy*, 34 (1987), 97–103.

Simpson, K. M., *The Protean Scot. The Crisis of Identity in Eighteenth-Century Scottish Literature* (Aberdeen, 1988).

Skinner, A. S., 'Economics and History – The Scottish Enlightenment', *Scottish Journal of Political Economy*, 12 (1965), 1–22.

Skinner, A. S., 'Natural History in the Age of Adam Smith', *Political Studies*, 12 (1967), 32–48.

Skinner, A. S., 'A Scottish Contribution to Marxist Sociology?', in I. Bradley and M. Howard (eds), *Classical and Marxian Political Economy: Essays in Honour of Ronald L. Meek* (London, 1982), pp. 79–107.

Skinner, Q., *The Foundations of Modern Political Thought*, 2 vols (Cambridge, 1978).

Skinner, Q., 'Meaning and Understanding in the History of Ideas', *History and Theory*, 8 (1969), 3–53.

Sloan, D. S., *The Scottish Enlightenment and the American College Ideal* (New York, 1971).

Sloane, T. O., *Donne, Milton, and the End of Humanist Rhetoric* (Berkeley, Calif., 1985).

Small, A. W., *Adam Smith and Modern Sociology* (Chicago, 1907).

Smart, I. M., 'The Political Ideas of the Scottish Covenanters, 1638–88', *History of Political Thought*, 1 (1980), 167–93.

Smout, T. C., 'Problems of Nationalism, Identity, and Improvement in Later Eighteenth-Century Scotland', in T. M. Devine (ed.), *Improvement and Enlightenment* (Edinburgh, 1989), pp. 1–21.

Snoddy, T. G., *Sir John Scot, Lord Scotstarvit* (Edinburgh, 1968).

Spadafora, D., *The Idea of Progress in Eighteenth-Century Britain* (New Haven, Conn., 1990).

Spurr, J., '"Virtue, Religion, and Government": the Anglican Uses of Providence', in T. Harris, P. Seaward and M. Goldie (eds), *The Politics of Religion in Restoration England* (Oxford, 1990), pp. 29–47.

Stein, P., 'From Pufendorf to Adam Smith: The Natural Law Tradition in Scotland', in N. Horn (ed.), *Europäisches Rechtsdenken in Geschichte und Gegenwart*, 2 vols (Munich, 1982), I, 667–79.

Stein, P., 'Law and Society in Eighteenth-Century Scottish Thought', in N. T. Phillipson and R. Mitchison (eds), *Scotland in the Age of Improvement* (Edinburgh, 1970), pp. 148–68.

Stephen, Sir L., *English Thought in the Eighteenth Century*, 2 vols (London, 1876).

Stewart, M. A., 'George Turnbull and Educational Reform', in J. J. Carter and J. H. Pittock (eds), *Aberdeen and the Enlightenment* (Aberdeen, 1987), pp. 95–103.

Stewart-Robertson, J. C., 'Cicero among the Shadows: Scottish Prelections of Virtue and Duty', *Rivista Critica di Storia della Filosofia*, 38 (1983), pp. 25–49.

Stocking, G. W., 'Scotland as the Model of Mankind: Lord Kames' Philosophical View of Civilization', in T. H. H. Thoresen (ed.), *Toward a Science of Man: Essays in the History of Anthropology* (The Hague, 1975), pp. 65–89.

Stout, H. S., *The New England Soul: Preaching and Religious Culture in Colonial New England* (Oxford, 1986).

Strawhorn, J., 'Ayrshire in the Enlightenment', in G. Cruikshank (ed.), *A Sense of Place. Studies in Scottish Local History* (Edinburgh, 1988), pp. 188–99.

Sutherland, S., 'The Presbyterian Inheritance of Hume and Reid', in R. H. Campbell and A. S. Skinner (eds), *The Origins and Nature of the Scottish Enlightenment* (Edinburgh, 1982), pp. 131–49.

Swingewood, A., 'Origins of Sociology: The Case of the Scottish Enlightenment', *British Journal of Sociology*, 21 (1970), 164–80.

Teichgraeber, R. F., *'Free Trade' and Moral Philosophy: Rethinking the Sources of Adam Smith's Wealth of Nations* (Durham, NC, 1986).

Thomas, Sir K., *Religion and the Decline of Magic*, 2nd issue (Harmondsworth, 1978).

Trevor-Roper, H. R., 'George Buchanan and the Ancient Scottish Constitution', *English Historical Review*, Suppl. 3, (1966).

Trevor-Roper, H. R., 'Scotland and the Puritan Revolution', in his *Religion, the Reformation, and Social Change* (London, 1967), pp. 392–444.

Trevor-Roper, H. R., 'The Scottish Enlightenment', *Studies on Voltaire and the Eighteenth Century*, 58 (1967), 1635–58.

Veitch, J., 'Philosophy in the Scottish Universities', *Mind*, 2 (1877), 74–91, 207–34.

Vickers, B. (ed.), *Public and Private Life in the Seventeenth Century: The Mackenzie-Evelyn Debate* (New York, 1986).

Viner, J., *The Role of Providence in the Social Order* (Philadelphia, 1972).

Walker, J., *The Theology and Theologians of Scotland*, 1560–1750 (Edinburgh, 1982).
Waszek, N., *The Scottish Enlightenment and Hegel's Account of 'Civil Society'*
    (Dordrecht, 1988).
Watson, J., *The Scot of the Eighteenth Century* (London, 1907).
Whitney, L., *Primitivism and the Idea of Progress in English Popular Literature of the
    Eighteenth Century* (Baltimore, Md., 1934).
Williamson, A. H., *Scottish National Consciousness in the Age of James VI: The
    Apocalypse, the Union, and the Shaping of Scotland's Public Culture* (Edinburgh,
    1979).
Winch, D., 'Adam Smith's enduring particular result' in I. Hont and M. Ignatieff
    (eds), *Wealth and Virtue: The Shaping of Political Economy in the Scottish
    Enlightenment* (Cambridge, 1983), pp. 253–69.
Wood, D., 'Constant in Edinburgh: Eloquence and History', *French Studies*, 40
    (1986), 151–66.
Wood, P., 'Science and the Aberdeen Enlightenment', in P. Jones (ed.), *Philosophy
    and Science in the Scottish Enlightenment* (Edinburgh, 1988), pp. 39–66.
Worden, B., 'Providence and Politics in Cromwellian England', *Past and Present*, 109
    (1985), 55–99.
Wormald, J., *Court, Kirk, and Community: Scotland, 1470–1625* (London, 1981).
Young, D. (ed.), *Edinburgh in the Age of Reason* (Edinburgh, 1967).
Young, D., 'Scotland and Edinburgh in the Eighteenth Century', *Studies on Voltaire
    and the Eighteenth Century*, 58 (1967), 1967–90.
Youngson, A. J., *The Making of Classical Edinburgh* (Edinburgh, 1966).
Zachs, W., *Without Regard to Good Manners: A Biography of Gilbert Stuart,
    1743–1782* (Edinburgh, 1992).

Unpublished Dissertations and Secondary Literature

Burke, U. P., 'Scottish Historians and the Feudal System: The Conceptualisation of
    Social Change' (unpublished conference paper, first presented in Pisa, 1978).
Clark, I. D. L., 'Moderatism and the Moderate Party in the Church of Scotland,
    1752–1805' (unpublished Ph.D. dissertation, University of Cambridge, 1963)
MacElroy, D. D., 'The Literary Clubs and Societies of Eighteenth-Century
    Scotland' (unpublished Ph.D. dissertation, University of Edinburgh, 1952).
Mason, R. A., 'Kingship and Commonweal: Political Thought and Ideology in
    Reformation Scotland' (unpublished Ph.D. dissertation, University of Edinburgh,
    1983).
Moore, P., 'The Nature of Theoretical History and its Application in the Works of
    William Robertson' (unpublished Ph.D. dissertation, University of Edinburgh,
    1975).

Index